UNITED ARAB EMIRATES YEARBOOK
2003

The UAE Yearbook project is a multimedia publishing programme undertaken by Trident Press in conjunction with the UAE Ministry of Information and Culture. In addition to this book the project includes operation of the Ministry's official web-site: www.uaeinteract.com, and production of the annual UAE CD-rom.

Editors and contributors:
Ibrahim Al Abed
Paula Vine
Gabrielle Warnock
Peter Hellyer
Peter Vine
Daniel Potts
Simon Aspinall
Andy Vine

Text copyright ©2003: Trident Press

Cover picture from a photograph by Lucy Monro

Photographs ©: Trident Press Ltd, Gulf News, Emirates News Agency (WAM), UAE Ministry of Information and Culture and credited photographers and agencies (see pages 319–320).

English edition design and typesetting: Jane Stark, Trident Press

Yearbook information is, by definition, subject to change. The current volume is based on available information at the time of printing. Whilst every care has been taken to achieve accuracy, the publishers cannot accept any liability for consequences arising from the use of information contained in this book.

Enquiries may be addressed to:
Ministry of Information and Culture
PO Box 17, Abu Dhabi, UAE.
Tel: (9712) 4453000; Fax (9712) 4450458
E-mail: admin@extinfo.gov.ae
Web site: www.uaeinteract.com

Published by Trident Press Ltd.
175 Piccadilly, Mayfair, London W1J 9TB
Tel: 0207 491 8770; Fax: 0207 491 8664
E-mail: admin@tridentpress.com
Web site: www.tridentpress.com

British Library Cataloguing in Publication Data
A CIP catalogue record for this book is available
from the British Library.

ISBN 1-900724-91-X (hardback); 1-900724-92-8 (paperback)

CONTENTS

FOREWORD	5
SHEIKH ZAYED	7
THE COUNTRY	31
HISTORY AND TRADITIONS	43
GOVERNMENT AND FOREIGN AFFAIRS	71
ECONOMIC DEVELOPMENT	93
INFRASTRUCTURE	179
SOCIAL DEVELOPMENT	215
CULTURE AND INFORMATION	247
ENVIRONMENT	267
SPORT AND LEISURE	279
EXHIBITIONS AND EVENTS	303
INDEX	315
PHOTO CAPTIONS AND CREDITS	319

FOREWORD

IN AN UNCERTAIN WORLD it is reassuring to pass familiar milestones. Publication of the *UAE Yearbook* has become one of those markers. It provides a valuable opportunity to look back on the previous year and to reflect on our recent experiences. Whilst the 2003 Yearbook highlights the UAE's successes over the past 12 months, and there have been many, it also reports on projects that have encountered difficulties, economic challenges and social issues that cannot be ignored; and political problems that may remain unsolved. Accurate, objective and regular chronicling of the UAE's development, such as that provided by the *UAE Yearbook*, plays a significant role in our international communications, presenting, as it were, an up to date curriculum vita for a rapidly growing nation. Its broad scope, dealing with the entire spectrum of development, helps to inform readers from differing backgrounds of issues outside their own fields of activity. 'Knowledge', Sheikh Zayed has said, 'is the foundation for our future well-being'. This book seeks to arm all those who have an involvement with the UAE with essential knowledge that will assist in their own activities.

The year 2002 was marked, within the UAE, by a renewed commitment on behalf of government to build a stable, prosperous and safe environment, not just nationally but also on the world stage. On the local level we once again gave great attention to our young people, providing high quality, stimulating education and training — both academically and in the fields of sports and social affairs. In order to achieve our goals it is essential that we retain a strong economy and continue to enhance our infrastructure and, as this book reports, we have made important progress in these fields. We have also continued to promote, among all our citizens, a sense of place, an appreciation for the UAE's heritage and a pride in living here.

On the world stage we have focused our attention on supporting genuine peacemakers and playing a positive role in helping innocent civilians who have been caught-up in conflict areas. Whilst our record in humanitarian aid has been praised by the United Nations, we are in no way complacent, but determined to do whatever we can to counter the scourge of violence with practical help and diplomatic assistance.

I take this opportunity to thank all those who have contributed towards this worthwhile record of our progress and hope that readers will find it useful.

Abdullah bin Zayed Al Nahyan
Minister of Information and Culture

SHEIKH ZAYED

PRESIDENT OF THE UAE

On 6 August 2002, His Highness Sheikh Zayed bin Sultan Al Nahyan completed 36 years as Ruler of the Emirate of Abu Dhabi, one of the seven emirates that together comprise the Federation of the United Arab Emirates (UAE), of which he has been President since its creation in December 1971. He has now provided leadership to the country for well over half a century.

Born around 1918 in Abu Dhabi, Sheikh Zayed is the youngest of the four sons of Sheikh Sultan bin Zayed Al Nahyan, Ruler of Abu Dhabi from 1922 to 1926. He was named after his grandfather, Sheikh Zayed bin Khalifa, who ruled the emirate from 1855 to 1909, the longest reign in the three centuries since the Al Nahyan family emerged as leaders of the Emirate of Abu Dhabi.

Abu Dhabi, like the other emirates of the southern Arabian Gulf formerly known as the Trucial States, was then in treaty relations with Britain. At the time Sheikh Zayed was born, the emirate was poor and undeveloped, with an economy based primarily on fishing and pearl diving along the coast and offshore and on simple agriculture in scattered oases inland. Part of the population was nomadic, ranging across a wide area of south-eastern Arabia in search of pasture.

Life, even for a member of the ruling family, was simple. Opportunities for education were generally confined to lessons in reading and writing, along with instruction in Islam from the local preacher, while modern facilities such as roads, communications and health care were conspicuous only by their absence. Transport was by camel or boat, and the harshness of the arid climate meant that survival itself was often a major concern.

In early 1926, following the death of Sheikh Sultan's successor, his brother Sheikh Saqr, a family conclave selected as Ruler Sheikh Shakhbut, Sheikh Sultan's eldest son. He was to hold the post until August 1966, when he stepped down in favour of his brother Zayed.

Throughout the late 1920s and 1930s, as Sheikh Zayed grew to manhood, he displayed an early thirst for knowledge that took him out into the desert with the bedu tribesmen to learn all he could about the way of life of the people and the environment in which they lived. He recalls with pleasure his experience of desert life and his initiation into the sport of falconry, which has been a lifelong passion.

In his book, *Falconry: Our Arab Heritage*, published in 1977, Sheikh Zayed noted that the companionship of a hunting party

> ... *permits each and every member of the expedition to speak freely and express his ideas and viewpoints without inhibition and restraint, and allows the one responsible to acquaint himself with the wishes of his people, to know their problems and perceive their views accurately, and thus to be in a position to help and improve their situation.*

From his desert journeys, Sheikh Zayed developed an understanding of the relationship between man and his environment and, in particular, the need to ensure that sustainable use was made of natural resources. Once an avid shot, he abandoned the gun for falconry at the age of 25, aware that hunting with a gun could lead rapidly to extinction of the native wildlife.

His travels in the remoter areas of Abu Dhabi provided Sheikh Zayed with a deep understanding both of the country and of its people. In the early 1930s, when the first oil company teams arrived to carry out preliminary surface geological surveys, he was assigned by his brother the task of guiding them around the desert. At the same time, he obtained his first exposure to the industry that was later to have such a great impact upon the country.

In the year 1946, Sheikh Zayed was chosen to fill a vacancy as Ruler's Representative in the Eastern Region of Abu Dhabi, centred on the oasis of Al Ain, approximately 160 kilometres east of the island of Abu Dhabi itself. Inhabited continuously for at least 5000 years, the oasis had nine villages, six of which belonged to Abu Dhabi and three, including Buraimi, by which name the oasis was also known, which belonged to the Sultanate of Oman. The job involved not only the task of administering the six villages but also the whole of the adjacent desert region, enabling Sheikh Zayed to learn the techniques of government as well as deepening his knowledge of the tribes. In the late 1940s and early 1950s, Saudi Arabia's territorial claims to Buraimi provided him with the opportunity to gain experience of politics on a broader scale.

Sheikh Zayed brought to his new task a firm belief in the values of consultation and consensus, in contrast to confrontation. Foreign visitors, such as the British explorer Sir Wilfred Thesiger, who first met him at this time, noted with approbation that his judgements 'were distinguished by their acute insights, wisdom and fairness'.

Sheikh Zayed swiftly established himself not only as someone who had a clear vision of what he wished to achieve for the people of Al Ain, but also as someone who led by example.

A key task in the early years in Al Ain was that of stimulating the local economy, which was largely based on agriculture. To do this, he ensured that the ancient subterranean water channels or falajes (*aflaj*) were cleaned out, and personally financed the construction of a new one, taking part in the strenuous labour that was involved. He also ordered a revision of local water ownership rights to ensure

a more equitable distribution, surrendering the rights of his own family as an example to others. The consequent expansion of the area under cultivation in turn generated more income for the residents of Al Ain, helping to re-establish the oasis as the predominant market centre for a wide area.

With development gradually beginning to get under way, Sheikh Zayed commenced the laying out of a visionary city plan, and, in a foretaste of the massive afforestation programme of today, he also ordered the planting of ornamental trees that, now grown to maturity, have made Al Ain one of the greenest cities in Arabia.

In 1953, Sheikh Zayed made his first visit abroad, accompanying his brother Shakhbut to Britain and France and attending an international arbitration tribunal on the legality of offshore oil concessions in the Emirate. He recalled later how impressed he had been by the schools and hospitals he visited, becoming determined that his own people should have the benefit of similar facilities:

There were a lot of dreams. I was dreaming about our land catching up with the modern world, but I was not able to do anything because I did not have the wherewithal in my hands to achieve these dreams. I was sure, however, that one day they would become true.

Despite constraints through lack of government revenues, Sheikh Zayed succeeded in bringing progress to Al Ain, establishing the rudiments of an administrative machinery, personally funding the first modern school in the emirate and coaxing relatives and friends to contribute towards small-scale development programmes.

Oil production was to provide Sheikh Zayed with the means to fund his dreams, with the export of the first cargo of Abu Dhabi crude in 1962. Although oil prices were then far lower than they are today, the rapidly growing volume of exports, from both onshore and offshore, revolutionised the economy of Abu Dhabi and its people began to look forward eagerly to receiving similar benefits to those already being enjoyed by their neighbours in Qatar, Bahrain, Kuwait and Saudi Arabia. The pearling industry, which had begun thousands of years earlier, had finally come to an end shortly after the Second World War, and little had emerged to take its place. Indeed, during the late 1950s and early 1960s, many people had left Abu Dhabi for other, oil-producing, Gulf states where there were opportunities for employment.

The economic hardships experienced by Abu Dhabi since the 1930s had accustomed the Ruler, Sheikh Shakhbut, to a cautious frugality. Despite the growing aspiration of his people for progress, he was reluctant to invest the new oil revenues in development. Attempts by members of his family, including Sheikh Zayed, and by the leaders of the other tribes in the emirate to persuade him to move with the times were unsuccessful, and eventually the Al Nahyan family decided that the time had come for him to step down. Sheikh Zayed's record over the previous 20 years in Al Ain and his popularity among the people made him the obvious choice as successor.

On 6 August 1966, Sheikh Zayed became Ruler, with a mandate from his family to press ahead as fast as possible with the development of Abu Dhabi. He was a man in a hurry. His years in Al Ain had not only given him valuable experience in government, but had also provided him with the time to develop a vision of how the emirate could progress. With revenues growing year by year as oil production increased, he was determined to use them in the service of the people, and a massive programme of construction of schools, housing, hospitals and roads got rapidly under way.

Of his first few weeks, Sheikh Zayed has said:

All the picture was prepared. It was not a matter of fresh thinking, but of simply putting into effect the thoughts of years and years. First I knew we had to concentrate on Abu Dhabi and public welfare. In short, we had to obey the circumstances: the needs of the people as a whole. Second, I wanted to approach other emirates to work with us. In harmony, in some sort of federation, we could follow the example of other developing countries.

One of Sheikh Zayed's early steps was to increase contributions to the Trucial States Development Fund, established a few years earlier. Abu Dhabi soon became its largest donor. At the beginning of 1968, when the British announced their intention of withdrawing from the Arabian Gulf by the end of 1971, Sheikh Zayed acted rapidly to initiate moves towards establishing closer ties with the other emirates.

Along with the late Ruler of Dubai, Sheikh Rashid bin Saeed Al Maktoum, who was to become Vice President and Prime Minister of the UAE, Sheikh Zayed took the lead in calling for a federation that would include not only the seven emirates that together made up the Trucial States, but also Qatar and Bahrain. When early hopes of a federation of nine states eventually foundered, Sheikh Zayed led his fellow rulers in achieving agreement on the establishment of the UAE, which formally emerged on the international stage on 2 December 1971.

While his enthusiasm for federation was a key factor in the formation of the UAE, Sheikh Zayed also won support for the way in which he sought consensus and agreement among his fellow rulers:

I am not imposing change on anyone. That is tyranny. All of us have our opinions, and these opinions can change. Sometimes we put all opinions together, and then extract from them a single point of view. This is our democracy.

Sheikh Zayed was elected by his fellow rulers as the first President of the UAE, a post to which he has been successively re-elected at five-year intervals.

The new state came into being at a time of political turmoil in the region. A couple of days earlier, on the night of 30 November and the early morning of 1 December, Iran had seized the islands of Greater and Lesser Tunb, part of Ra's al-Khaimah, and had landed troops on Abu Musa, part of Sharjah (see section on Foreign Policy).

On land, demarcation of the borders between the individual emirates and with the federation's neighbours had not been completed, although a preliminary agreement had been reached between Abu Dhabi and Oman.

Foreign observers, who lacked an understanding of the importance of a common history and heritage in uniting the people of the UAE, predicted that the new state would survive only with difficulty, pointing to disputes with its neighbours and to the wide disparity in the size, population and level of development of the seven emirates.

Better informed about the character of the country, Sheikh Zayed was naturally more optimistic. Looking back a quarter of a century later he noted:

Our experiment in federation, in the first instance, arose from a desire to increase the ties that bind us, as well as from the conviction of all that they were part of one family, and that they must gather together under one leadership.

We had never (previously) *had an experience in federation, but our proximity to each other and the ties of blood relationship between us are factors which led us to believe that we must establish a federation that should compensate for the disunity and fragmentation that earlier prevailed.*

That which has been accomplished has exceeded all our expectations, and that, with the help of God and a sincere will, confirms that there is nothing that cannot be achieved in the service of the people if determination is firm and intentions are sincere.

The predictions of those early pessimists have been overwhelmingly shown to be unfounded. Over the past 31 years, the UAE has not only survived, but has developed at a rate that is almost without parallel. The country has been utterly transformed. Its population has risen from around 250,000 in 1971 to an estimate of around 3.48 million in mid-2002. Progress, in terms of the provision of social services, health and education, as well as in sectors such as communications and the oil and non-oil economy, has brought a high standard of living that has spread throughout the seven emirates, from the ultra-modern cities to the remotest areas of desert and mountains. The change has, moreover, occurred against a backdrop of enviable political and social stability, despite the insecurity and conflict that has dogged much of the rest of the Gulf region.

The country has also established itself firmly on the international scene, both within the Arab region and in the broader community of nations. Its pursuit of dialogue and consensus and its firm adherence to the tenets of the Charter of the United Nations, in particular those dealing with the principle of non-interference in the affairs of other states, have been coupled with a quiet but extensive involvement in the provision of development assistance and humanitarian aid that, in per capita terms, has few parallels.

There is no doubt that the experiment in federation has been a success and the undoubted key to the achievements of the UAE has been the central role played by Sheikh Zayed.

During his years in Al Ain he was able to develop a vision of how the country should progress, and, since becoming first Ruler of Abu Dhabi and then President of the UAE, he has devoted three and a half decades to making that vision a reality.

One foundation of his philosophy as a leader and statesman is that the resources of the country should be fully used to the benefit of the people. The UAE is fortunate to have been blessed with massive reserves of oil and gas and it is through careful utilisation of these, including the decision in 1973 that the Government of Abu Dhabi, the emirate with the lion's share of reserves, should take a controlling share of the oil reserves to complement its total ownership of associated and non-associated gas, that the financial resources necessary to underpin the development programme have always been available. Indeed there has been sufficient to permit the setting aside of large amounts for investment on behalf of future generations and, through the Abu Dhabi Investment Authority created by Sheikh Zayed, the country now has financial reserves unofficially estimated at around US $300 billion.

The financial resources, however, have always been regarded by Sheikh Zayed not as a means unto themselves, but as a tool to facilitate the development of what he believes to be the real wealth of the country – its people, and, in particular, the younger generation. As he has stated:

Wealth is not money. Wealth lies in men. This is where true power lies, the power that we value. They are the shield behind which we seek protection. This is what has convinced us to direct all our resources to building the individual, and to using the wealth with which God has provided us in the service of the nation, so that it may grow and prosper.

Unless wealth is used in conjunction with knowledge to plan for its use, and unless there are enlightened intellects to direct it, its fate is to diminish and to disappear. The greatest use that can be made of wealth is to invest it in creating generations of educated and trained people.

Addressing the graduation ceremony of the first class of students from the Emirates University in 1982, Sheikh Zayed said:

The building of mankind is difficult and hard. It represents, however, the real wealth [of the country]. This is not found in material wealth. It is made up of men, of children, and of future generations. It is this which constitutes the real treasure.

Within this framework, Sheikh Zayed believes that all of the country's citizens have a role to play in its development. Indeed he defines it not simply as a right, but as a duty. Addressing his colleagues in the Federal Supreme Council, he noted:

The most important of our duties as Rulers is to raise the standard of living of our people. To carry out one's duty is a responsibility given by God, and to follow up on work is the responsibility of everyone, both the old and the young.

Both men and women, he believes, should play their part. Recognising that in the past a lack of education and development had prevented women from playing a full role in much of the activity of society, he has taken action to ensure that this situation does not continue. Although women's advocates might argue that there is still much to be done, the achievements have been remarkable, and the country's women are now increasingly playing their part in political and economic life by taking up positions at all levels in the public and private sectors. In so doing, they have enjoyed full support from the President:

Women have the right to work everywhere. Islam affords to women their rightful status, and encourages them to work in all sectors, as long as they are afforded the appropriate respect. The basic role of women is the upbringing of children, but, over and above that, we must offer opportunities to a woman who chooses to perform other functions. What women have achieved in the Emirates in only a short space of time makes me both happy and content. We sowed our seeds yesterday, and today the fruit has already begun to appear. We praise God for the role that women play in our society. It is clear that this role is beneficial for both present and future generations.

Remarkable progress has now been achieved by the women of the Emirates, due in no small measure to initiatives taken by President Sheikh Zayed and by his wife, the UAE First Lady, HH Sheikha Fatima bint Mubarak, who is the President of the country's General Women's Union. With women already playing a prominent role in the civil service, health, education and business, they are now set to raise the profile in the political process, through membership in the various consultative and legislative bodies.

Talking to the Egyptian newspaper *Al Ahram* in October 2002, Sheikh Zayed noted that:

The Woman is the mother, sister, aunt and wife of Man, and we should not, therefore, deprive women of their rights, which God has instructed us to respect and observe. Women should be respected and encouraged in whatever work they may do.

The UAE General Women's Union has contributed actively to the enhancement of the role of and contribution of women, while at the same time, together with this contribution, UAE women have maintained and preserved the values of our society.

Sheikh Zayed has made it clear that he believes that the younger generation, those who have enjoyed the fruits of the UAE's development programme throughout their lives, must now take up the burden once carried by their parents. Within his immediate family, Sheikh Zayed has ensured that his sons have taken up posts in government at which they are expected to work, and not simply enjoy as sinecures. Young UAE men who have complained about the perceived lack of employment opportunities at a realistic salary level have been offered positions on farms as agricultural labourers, so that they may learn the dignity of work:

Work is of great importance, and of great value in building both individuals and societies. The size of a salary is not a measure of the worth of an individual. What is important is an individual's sense of dignity and self-respect. It is my duty as the leader of the young people of this country to encourage them to work and to exert themselves in order to raise their own standards and to be of service to the country. The individual who is healthy and of a sound mind and body but who does not work commits a crime against himself and against society.

We look forward in the future to seeing our sons and daughters playing a more active role broadening their participation in the process of development and shouldering their share of the responsibilities, especially in the private sector, so as to lay the foundations for the success of this participation and effectiveness. At the same time, we are greatly concerned to raise the standard and dignity of the work ethic in our society, and to increase the percentage of citizens in the labour force. This can be achieved by following a realistic and well-planned approach that will improve performance and productivity, moving towards the long-term goal of secure and comprehensive development.

In this sphere, as in other areas, Sheikh Zayed has long been concerned about the possible adverse impact upon the younger generation of the easy life they enjoy, so far removed from the resilient, resourceful lifestyle of their parents. One key feature of Sheikh Zayed's strategy of government, therefore, has been the encouragement of initiatives designed to conserve and cherish features of the traditional culture of the people, in order to familiarise the younger generation with the ways of their ancestors. In his view, it is of crucial importance that the lessons and heritage of the past are not forgotten. They provide, he believes, an essential foundation upon which real progress can be achieved:

History is a continuous chain of events. The present is only an extension of the past. He who does not know his past cannot make the best of his present and future, for it is from the past that we learn. We gain experience and we take advantage of the lessons and results [of the past]. Then we adopt the best and that which suits our present needs, while avoiding the mistakes made by our fathers and grandfathers. The new generation should have a proper appreciation of the role played by their forefathers. They should adopt their model, and the supreme ideal of patience, fortitude, hard work and dedication to doing their duty.

Once believed to have been little more than a backwater in the history of the Middle East, the UAE is now known to have been a country that has played a vital role in the development of civilisation in the region for thousands of years.

The first archaeological excavations in the UAE took place over 40 years ago, in 1959, with the archaeologists benefiting extensively from the interest shown in their work by Sheikh Zayed. Indeed, he himself invited them to visit the Al Ain area to examine remains in and around the oasis that proved to be some of the most

important yet found in south-eastern Arabia. In the intervening decades, Sheikh Zayed has continued to support archaeological studies throughout the country, eager to ensure that the achievements of the past become known to the people of today.

Appropriately, one of the UAE's most important archaeological sites has been discovered on Abu Dhabi's western island of Sir Bani Yas, which for 25 years has been a private wildlife reserve created by Sheikh Zayed to ensure the survival of some of Arabia's most endangered species.

If the heritage of the people of the UAE is important to Sheikh Zayed, so too is the conservation of its natural environment and wildlife. He believes the strength of character of the Emirati people derives, in part, from the struggle that they were obliged to wage in order to survive in the harsh and arid local environment.

His belief in conservation of the environment owes nothing to modern fashions. Acknowledged by the presentation to him of the prestigious Gold Panda award of the Worldwide Fund for Nature, and by the inauguration, early in 2001, of the Zayed International Prize for the Environment (whose first recipient was former US President and Nobel Peace Prize winner Jimmy Carter), it derives, instead, from his own upbringing, where a sustainable use of resources required man to live in harmony with nature. This has led him to ensure that conservation of wildlife and the environment is a key part of government policy. At the same time he has stimulated and personally supervised a massive programme of afforestation that has now seen over 150 million trees planted.

In a speech given on the occasion of the UAE's first Environment Day in February 1998, Sheikh Zayed spelt out his beliefs:

We cherish our environment because it is an integral part of our country, our history and our heritage. On land and in the sea, our forefathers lived and survived in this environment. They were able to do so only because they recognised the need to conserve it, to take from it only what they needed to live, and to preserve it for succeeding generations.

With God's will, we shall continue to work to protect our environment and our wildlife, as did our forefathers before us. It is a duty, and, if we fail, our children, rightly, will reproach us for squandering an essential part of their inheritance, and of our heritage.

Like most conservationists, Sheikh Zayed is concerned wherever possible to remedy the damage done by man to wildlife. His programme on the island of Sir Bani Yas for the captive breeding of endangered native animals such as the Arabian oryx and the Arabian gazelle has achieved impressive results, so much so that not only is the survival of both species now assured, but animals are also being carefully reintroduced to the wild.

As in other areas of national life, Sheikh Zayed has made it clear that conservation is not simply the task of government. Despite the creation of official institutions like the Federal Environment Agency and Abu Dhabi's Environmental Research and Wildlife Development Agency, the UAE's President has stressed that there is also a role for the individual and for non-governmental organisations, both of citizens and expatriates.

He believes that society can only develop and flourish if all of its members acknowledge their responsibilities. This applies not only to concerns such as environmental conservation, but to other areas of national life as well.

Members of the Al Nahyan family, of which Sheikh Zayed is the current head, have been rulers of Abu Dhabi since at least the beginning of the eighteenth century, longer than any other ruling dynasty in Arabia. In Arabian *bedu* society, however, the legitimacy of a ruler, and of a ruling family, derives essentially from consensus and from consent and the legitimacy of the political system today derives from the support it draws from the people of the UAE. The principle of consultation (*shura*) is an essential part of that system.

At an informal level, that principle has long been practiced through the institution of the *majlis* (council) where a leading member of society holds an 'open-house' discussion forum, at which any individual may put forward views for discussion and consideration. While the majlis system – the UAE's form of direct democracy – still continues, it is, naturally, best suited to a relatively small community.

In 1970, recognising that Abu Dhabi was embarking on a process of rapid change and development, Sheikh Zayed established the Emirate's National Consultative Council, bringing together the leaders of each of the main tribes and families which comprised the population. A similar body was created in 1971 for the entire UAE, the Federal National Council, the state's parliament.

Both institutions represent the formalisation of the traditional process of consultation and discussion, and their members are frequently urged by Sheikh Zayed to express their views openly, without fear or favour.

At present members of both Councils, as well as lower-level Municipal Councils, continue to be selected by Sheikh Zayed and the other rulers, in consultation with leading members of the community in each emirate. In the future, Sheikh Zayed has said, however, a formula for direct elections will be devised. He notes, though, that in this, as in so many other fields, it is necessary to move ahead with care in order to ensure that only such institutions as are appropriate for Emirati society are adopted.

Questioned in 1998 by the *New York Times* on the topic of the possible introduction of an elected parliamentary democracy, Sheikh Zayed replied:

Why should we abandon a system that satisfied our people in order to introduce a system that seems to engender dissent and confrontation? Our system of government is based upon our religion, and is what our people want. Should they seek alternatives, we are ready to listen to them. We have always said that our people should voice their demands openly. We are all in the same boat, and they are both captain and crew.

Our doors here are open for any opinion to be expressed, and this is well known by all our citizens. It is our deep conviction that God the Creator has created people free, and has prescribed that each individual must enjoy freedom of choice. No-one should act as if he owns others. Those in a position of leadership should deal with their subjects with compassion and understanding, because this is the duty enjoined upon them by God Almighty, who enjoins us to treat all living creatures with dignity. How can there be anything less for man, created as God's vicegerent on earth? Our system of government does not derive its authority from man, but is enshrined in our religion, and is based on God's book, the Holy Quran. What need have we of what others have conjured up? Its teachings are eternal and complete, while the systems conjured up by man are transitory and incomplete.

Sheikh Zayed imbibed the principles of Islam in his childhood and they remain the foundation of his beliefs and principles today. Indeed, the ability with which he and the people of the UAE have been able to absorb and adjust to the remarkable changes of recent decades can be ascribed largely to the fact that Islam has provided an immutable and steadfast core of their lives. Today, it provides the inspiration for the UAE judicial system and its place as the ultimate source of legislation is enshrined in the country's Constitution.

Islam, like other divinely-revealed religions, has those among its claimed adherents who purport to interpret its message as justifying harsh dogmas and intolerance. In Sheikh Zayed's view, however, such an approach is not merely a perversion of the message but is in direct contradiction of it. Extremism, he believes, has no place in Islam. In contrast, he stresses that:

Islam is a civilising religion that gives mankind dignity. A Muslim is he who does not inflict evil upon others. Islam is the religion of tolerance and forgiveness, and not of war, of dialogue and understanding. It is Islamic social justice which has asked every Muslim to respect the other. To treat every person, no matter what his creed or race, as a special soul is a mark of Islam. It is just that point, embodied in the humanitarian tenets of Islam, that makes us so proud of it.

Within that context, Sheikh Zayed has set his face firmly against those who preach intolerance and hatred:

In these times, we have seen around us violent men who claim to talk on behalf of Islam. Islam is far removed from their talk. If such people really wish for recognition from Muslims and the world, they should themselves first heed the words of God and His Prophet. Regrettably, however, these people have nothing whatsoever that connects them to Islam. They are apostates and criminals. We see them slaughtering children and the innocent. They kill people, spill their blood and destroy their property, and then claim to be Muslims.

In September 2001, following the terrorist attacks against the United States, Sheikh Zayed noted that:

the UAE clearly and unequivocally condemns the criminal acts that took place in New York and Washington, resulting in the deaths and injuries of thousands . . . There should be a direct move and a strong international alliance to eradicate terrorism, and all those who provide assistance to it or harbour it.

'The UAE condemns all acts of terrorism everywhere,' he said, expressing the UAE's 'condemnation of the daily and continuous acts of terrorism being committed by Israeli occupation forces in the occupied Palestinian territories against the unarmed Palestinian people.'

Besides the international campaign against the types of terrorism, Sheikh Zayed also noted that there should be a strong international alliance that worked, in parallel, to exert real and sincere efforts to bring about a just and lasting solution to the Middle East conflict. 'The Arabs and the Islamic world cannot accept what is happening in the occupied Palestinian territories – the daily killings, deportations and destruction. All of this is politically and morally unacceptable.'

In his interview with *Al Ahram* in October 2002, Sheikh Zayed also reiterated his belief that there is no connection between Islam and terrorism:

Muslims stand against any person of Muslim faith who will try to commit any terror act against a fellow human being. A terrorist is an enemy of Islam and of humanity, while the true Muslim is friendly to all human beings and a brother to other Muslims and non-Muslims alike. This is because Islam is a religion of mercy and tolerance.

Sheikh Zayed is an eager advocate of tolerance, discussion and a better understanding between those of different faiths, and in particular, has been an ardent advocate of dialogue between Muslims and Christians, recognising that this is essential if mankind is ever to move forward in harmony. His faith is well summed up by a statement explaining the essential basis of his own beliefs: 'my religion is based neither on hope, nor on fear. I worship my God because I love Him.'

That faith, with its belief in the brotherhood of man and in the duty incumbent upon the strong to provide assistance to those less fortunate than themselves, is fundamental to Sheikh Zayed's vision of how his country and people should develop. It is, too, a key to the foreign policy of the UAE, which he has devised and guided since the establishment of the state. That faith, with its belief in the brotherhood of man and in the duty incumbent upon the strong to provide assistance to those less fortunate than themselves, is fundamental to Sheikh Zayed's vision of how his country and people should develop. It is, too, a key to the foreign policy of the United Arab Emirates, which he has devised and guided since the establishment of the state.

The UAE itself has been able to progress only because of the way in which its component parts have successfully been able to come together in a relationship of harmony, working together for common goals. That approach has also been applied in the sphere of foreign policy.

Within the Arabian Gulf region, and in the broader Arab world, the UAE has sought to enhance cooperation and to resolve disagreement through a calm pursuit of dialogue and consensus. Thus one of the central features of the country's foreign policy has been the development of closer ties with its neighbours in the Arabian Peninsula. The Arab Gulf Cooperation Council, (AGCC) grouping the UAE, Kuwait, Saudi Arabia, Bahrain, Qatar and Oman, was founded at a summit conference held in Abu Dhabi in May 1981, and has since become, with strong UAE support, an effective and widely-respected grouping.

Intended to facilitate the development of closer ties between its members and to enable them to work together to ensure their security, the AGCC has faced two major external challenges during its short lifetime, first the long and costly conflict in the 1980s between Iraq and Iran, which itself prompted the Council's formation, and then the August 1990 invasion by Iraq of one of its members, Kuwait.

Following the invasion of Kuwait, President Zayed was one of the first Arab leaders to offer support to its people and units from the UAE Armed Forces played a significant role in the alliance that liberated the Gulf state in early 1991.

While fully supporting the international condemnation of the policies of the Iraqi regime and the sanctions imposed on Iraq by the United Nations during and after the conflict, the UAE has, however, expressed its serious concern about the impact that the sanctions have had upon the country's people. As the possibility of a further conflict in the region grew in late 2002, President Sheikh Zayed reaffirmed his belief that a peaceful solution needed to be found to the crisis.

'War never solves a problem,' he said. 'Listening to the sense of reason is the right way to resolve differences between countries . . . This must be based on the principles of justice and the rule of law.'

'The Arabs should do everything that they can in order to avert war against Iraq. We hope that diplomatic means will be given a full chance,' he added. In subsequent talks with a visiting Iraqi envoy, the UAE President also stressed that the Iraqi Government should recognise the demand of the international community that it should abide by, and implement the terms of, all relevant United Nations Security Council resolutions.

Another key focus of the UAE's foreign policy in an Arab context has been the provision of support to the Palestinian people in their efforts to regain their legitimate rights to self-determination and to the establishment of their own State. As early as 1968, before the formation of the United Arab Emirates, Sheikh Zayed extended assistance to Palestinian organisations, and has done so throughout the last three and a half decades, although he has always believed that it is for the Palestinians themselves to determine their own policies.

Following the establishment of the Palestinian Authority in Gaza and on parts of the occupied West Bank, the UAE has provided substantial help for the building of a national infrastructure, including not only houses, roads, schools and hospitals, but also for the refurbishment of Muslim and Christian sites in the city of Jerusalem. While much of the aid has been bilateral, the UAE has also taken part in development programmes funded by multilateral agencies and groupings and has long been a major contributor to the United Nations Relief Works Agency (UNRWA). With the outbreak of the second Palestinian Intifada (Uprising) in September 2000, the UAE, acting on the instructions of Sheikh Zayed, stepped up its assistance to the Palestinian Authority, and has also been a vocal, and forceful, critic not only of the repressive policies of the Israeli Government, but also of the failure of the international community, in particular the United States, to force the Israelis to desist.

Substantial amounts of aid have also been given to a number of other countries in the Arab world. In Lebanon, for example, the UAE has funded a major programme of clearing the many hundreds of thousands of land mines left behind by the Israelis when they were forced to withdraw in 2000, so that the Lebanese civilian population may return to their homes and land. Other countries like Egypt, Syria, Jordan, Yemen and Morocco have received substantial loans and other aid for their infrastructural development programmes.

Sheikh Zayed has a deeply held belief in the cherished objective of greater political and economic unity within the Arab world. At the same time, however, he has long adopted a realistic approach on the issue, recognising that any unity, to be effective, must grow slowly, and with the support of the people. Arab unity, he believes, is not something that can simply be created through decrees of governments that may be simply temporary, political phenomena.

That approach has been tried and tested both at the level of the UAE itself, which is the longest-lived experiment in recent times in Arab unity, and at the level of the Arabian Gulf Cooperation Council.

On a broader plane, Sheikh Zayed has sought consistently to promote greater understanding and consensus between Arab countries and to reinvigorate the League of Arab States.

Relations between the Arab leaders, he believes, should be based on openness and frankness:

They must make it clear to each other that each one of them needs the other, and they should understand that only through mutual support can they survive in times of need. A brother should tell his brother: you support me, and I will support you, when you are in the right. But not when you are in the wrong. If I am in the right, you should support and help me, and help to remove the results of any injustice that has been imposed on me.

Wise and mature leaders, he feels, 'should listen to sound advice, and should take the necessary action to correct their mistakes. As for those leaders who are unwise or immature, they can be brought to the right path through advice from their sincere friends.'

Within that context, Sheikh Zayed consistently argued throughout the 1990s for the holding of a new Arab summit conference, at which the leaders could honestly and frankly address the disputes between them. Only thus, he believes, can the Arab world as a whole move forward to tackle the challenges that face it, both internally and on the broader international plane:

I believe that an all-inclusive Arab summit must be held, but before attending it, the Arabs must open their hearts to each other and be frank with each other about the rifts between them and their wounds.

They should then come to the summit, to make the necessary corrections to their policies, to address the issues, to heal their wounds and to affirm that the destiny of the Arabs is one, both for the weak and the strong. At the same time, they should not concede their rights, or ask for what is not rightfully their's.

Welcoming the holding of the first of the annual summits, in Jordan in March 2001, Sheikh Zayed noted that:

The spirit of understanding and brotherhood that has prevailed during (the) sessions and discussions has brought me great satisfaction. (The) serious deliberations on the key issues . . . have proved that sincere intentions and frankness are the way for us to achieve success . . . Dialogue is essential between brothers, and we are happy because the Arabs recognise the correct path to follow towards reconciliation and solidarity, and to surmount the negative elements and mistakes of the past, in order to move away from divisions and rifts.

At the same time, however, the UAE President acknowledges that unanimity, although desirable, cannot always be achieved. He has, therefore, been the only Arab leader to openly advocate a revision of the Charter of the League of Arab States to permit decisions to be taken on the basis of the will of the majority. Such has been the experience of the society from which he comes, and such has been one of the foundations of the success of the federal experiment in the UAE. It is time, he believes, that a similar approach was adopted within the broader Arab world.

That should not, however, mean that essential rights and principles should be set aside. These include, of course, the principle of the inviolability of the integrity of Arab territories.

This principle has been a matter of major concern to the United Arab Emirates since its formation, because of the Iranian occupation in 1971 of the UAE islands of Abu Musa and Greater and Lesser Tunb. President Sheikh Zayed and other senior UAE

Government officials have made repeated calls for the occupation to be brought to an end peacefully, either through direct negotiations, or by referral to the International Court of Justice or to international arbitration. Recent developments on the issue, including a visit to Tehran in 2002 by Minister of State for Foreign Affairs Sheikh Hamdan bin Zayed Al Nahyan, suggest that there is now some hope for a solution of the dispute.

In an interview with Egypt's *Al Ahram* in October 2002, Sheikh Zayed commented:

Our relations with Iran are based on the best interests of the people of the two countries. Apart from the issue of the occupied islands, our relations have not been subjected to any kind of difficulties, and it is against this background that we have repeatedly urged Iran to join us in finding a peaceful solution to this problem through mediation and understanding . . . On the basis of this belief, we have constantly called upon the rest of the world to seek peaceful solutions to problems, within the framework of international law, rather than engage in confrontation and war.

The UAE now looks forward, he said, to 'the beginning of a new era' in relations between the two countries.

Here, as on other foreign policy issues, Sheikh Zayed has consistently adopted a firm but calmly worded approach, eschewing rhetoric that could make the search for a solution to problems more difficult.

In recent years, the conflicts ensuing from the disintegration of the former Yugoslavia have been the cause of considerable concern to the UAE President. The lessons of these conflicts were not, however, lost on him. The time had come, he recognised, for the United Arab Emirates itself to play a more pro-active role in international peacekeeping operations.

The UAE Armed Forces had already begun to establish a record in such peacekeeping activities, first as part of the joint Arab Deterrent Force that sought for a few years to bring to an end the civil strife in Lebanon, and then through participation in UNISOM TWO, the United Nations peacekeeping and reconstruction force in Somalia.

In early 1999, as a new campaign of Serbian atrocities began to get under way against the Albanian population of Kosovo, Sheikh Zayed was among the first world leaders to express support for the decision by the North Atlantic Treaty Organisation (NATO) to launch its aerial campaign to force Serbia to halt its genocidal activities.

Recognising early on in the campaign that there would be a need for an international peacekeeping force once the NATO campaign ended, Sheikh Zayed ordered that the UAE Armed Forces should be a part of any such force operating under the aegis of the United Nations. In late 1999, with the UN's KFOR force in place in Kosovo, the contingent from the United Arab Emirates was the largest taking part from any of the non-NATO states, and the only one from an Arab or Muslim country. By the time the unit was withdrawn, in late 2001, it had done much not only in terms of contributing to the rebuilding of peace and security in Kosovo, but also to strengthening the UAE's reputation on the international plane.

While ensuring that the UAE should now increasingly come to shoulder such international responsibilities, however, Sheikh Zayed has also made it clear that the UAE's role is one that is focused on relief and rehabilitation.

In the Balkans, and in other countries, the policy adopted by the United Arab Emirates clearly reflects the desire of Sheikh Zayed to utilise the good fortune of his country to provide assistance to those less fortunate. Through bodies like the Zayed Foundation and the Abu Dhabi Fund for Development, established by Sheikh Zayed before the foundation of the UAE, as well as through institutions like the Red Crescent Society, chaired by his son, Sheikh Hamdan bin Zayed Al Nahyan, the country now plays a major role in the provision of relief and development assistance worldwide.

The UAE itself has been able to progress only because of the way in which its component parts have successfully been able to come together in a relationship of harmony, working together for common goals.

Within the Arabian Gulf region, and in the broader Arab world, the UAE has sought to enhance cooperation and to resolve disagreement through a calm pursuit of dialogue and consensus. However, the pursuit of agreement and consensus does not, in Sheikh Zayed's view, justify the setting aside of essential rights and principles. These include not only support for the basic fundamentals of human and civil rights but also the principle of the inviolability of the territorial integrity of states, whether Arab or others.

Pursuit of these rights and principles has characterised the foreign policy of the state, bringing Sheikh Zayed's own philosophy and humanitarianism to bear far from the boundaries of the state itself. In essence, the philosophy of Sheikh Zayed, derived from his deeply-held Muslim faith, is that it is the duty of man to seek to improve the lot of his fellow man.

His record in over half a century of government, from local to international level, is an indication of the dedication and seriousness with which he has sought to carry out that belief.

THE COUNTRY

LOCATION

THE UNITED ARAB EMIRATES (UAE) IS SITUATED along the south-eastern tip of the Arabian Peninsula between 22°50 and 26°N and between 51° and 56°25 E. Qatar lies to the west and north-west, Saudi Arabia to the west and south and Oman to the north, east and south-east. Occupying a total area of about 83,600 square kilometres (32,400 square miles) – roughly the size of Portugal – the UAE has 700 kilometres of coastline, 600 kilometres along the Arabian Gulf and 100 kilometres bordering the Gulf of Oman.

PHYSICAL FEATURES

Desert
Despite the fact that four-fifths of its land area is arid desert, the UAE is a country of contrasting landscapes. To the north and west is an extensive area of coastal salt flats (*sabkha*). Isolated *sabkha*, otherwise surrounded by dune and gravel desert, also exists inland (particularly in Abu Dhabi's Western Region). The sandy desert begins behind the coastal *sabkha*, with little white dune ripples eventually forming an expanse of large orange-red dunes in the south-west. About 100 kilometres inland, towering dunes rising to 200 metres are common. These form part of the Empty Quarter or Rub al-Khali, a vast desert which stretches beyond the UAE's southern border.

Mountain
The sand and gravel desert dominating most of the south and west of the country extends east to the jagged Hajar Mountain chain that divides the UAE from north to south in the Northern Emirates and forms the eastern boundary of the UAE further to the south. The rocky slopes rise to 1300 metres within UAE territory, falling steeply to the UAE's East Coast on the Gulf of Oman where an alluvial gravel plain separates the precipitous mountains from the ocean. To the north-east, a fertile plain also divides the mountains from the coast around Ra's al-Khaimah.

Sea
Small sandy islets, patch and fringing coral reefs, seagrass beds, mangrove stands and *khors* (tidal inlets) as well as long sandy beaches abound along the UAE's shallow Arabian Gulf coast. For the most part seawater depth is less than 10 metres

with an average overall depth of 31 metres and a narrow tidal range (ca. 0.5–1.5 metres). Water temperatures in the Gulf exceed 33°C in summer, falling in winter to 16°C in the north and 22–24°C in the south.

Offshore in the Arabian Gulf, islands such as Dalma, Sir Abu Nu'air, Sir Bani Yas, Qarnein and Zirku are mostly the elevated portions of salt domes.

The Gulf of Oman and Arabian Sea area is a much deeper body of water. Here upwellings of oceanic nutrient-rich waters and abundant plankton combine to support commercially important fisheries.

CLIMATE

Sun

Straddling the Tropic of Cancer, the UAE is warm and sunny in winter and hot and humid during the summer months. Winter daytime temperatures average a very pleasant 26°C, although nights can be relatively cool, between 12–15°C on the coast, and less than 5°C in the depths of the desert or high in the mountains. Local north-westerly winds (*shamal*) frequently develop during the winter, bringing cooler windy conditions. Summer temperatures are in the mid-40s, but can be higher inland. Humidity in coastal areas averages between 50 and 60 per cent, touching over 90 per cent in summer and autumn. Inland it is far less humid.

Rainfall

Rainfall is sparse and intermittent. In most years it rains during the winter months, usually in February or March, but occasionally earlier. Winter rains take the form of short sharp bursts, which, if occurring in the Hajar Mountains, run off rapidly into wadis and onto the downwashed gravel plains. Localised thunderstorms occasionally occur during the summer. Generally appearing over the mountains of the south and east of the country, these rumbling cloudbursts can give rise to severe flash floods.

Some years are totally dry and it is only through the regular formation of dew that vegetation and wildlife can survive. This applies even to those places that experience a relatively high annual rainfall: at the Hajar Mountain town of Masafi, for example, 350 millimetres may fall in a 'wet' year, whereas as little as 30 millimetres may be recorded in a 'dry' year.

SEVEN EMIRATES

Abu Dhabi

Abu Dhabi, occupying over 86 per cent (67,340 square kilometres) of the country's total landmass, is the largest of the seven emirates that constitute the federation known as the United Arab Emirates. Abu Dhabi City, capital of the emirate and of the UAE, is situated on an island (8 kilometres wide by 14.5 kilometres long) which is connected to the mainland by the Maqta and Mussafah Bridges.

Table 1. Mean monthly maximum temperature (Bateen airport, Abu Dhabi) and national mean monthly rainfall.

	J	F	M	A	M	J	J	A	S	O	N	D
°C	24	25	29	33	38	39	40	40	39	35	30	26
mm	11	38	34	10	3	1	2	3	1	2	4	10

Sheikh Zayed, President of the UAE, has his home in Abu Dhabi City. Federal Government offices, the Federal National Council (Parliament) building, and foreign embassies are also located here. Since Abu Dhabi Emirate possesses more than 90 per cent of the UAE's oil reserves and produces over 85 per cent of its oil, the city is also the headquarters of the main oil companies and a major business, manufacturing and trading centre.

Architecturally, Abu Dhabi is a fascinating place where the domes and minarets of traditional mosques sit comfortably in the shade of gleaming futuristic skyscrapers. Tree-lined boulevards, manicured roundabouts, dazzling fountains and extensive parks soften the modern cityscape. A short distance from the city centre the wonderfully engineered Abu Dhabi Corniche runs for 10 kilometres along the island's mangrove-fringed and white sandy shores. Many of the city's top class hotels and restaurants are located along the downtown section of this scenic stretch.

Al Ain, the capital of Abu Dhabi's mainland Eastern Region, is a green, low-rise city nestling in the shade of Jebel Hafit. The surrounding district, blessed with substantial groundwater resources, is a rich agricultural area and is also home to the UAE's main university.

Bida Zayed (Zayed City) is the capital of the Western Region, Abu Dhabi Emirate's third administrative sector. This area has undergone extensive afforestation in recent years, including the planting of millions of evergreens, covering at least 100,000 hectares. The country's main onshore oil fields are located in this region, as is the largest oil refinery (Ruwais). Liwa, a series of oasis villages and the site of spectacular high dunes on the edge of the Empty Quarter, is situated to the south-west.

Abu Dhabi Emirate also possesses a number of important islands, including Das, Mubarraz and Zirku, near where the main offshore oil fields are located. Closer inshore are many more islands, including Dalma, Sir Bani Yas, Marawah, Abu al-Abyadh, and Saadiyat.

Dubai

The Emirate of Dubai extends approximately 72 kilometres along the Arabian Gulf coast of the UAE. Dubai has an area of c. 3885 square kilometres, equivalent to 5 per cent of the country's total landmass.

Dubai City is built along the edge of a narrow 10-kilometre winding creek that divides the southern section of Bur Dubai, the city's traditional heart, from the northern area, Deira, a bustling commercial centre containing a range of retail outlets, souqs and hotels. Al Maktoum and Al Garhoud Bridges and Al Shindagha Tunnel link Bur Dubai and Deira.

About 20 minutes from Dubai city, Jumeirah Beach is a major tourism area with a number of award-winning hotels and a delightful sandy beach. Jebel Ali, home of a huge man-made port and the largest free-trade zone in Arabia, is located about 30 kilometres away. Inland is the attractive mountain resort town of Hatta.

SEVEN EMIRATES – ONE NATION

Dubai

Abu Dhabi

Ajman

Umm al-Qaiwain

THE COUNTRY

SEVEN EMIRATES – ONE NATION

Ra's al-Khaimah

Sharjah

Fujairah

Dubai has four offshore oil fields, Fateh, Southwest Fateh, Rashid and Falah, and an onshore gas and condensate field at Margham.

Sharjah

Sharjah Emirate, occupying an area of 2590 square kilometres, equivalent to 3.3 per cent of the country's total landmass, has the distinction of being the only emirate to have land on both coasts. Although the main city is situated on the Arabian Gulf coast between Dubai and Ra's al-Khaimah, enclaves belonging to Sharjah (Kalba, Khor Fakkan and Dibba al-Husn) are located across the Hajar Mountains on the Gulf of Oman. Two offshore islands in the Arabian Gulf also belong to Sharjah: Abu Musa, which has been under military occupation by Iran since 1971, and Sir Abu Nu'air.

Sharjah City, the main administrative and commercial centre, has some fine restored traditional buildings, together with a number of impressive museums. Distinctive landmarks are the two major covered souqs reflecting Islamic design, and the many elegant mosques. In 1998 Sharjah city was designated by UNESCO as the cultural capital of the Arab world for its commitment to art, culture and the preservation of its heritage.

Khor Khalid, a tidal creek, runs inland from the city's main port. The outer narrow section shelters an active dhow fleet whilst inland the creek widens to a large lagoon aerated by a 100-metre-high fountain, and is circled by the impressive Buhaira Corniche.

Sharjah also encompasses some important oasis areas, the most famous of which is the inland agricultural area of Dhaid, whilst on the East Coast precipitous mountains sweep down to sandy beaches washed by the clear blue Indian Ocean. Khor Fakkan provides Sharjah with a major East Coast port. Dibba, to the north of Khor Fakkan, has a long and valiant history whilst Khor Kalba to the south is the location of an extensive mangrove stand that has been designated a nature reserve.

Sharjah's Mubarak oilfield is located near the Arabian Gulf island of Abu Musa. The emirate also has an important onshore gas and condensate field at Saja'a.

Ajman

Ajman, located a short distance north-east of Sharjah City, has a beautiful 16-kilometre coastline fringed by a sandy beach. It is the smallest of the seven emirates in terms of its physical size, covering about 259 square kilometres, equivalent to 0.3 per cent of the country's total landmass.

The capital city, Ajman, has an historic fort at its centre and is blessed with a natural harbour in which the Port of Ajman is situated. Fishing and dhow building are still important industries. Ajman has also capitalised on its boat-building skills by establishing a major ship repair company.

Ajman has two inland enclaves: Masfut is an agricultural village located in the mountains 110 kilometres to the south-east of the city, whilst Manama is situated approximately 60 kilometres to the east.

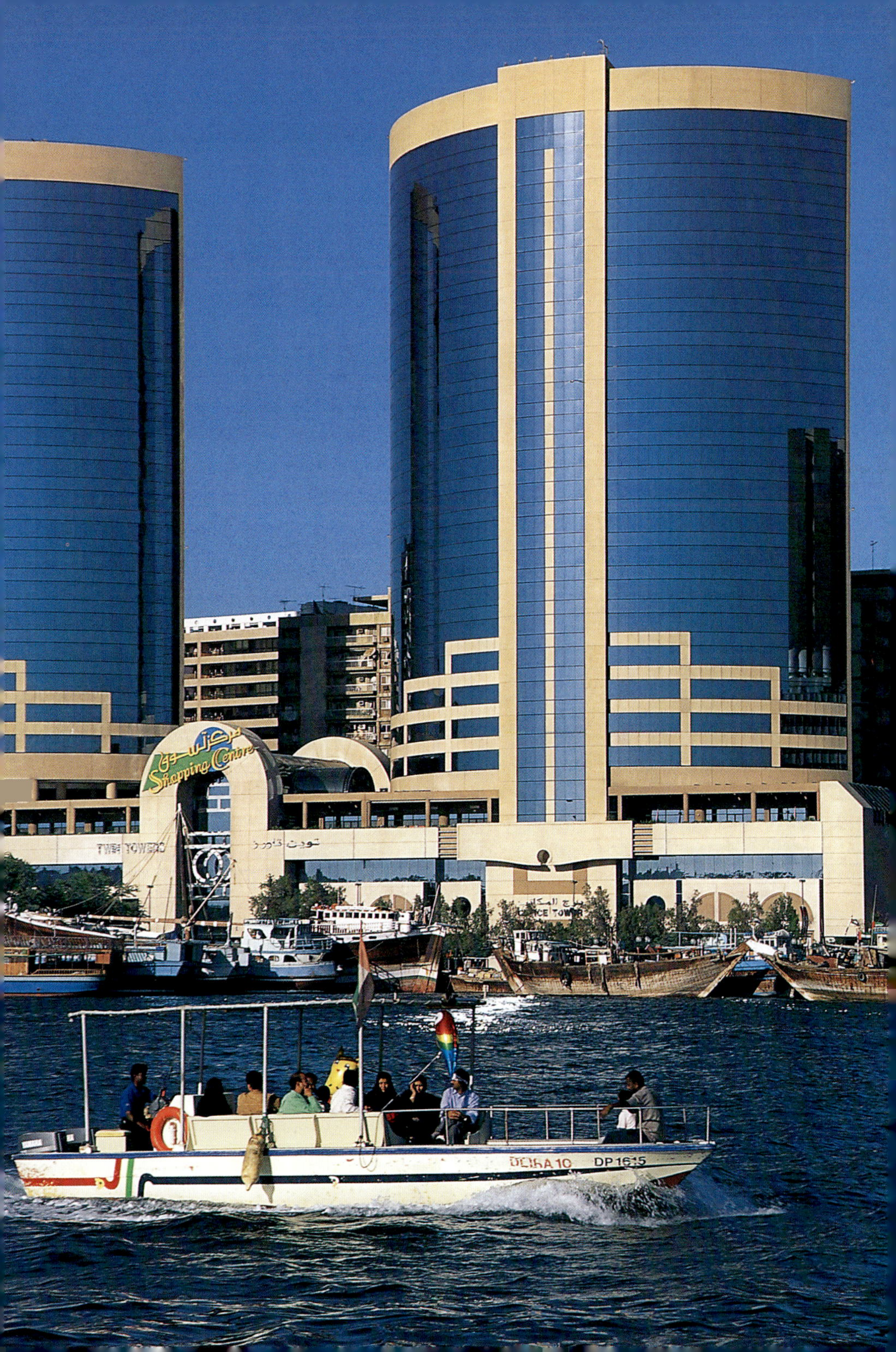
Shopping Centre
TWIN TOWERS
DEIRA 10
DP 1615

Umm al-Qaiwain

Umm al-Qaiwain is located on the Arabian Gulf coast, between Sharjah to the south-west and Ra's al-Khaimah to the north-east. The total area of the emirate, which has a coastline stretching to 24 kilometres, is approximately 777 square kilometres, equivalent to 1 per cent of the country's total landmass.

Umm al-Qaiwain City, capital of the emirate, is situated on a narrow peninsula encircling a large creek 1 kilometre wide by 5 kilometres long. The preserved remains of an old fort museum, its main gate flanked by defensive cannons, are a delightful feature of the city. Traditional occupations of fishing and date cultivation are still important, but a mariculture research centre and an innovative free zone, along with a cement industry, have helped to develop the emirate.

Sinayah Island, lying a short distance offshore, has important mangrove areas together with a breeding colony of endangered Socotra cormorants. Falaj al-Mu'alla, an attractive natural oasis belonging to Umm al-Qaiwain, is located 50 kilometres south-east of Umm al-Qaiwain City.

Ra's al-Khaimah

Ra's al-Khaimah, the most northerly emirate on the UAE's west coast, has an impressive coastline of approximately 64 kilometres bordering the Arabian Gulf. This is backed by a fertile palm-filled plain that is overshadowed by the precipitous Hajar Mountains to the east. In the north, close to the emirate's border with the Sultanate of Oman, the sheer rocky slopes seem to rise straight out of the sea. The area of the emirate is 1680 square kilometres, equivalent to 2.2 per cent of the UAE's total landmass. Ra's al-Khaimah also possesses a number of islands including those of Greater and Lesser Tunb, occupied by Iran since 1971.

A winding creek, Khor Ra's al-Khaimah, divides Ra's al-Khaimah City into two distinct areas connected by a large modern bridge. The old fort housing Ra's al-Khaimah National Museum and the old souq are located in the western section, old Ra's al-Khaimah, whilst the eastern area, Al Nakheel, is a modern commercial centre.

For centuries Ra's al-Khaimah depended on seafaring, fishing and agriculture and these occupations are still important today, albeit with a distinctly modern outlook. Digdagga in the fertile hinterland is now a major agricultural area supplying fruit and vegetables to the other emirates. Mina Saqr, to the north of Ra's al-Khaimah City, is an important modern port and fishermen from the traditional fishing district of Rams now ply their trade in motorised fishing boats. Cement manufacture, stone quarrying in the mountains, and oil production from the offshore Saleh field have also helped to fund prosperity.

Fujairah

Fujairah, with a breathtaking coastline of more than 90 kilometres, is the only emirate situated along the Gulf of Oman, although it also has outlying areas to the west of the Hajar Mountains. The emirate occupies an area of 1165 square kilometres, equivalent to 1.5 per cent of the country's total landmass.

Fujairah is a place of considerable natural beauty where rugged mountains and valleys sweep down to the settled palm-fringed coastal plain. There are some stunning beaches and good diving locations along the coast, whilst both the coastal strip and the hinterland contain many cultural and historic sites. Agriculture and fishing, two traditional mainstays of the economy, still feature prominently.

Fujairah City is an attractive town and a rapidly developing commercial and tourist centre. Its strategic location outside the Straits of Hormuz, which provides easy access to international shipping routes, has played a key role in its development as one of the world's top oil-bunkering ports.

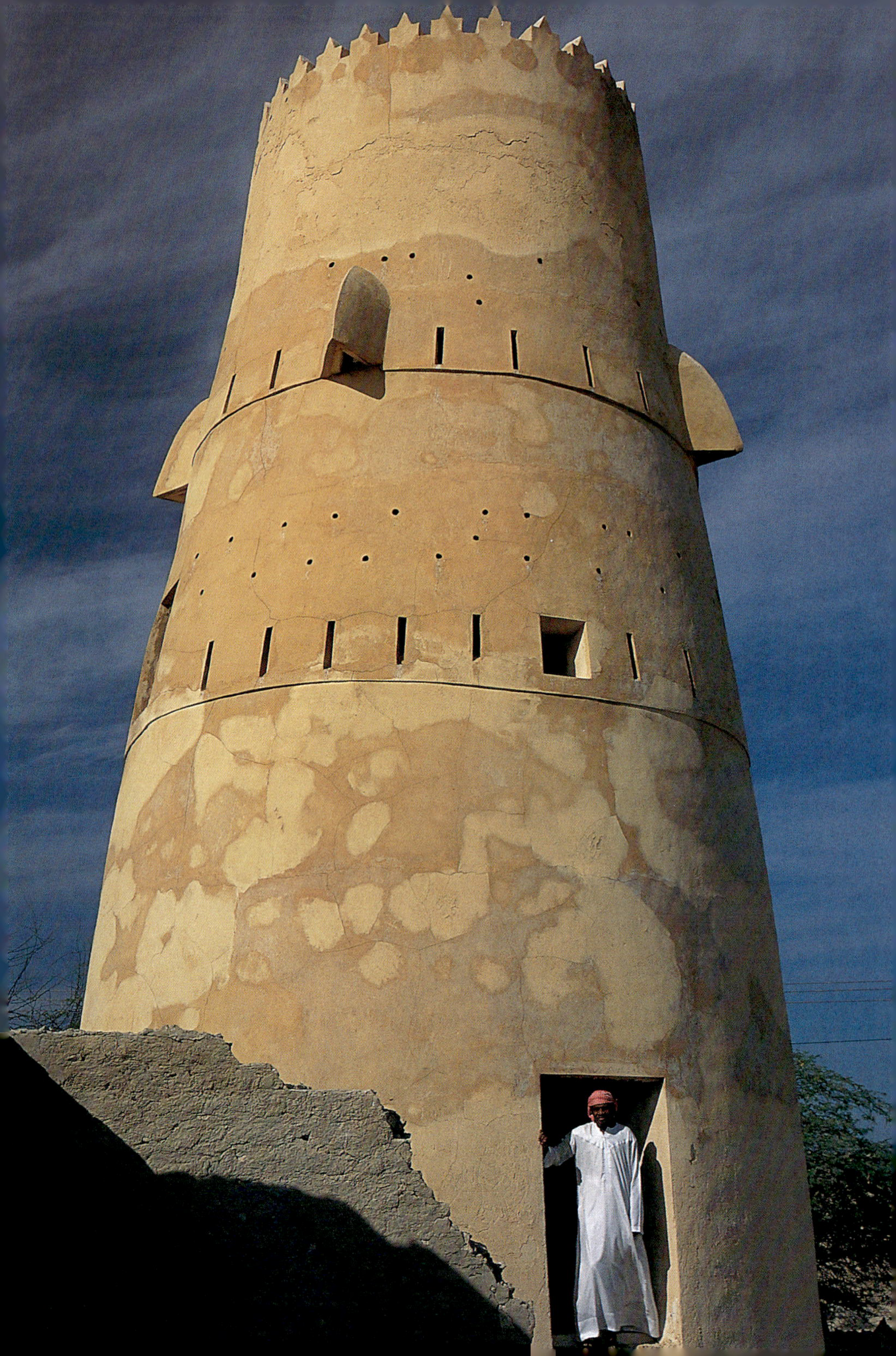

HISTORY AND TRADITIONS

EARLY INHABITANTS

MANKIND HAS EXPLOITED THE LAND now known as the United Arab Emirates (UAE) since the Late Stone Age (5500 BC) when the climate was wetter and more humid than it is today. Game such as gazelle and oryx would have been abundant on the savannah and neighbouring grasslands and even in the deep sands the basic necessities of life would have been available. So, far from being an inhospitable desert, the land and waters of the region presented its ancient inhabitants with an enormous variety of exploitable, economically important resources. At this time the sea level in the Gulf was about half a metre higher than it is today.

The earliest known inhabitants of the UAE were probably skilled herders who would have used finely made stone tools. More than likely, they lived along the coasts and offshore islands in the winter, when fishing and shellfish gathering (including the harvesting of pearls) would have been the main pursuits, and moved to the interior in summer, where pastoralism and, eventually, horticulture, were practiced. This was a pattern of seasonal resource utilisation that was to be repeated throughout the history of the region. These were not an isolated people as there is ample evidence of contacts with the outside world, especially with civilisations to the north such as Mesopotamia (southern Iraq), indicated by finds of painted pottery (Ubaid type) which originated in these areas.

While the stone tools of the UAE's early inhabitants have been found at dozens of sites from Bida al-Mutawa in the west to Khatt in the north, few settlements are known. Of these, undoubtedly the most impressive is Al Buhays 18, currently under excavation.

HAFIT TOMBS

At the end of the fourth millennium (c. 3100–3000 BC), the first archaeological structures in the form of above-ground tombs built of unworked stone (Hafit tombs) appear at two sites in the UAE, Jebel Hafit (including Mazyad) near Al Ain and Jebel al-Emalah south of Dhaid. These collective tombs contain pottery (Jamdat Nasr type) imported from south-central Iraq. Other imported finds also point to foreign contact and it is thought that trade in copper from the Hajar Mountains was the likely motivation for communication with the outside world. Certainly early 'Archaic texts' (3400–3000 BC) from Uruk in southern Mesopotamia refer to copper from Dilmun, later identified with Bahrain, but as there is no copper in this area it is usually assumed that the precious metal came from further afield, i.e the copper source which stretches from Fujairah in the north to lower Oman in the south. To date the settlements of the population buried in the Hafit tombs of south-eastern Arabia have yet to be discovered.

UMM AL-NAR

Around 3000 BC the arid climate that is evident today set in. The following era, known as the Umm al-Nar period (2500–2000 BC), was characterised by numerous oasis towns (e.g. at Hili, Tell Abraq, Bidiya, Kalba) dominated by imposing large, circular fortresses. These agriculturally based settlements were possible because of the domestication of the date palm (*Phoenix dactylifera*). Without this blessed tree, the shade necessary for the growth of other less hardy plants, including cereals, vegetables and fruits, would have been lacking. Water was available from the many wells that tapped the relatively abundant and shallow lenses of sweet water found throughout much of the UAE. During this period, the dead were buried in round communal tombs of finely masoned stone blocks (there is a particularly fine reconstruction at Hili). These graves yield much evidence of wide-ranging trade contact with Mesopotamia, Iran, the Indus Valley, Baluchistan and Bactria (Afghanistan). Significantly, textual sources from Mesopotamia referred to the area as *Magan* around this time and the towers of the Umm al-Nar period may have been the power centres for the 'lords of Magan' against whom several of the Old Akkadian emperors (from southern Mesopotamia) campaigned in the twenty-third century BC, as these ancient texts record. There is also ample evidence from this period of the first intensive use of the copper resources found in the Hajar Mountains. Certainly, by 2300 BC, bronze (an alloy of copper and tin) was becoming increasingly popular as a material for manufacturing tools.

WADI SUQ

The Wadi Suq period (2000–1300 BC) was one in which there were fewer towns, although those that continued to be inhabited on a full-time basis (such as Tell Abraq) showed no signs of a cultural decline. It seems, however, that marine resources (fish and shellfish) became more important than they had been in the late third millennium. There was a change in burial customs to long, generally narrow collective tombs (as at Shimal, Ghalilah and Dhayah). Wadi Suq tombs have yielded literally hundreds of weapons and vessels. Where the Umm al-Nar period was characterised by daggers and spears, the Wadi Suq period witnessed the introduction of the long sword, the bow and arrow. The appearance of these weapons, along with hundreds of cast bronze, lanceolate arrowheads with a raised flattened midrib, suggest an evolution in the technology of warfare. Gold and electrum plaques in the form of two animals, standing back to back, often with their tails curled up in a spiral, are indications of the accumulation of wealth during this period, some of which may have been earned by long-distance trade in copper through Dilmun (Bahrain).

In the late third millennium a distinctive industry arose in the manufacture of soft-stone vessels – generally bowls, beakers and compartmented boxes – decorated with dotted circles made using a bow drill. During the Wadi Suq period the numbers of soft-stone vessels deposited in tombs increased vastly and new shapes and decorations were developed.

IRON AGE

Domestication of the camel at the end of the second millennium revolutionised the economies of south-eastern Arabia, opening up new possibilities for transport. At the same time the discovery of the principles of using sub-surface water channels for the transportation of water from mountain aquifers to lower-lying gardens (*falaj* irrigation) made possible the extensive irrigation of gardens and agricultural plots that resulted in a veritable explosion of settlement across the Oman peninsula. This era (1300–300 BC) is termed the Iron Age, although iron was not widely used in this region. Fish and shellfish continued to be important in the diet of the Iron Age inhabitants, although domesticated sheep, goat and cattle were kept, and gazelle, oryx, dugong, turtle and cormorant were exploited as well. Domesticated wheat and barley were cultivated and the date palm remained as important as ever. There seems to have been some form of centralised power. A cuneiform inscription from Nineveh in Assyria (northern Mesopotamia) speaks of the existence of at least one 'king' in the area, an individual named Pade, king of Qade, who lived at Is-ki-e (modern Izki in Oman) and sent tribute to the Assyrian emperor Assurbanipal in or around this time. Political and economic control by central bodies may also be implied by the appearance at this time of a tradition of stamp seal manufacture. There is also strong evidence of foreign contacts and a pendant found at Tell Abraq, the earliest depiction of a boat with a lateen sail yet discovered, gives us some indication of how such contacts took place.

MLEIHA PERIOD

We know that in the late sixth century BC, the Persian empire, under Darius the Great, extended its influence to the area, then known as Maka. However, by the third century BC south-eastern Arabia was free of foreign political influence. Alexander the Great's conquests never touched the Arabian side of the Gulf and none of his Seleucid successors was able to establish any sort of Greek dominance in the region. This era has been designated the Mleiha period (300 BC–0 BC) after a flourishing town at Mleiha, a sprawling settlement on the gravel plain south of Dhaid in the interior of Sharjah. To date, there are no other settlements in the region attributable to this time span. At Mleiha the earliest post-Iron Age settlement probably consisted of *'arish*, palm-frond houses, eminently suited to the hot climate of south-eastern Arabia. Dates were grown and wheat was harvested. Mleiha's dead were buried in mudbrick cists surmounted by a solid tower of brick and capped by crenellated stone ornaments, similar to the funerary towers of Palmyra (Syria) and the early periods at Petra (Jordan).

Some of the most interesting finds include far-flung imports from Greece (black-glazed pottery and Rhodian amphorae), and South Arabia (alabaster unguent jars). Several items (stone stelae, bronze bowls) are inscribed in South Arabian characters and several coins found at Mleiha are also of South Arabian origin, pointing to cultural links with this region. These were important finds in the light of stories of the Azd migration from Yemen to the region. The Mleiha period also witnessed the appearance of iron in large quantities for the first time in the archaeological record of this region.

AD DOOR PERIOD

The first century AD (Ad Door period 0–250 AD) heralded a time for which there is considerably more literary documentation. The Roman writer Pliny the Younger (23/24–79 AD) completed his *Natural History* in 77 AD and to judge from his account of the peoples and places of south-eastern Arabia, combined with information from the second century AD map by Ptolemy, the area of the UAE was full of settlements, tribes and physical features. The town of Omana, at that time the most important port in the lower Gulf, has been linked with the ancient settlement of Ad Door in Umm al-Qaiwain, a vast area containing private houses, graves, a fort and a temple (built of beach rock), along with areas of *'arish* habitation. Overland caravan traffic between Syria and cities in southern Iraq, followed by seaborne travel to Omana and thence to India, was an alternative to the Red Sea route used by the Romans, as is clear from finds of Roman glass, brass and coinage.

While Ad Door was the prime settlement, other minor sites have been found on the islands of Abu Dhabi, and in the interior Mleiha prospered. There was also a massive production of local coinage by a ruler called Abi'el, who appears to have been an important figure in the region during this era. That Aramaic was the language of the populations of Mleiha and Ad Door at this time is confirmed not only by its use on coinage, but also by the discovery of other inscribed objects.

The *Periplus of the Erythraean Sea*, composed around 60–75 AD, informs us that pearls, purple dye, clothing, wine, a great quantity of dates, gold and slaves were exported from Omana.

Pearls were already in use in the prehistoric era, but it was during the Roman era that the trade reached new heights. Pearling was certainly practised at Ad Door, as the recovery of a bell-shaped, lead pearl diver's weight, complete with iron ring attachment for a rope attests. Moreover, stacks of pearl oyster shells were found outside the entrance to one of the monumental graves.

PRE-ISLAMIC ERA

The rise of the Sasanian dynasty in south-western Iran in 240 AD brought Sasanian influence to most of eastern Arabia, including the UAE, as is indicated by finds of coins and ceramics at Kush (Ra's al-Khaimah), Umm al-Qaiwain and Fujairah. Indian Ocean trade and communications with the Near East continued during this period. Contact with the outside world was reflected in the spread of religious influences at this time, influences that would have varied from Arab paganism to Sasanian Zoroastrianism and Nestorian Christianity. Certainly by the fourth or fifth centuries AD at least one Nestorian monastery, complete with carved stucco ornamentation, including several crosses, was established on Sir Bani Yas – an island off the coast of Abu Dhabi. Another probable monastery has been located on the island of Marawah. Sea faring and trading were still a mainstay of the coastal areas during this period. Ibn Habib in his *Kitab al-Muhabbar* records the staging of a 'fair' at Dibba, a major port now situated on the UAE's East Coast. Ibn Habib recounts that Dibba was 'one of the two ports of the Arabs [the other being Sohar] merchants from Sind, China, people of the East and West came to it. This fair was held on the last day of Tagab. Merchants traded here by bargaining'.

COMING OF ISLAM

Religious diversity came to an end in 630 AD with the arrival of envoys from the Prophet Muhammad and the subsequent conversion of the people of the region to Islam. The death of the Holy Prophet in 632 AD was followed by a widespread revolt that was subsequently quashed by the army of the first Caliph, Abu Bakr. During this time, a battle at Dibba is said to have resulted in the deaths of over ten thousand rebels. Their graves can still be seen on the outskirts of the town.

By 637 AD, the Islamic armies were using Julfar (Ra's al-Khaimah) as a staging post for the conquest of Iran. Indeed well known historians of early Islam, such as al-Tabari, and local sources indicate that this area was of considerable interest to successive Umayyad and Abbasid rulers. In 892 AD we find Julfar being used again, this time as an entry point for the Abbasid invasion of Oman. In the tenth century the area of Oman and the UAE came under the control of the Buyid dynasty (reflected in the discovery of a hoard of Buyid coins in Ra's al-Khaimah in 1965). Julfar continued to be a port and pearling centre of considerable importance, mentioned by al-Maqdisi in the tenth, al-Idrisi in the twelfth and Yaqut in the thirteenth centuries. From here, perpetuating a 5000-year-old tradition, great wooden dhows ranged far and wide across the Indian Ocean, trading as far away as Mombasa in Kenya, Sri Lanka, Vietnam and China.

The growth of Sohar, an important trade emporium on the Batinah coast of Oman, resulted in a proliferation of domestic trade routes leading to Julfar in the north and Tu'am (Al Ain/Buraimi) in the west. By the fourteenth and fifteenth centuries, the UAE had established close commercial contact with the Kingdom of Hormuz based on Jarun Island in the Straits of Hormuz. But this relationship was upset in 1498 following the Portuguese circumnavigation of Cape of Good Hope by Vasco da Gama using Arab navigational information.

IBN MAJID

Ibn Majid, the 'Lion of the Sea' and a legendary figure in UAE history was one of those navigators whose vast store of navigational knowledge was used by the Portuguese to reach India. Born in Julfar, close to present day Ra's al-Khaimah, in around 1432–37, Ibn Majid came from a long line of intrepid sailors. His reputation as a navigator is based upon 40 surviving works, 39 of which are in verse. Some are brief, others, such as the 805-verse al-Sofaliya describing the sea route from India to Sofala on the Mozambique coast, are of considerable length. One treatise (the *Fawa'id*) is a lengthy opus that not only summarises all of Ibn Majid's own knowledge of navigation, but also draws extensively on the work of early Arab astronomers. His last known poem was written in 1500 AD and it is believed that he died soon after, at a little over 70 years of ages.

PORTUGUESE PRESENCE

The Portuguese arrival in the Gulf had bloody consequences for the Arab populations of Julfar and East Coast ports like Dibba, Bidiya, Khor Fakkan and Kalba. A string of forts established in these towns, often described as 'Portuguese', are in fact better considered strongholds of local Arab sheikhs, allies of the Portuguese.

The Portuguese author, Duarte Barbosa, writing in 1517 noted that the people of Julfar were 'persons of worth, great navigators and wholesale dealers. Here is a very great fishery as well, of seed pearls as well as large pearls'. The Portuguese traveller Pedro Teixeira mentions that a fleet of 50 terradas sailed from Julfar every year to the pearl beds. There was even a kind of pearl found near Julfar named after the latter, and it was the growing interest of the Europeans in 'Gulf pearls' that led to the tour of the Venetian state jeweller, Gasparo Balbi in 1580. Interestingly, his description of the UAE coast from Qatar to Ra's al-Khaimah includes the first European record of the Bani Yas tribe in Abu Dhabi.

BANI YAS

The ancestors of the bedouin, who made the sandy deserts of Abu Dhabi and Dubai their home, created date gardens and built themselves date frond houses in the hollows of the dunes where adequate water was found. These *'arish* habitations eventually formed about 40 settlements, some of which were inhabited all the year round. This half moon arc of villages, called Liwa, was the focus of economic and social life for the Bani Yas at least since the sixteenth century. By the early 1790s however,

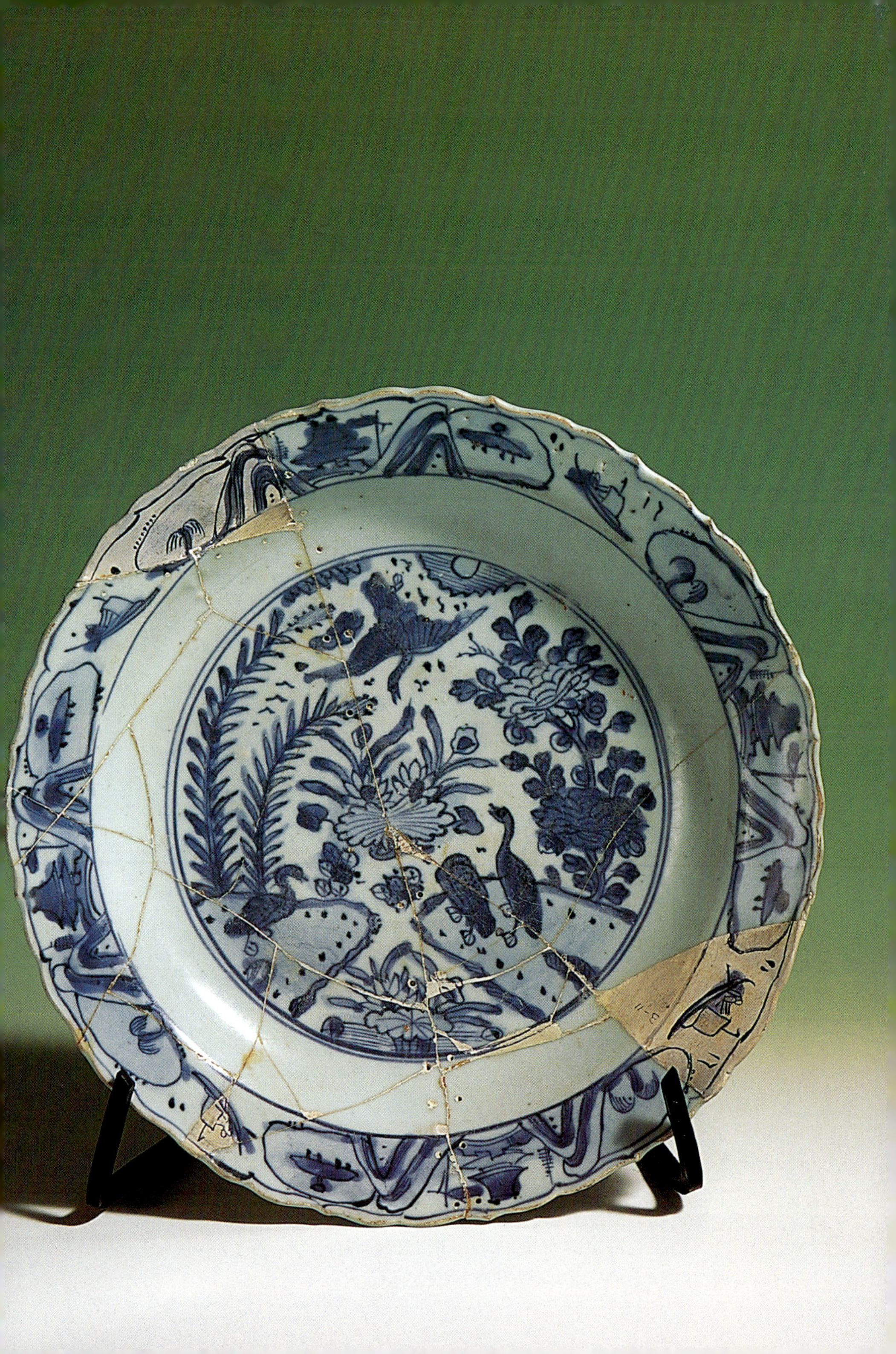

the town of Abu Dhabi had already become so important a centre of activity that the political leader of all the Bani Yas groups transferred his residence there from the Liwa. Early in the nineteenth century, members of the Al Bu Falasah, a branch of the Bani Yas, settled by the Creek in Dubai and established Maktoum rule in that emirate.

QAWASIM

While European powers like Portugal, Holland and eventually Britain competed for regional supremacy, a local power, the Qawasim were gathering strength and at the beginning of the nineteenth century had built up a fleet of over 60 large vessels and could put nearly 20,000 sailors to sea. Their strength posed a serious challenge to the British, then emerging as the dominant power in the Indian Ocean, and in the first two decades of the nineteenth century a series of clashes between the two sides ended in the virtual destruction of the Qasimi fleet and the consolidation of British influence in the Gulf. Based on British claims that the Qasimi vessels had engaged in piracy, the area gained the name 'The Pirate Coast'. However HH Dr Sheikh Sultan bin Mohammed Al Qasimi, Ruler of Sharjah, has shown in his book *The Myth of Arab Piracy in the Gulf* that the British offensive was based on their desire to control the maritime trade routes between the Gulf and India.

THE TRUCIAL STATES

Following the defeat of the Qawasim, the British signed a series of agreements with the sheikhs of the individual emirates that, later augmented with treaties on preserving a maritime truce, resulted in the area becoming known as 'The Trucial States'. The treaties with Britain meant that the sheikhs could not engage in independent relations with foreign powers, and were obliged to accept the advice of Britain in certain defined areas.

However, peace at sea facilitated uninterrupted exploitation of the ancient pearl fisheries in the lower Gulf, and once again fine pearls from the emirates were exported not only to India, but also away to the growing market in Europe. The pearling industry thrived during the nineteenth and early twentieth centuries, providing both income and employment to the people of the Arabian Gulf coast. By the beginning of the twentieth century there were, according to one calculation, over 1200 pearling boats operating out of the Trucial States, each carrying an average crew of 18 men. This meant that during the summer most able-bodied men, numbering more than 22,000 were absent on the pearl banks.

On land, freed from the damaging effects of warfare at sea, but lacking any real economic resources, the emirates developed only slowly during the late nineteenth and early twentieth centuries. One of the greatest figures of the period was Sheikh Zayed bin Khalifa of Abu Dhabi, who ruled that emirate for over 50 years from 1855 to 1909, earning the title 'Zayed the Great'.

HARD TIMES

The First World War had already dealt a heavy blow to the pearl fishery, but it was the world economic depression of the late 1920s and early 1930s, coupled with the Japanese invention of the cultured pearl that eventually finished it off. This was a catastrophic blow to the area.

The population was resourceful and hardy, nevertheless, there is no denying the difficulties that they faced. Opportunities for education were generally confined to lessons in reading and writing, along with instruction in Islam from the local preacher, while modern facilities such as roads, communications and health care were conspicuous only by their absence. Transport was by camel or boat, and the harshness of the arid climate meant that survival itself was often a major concern.

Zayed the Great's son, Sheikh Sultan, father of the present ruler, Sheikh Zayed, was in power in Abu Dhabi from 1922 to 1926, and then, after a brief reign by a brother, one of Sheikh Sultan's sons, Sheikh Shakhbut, came to the throne at the beginning of 1928.

THE DISCOVERY OF OIL

In the early 1930s the first oil company teams arrived to carry out preliminary surface geological surveys and the first cargo of crude was exported from Abu Dhabi in 1962. With revenues growing year by year as oil production increased, Sheikh Zayed, who was chosen as Ruler of Abu Dhabi on 6 August 1966, undertook a massive programme of construction of schools, housing, hospitals and roads. One of Sheikh Zayed's early steps was to increase contributions to the Trucial States Development Fund, established a few years earlier by the British. Abu Dhabi soon became its largest donor.

In the meantime Sheikh Rashid bin Saeed Al Maktoum, de facto ruler of Dubai since 1939, had developed facilities for shipping along the Creek in a determined effort to replace pearling revenues. When Dubai's oil exports commenced in 1969 Sheikh Rashid was also able to use oil revenues to improve rapidly the quality of life of his people.

FEDERATION

At the beginning of 1968, when the British announced their intention of withdrawing from the Arabian Gulf by the end of 1971, Sheikh Zayed acted rapidly to initiate moves towards establishing closer ties with the emirates. Along with Sheikh Rashid, who was to become Vice President and Prime Minister of the newly formed state, Sheikh Zayed took the lead in calling for a federation that would include not only the seven emirates that together made up the Trucial States, but also Qatar and Bahrain. Following a period of negotiation however, agreement was reached between the rulers of six of the emirates (Abu Dhabi, Dubai, Sharjah, Umm al-Qaiwain, Fujairah and Ajman) and the federation, to be known as the United Arab Emirates

(UAE) was formally established on 2 December 1971. The seventh emirate, Ra's al-Khaimah, formally acceded to the new federation on 10 February 1972.

TRADITIONAL LIFE

The tribe has been the principal building block of UAE society since successive waves of migrations, beginning in the middle of the first millennium BC, brought Arab tribes to the region, initially from Yemen through Oman and later from central and northern Arabia. The varied terrain that these tribes inhabited, i.e. desert, oasis, mountain and coast, dictated the traditional lifestyles that evolved over the centuries, but a universal thread was the resourcefulness that the people displayed in exploiting to the limit their harsh environment. This sustainable use of meagre resources was assisted by the age-old social structure in which each family was traditionally bound by obligations of mutual assistance to its immediate relatives and to the tribe as a whole. This was an homogenous society where tribal affinities were reinforced by a common religion, Islam, and a common language, Arabic.

The largest tribe of the UAE, the Bani Yas, roamed the vast sandy areas that cover almost all of the emirates of Abu Dhabi and Dubai. Other tribes, too, such as the Awamir and Manasir, shared this challenging environment for numerous generations, guarding their much-prized knowledge of where to obtain water in the harsh terrain.

The patterns of their economic exploitation varied over time, but all the subtribes and clans were accustomed to wander great distances with their camels in search of grazing, moving as entire family units. Almost all Bani Yas families, with the exception of fishing groups like the Al Rumaithat, returned to a home in one of the oasis settlements at certain times of the year.

Much-prized date gardens were cultivated in the hollows of the huge dunes at Liwa, tapping the water trapped beneath the absorbent sands. In the oasis of Al Ain the luxuriant date gardens cultivated by the Dhawahir were nurtured by an efficient traditional irrigation system (*falaj*) bringing water from aquifers in the mountains, a system which is still in use today. In these favourable conditions other trees besides palms could grow, such as figs, mangoes, oranges, pomegranates, grapes, bananas and, in particular, limes. Lucerne for animal fodder and a limited variety of vegetables, mostly sweet potatoes and onions, were cultivated inside walled palm groves.

Pearling constituted just another means of exploiting all the resources available to the tribal people. As pearling flourished, an increasing number of the able-bodied men participated in the diving expeditions (*ghaus*) during four months in the summer, tending their date gardens in the winter. These long periods away from home meant that great responsibility was placed on the women of the family, both economically and socially.

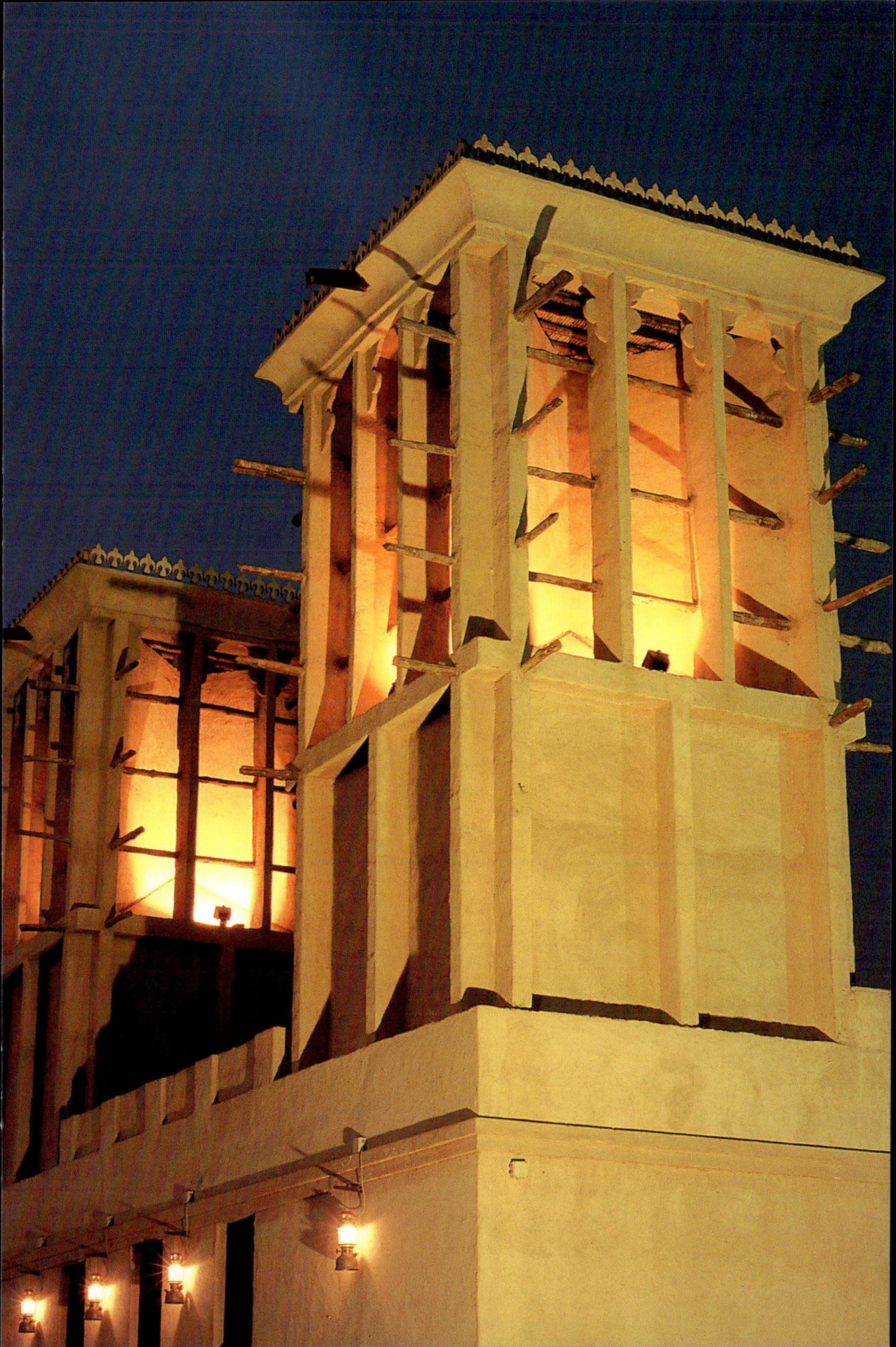

Eventually many of the Liwa-based sub-tribes of the Bani Yas formed cooperatives which jointly owned a boat and shared the proceeds of the sale of the pearls according to an established arrangement, giving the biggest share to the captain, a larger share to the divers than the haulers and leaving some money aside to finance the preparations for the following year. It was due to pearling that, over several generations, some tribes became more specialised in one economic activity or another and became tied to particular locations.

Life in the mountains presented its own challenges. Here fertile soil can be found in many places, such as in the wadis and the outwash plains on either side of the rugged peaks. In the narrow wadis, *falaj*-like watercourses (*ghayl*) were used to irrigate terraced gardens tended by extended families. Domestic animals, sheep, goats and some cows, were kept by the wadi-dwellers. Donkeys were the preferred beast of burden, but camels and bulls were also used for tasks such as drawing water.

Important mountain oases such as Masafi and Manama are situated away from the wadis in areas where good soil on level ground permitted more intensive cultivation. Extensive date gardens watered by ground water trapped under the gravel plains were cultivated on the Ra's al Khaimah coastal strip on the western flank of the Hajar Mountains and on the East Coast plain bordering the Indian Ocean.

Because of the ready access to trading, fishing, agriculture and husbandry, the inhabitants of the East Coast and the plains near Ra's al-Khaimah traditionally led a more settled existence than their western desert counterparts for whom travel over considerable distances was an essential survival strategy.

THE CAMEL

The camel, uniquely adapted to life in the desert, was the mainstay of the bedouin. Not only a useful mount and beast of burden on long treks across inhospitable terrain, it also provided food, clothing, household items and recreation, and at the end of the day was a primary source of wealth. In many cases camel milk and the products derived from it were the only source of protein for the entire family for months on end. Young male camels were slaughtered to provide meat for feasts. Informal camel races were held during festivities and camel hide was used to make bags and other useful utensils, while fine cloaks (*bisht*) were woven from camel hair.

In the winter camel herders wandered for weeks in search of grazing provided by dormant vegetation rejuvenated by rainfall. Their camels were capable of surviving for long periods without water, while camels' milk quenched the thirst of their herders. In the arid summer the camels were kept close to a well to which they returned daily to drink. Camel owners who had sufficient summer grazing close to their date-palm plantations were particularly fortunate as they could harvest whilst watering their livestock at the wells that supplied the local communities.

Although 4WD vehicles are primarily used for desert transport, camels still feature

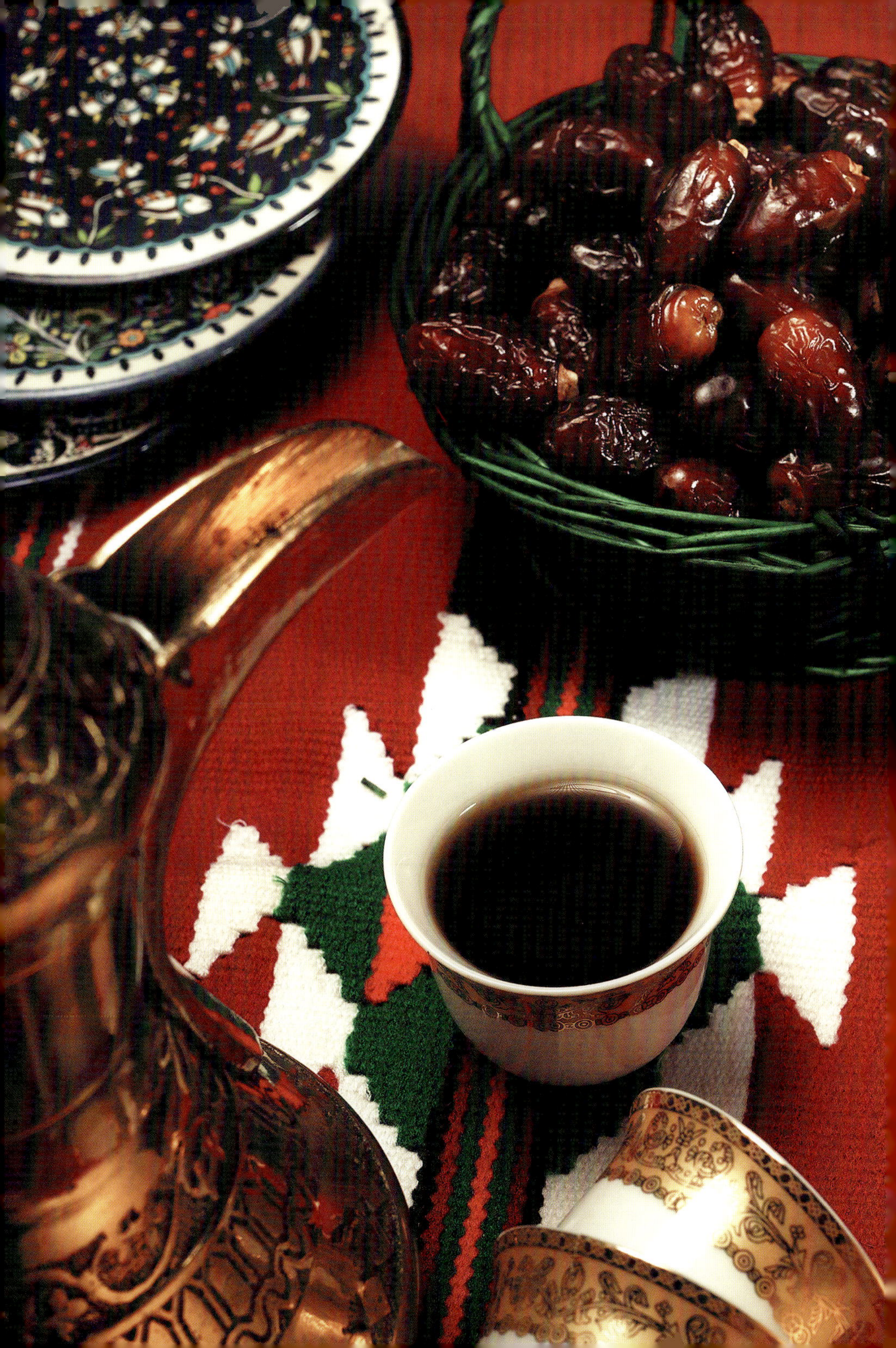

prominently in the UAE. Modern technology has been applied to camel breeding and formal camel races are now held on dedicated camel tracks.

DATE PALM

The date palm (*Phoenix dactylifera*), capable of survival even in the midst of the most inhospitable dunes, rivals the camel in its adaptation to life in one of the severest climates in the world. The date palm can tolerate very high salinity and thrives even in intense heat.

As a cultivated fruit tree, the date palm is propagated from side shoots that grow out from the base of a mature trunk. Today, tissue culture is also used to propagate plants. The newly planted saplings need to be watered regularly. In the desert the water is carried from the well – one leather bagful at a time. After months, or even years, the young bushy plant's roots will reach the water table and be self-sufficient. However, its rate of growth and eventual yield of dates is significantly influenced by the amount and quality of the water available. Obviously, date gardens watered by aflaj or modern irrigation systems are more likely to thrive.

Care for the date tree is a year-long activity involving much more than watering. The outer branches sprouting at ground level are trimmed every year and as the tree grows these branches are cut higher up, and eventually the trunk is formed. After three or more years, depending on the amount of available water, the tree will flower in spring; flowers of the female tree must then be hand-pollinated with the panicles from a male tree, of which only very few are planted. Harvesting takes place during the hottest period of the year, between late June and early October, depending on the type of date tree – there are more than 50 varieties in the UAE alone.

The harvested dates were essential for the survival of the inhabitants in the desert. The ripe dates were lightly boiled and compressed into a congealed substance called *tamr* that can be kept almost indefinitely because the high sugar content acts as a preservative. The dried palm fronds were plaited into containers in which the nourishing, vitamin-rich staple diet could be taken on journeys through the desert, into the mountains, or out to sea. The dates were also stacked in small storerooms with underlying drainage for collecting the valuable date syrup.

Palm fronds were used in construction of walls and roofs for *'arish* houses and as roof matting for the more sturdy coral block constructions. Palm tree trunks supported the roofs of mudbrick and stone castles and towers. Palm fronds are still woven into baskets, bags, bowls, food covers, floor mats and made into sweeping brushes. Even boats (canoe-like *shashah*) are made from the midrib of the palm frond. These can still be seen on the beach at Kalba. The palm trunk was often hollowed out to form a mortar for crushing wheat with the tree stump shaped into a pestle.

In an area of very limited resources, the inhabitants of the UAE certainly considered themselves to have been doubly blessed with both the camel and the date palm.

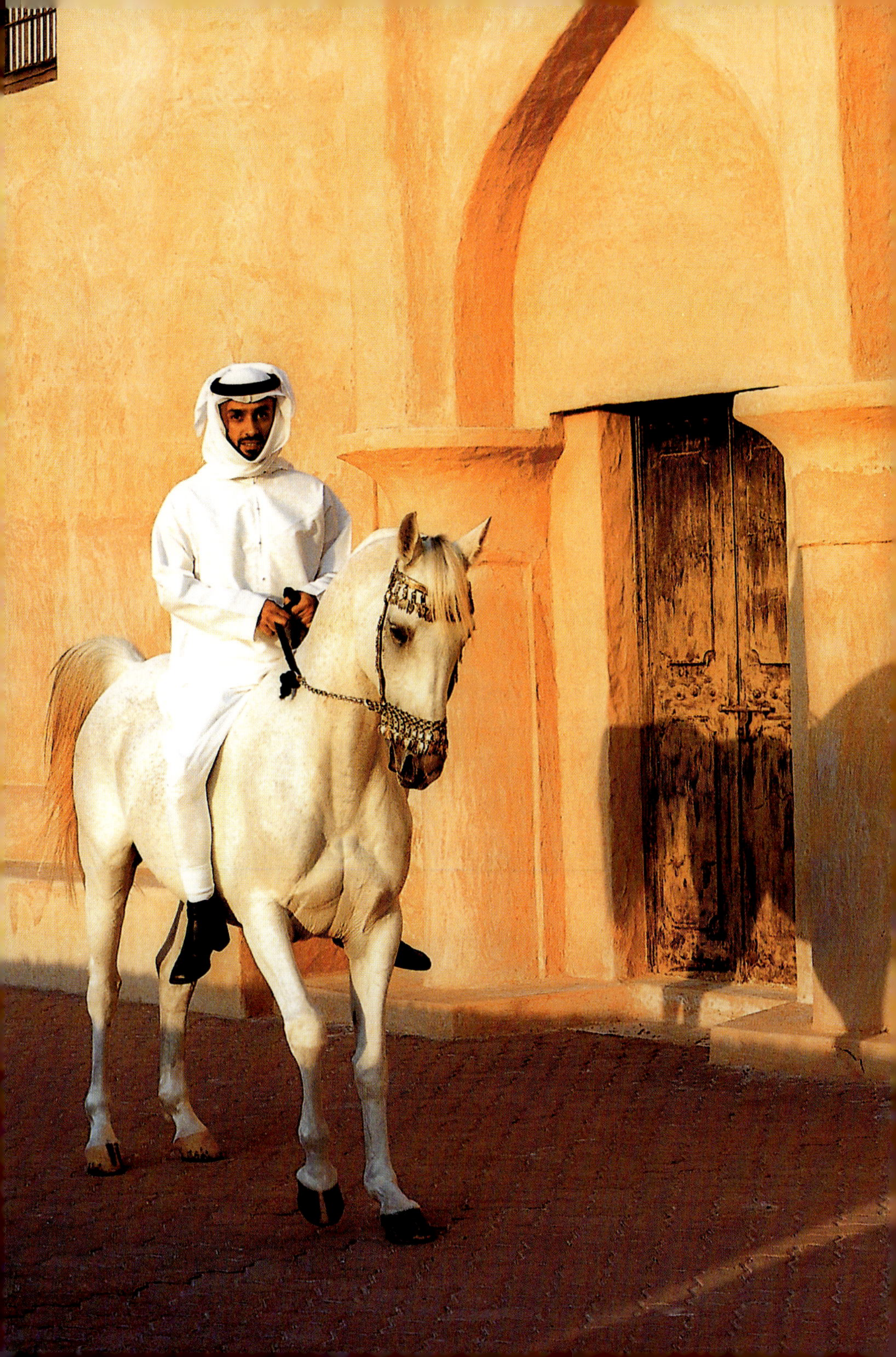

Prosperity reduced dependence on dates, however in recent years modern technology and intensive planting (there are now over 40 million date palms in the UAE) have transformed the subsistence nature of date-palm cultivation into a major agricultural industry serving export and domestic markets.

FISHING

The inhabitants of the UAE made every possible use of the resources to be found on the beaches, sand banks, creeks and inshore islands of the country's 600-kilometre-long Arabian Gulf coast. They also colonised the many more distant islands. The extensive tidal shallows, which are characteristic of much of this coast, were ideal for fishing with traps or cast nets. Fish traps were of two types – the fixed, v-shaped *hadra* by which fish were guided along a stake-fence and finally into a small enclosure where they were harvested at low tide, or the small moveable *garghour* traps woven from palm fronds, weighted down by stones, and baited to entice fish to enter through a narrow hole. In addition to fish, turtles and dugongs also provided valuable protein. The latter were stalked through the shallows, generally from a canoe – but catching them depended ultimately on the hunter's ability to dive in and grapple physically with his prey. Turtle and bird eggs were collected from well-known nesting beaches.

On the East Coast, where the fisheries are replenished by upwellings from the Indian Ocean, sardines were the most profitable catch. Wooden boats manned by about 20 people were used to set a weighted net of about 100 metres in length parallel to the beach. For larger fish such as tuna or shark, heavier tangle nets and landlines were used. Fishermen on the East Coast also fish from palm-frond *shashah*.

Fish that were not consumed fresh were spread on the beach or hung up in the sun to dry, or treated with salt and taken to the inland settlements where this additional protein was very welcome. Some of the small fish were dried and used as camel fodder or as fertiliser for the gardens.

BOAT-BUILDING

The area now known as the UAE was famous for the prowess of its sailors and the sleek lines of their trading vessels, graceful wooden dhows that plied the Indian Ocean. Pearling also depended upon dhows, but the craft used were designed as working platforms and places to live for months on end rather than as ocean voyagers.

Although many of the larger vessels were built in India, there was also an indigenous boat-building industry using imported wood, especially when pearling was at its climax. The construction of dhows remains very much a living tradition in the Emirates with at least as many traditional craft being built now as at the beginning of the last century. At that time Umm al-Qaiwain was an important boat-building centre. Today Ajman has the largest dhow-building yard on the coast, but

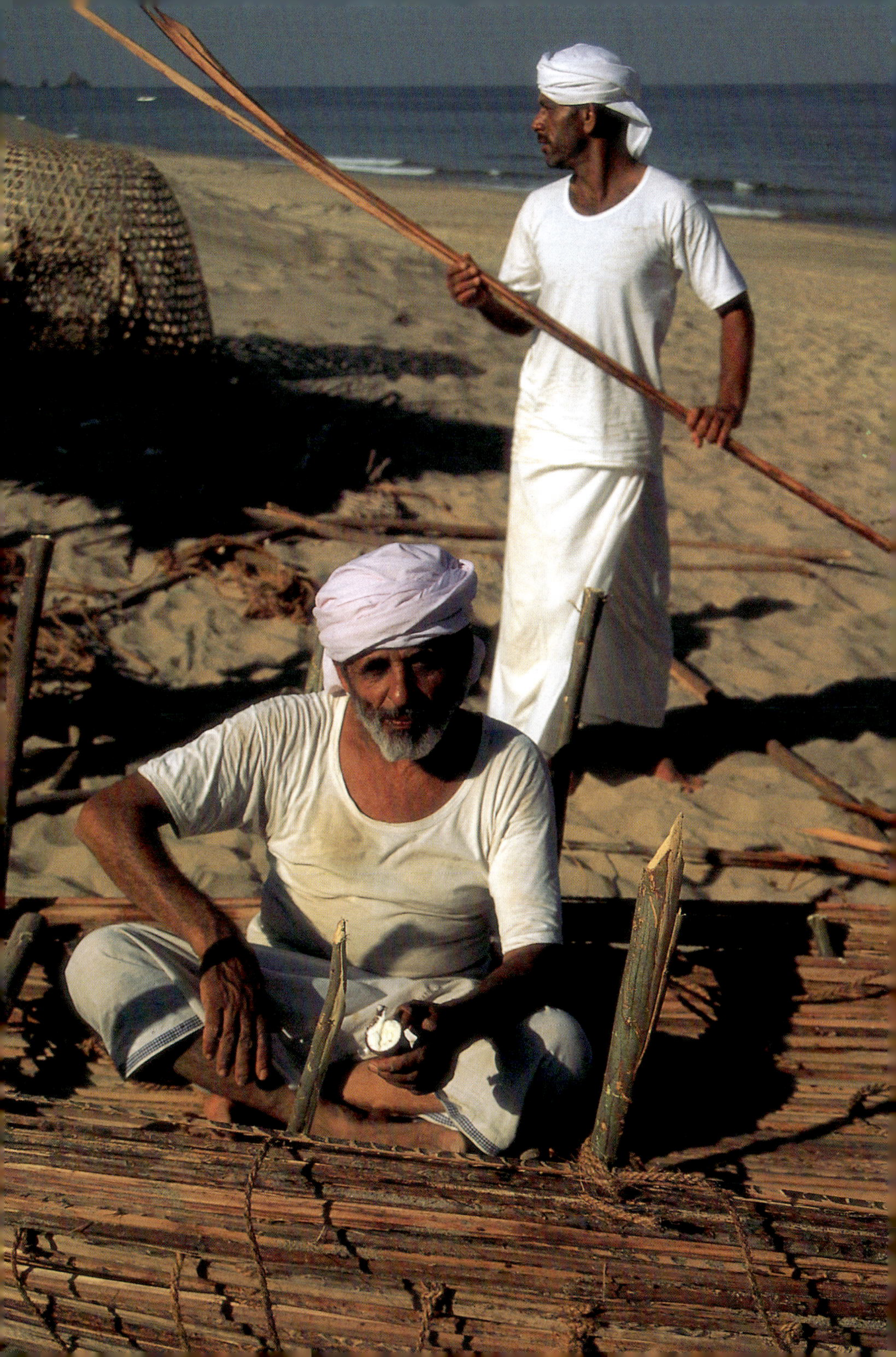

most of the emirates have boat-building yards, enormously atmospheric places to visit. Dhows with inboard motors are still used for trade and fishing and specially constructed vessels compete in traditional sailing and rowing races in the UAE.

The construction methods by which these elegant craft are fashioned have remained the same for centuries. Shell construction involving the fitting of planks first and ribs later contrasts with the European method of forming a skeleton of ribs prior to planking. Boats are all carvel-built with planks laid edge to edge. Hundreds, sometimes thousands, of holes are hand-drilled to avoid splitting the wood and long thin nails wrapped in oiled fibre are driven through to secure the planks to the frames. All the construction work is carried out without the aid of plans and drawings, measurements being made solely by eye and experience. Templates are, however, used to shape the hull planking. Although it appears that accuracy depends solely on the instinct of the boat-builders, in fact a highly experienced master-craftsman (*ustadh*) usually oversees the calculations. The tools used in building boats are very simple: hammer, saw, adze, bow-drill, chisel, plane and caulking iron. The building of a large vessel could take anything up to ten months, while a smaller one, a *shu'i* for instance, would be finished in one to four months.

FALCONRY

Falconry, once an important way of supplementing the diet of the UAE's desert inhabitants, is now enjoyed as a traditional pastime. The most popular hunting birds remain the saker falcon and the peregrine falcon, which were traditionally trapped along the coast during their autumn migration, trained, used for hunting, and then released in the spring.

Once the falconers managed to trap one of the highly prized birds, they had only two to three weeks to train it before the migrating houbara bustards started to arrive. This was done by developing a strong bond of trust between a wild captured bird and its handler, a unique skill that commands the respect of bird handlers worldwide. Ideally, the training of the falcon was completed by the day when the first houbara arrived and the bedouin would hunt the bustards with his falcon throughout the winter months. Although houbara were the favoured quarry, falcons were also used in the past to take stone curlews and hares, and sometimes with saluki hunting dogs to take gazelle.

Today, many birds are caught abroad and are imported. In fact, most falconry now takes place outside the Emirates, and the UAE is a leader in research into conservation of falcons. A captive breeding programme is reducing the number of birds taken from the wild, while the Environmental Research and Wildlife Development Agency (ERWDA) is satellite tracking released birds to monitor migration and the bird's survival rates when freed after the hunting season has ended. The breeding of houbara has also been pioneered in the UAE and wild houbara have been tracked by satellite from Abu Dhabi to China and back again.

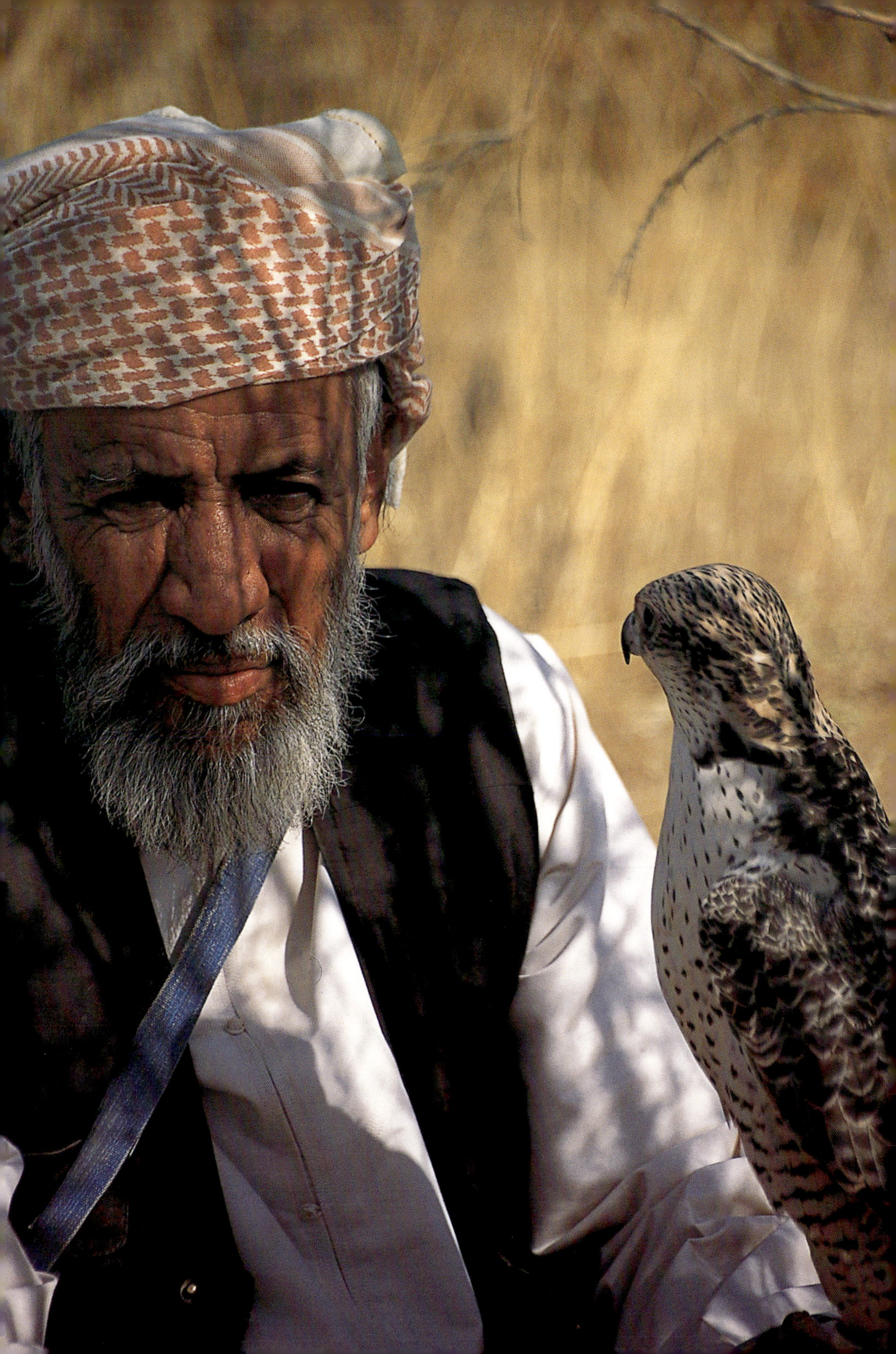

ARABIAN HORSE

Ancestor of today's racing thoroughbreds, the Arabian horse has played a noble part in the history of Arabia. Excavations at Mleiha, in Sharjah, show that over 2000 years ago, prized stallions, decorated with gold trappings, were buried close to their owners, evidence of their place in local society. The loyal, gentle and stout heart of the Arabian horse has been the inspiration of much of the finest Arab poetry. Today, the UAE is one of the world's top breeding centres for the breed, and is playing a major role in its preservation. The UAE also sponsors special races for Arabian horses in many countries, including Germany. Lacking the speed of the thoroughbred, the Arabian horse is noted for its ability to endure hardship and to be ridden over long distances. Some endurance races last over a distance of 100 kilometres or more. Riders from the Emirates are among the world's top practitioners of this sport, which tests both man and horse to the limits (see Sport and Leisure).

TRADITIONAL USES OF PLANTS

At one with the desert and its wildlife, the bedu of the UAE were familiar with the medicinal properties of many plants. Even today local people make good use of such herbs. Seeds of *Cassia italica*, the senna plant, are used as a laxative and the bedu claim it will heal any kind of stomach pain. Seeds of the desert squash, *Citrullus colocynthis*, are highly acclaimed as a cure for diabetes. The bitter sap of the milkweed *Calotropis procera* was even dried and used to fill aching hollow teeth, while the woody parts of this plant were burned to make charcoal, which was an ingredient for gunpowder in the old days. Poultices made of the leaves were applied to joints to heal rheumatism. The leaves also served as fertiliser – dug into the ground around the roots of an ailing palm tree, they help to make the tree more vigorous. *Salsola imbricata* and several *Suaeda* species were dried and powdered to be used as snuff to clear the sinuses.

The best known cosmetic use of a plant is that of henna to dye hair and to beautify hands and feet on special days like weddings and Eid celebrations. To make the henna paste, crushed dried berries and leaves are mixed with medicinal herbs, including one containing a blue dye, and applied to the skin in intricate designs. Poultices of the henna plant leaves are also used to relieve headaches. The poisonous plant *Rhazya stricta* is used in small quantities to settle gastric upsets. An important plant for combating fevers is *Teucrium stocksianum*, a most fragrant herb, similar to a sage. The seeds of garat (*Acacia nilotica*) are ground to a powder to dry out second-degree burns.

Today this traditional knowledge has become the basis for scientific investigation of local plantlife and their biochemical properties. The Zayed Complex for Herbal Research and Alternative Medicine, which has been established in the Mafraq area, utilises modern technology to conduct research into traditional herbal medicine with the aim of establishing an advanced pharmaceutical industry, wholly dependent on natural remedies.

ARCHAEOLOGY REVIEW

While the mining and smelting of copper ores in the mountains of the UAE has been well documented over the last 40 years, little is yet known of other aspects of the past exploitation of the country's mineral resources. During early 2002, a fourth phase of work at a large complex of sulphur mines at Jebel Dhanna, in Abu Dhabi's Western Region, has, however, permitted some preliminary conclusions to be drawn about this little known aspect of the UAE's past.

Originally identified by a team from the Abu Dhabi Islands Archaeological Survey (ADIAS) in 1998, the complex includes 12 separate groups of mines, with a total of at least 150 individual shafts, some connecting to underground tunnels and chambers. Between 60 and 90 tonnes of high grade sulphur are estimated to have been mined at the site. In the absence of archival evidence, it has proved difficult to determine the precise period when the mines were in use, but a combination of radiocarbon dating and pottery analysis suggests that the peak period of use was from the late seventeenth century until the late eighteenth century AD, with the sulphur itself probably being exported. The only evidence of sulphur mines yet identified in the Emirates, the Jebel Dhanna site lies within the oil export terminal complex of the Abu Dhabi Company for Onshore Oil Operations (ADCO) which has instituted a formal programme of protection for this important part of the UAE's pre-oil industrial heritage.

During the year under review, ADIAS also continued its programme of surveys on Abu Dhabi's coast and islands, focusing, in particular, on the island of Abu al-Abyadh, where artefacts and radiocarbon dating suggest occupation throughout the period from the Late Stone Age onwards, and on the island of Futaisi, just west of Abu Dhabi, where over 30 sites of a Late Islamic date were identified. Further work was also undertaken at the end of 2002 on a major Late Stone Age site at Abu Dhabi International Airport. Several hundred archaeological finds, including both several hundred fragments of worked flint and a smaller number of fragments of pottery, were collected during the two weeks of fieldwork on the site, one of the largest in the country. The pottery dates primarily to the early part of the local Bronze Age, while the flint material dates to the Late Stone Age or Arabian Neolithic period. The detailed study of the whole of the site has shown that occupation in the Late Stone Age covered a much larger area than had previously been recognised. Further details of ADIAS activity can be found on www.adias-uae.com.

In Abu Dhabi's Eastern Region, centred on Al Ain, a major focus of work early in the year was a Bronze Age pit-grave at Hili. First discovered nearly 20 years ago, the grave, in the Hili Archaeological Park, has been the focus of several seasons of detailed excavation by a joint team from the Department of Antiquities and Tourism in the Eastern Region and a French group. The remains of over 360 people have so far been recovered from the tomb, and studies of the skeletons have indicated that the disease

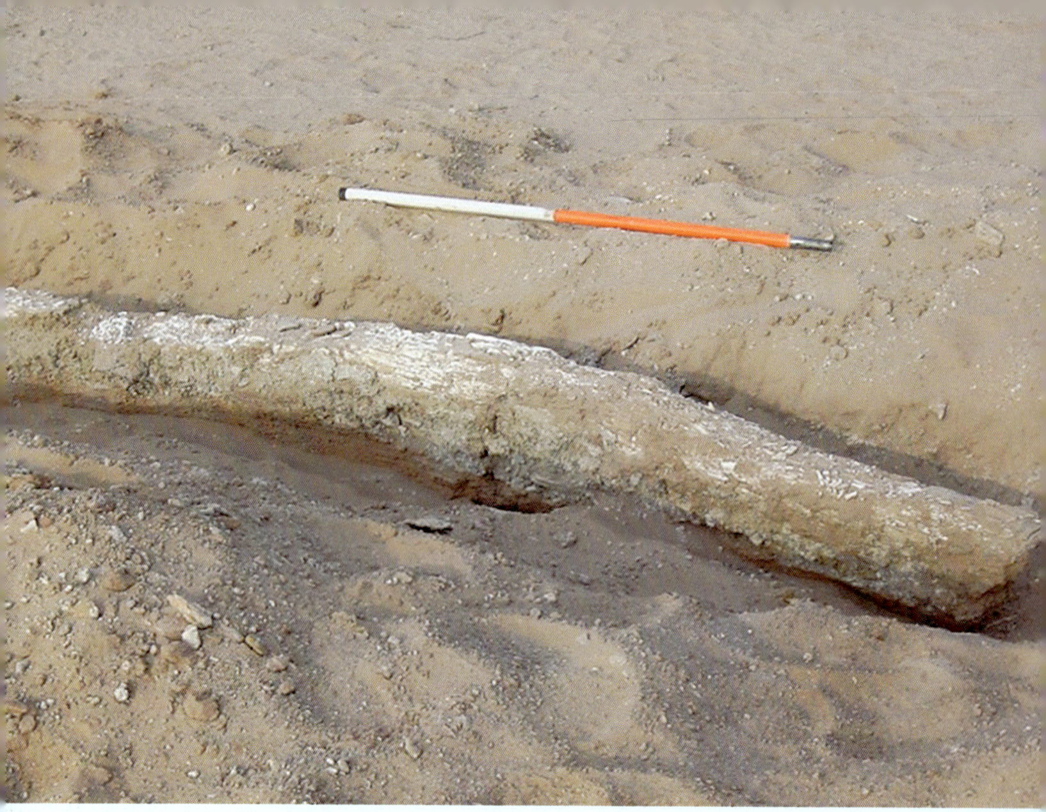

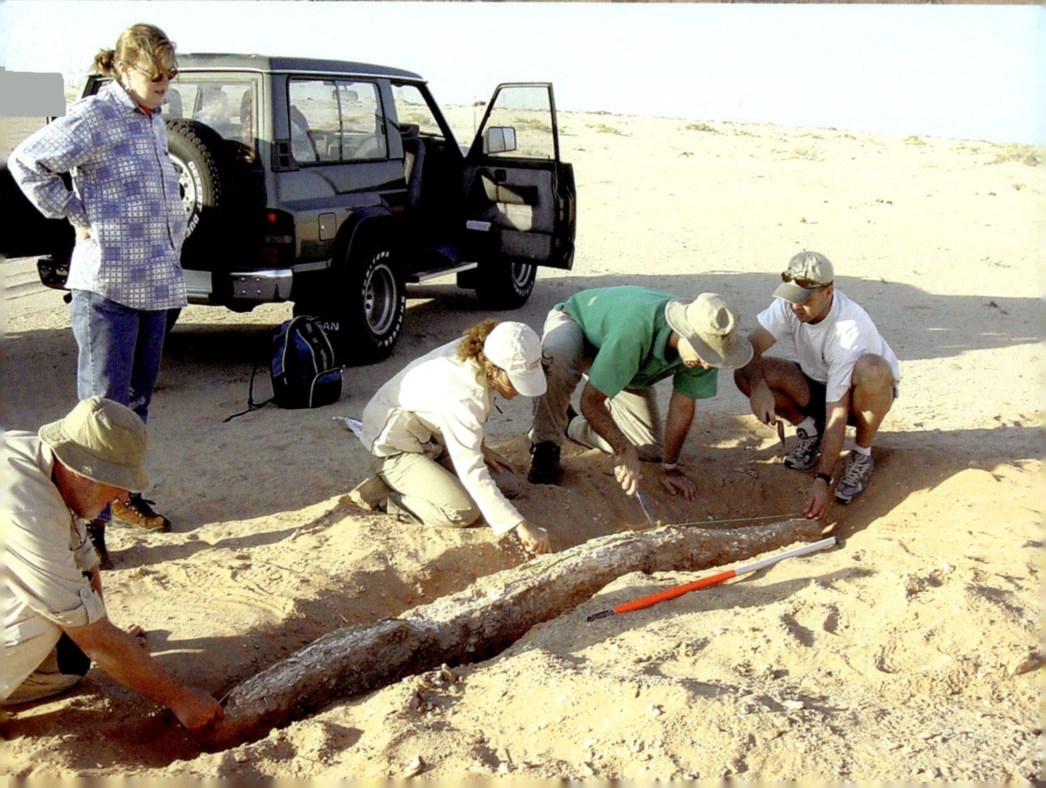

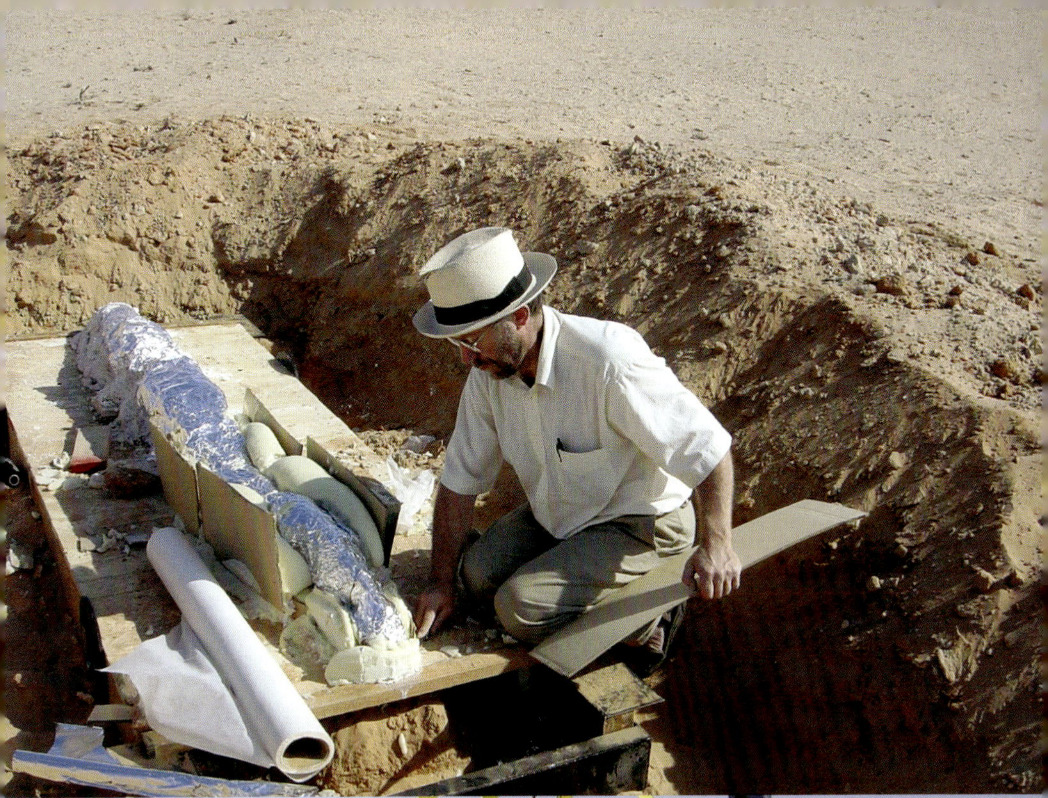
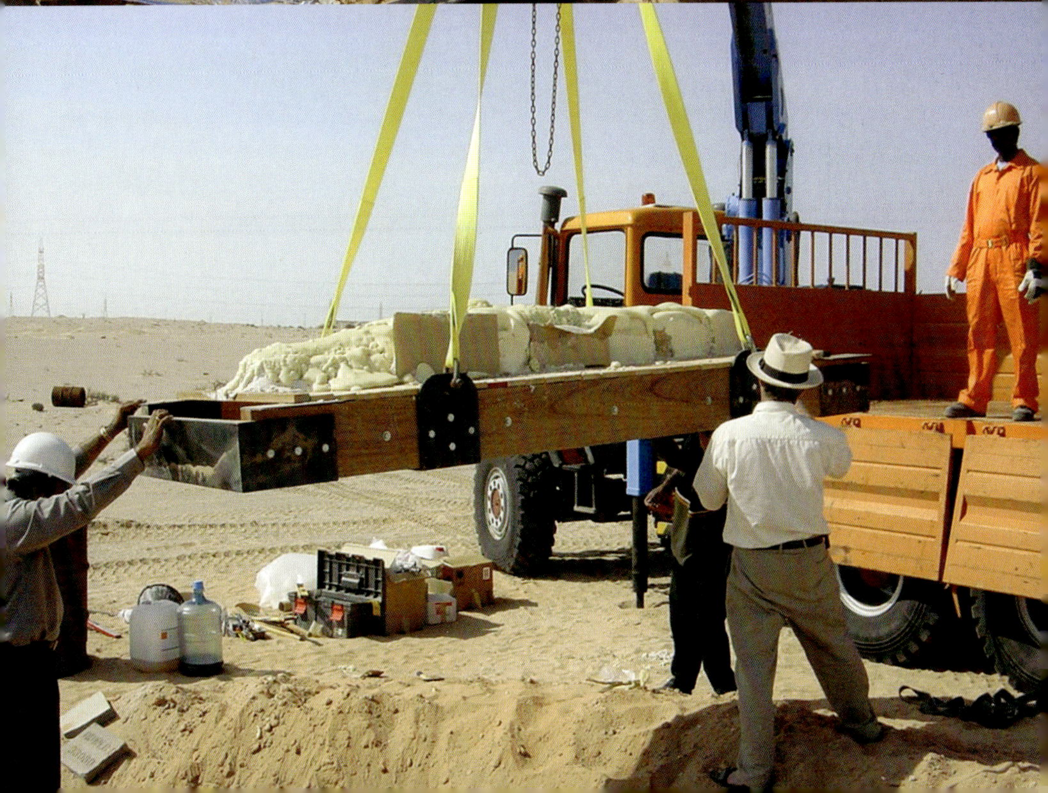

thalassemia was prevalent in the area around 4000 years ago. The studies indicated that infant mortality was high, while most people had died before the age of 45.

In the Emirate of Ra's al-Khaimah, the Department of Antiquities and Museums continued work in the prehistoric cemetery of Qarn al-Harf, where more than 65 tombs are spread along the foot of a massive rock outcrop. Most of them had previously been dated to the early third millennium BC. Excavation of a tomb threatened by development at the southern end of the cemetery, however, provided the surprising date of the early second millennium BC, (Wadi Suq period), this being proven by its U-shaped chamber and the presence of several typical pottery and stone vessels and beads. The presence of several incised arrowheads and glass beads are indications of re-use during the Iron Age and the Late Pre-Islamic period. The tomb, therefore, fills in a previously existing geographical gap in the distribution of known cemeteries of the Wadi Suq period along the foot of the Ru'us al-Jebal.

Dr Derek Kennet from Durham University conducted an intensive survey in the mountains of the Ru'us al-Jebal, overlooking the coastal plain of Ra's al-Khaimah, focusing on old settlements and field systems in the steep and infertile mountain ranges. The field systems have been built over the last 500 years with enormous expense of labour and time in order to enlarge the cultivable area and the study represented the first of its kind in the UAE mountains. Terraced fields with large retaining walls were fed by sophisticated channels, which caught the run-off of rainfall. Cisterns were shown to be the only source of water, while small stone dwellings were built for temporary use.

Carrying out the survey proved to be a strenuous task, since most of the settlements could only be reached along small mountain trails, involving several hours of walking and, on occasion, climbing to a height of around 1000 metres. In most cases, the survey work was carried out with the involvement and support of Gary Feulner, Chairman of the Dubai Natural History Group, who is an expert on the Ru'us al-Jebal.

The Ra's al-Khaimah Department provided computer-enhanced aerial photographs as a basis for the ground survey. Data collected included the number and size of fields, houses, cisterns and cemeteries, as well as the results of a pick-up of pottery sherds, to facilitate dating. When analysed, the data will shed important new light on this fascinating aspect of former occupation of the mountains of the Musandam Peninsula.

The Ra's al-Khaimah Department also carried out further work at the site of a fortified farm of Falayah, the summer residence of the ruling Qawasim family of Ra's al-Khaimah. This farm is of historical significance for the United Arab Emirates, as the first peace treaty of 1820 between the British and the sheikhs of the Gulf was signed there. Excavations took place in several areas, revealing the remains of two small farms in the vicinity of the main fortified complex. These are important for an understanding of building traditions in the palm gardens during the last 200 years, because little has survived from this period. Both farms were originally surrounded by mudbrick walls, forming rectangular compounds, quite like modern residences. Each possessed a *madbasa* (date press), which confirms the original function of the complexes. The older of the two farms was built of *'arish* (palm-fronds), and predates the summer residence of the Qawasim family. In contrast, the second farm was made from mudbrick buildings and may have been used after the fortified structure had already been abandoned.

In the Emirate of Sharjah, excavations were carried out during late 2001 and 2002 by both archaeologists from Sharjah's Directorate of Antiquities and by foreign teams. The local team, working in collaboration with a team from Germany's University of Tubingen, continued a further season of work at the Late Stone Age cemetery at Jebel Buhays, south of the town on Dhaid on the western edge of the Al Madam plain. The cemetery, site Buhays 18, now appears to have extended over an area of over 100 square metres, and may have contained as many as 1000 burials.

Further survey work in the Jebel Buhays area identified a number of previously unrecorded sites that may provide further information on the patterns of land-use by the Late Stone Age population in the area in the fifth millennium BC.

Of much greater potential significance, though, was the discovery by Adelina Uerpmann at Jebel Emalah, north of Jebel Buhays, of a number of stone artefacts that appear to be of possible Middle Palaeolithic date. The typology of the artefacts and the environmental history of the UAE in the Pleistocene period suggests that they may date from an inter-glacial period (a period between the great Ice Ages), either during the last inter-glacial (135,000–100,000 years ago), or, more probably, during the previous inter-glacial, around 240,000 years ago.

Prior to this discovery, the earliest known evidence of human occupation of the United Arab Emirates was dated to the early part of the Late Stone Age, around 7500 years ago. Further work in the Jebel Emalah area is planned, with the objective of identifying more evidence from this early period.

Work also continued during the year at the Iron Age site of Muwailah, close to Sharjah International Airport, and 13 kilometres from the centre of modern Sharjah. Work here commenced in 1994, being undertaken by an international team of archaeologists in collaboration with Sharjah Archaeological Museum. Prior to 2001, excavations and geophysical survey had revealed evidence for at least two large buildings surrounded by an enceinte or fortification wall (Area C). Through many carbon14 (C14) assays it has been determined that the settlement came into existence around 900 BC and was destroyed sometime after 750 BC.

Recent research at Muwailah has taken the form of post-excavation analysis. This has included further C14 dating of a number of campsites that are located outside Area C. These indicate that the landscape was used by nomads, probably travelling between the coast and inland, shortly before and/or during the main occupation in Area C. A project is now in train to examine the many ceramics from the site using ICP-MS

(Inductively Coupled Plasma – Mass Spectometry) to determine patterns of trade and exchange with other communities in the Gulf and further afield. The ongoing analysis of the archaeozoological data by Professor Margarethe Uerpmann (Tübingen University) is continuing to shed light on the subsistence strategies at the settlement.

Since 2001, the results of Ground Penetrating Radar have been analysed to determine the existence of other buildings at the site. These have pinpointed several areas of interest within Area C that will guide future work, and, armed with this information a new programme of excavations commenced at the site in December 2002.

In Sharjah's East Coast port town of Khor Fakkan, part of the site of a fort dating to the Islamic period was excavated by a team from Japan's University of Kanazawa, with Chinese and South-East Asian pottery from the fifteenth and sixteenth centuries being identified. Local reports suggest that the fort was once used by the Portuguese during their occupation of parts of the northern UAE coastline.

Just south of Khor Fakkan, at the town of Qidfa, part of the Emirate of Fujairah, a study of an area close to the new water desalination plant was undertaken by the Abu Dhabi Islands Archaeological Survey (ADIAS) under the sponsorship of HH the Ruler of Fujairah and the UAE Offsets Programme. Here, as at a number of other points along the East Coast, agricultural settlement appears to have been more extensive from around the fifteenth to eighteenth centuries than it is today, with a number of abandoned structures and wells being identified.

Elsewhere in Fujairah, a team from France's Centre Nationale des Recherches Scientifiques (CNRS) undertook a season of excavations on Iron Age sites at the village of Bithna, in the Wadi Ham, identifying a number of buildings and adding to the emerging picture of widespread occupation of the UAE mountains during the Iron Age. Although further investigation of the ancient environment is required, the extent of occupation at Bithna, and elsewhere, may suggest that the UAE climate at the time was less arid than it is today.

Besides archaeological work undertaken within the framework of the planned programmes of the various Departments and Directorates of Antiquities in the Emirates, often in association with foreign archaeological teams, a number of important discoveries have also been made as a result of government legislation requiring the carrying out of environmental impact assessments prior to the construction of any major new projects. Of these, the most important finds have been in southern Ra's al-Khaimah and in Abu Dhabi's Western Region, near Ruwais.

The first, identified during a survey of a water pipeline route commissioned by the Union Water and Electricity Company (UWEC) part of the UAE Offsets Group, was a large copper-mining and smelting complex in the mountains near the village of Muna'i. According to the Ra's al-Khaimah Department of Antiquities and Museums, the complex, yet to be properly studied, is mainly of early to mid-Islamic date, and is the best preserved such complex yet found in the Emirates. Following its discovery, UWEC demonstrated their commitment to preservation of the UAE's archaeological heritage by diverting the route of the pipeline away from the site.

Another important find, of fossils from the Late Miocene period, around 5 to 7 million years ago, was made by ADIAS in the Ruwais region, while surveying the proposed site for a plant to be built by TAKREER, part of the Abu Dhabi National Oil Company (ADNOC) Group. Among fossils found at the site were a complete elephant tusk, just over 2.5 metres in length (and the largest such tusk so far discovered), teeth and leg bones of small mammals and a large skull, probably that of an elephant or hippopotamus. In keeping with ADNOC guidelines on conservation, TAKREER then agreed with ADIAS on plans for further work in the area. A detailed programme of survey was under way at the end of 2002.

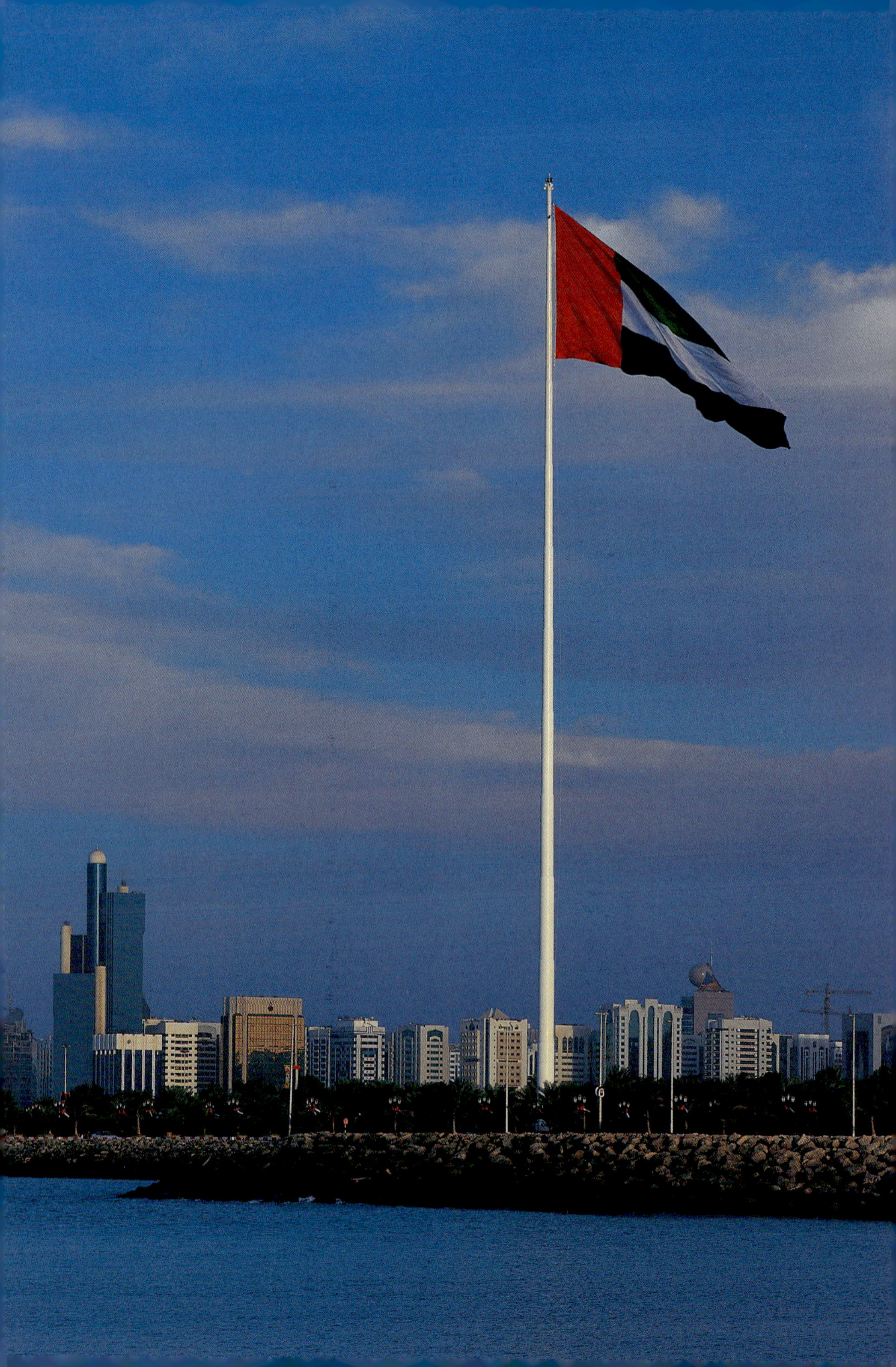

GOVERNMENT AND FOREIGN AFFAIRS

POLITICAL SYSTEM

SINCE THE ESTABLISHMENT OF THE FEDERATION in 1971, the seven emirates that comprise the United Arab Emirates (UAE) have forged a distinct national identity through consolidation of their federal status and now enjoy an enviable degree of political stability. The UAE's political system, which is a unique combination of the traditional and the modern, has underpinned this political success, enabling the country to develop a modern administrative structure while, at the same time, ensuring that the best of the traditions of the past are maintained, adapted and preserved.

Known until 1971 as the Trucial States, which had separate treaty relationships with Britain, the seven emirates came together to establish a a federal state officially entitled *Dawlat al Imarat al Arabiyya al Muttahida* (State of the United Arab Emirates).

The philosophy behind the UAE was explained in a statement that was released on 2 December 1971 as the new state was formally established:

The United Arab Emirates has been established as an independent state, possessing sovereignty. It is part of the greater Arab nation. Its aim is to maintain its independence, its sovereignty, its security and its stability, in defence against any attack on its entity or on the entity of any of its member Emirates. It also seeks to protect the freedoms and rights of its people and to achieve trustworthy co-operation between the Emirates for the common good. Among its aims, in addition to the purposes above described, is to work for the sake of the progress of the country in all fields, for the sake of providing a better life for its citizens, to give assistance and support to Arab causes and interests, and to support the charter of the United Nations and international morals.

Each of the component emirates of the Federation already had its own existing institutions of government prior to 1971 and, to provide for the effective governing of the new state, the rulers agreed to draw up a provisional Constitution specifying the powers that were to be allocated to new federal institutions, all others remaining the prerogative of the individual emirates.

Assigned to the federal authorities, under Articles 120 and 121 of the Constitution, were the areas of responsibility for foreign affairs, security and defence, nationality and immigration issues, education, public health, currency, postal, telephone and other communications services, air traffic control and licensing of aircraft, in addition to a number of other topics specifically prescribed, including labour relations, banking, delimitation of territorial waters and extradition of criminals.

In parallel, the Constitution also stated in Article 116 that 'the Emirates shall exercise all powers not assigned to the Federation by this Constitution'. This was reaffirmed in Article 122, which stated that 'the Emirates shall have jurisdiction in all matters not assigned to the exclusive jurisdiction of the Federation, in accordance with the provision of the preceding two Articles'.

The new federal system of government included a Supreme Council, a Cabinet, or Council of Ministers, a parliamentary body, the Federal National Council, and an independent judiciary, at the apex of which is the Federal Supreme Court.

In a spirit of consensus and collaboration, the rulers of the seven emirates agreed during the process of federation that each of them would be a member of a Supreme Council, the top policy-making body in the new state. They agreed also that they would elect a President and a Vice President from amongst their number, to serve for a five-year term of office. The Ruler of Abu Dhabi, Sheikh Zayed bin Sultan Al Nahyan, was elected as the first President, a post to which he has been re-elected at successive five-yearly intervals, while the Ruler of Dubai, Sheikh Rashid bin Saeed Al Maktoum, was elected as first Vice President, a post he continued to hold until his death in 1990, at which point his eldest son and heir, Sheikh Maktoum bin Rashid Al Maktoum, was elected to succeed him.

Supreme Council Members

HH President Sheikh Zayed bin Sultan Al Nahyan, Ruler of Abu Dhabi
HH Vice President and Prime Minister Sheikh Maktoum bin Rashid Al Maktoum, Ruler of Dubai
HH Dr Sheikh Sultan bin Mohammed Al Qasimi, Ruler of Sharjah
HH Sheikh Saqr bin Mohammed Al Qasimi, Ruler of Ra's al-Khaimah
HH Sheikh Hamad bin Mohammed Al Sharqi, Ruler of Fujairah
HH Sheikh Rashid bin Ahmed Al Mu'alla, Ruler of Umm al-Qaiwain
HH Sheikh Humaid bin Rashid Al Nuaimi, Ruler of Ajman

Crown Princes and Deputies of the Rulers

HH Sheikh Khalifa bin Zayed Al Nahyan, Crown Prince of Abu Dhabi and Deputy Supreme Commander of the UAE Armed Forces, Chairman of the Executive Council of the Emirate of Abu Dhabi
HE Sheikh Hamdan bin Rashid Al Maktoum, Deputy Ruler of Dubai, Minister of Finance and Industry
General HE Sheikh Mohammed bin Rashid Al Maktoum, Crown Prince of Dubai, Minister of Defence
HE Sheikh Sultan bin Mohammed Al Qasimi, Crown Prince, Deputy Ruler of Sharjah
HE Sheikh Khalid bin Saqr Al Qasimi, Crown Prince, Deputy Ruler of Ra's al-Khaimah
HE Sheikh Saud bin Rashid Al Mu'alla, Crown Prince of Umm al-Qaiwain

HE Sheikh Ammar bin Humaid Al Nuaimi, Crown Prince of Ajman
HE Sheikh Ahmed bin Sultan Al Qasimi, Deputy Ruler of Sharjah
HE Sheikh Hamad bin Saif Al Sharqi, Deputy Ruler of Fujairah
HE Sheikh Sultan bin Saqr Al Qasimi, Deputy Ruler of Ra's al-Khaimah

The Federal Supreme Council is vested with legislative as well as executive powers. It ratifies federal laws and decrees, plans general policy, approves the nomination of the Prime Minister and accepts his resignation. It also relieves him from his post upon the recommendation of the President. The Supreme Council elects the President and his deputy for five-year terms; both may be re-elected.

At an historic meeting on 20 May 1996 the Federal Supreme Council approved a draft amendment to the country's provisional Constitution, making it the permanent Constitution of the UAE. The amendment also named Abu Dhabi as the capital of the state.

The Council of Ministers or Cabinet, described in the Constitution as 'the executive authority' for the Federation, includes the usual complement of ministerial portfolios, and is headed by a Prime Minister, chosen by the President in consultation with his colleagues on the Supreme Council. The Prime Minister, currently the Vice President (although this has not always been the case), then selects the ministers, who may be drawn from any of the Federation's component emirates, although, naturally, the more populous emirates have generally provided more members of each Cabinet.

The current 21-member Cabinet was appointed on 25 March 1997 under the terms of Decree No. 67 of 1997 and according to the proposal of Vice President HH Sheikh Maktoum bin Rashid Al Maktoum, who was requested by the President to form a new Government.

Members of the Cabinet
Prime Minister: Vice President HH Sheikh Maktoum bin Rashid Al Maktoum
Deputy Prime Minister: Sheikh Sultan bin Zayed Al Nahyan
Minister of Finance and Industry: Sheikh Hamdan bin Rashid Al Maktoum
Minister of Defence: Gen. Sheikh Mohammed bin Rashid Al Maktoum
Minister of State for Foreign Affairs: Sheikh Hamdan bin Zayed Al Nahyan
Minister of Information and Culture: Sheikh Abdullah bin Zayed Al Nahyan
Minister of Planning: Sheikh Humaid bin Ahmed Al Mu'alla
Minister of Higher Education and Scientific Research: Sheikh Nahyan bin
    Mubarak Al Nahyan
Minister of Economy and Commerce: Sheikh Fahim bin Sultan Al Qasimi
Minister of State for Supreme Council Affairs: Sheikh Majed bin Saeed Al Nuaimi
Minister of Foreign Affairs: Rashid Abdullah Al Nuaimi
Minister of Interior: Lt Gen. Dr Mohammed Saeed Al Badi
Minister of Health: Hamad Abdul Rahman Al Madfa

Minister of Electricity and Water: Humaid bin Nasir Al Owais
Minister of State for Cabinet Affairs: Saeed Khalfan Al Ghaith
Minister of Agriculture and Fisheries: Saeed Mohammed Al Raqbani
Minister of Communications: Ahmed Humaid Al Tayer
Minister of Public Works and Housing: Rakad bin Salem Al Rakad
Minister of Petroleum and Mineral Resources: Obeid bin Saif Al Nassiri
Minister of Education and Youth: Dr Abdul Aziz Al Sharhan
Minister of Justice, Islamic Affairs and Awqaf: Mohammed Nukhaira Al Dhahiri
Minister of Labour and Social Affairs: Mattar Humaid Al Tayer
Minister of State for Financial and Industrial Affairs: Dr Mohammed Khalfan bin Kharbash.

The Director General of the President's Office, Sheikh Mansour bin Zayed Al Nahyan, also has ministerial status.

FEDERAL NATIONAL COUNCIL

The Federal National Council (FNC) has 40 members drawn from the emirates on the basis of their population, with eight for each of Abu Dhabi and Dubai, six each for Sharjah and Ra's al-Khaimah, and four each for Fujairah, Umm al-Qaiwain and Ajman. The selection of representative members is left to the discretion of each emirate and the members' legislative term is deemed to be two calendar years.

Day-to-day operation of the FNC is governed by standing orders based on the provisions of Article 85 of the Constitution. These orders were first issued in 1972 and subsequently amended by Federal Decree No. 97 of 1977.

The FNC plays a vital role in serving the people and the nation and consolidating the principles of *shura* (consultation) in the country. Presided over by a speaker, or either of two deputy speakers, elected from amongst its members, the FNC has both a legislative and supervisory role under the Constitution. This means that it is responsible for examining, and, if it so requires, amending, all proposed federal legislation, and is empowered to summon and to question any federal minister regarding ministry performance. One of the main duties of the FNC is to discuss the annual budget. Specialised sub-committees and a Research and Studies Unit have been formed to assist FNC members to cope with the increasing demands of modern government.

Since its inception the Council has been successively chaired by the following Speakers:
Thani bin Abdulla
Taryam bin Omran Taryam
Hilal bin Ahmed bin Lootah
Al-Haj bin Abdullah Al Muhairbi
Mohammed Khalifa Al Habtoor
Saeed Mohammed Al Ghamdi

At an international level, the FNC is a member of the International Parliamentary Union (IPU) as well as the Arab Parliamentary Union (APU) and participates actively in these bodies.

FEDERAL JUDICIARY

The federal judiciary, whose total independence is guaranteed under the Constitution, includes the Federal Supreme Court and Courts of First Instance. The Federal Supreme Court consists of five judges appointed by the Supreme Council of Rulers. The judges decide on the constitutionality of federal laws and arbitrate on inter-emirate disputes and disputes between the Federal Government and the emirates.

LOCAL GOVERNMENT

Parallel to, and, on occasion, interlocking with, the federal institutions, each of the seven emirates also has its own local government. Although all have expanded significantly as a result of the country's growth over the last 30 years, these differ in size and complexity from emirate to emirate, depending on a variety of factors such as population, area, and degree of development.

Thus the largest and most populous emirate, Abu Dhabi, has its own central governing organ, the Executive Council, chaired by the Crown Prince, Sheikh Khalifa bin Zayed Al Nahyan. The Eastern and Western Regions are headed by an official with the title of Ruler's Representative. There is also a Ruler's Representative on the important oil terminal island of Das.

The main cities, Abu Dhabi and Al Ain, the latter also the capital of the Eastern Region, are administered by municipalities, each of which has a nominated municipal council. A new set of members for the Abu Dhabi Municipal Council was appointed in November 2001.

Abu Dhabi's National Consultative Council, chaired by a Speaker, and with 60 members selected from among the emirate's main tribes and families, undertakes a role similar to that of the FNC on a country-wide level, questioning officials and examining and endorsing local legislation. It is also a source of vocal suggestion for the introduction or revision of federal legislation. A new set of members was appointed in December 2002.

Administration in the emirate is implemented by a number of local departments, covering topics such as public works, finance, customs and management. Some have a responsibility for the whole of the emirate, although in certain spheres there are also departments covering only the Eastern Region.

A similar pattern of municipalities and departments occurs in each of the other emirates, while Sharjah, with its three enclaves on the country's east coast, has also adopted the practice of devolving some authority on a local basis, with branches of the Sharjah Emiri Diwan (Court), in both Kalba and Khor Fakkan. Dubai and Sharjah have also created Executive Councils for their respective emirates.

In smaller or more remote settlements, the ruler and government of each emirate may choose a local representative, an emir or wali, to act as a conduit through which the concerns of inhabitants may be directed to government. In most cases, these are the leading local tribal figures, whose influence and authority derive both from their fellow tribesmen and from the confidence placed in them by the ruler, an example of the way in which local leaders within the traditional system have become involved with, and lend legitimacy to, the new structures of government.

FEDERAL AND LOCAL GOVERNMENT

The powers of the various federal institutions and their relationship with the separate institutions in each emirate, laid down in the Constitution, have evolved and changed since the establishment of the state. Under the terms of the Constitution, rulers may, if they wish, relinquish certain areas of authority, prescribed as being the responsibility of individual emirates, to the Federal Government, one significant such decision being that to unify the armed forces in the mid-1970s. The 1971 Constitution also permitted each emirate to retain, or to take up, membership in the Organisation of Petroleum Exporting Countries (OPEC) and the Organisation of Arab Petroleum Exporting Countries (OAPEC), although none have done so; the only emirate to be a member in 1971, Abu Dhabi, having chosen to relinquish its memberships in favour of the Federation.

In line with the dramatic social and economic development that has taken place since the foundation of the state, the organs of government, both federal and local, have also developed impressively, and their influence now affects almost all aspects of life, for both UAE citizens and expatriates. As with other relatively young states, new institutions that were created for the first time have derived their legitimacy and status from the extent of their activities and achievements, and from acknowledgement and appreciation of their role by the people.

The relationship between the new systems of government, federal and local, has itself evolved in a highly constructive manner. As the smaller emirates have benefited from significant development in terms of, for example, education and vocational training, so they have been able to provide from their own local governments the personnel to extend the variety of services (e.g. tourism) which had once been handled on their behalf by federal institutions. At the same time, in other areas, such as the judiciary, there has been an evolving trend towards a further voluntary relinquishment of local authority to the federal institutions. These new systems of government have not, however, replaced the traditional forms which coexist and evolve alongside them.

TRADITIONAL GOVERNMENT

Traditionally, the ruler of an emirate, the sheikh, was the leader of the most powerful, though not necessarily the most populous, tribe, while each individual tribe, and often its various sub-sections, also generally had a chief or sheikh. Such rulers and chiefs maintained their authority only insofar as they were able to retain the loyalty and support of their people, in essence a form of direct democracy, though without the paraphernalia of western forms of suffrage. Part of that democracy was the unwritten but strong principle that the people should have free access to their sheikh, and that he should hold a frequent and open *majlis*, or council, in which his fellow tribesmen could voice their opinions.

Such a direct democracy, which may be ideally suited to small and relatively uncomplicated societies, becomes steadily more difficult to maintain as populations grow, while the increasing sophistication of government administration means that on a day-to-day basis many of the inhabitants of the emirates now find it more appropriate to deal directly with these institutions on most matters, rather than to seek to meet personally with their ruler or sheikh.

Nevertheless, a fascinating aspect of life in the UAE today, and one that is essential to an understanding of its political system, is the way in which the institution of the *majlis* has continued to maintain its relevance. In larger emirates, not only the ruler, but also a number of other senior members of his family, continue to hold open majlises (or *majalis*), in which participants may raise a wide range of topics, from a request for a piece of land, or a scholarship for a son or daughter to go abroad, to more weighty subjects such as the impact of large-scale foreign immigration upon society or complaints about perceived flaws in the practices of various ministries and departments.

In smaller emirates, the *majlis* of the ruler himself, or of the crown prince or deputy ruler, remains the main focus. The Ruler of Fujairah, for example, holds an open *majlis* at least once a week (daily during the Muslim holy fasting month of Ramadan), which may be attended by both citizens and expatriates. To these majlises come traditionally-minded tribesmen who may have waited several months for the opportunity to discuss with their ruler directly, rather than choose to pursue their requests or complaints through a modern governmental structure.

In modern society, of course, as President Sheikh Zayed himself has commented, it is naturally easier for a ruler to go to meet his people than for them to come to meet him. Sheikh Zayed frequently travels within the UAE, providing opportunities for him to meet with citizens away from the formal surroundings of an office or palace. During his regular inspection tours of projects, he also takes pains to ensure that citizens living nearby are guaranteed easy access to him.

Just as the modern institutions have developed in response to public need and demand, however, so the traditional forms of tribal administration have adapted. With many relatively routine matters now being dealt with by the modern institutions, traditional institutions, like the *majlis*, have been able to focus on more complex issues rather than on the routine matters with which they were once heavily involved.

In the majlises, for example, it is possible to hear detailed, and often heated, discussions between sheikhs and other citizens on questions such as the policy that should be adopted towards the evolution of the machinery of government, or the nature of relations with neighbouring countries. On matters more directly affecting the individual, such as the highly relevant topic of unemployment among young UAE graduates, debates often tend to begin in the majlises, where discussion can be fast and furious, before a consensus approach evolves that is subsequently reflected in changes in government policy.

Through such means, the well-tested traditional methods of government in the United Arab Emirates have been able to retain both their essential relevance and unique vitality, and they continue to play an important, although often unpublicised, role in the evolution of the state today.

A BALANCED APPROACH

When the rulers of the seven emirates met 31 years ago to agree on the forms of government for their new federal state, they deliberately chose not simply to copy from others. They chose, instead, to work towards a society that would offer the best of modern administration, while at the same time retaining the traditional forms of government, that, with their inherent commitment to consensus, discussion and direct democracy, offered the best features of the past.

With the benefit of hindsight, it is evident that they made the correct choice, for, despite the massive economic growth and the social dislocation caused by an explosion in the population, the state has enjoyed political stability. During the last few decades there have been numerous attempts to create federal states, both in the Arab world and elsewhere. The UAE is the only one in the Arab world to have stood the test of time.

FOREIGN POLICY

In common with the rest of the world, the United Arab Emirates found that three major foreign policy issues dominated the international scene during the course of the year 2002. The aftermath of the attacks of September 2001 against the United States continued to demand attention, in particular in relation to international efforts to restore stability to Afghanistan, following the removal of the Taliban Government and the installation of the new Government headed by President Hamid Karzai, and the international campaign to eradicate terrorist groupings and their sources of finance.

In the latter part of the year, rising concern was felt locally over the possibility of another conflict between the United States and Iraq, a possibility that remained present as this book went to press.

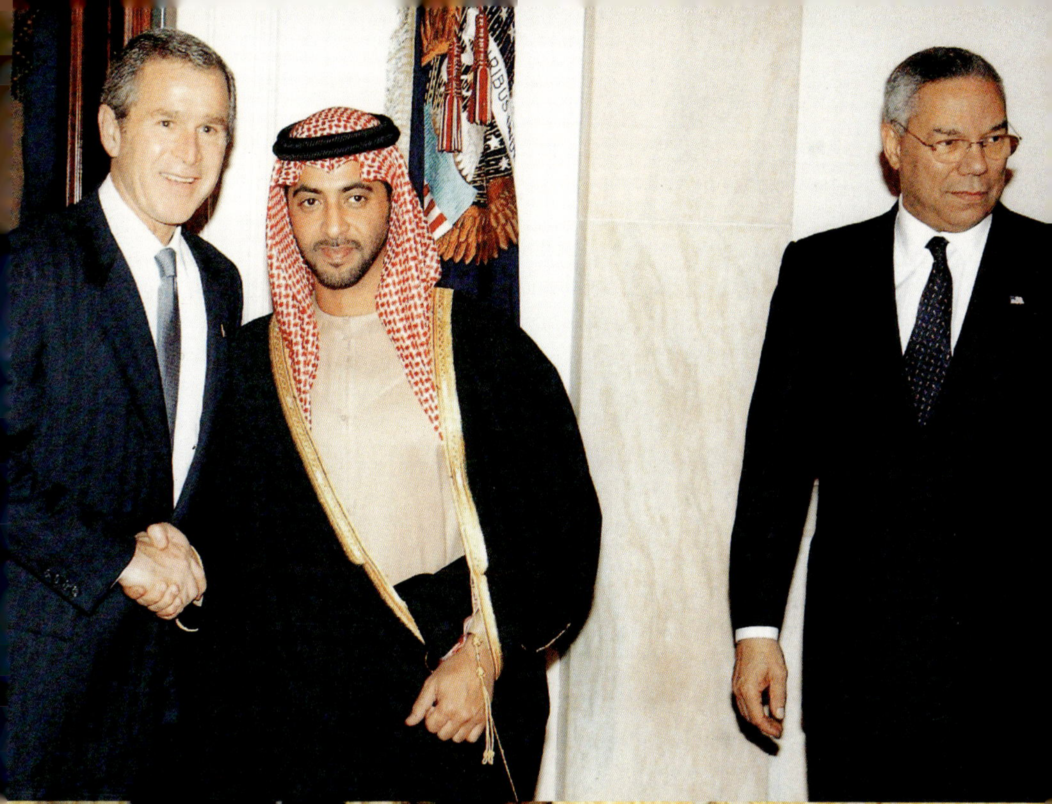

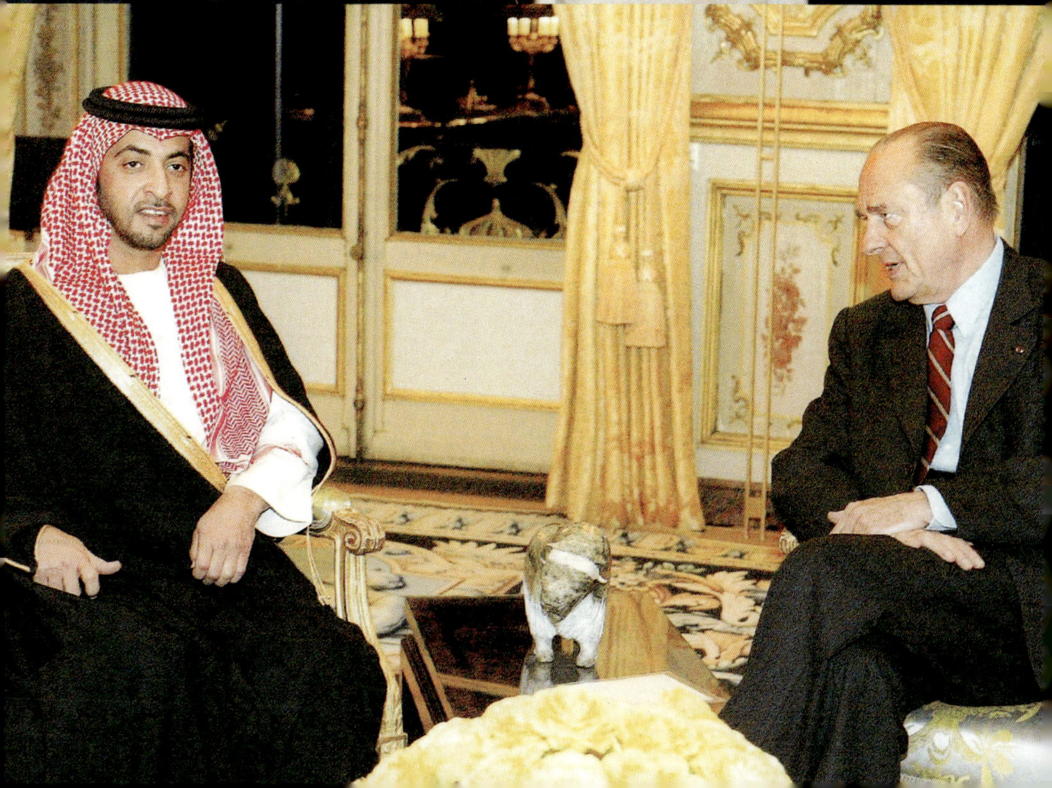

Also of major concern, throughout 2002, was the cycle of violence caused by Israel's attempts to crush the second Palestinian Intifada (Uprising), and the consequent de-railing of all international efforts to revive the Middle East peace process.

Issues of a more local significance also played a role in UAE foreign policy during the year. At the level of the Arabian Gulf, the country has pursued, especially since the formation of the Arab Gulf Cooperation Council in 1981, a policy of enhancing ties with other Gulf states. One milestone reached during the past year was the ratification and signing, in June 2002, of documents completing the demarcation of the border between the UAE and its neighbour, Oman. The agreements were signed during a visit by Oman's Sultan Qaboos to the UAE.

The consolidation of ties between the six GCC states, Kuwait, Saudi Arabia, Bahrain, Qatar, Oman and the UAE, was a central part of discussions at the fourth GCC Consultative Summit, held in Jeddah, Saudi Arabia, in May.

One issue of regional concern since the foundation of the UAE has been the occupation by Iran, in late November 1971, of the three UAE islands of Greater and Lesser Tunb and Abu Musa. Since then, the UAE has adopted a steady policy of seeking a resolution of the problem through diplomatic means or through arbitration, gathering substantial support for its approach from the international community.

Minister of State for Foreign Affairs Sheikh Hamdan bin Zayed Al Nahyan visited Tehran early in the year to hold talks on the issue with leading Iranian officials, and a visit by Iran's President Mohammed Khatami is expected. In an interview with the daily *Al Ittihad* on 1 December, Sheikh Hamdan expressed hopes that a solution to the long-drawn out problem was now approaching.

'Such optimism is based on principles and references related to these issues,' he said. 'I'm sure we are going to see significant progress in the next few months . . . We are looking forward to reaching a final solution to the existing issues between us.'

Commenting on the issue during a speech to the General Assembly of the United Nations in October, Foreign Minister Rashid Abdullah expressed the UAE's hope that exchanges of visits 'will contribute to bringing both points of view closer and to reaching a peaceful solution to the issue, in accordance with the principles of dialogue, peaceful co-existence, trust and good neighbourliness.'

In remarks published on 6 October, President HH Sheikh Zayed reaffirmed his hopes that Iran would respond to the overtures made by the UAE for a peaceful resolution of the issue. He went on to state that in the future, relations between the two countries should adopt a positive tone that would 'result in the eradication of all hurdles that stand in the way of achieving a real improvement in our relations.'

On the broader issue of relations between the countries of the Arab world, the UAE continued to advocate an approach based on efforts to resolve differences through dialogue. With a spirit of forgiveness, Sheikh Zayed believes, it should be possible for all countries to resume brotherly relations, this then permitting a review of existing policies and attitudes so that disputes can be resolved. Only thus, he believes, can the Arab nation once again be united and take its proper place in the world.

Within this context, the UAE participated actively in the Arab summit conference held in the Lebanese capital of Beirut in March. The delegation, led by Vice President and Prime Minister HH Sheikh Maktoum bin Rashid Al Maktoum, actively supported the Middle East peace initiative launched by Saudi Arabia's Crown Prince Abdullah bin Abdul Aziz.

A key part of the UAE's approach to affairs within the broader Arab region is that of support for the Palestinian people, and their desire to exercise their legitimate rights, to end occupation of their land and to establish their own independent state on their own land, with Jerusalem as its capital. Support for the second Palestinian Intifada and for the resistance of the Palestinian people to Israeli violence has, naturally, been an important component of this policy.

Meeting on 14 January 2002 with US Assistant Secretary of State for Middle East Affairs William Burns, Sheikh Zayed emphasised his belief that since the United States is a prime sponsor of the Middle East peace process, it has a duty to act by ordering an immediate end to Israeli attacks. He stated that the Israeli policies of aggression against Palestinians pose a threat to the security of all countries in the region. 'The continuation of the serious situation prevailing in the occupied Palestinian territories as a result of the aggressive Israeli polices, which claim the lives of many Palestinians, poses a threat to the security of all countries in the region, and to international efforts aimed at achieving a comprehensive and just peace,' the President told the US envoy.

It was important that the international campaign against terrorism should not overlook Israeli terrorism in Palestine, he added.

Sadly, the conflict between the Palestinians and occupying Israeli forces continued throughout the year, with little progress having been achieved by the end of the year in terms of bringing new life back into the peace process. While the UAE continued to urge the international community to take action to restrain Israel, it also showed its support for the Palestinians, both Muslims and Christians, through an extensive programme of relief aid and of support for the reconstruction of facilities and buildings damaged as a result of Israeli military activity. The support included funds for the re-building of the Jenin refugee camp, destroyed by Israeli action in April and also for repairs to the Church of the Nativity in Bethlehem, damaged by Israeli attacks over the Easter period (see Overseas Aid).

Within this framework of support for the Palestinians, the UAE welcomed the speech by US President George W. Bush in which he recognised the necessity for the establishment of a Palestinian state as part of a lasting, just and comprehensive peace settlement. At the same time, however, as Foreign Minister Rashid Abdullah noted in his speech to the UN General Assembly in October, it was essential that 'Israel ends its continuous violation of the agreements made within the framework of the peace process and resume peace talks in accordance with UN Security Council resolutions.'

In comments released on 29 November, to coincide with the International Day of Solidarity with the Palestinian people, Sheikh Zayed returned once again to the issue, expressing his concern at 'the continued impotence' of the international community in obliging Israel to abide by international resolutions and to cease 'its systematic aggression against and occupation of Palestinian territories.'

Describing Israel's activities as being both against international laws and norms and in conflict with the principles of international relations, the President added: 'Bringing peace in our Arab region requires a genuine political will and a more serious approach by the United Nations to force Israel to implement UN resolutions related to the Arab-Israeli conflict.'

'As a first step to contain the cycle of violence in the region,' he said, 'we reiterate the need for Israel to withdraw from all areas it has occupied since September 2000, and to stop the daily atrocities it commits against the Palestinian people, in addition, of course, to Israel's withdrawal from other Palestinian and Arab lands . . . occupied since June 1967.'

Although the issue of the Palestine conflict took centre stage for much of the year, the UAE also viewed with considerable concern the increasing tension between the United States and Iraq. On 28 March, for example, Sheikh Hamdan bin Zayed told the local Arabic language daily *Al Ittihad* that 'there should be peaceful means to resolve any issue or conflict, because the biggest and only loser in any (military) strikes is the people.'

As diplomatic activity designed to try to avert a war built up in the latter part of the year, United Nations Secretary General Kofi Annan visited Abu Dhabi as part of a regional tour, meeting with Sheikh Zayed on 23 October to discuss not only the issue of Iraq, but also the situation in the occupied territories of Palestine and the international campaign against terrorism.

The President expressed his belief that war should be averted at all costs, and also reiterated the need for international law to be upheld in any attempts to resolve conflicts, while noting, in agreement with the UN Secretary General, that it was essential that Iraq should comply with all relevant United Nations resolutions.

The UAE welcomed the adoption of UN Security Council resolution 1441, laying down the terms for the re-admission of UN weapons inspectors to Iraq, and also the acceptance of this resolution by the Government in Baghdad. This, Sheikh Hamdan bin Zayed said in a statement, was a positive step, going on to express the hope of the UAE that the UN inspectors would discharge their duties with the utmost transparency, objectivity and neutrality. He also expressed the hope that the Iraqi acceptance of the resolution, and its agreement to re-admit the inspectors, would pave the way to a peaceful resolution of the crisis, would protect Iraq's sovereignty, and would lead to the lifting on UN sanctions on the country, thus allowing it to resume its rightful place in the Arab, Islamic and international communities.

As part of this process of Iraq rejoining the international community, the UAE continued throughout the year to argue for a lifting of UN sanctions on the country, while, at the same time, urging Iraq to take the necessary steps to improve its relations with its neighbour, Kuwait, by freeing Kuwaiti prisoners held since 1990, returning any Kuwaiti property still held and by displaying its respect for Kuwaiti sovereignty.

In its pursuit of efforts to try to contribute to a peaceful resolution of the crisis between the United States and Iraq, Sheikh Hamdan bin Zayed made important visits in November to the United States and France.

In Washington, Sheikh Hamdan met with President George W. Bush, Vice President Richard Cheney, Secretary of State Colin Powell and National Security Adviser Condoleezza Rice, taking the opportunity to urge the United States to put pressure on Israel to end its occupation of Palestinian land and, thus, to bring to an end the sufferings of the Palestinian people. He also emphasised the UAE's belief in the necessity of the revival of activity by the Quartet group of powers in pursuit of Middle East peace.

Meeting with French President Jacques Chirac in Paris on 15 November, Sheikh Hamdan reiterated the view of the UAE that it was important to work hard to bring about an end to Israel's occupation of the West Bank and Gaza and to resume peace negotiations between the Israelis and the Palestinians, in accordance with international resolutions, and the agreements signed by both parties.

Throughout the year, the United Arab Emirates extended all possible support to the international fight against terrorism, while emphasising the necessity both of a clear definition of terrorism and of ensuring that terrorism perpetrated by states, such as Israel, should not be overlooked.

Addressing the United Nations General Assembly in October, Foreign Minister Rashid Abdullah noted the UAE's view that 'international terrorism is a direct threat to the stability of nations and to international peace . . . The UAE denounces all acts of terrorism, whatever their reasons and origins (and) renews its call for an international conference on terrorism, to produce a clear definition of terrorism, based on the principles of the Charter of the United Nations and international treaties, conventions and covenants.'

Within that framework, the UAE's financial authorities continued to collaborate with efforts to trace and freeze sources of finance for terrorism.

Within the broad Indian Ocean, the UAE viewed with considerable concern the escalation of tension between India and Pakistan, both neighbours and friends, calling on both states to deal with their disputes through bilateral negotiations, and by peaceful means, so as to maintain regional peace and security.

Elsewhere, the UAE has continued to promote the development of its political and economic relations with both developed and developing countries, particular progress being achieved within the Arab world, and also with the countries of the European Union, the US and Japan and the Muslim states of Central Asia. Numerous bilateral Ministerial visits were exchanged between the UAE and other countries, focusing on issues ranging from economics and defence to regional affairs and cultural exchange, while successful meetings of bilateral joint commissions were held with a number of countries, including France and Finland.

One unusual visit, in October, was by the First Minister and Finance Minister of Jersey, a British dependency that had not previously sent a delegation to the Emirates, with the visit being concerned, in particular, with the further development of financial ties between the two sides.

Since the establishment of the United Arab Emirates in 1971, it has enjoyed a marked consistency in its foreign policy, this being due to a very large extent to the leadership of President Sheikh Zayed. Over the past year, as in previous years, this has helped to consolidate the country's reputation within the international community as a responsible state that seeks to promote dialogue and consensus as a tool for the resolution of disputes and which endeavours to strengthen the legitimacy and authority of international organisations and institutions.

At the end of 2002, the UAE had diplomatic relations with 143 countries and hosted 71 embassies, compared to three in 1971. There are 35 non-resident ambassadors and 52 consulates in Dubai. The UAE has 44 embassies and 7 consulates abroad and two Permanent Missions to the United Nations in New York and Geneva.

The country is a member of more than 25 regional and international organisations, and has signed 45 international treaties and conventions, apart from numerous bilateral agreements, including over 60 investment protection agreements, 65 civil aviation agreements and more than 52 cultural agreements.

OVERSEAS AID

Over the course of the last year, the United Arab Emirates has continued to demonstrate its commitment to the alleviation of hardship in other developing countries and to the provision of emergency relief assistance for those affected by conflict and by natural disasters.

ABU DHABI FUND FOR DEVELOPMENT

The overseas aid programme was originally born out of the belief that a country like the UAE, well-endowed with natural resources thanks to its hydrocarbon reserves, had a duty to help others who were less fortunate. In 1971, therefore, on the instructions of President HH Sheikh Zayed bin Sultan Al Nahyan, the Abu Dhabi Fund for Arab

Economic Development (ADFAED), now known as the Abu Dhabi Fund for Development (ADFD), was established. Over the three decades since then, concessionary loans made by the Fund, or made by government and administered by the Fund, have amounted to nearly US$6.2 billion to over 50 developing countries throughout the Arab world, Africa and Asia, a very substantial sum for what is, after all, a small country with a small population.

In the period from December 2001 to October 2002, the Fund signed new loan agreements worth around US$625 million. Among these were a loan of US$300 million to Morocco for the funding of a major free port complex on the northern coast, one of US$100 million to Algeria for housing projects, US$100 million to Egypt for the Toshka water project in southern Egypt and US$100 million to Sudan for another project related to the tapping of the waters of the Nile, a hydro-electric power project at Meroe, north of Khartoum.

Another loan, worth around US$25 million was given to Tunisia for the building of 20 dams to provide water for agricultural development.

Fund officials also held talks during the year with officials from a number of other Asian and African countries on new loan agreements, including Indonesia, Yemen and Eritrea, the latter already having received a loan of US$30 million in 2001 for refurbishment and development of its major Red Sea port of Massawa.

The commitment by the Government of the United Arab Emirates to global development extends, however, well beyond the loans made by, or administered by, the ADFD. The UAE is, for example, a major contributor to a number of the specialised organisations of the United Nations, such as UNRWA, UNICEF, UNESCO and FAO, while direct contributions have also been made by senior government officials, including Sheikh Zayed. As a result, therefore, the country has an impressive record as a provider of development assistance not only in terms of the value of its aid, but also in terms of its performance in relation to its Gross National Product.

OPERATION EMIRATES SOLIDARITY

When Israeli forces withdrew from southern Lebanon in May 2000, it seemed as if one of the last obstacles to re-occupation of this troubled region was finally removed. But decades of war had left a bitter aftermath with over 150,000 landmines still threatening local people, making farmers fearful of tilling their land; children petrified of leaving their homes; ordinary people unsure of each new step. This is still true of parts of southern Lebanon today but thanks to a unique overseas aid project established by the UAE, the situation has been changing very rapidly. Operation Emirates Solidarity or OES was set-up in order to provide a lasting solution to what seemed to be an intractable problem. It is a unique partnership between the Lebanese Government, the United Nations and the United Arab Emirates (which pledged up to US$50 million). The main phase of OES, involving clearance of over

150 minefields and support for local communities to rebuild their battered lives, was initially scheduled to run for two years but is being completed in approximately half that time thanks to skilled management, discipline and technical expertise of the contracted companies, Minetech and Bactec. Quality assurance was supplied by the UN MAC office in South Lebanon. A film about the project, entitled *Lethal Legacy*, is being made for international broadcast.

RCS AND OTHER NGOS

In recent years, the formal government aid contributions have been supplemented by very substantial sums donated by non-governmental organisations and by charitable foundations, as well as by individual citizens and residents of the country.

In this process, a leading role has been played by the country's Red Crescent Society (RCS) headed by Sheikh Hamdan bin Zayed Al Nahyan, who is also the UAE's Minister of State for Foreign Affairs. The Society has contributed several hundred million dollars in relief assistance over the past few years, with particular effort being paid towards those suffering from the results of conflict of natural disasters.

In the first half of 2002 alone, the Society spent over Dh203 million (US$55 million), with beneficiaries including victims of a train crash in Tanzania, the needy in Benin, victims of drought and disease in Somalia, flood victims in Sudan, Yemen, Syria and Bangladesh, earthquake victims in Iran and refugees from the conflicts in Southern Sudan, Afghanistan and Chechnya. The Society is also sponsoring the expenses of 17,200 orphans in 16 countries around the world, as well as within the UAE.

A major focus of activity by the Red Crescent Society during 2002, of course, has been the victims of the continuing and devastating Israeli assault against the civilian population of the Palestinian West Bank and Gaza Strip. In the period from the breaking-out of the second Palestinian Intifada in September 2000 until the end of June 2002, the Society had supplied Dh285 million (US$77.6 million) in assistance of various forms, including the air-lifting of relief supplies, distribution of food to the needy and the establishment of health centres and hospitals, these sums being additional to those mentioned above.

Among other commitments were a contribution of US$27 million for the rebuilding of the Jenin refugee camp in the West Bank, destroyed during an Israeli armoured onslaught in April, the largest such contribution offered from any country, and one which attracted special thanks from the Commissioner-General of the UN Relief Works Agency, UNRWA. Work on the rebuilding programme is being carried out in association with UNRWA and the Palestinian Public Works Ministry

The ferocious Israeli assaults in April and May, as well as later in 2002, affected many other Palestinian towns and cities, including the city of Bethlehem, where the Church of the Nativity, built over the birthplace of Jesus, was damaged, as well as the historic Omar Mosque. Here again, on the instructions of Sheikh Zayed, the UAE

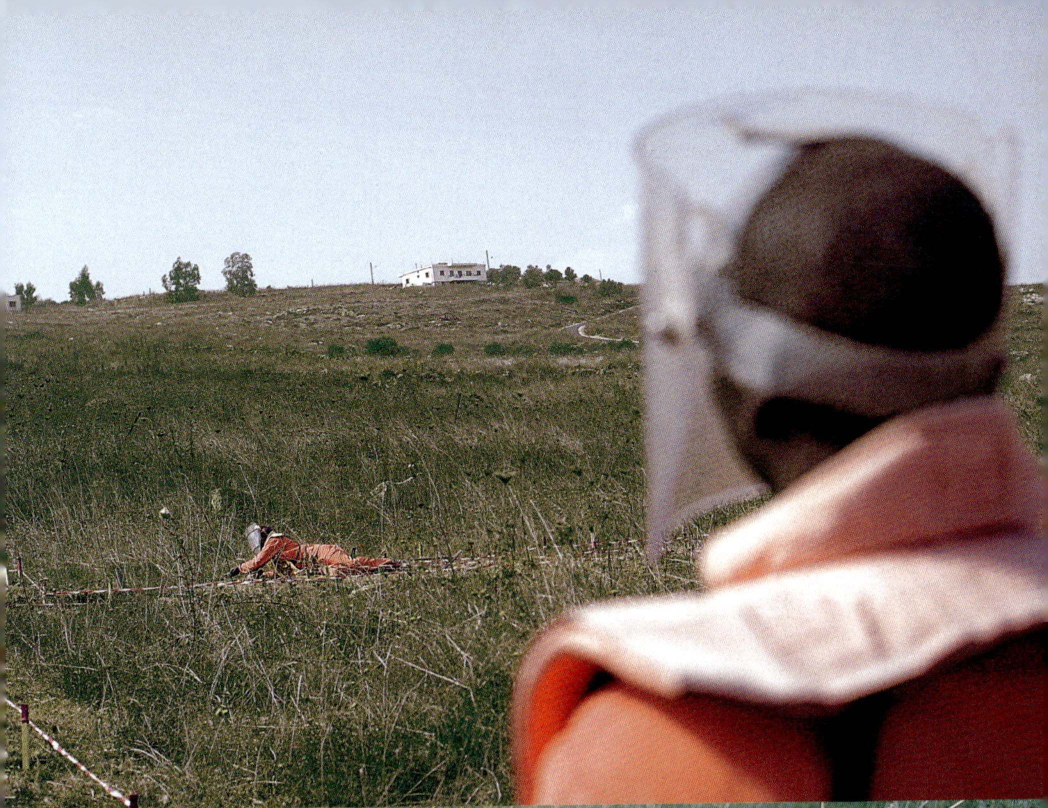

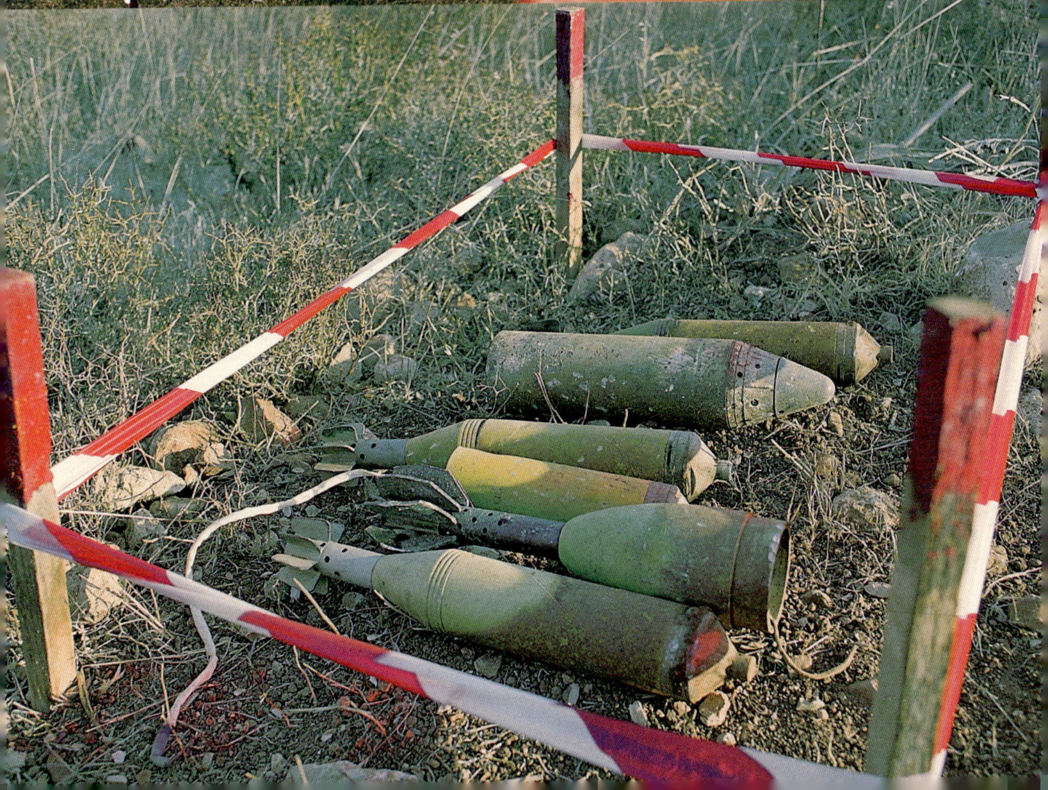

has committed all necessary funds for the restoration of these two important religious sites. The Red Crescent Society also continued to support projects to restore religious buildings in Jerusalem. One major project during the year, also partly financed by other Arab and Muslim countries, was the funding of restoration of the long-neglected Marawani mosque, near the Al Aqsa Mosque. Work on the mosque had previously been prevented by Israeli authorities. The Yousufi cemetery, also near Al Aqsa, where a number of the companions of the Prophet Mohammed are buried, is also being restored by the RCS, as is the Al Ghadriya Islamic school.

Two UAE women have also made major private contributions to providing long-term funding for maintenance of the Al Aqsa Mosque and adjacent buildings by purchasing residential accommodation whose rental income will be added to the Al Aqsa endowments. A total of over US$2.1 million has been provided by the two women, whose donation is being administered by the Red Crescent Society. Towards the end of the year, a third project, the purchase of a nearby hotel at a cost of US$600,000, was also being negotiated.

The RCS also funded fencing for the Al Quds University, at a cost of US$425,000 million, to protect land under threat of expropriation by Israeli authorities, and has donated US$900,000 to the University to help it pay salaries of its staff.

Other activity by the Society in Jerusalem has included the provision of equipment to a health clinic in the Abu Dis area, at a cost of Dh870,000, and relief aid distributed to needy Palestinians in the city, which is estimated to have amounted to around US$1.6 million over the last year.

During a fund-raising campaign for Palestine carried out in the UAE early in 2002, with the help of local media organisations, a total of Dh350 million (US$95.3 million) was raised. Expressing thanks for the donations, Sheikh Hamdan told the Emirates News Agency, WAM that 'This tremendous response shows the solidarity of the UAE people, both citizens and other residents, with the Palestinian people who are living in tragic and inhuman circumstances.'

As a result of the fund-raising campaign, an Emirates Committee for the Relief of the Palestinian People was established in April, which includes representatives of seven charitable organisations: the Mohammed bin Rashid Al Maktoum Charitable and Humanitarian Foundation; Dubai Charity Foundation; International Islamic Relief Organisation of Sharjah; Human Appeal International; Sharjah Charity Association; Fujairah Charity Association and Dar Al Bir of Dubai. The objective of the new committee was to co-ordinate the individual fund-raising efforts of these groups, as well as to help to ensure that the distribution of their assistance to intended recipients was undertaken in an efficient and cost-effective manner.

While the Palestinian people were, naturally, a focus of attention during the course of the year, support from the UAE's various aid donors continued to be given to other areas hit by conflict as well, key amongst these being Afghanistan and Kosovo.

جسر جوي لنقل مساعدات إنسانية إلى كادقلي بالسودان.
2002

The UAE's involvement in relief aid to Balkan states dates back to the early 1990s, as the former state of Yugoslavia collapsed into anarchy, blood-letting and ethnic cleansing. A contingent of the UAE Armed Forces served with distinction in the international peace-keeping force in Kosovo, and although this was eventually withdrawn in late 2001, assistance continues to be given by the Red Crescent Society and Dubai's Mohammed bin Rashid Al Maktoum Charitable and Humanitarian Foundation to the people of Kosovo as they seek to rebuild their lives. Much of this assistance has been devoted to helping in the restoration of the Kosovan infrastructure, with projects during the year including two schools, at Vucitra and Salatina, and the construction of a complete village, with the total cost being in excess of US$1.3 million.

In Afghanistan, the involvement of the United Arab Emirates in relief operations again dates back several years, with the Red Crescent Society and the Mohammed bin Rashid Foundation long having provided assistance to refugee camps in Pakistan. The increase in the refugee flow late in 2001, however, with tens of thousands more refugees flooding across the border into Pakistan's Baluchistan and North West Frontier areas, prompted a major increase in aid. One landmark project, run by the Red Crescent Society, was the setting up of a field hospital in the Chaman area of Baluchistan, close to the Afghan border, which treated around 60,000 patients during the period from October 2001 to March 2002, while the Society also distributed over 1800 tonnes of relief supplies to refugees.

Another project, run by the Mohammed bin Rashid Foundation, was the establishment of a refugee camp at Spin Boldak which, by mid 2002, had provided temporary homes for over 27,000 people.

With the installation of a new government in Afghanistan, however, and the beginnings of reconstruction, a new phase of assistance commenced, that of helping refugees to return to their homes, and to rebuild their villages. The UAE Red Crescent Society undertook in December 2001 to be responsible for the repair and maintenance of the hospital of the Afghan Red Crescent Society in the country's capital, Kabul, and has worked closely with its sister Society to reintroduce proper medical services in the city.

With the flow of refugees returning home, the Spin Boldak camp was closed in late 2002, with every family of refugees being given a cash sum as well as food supplies, to provide them with help to resume their lives. Overall, an estimated 15,000 families are expected to benefit from the Foundation's activities, which are being carried out in association with the Islamic Relief Agency and the Afghan Cultural Centre.

The Foundation is also building five villages in rural areas of Afghanistan and, an important move in a country that has been so long ravaged by conflict, is funding the construction of two factories to make artificial limbs. Other projects designed to help Afghanistan in its efforts to return to normality include a Dh11 million (US$3 million) programme for drilling water wells.

In adjacent Pakistan, the beneficiary of a major ADFD loan package worth Dh974 million (US$265 million) in 2001, another major aid project came to fruition in 2002, with the opening of a 500-bed hospital at the Sheikh Zayed Medical Complex in Lahore. The complex, which also includes a medical sciences university and an institute for training of nurses, named after the UAE First Lady, Sheikha Fatima bint Mubarak, was wholly funded by the UAE President.

While the main focus of relief aid during the past year has been on areas of conflict, the UAE'S charitable organisations also responded swiftly and constructively to victims of natural disasters around the world, and also gave support for the construction of a wide range of small-scale development and infrastructure projects. Among countries to receive such support, besides those already mentioned above, were Mali, Mauretania, Senegal, Nigeria, Sierra Leone, Sudan, Egypt, Ethiopia, Namibia, Iran and Indonesia, with support ranging from aid for victims of floods and earthquakes, funds to build hospitals, schools, mosques and clinics, well-drilling programmes to improve water supply, and computers, electronic instruments and books to support educational programmes.

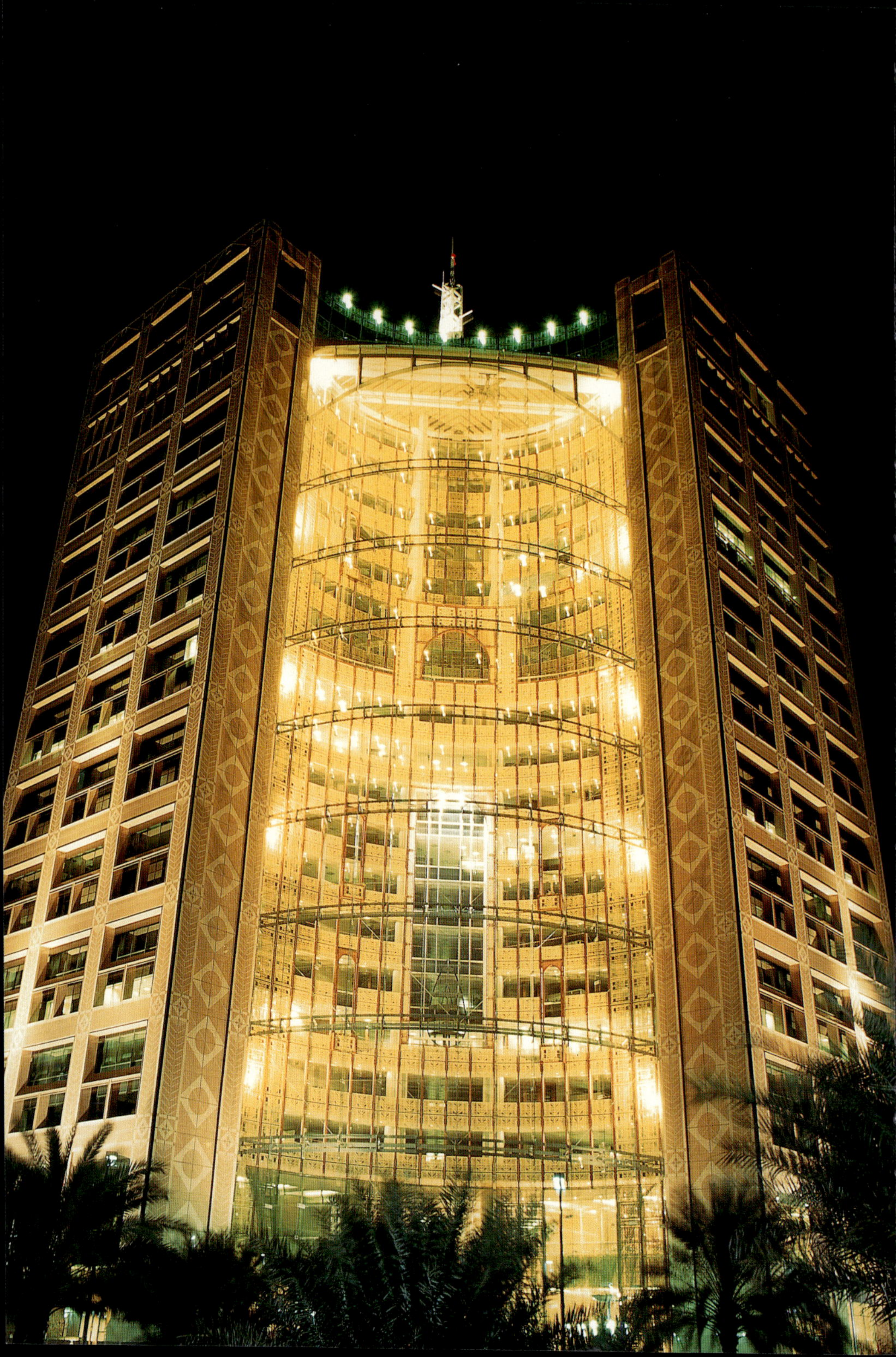

ECONOMIC DEVELOPMENT

THE ECONOMY*

CONTINUED FLUCTUATIONS IN THE INTERNATIONAL oil market have underpinned the importance of the UAE's policy of economic diversification. Whilst there have been considerable achievements in the non-oil sector, oil and gas remain the UAE's most important sources of income and there has been a concentrated focus on ensuring that the maximum benefits accrue to the country as a result of the exploitation of these non-renewable resources. Although known oil reserves, at current production rates, should last for over 150 years, this does not mean that there is any complacency regarding the importance of laying down firm foundations for the future prosperity and well being of the country and its citizens. The stark reality of oil wells beginning to dry up has already been experienced in Dubai where economic diversification projects are most visible. In a very real sense Dubai's energetic determination to overcome economic hurdles is an example to other emirates, and indeed to other oil producing countries, of what can be achieved with good planning, professional management, active participation of the private sector and, most importantly, the vision and support of the nation's leaders.

The UAE follows a free market economy in which there are no constraints on imports and exports or movement of capital. The country enjoys a solid financial reputation supported by a highly organised and controlled banking system that is on a par with that of major industrial countries.

Economic growth has been greatly stimulated by the development of the many free zones spread throughout the UAE. The largest of these, established in 1985, is the Jebel Ali Free Zone (JAFZ) in Dubai. Two impressive recent additions to that emirate's free zones include the Dubai Internet City (DIC) and Dubai Media City (DMC). These are considered to be the world's first ever e-commerce free zones. The Dubai International Finance Centre (DIFC) and the Dubai Metals and Commodities Centre (DMCC), an international market for the exchange and trade of valuable commodities and metals, are also under way.

---

*Figures quoted in this section of the UAE 2003 *Yearbook*, unless otherwise stated, are based on information provided by the UAE Central Bank in its 2001 Annual Report and its 2002 Economic Bulletin.

The free zones offer 100 per cent foreign ownership and investors enjoy exemption from customs duty which is only levied on commodities manufactured in these zones if they are sold within the UAE or GCC markets. There is also a tax holiday on corporate tax, whilst no income tax is imposed. Another incentive is access to low-cost energy.

During 1995–2001 the gross domestic product (GDP) of the country grew at an annual rate of 8.4 per cent, while the population (both nationals and expatriates) increased by 6.35 per cent. The size of the workforce grew at a rate of 9.5 per cent to more than 1,853,000 by the end of 2001.

As there is no federal tax on personal incomes or profits, government expenses depend primarily on oil revenues. Whilst oil accounted for 76.59 per cent of the total government revenues in 1994 the ratio has been falling slightly and amounted to 71.39 per cent of the total revenues in 2001. This was mainly due to the government investments made in non-oil sources of income.

The Central Bank maintains an exchange rate of Dh3.6725 to the US dollar. Banking policy plays a very important role in organising cash flows within the country and with the rest of the world. The Central Bank provides local banks with their requirements of bank notes and the amount of the UAE currency in circulation outside the banks has increased from Dh6.4 billion as of December 1995 to Dh10.9 billion in September 2002. Bank deposits have jumped from Dh14.4 billion in 1995 to Dh34.14 billion as of September-end 2002, reflecting a growth in economic activity over this period. Meanwhile, government deposits rose from Dh22.09 billion in 1995 to Dh40.45 billion by the end of September 2002.

The net foreign assets of the country (excluding investments of the Abu Dhabi Investment Authority) have increased from Dh63.89 billion as of 1995 to Dh120.69 billion by the end of 2001 and to Dh125.24 billion towards the end of the third quarter 2002.

ECONOMIC PERFORMANCE

According to the Central Bank, the deficit widened by 166.1 per cent in 2001, to stand at Dh25.8 billion, against a deficit of Dh9.7 billion in 2000. The Ministry of Planning (MOP) figures for the deficit in 2001 are somewhat lower, at Dh17.9 billion, caused by MOP providing higher income estimates (primarily from non-oil sources) and lower than projected expenditure. According to the MOP there has been an accumulated deficit in the consolidated accounts of around Dh164.5 billion (US$44.8 billion) since 1993. However, much of this has been compensated by returns from the UAE's massive overseas investments rather than from borrowing.

General Summary

Non-oil economic sectors in the UAE witnessed marked activity during 2001, together with an increase in their respective growth rates, despite fluctuations in oil prices. Monetary and credit policy succeeded in keeping growth rates in domestic liquidity and credit expansion in harmony with non-oil GDP growth rates, hence slowing increases in domestic prices.

Gross domestic product (GDP) at fixed prices for the year 1995 grew by 1.3 per cent in 2001 over its level in 2000, reaching Dh217.0 billion. The increase in non-oil sectors reached 3.7 per cent, while the growth of the oil and natural gas sector dropped.

Non-oil output was Dh169.0 billion in 2001, accounting for 77.9 per cent of GDP, against Dh163.0 billion and a ratio of 76.1 per cent in 2000. The output of the commodity sectors reached Dh112.0 billion, accounting for 51.6 per cent of GDP in 2001, against Dh114.48 billion and a ratio of 53.4 per cent in 2000.

On the other hand, the oil sector output dropped from Dh51.3 billion in 2000 to Dh48.0 billion in 2001 (-6.5 per cent). The contribution of this sector to GDP decreased from 23.9 per cent in 2000 to 22.1 per cent in 2001. This was mainly attributed to the drop in average oil prices from US$27.2 a barrel in 2000 to US$23.3 a barrel in 2001 (-14.3 per cent).

Balance of payments entries showed a marked decline in 2001 as a result of the fall in oil prices. The overall surplus fell by 82.9 per cent below the level achieved in 2000. The current account surplus also declined by 35.6 per cent while the surplus in the trade balance decreased by 29.9 per cent since 2000.

With regard to monetary and banking developments in 2001 over 2000, money supply (M1) rose by 15.8 per cent to reach Dh39.46 billion. As a result of this increase, and of an increase of Dh9.54 billion (8.9 per cent) in quasi-monetary deposits, private domestic liquidity (M2) expanded by Dh14.94 billion (10.6 per cent) to reach Dh156.48 billion.

An analysis of the factors affecting private domestic liquidity shows that the impact of net foreign assets was expansionary, increasing by Dh5.64 billion (4.9 per cent). The impact of net domestic credit was also expansionary as it rose by Dh12.65 million (12.8 per cent). The impact of net other factors (capital, reserves, provisions and other items), which grew by Dh3.35 billion (4.7 per cent), on private domestic liquidity (M2) was also contractionary.

Gross Domestic Product (GDP)

Preliminary estimates published by the Ministry of Planning indicate that GDP at base price and at fixed 1995 prices rose from Dh214.3 billion in 2000 to 217.0 billion in 2001 (1.3 per cent). The rate of increase in the non-oil sectors reached 3.7 per cent while the output of the oil and natural gas sector dropped by 6.5 per cent in 2001 over 2000, owing to the decline in oil prices by 14.3 per cent to reach US$23.3 a barrel. Accordingly, the value added of this sector dropped from Dh51.3 billion in 2000 to Dh48.0 billion in 2001 and hence its contribution to GDP fell to 22.1 per cent in 2001 compared to 23.9 per cent in 2000.

Table 2 shows the development achieved in various non-oil sectors during 2001, which in turn helped in partially alleviating the negative impact of the fluctuations in

Table 2: Gross Domestic Product at Base Price by Economic Sectors (at fixed 1995 prices)

(In Millions of AEDs)

Sectors	2000	2001*
(1) Non-Financial Enterprises Sector	178,275	177,662
- Agriculture, Livestock and Fishery	8,733	9,300
- Mining	51,972	48,672
A. Crude Oil & Natural Gas	51,310	48,000
B. Quarries	662	672
- Manufacturing	33,120	32,785
- Electricity, Gas and Water	4,487	4,748
- Building & Construction	16,170	16,490
- Wholesale/Retail Trade and Maintenance	20,676	21,146
- Restaurants and Hotels	4,645	4,970
- Transportation, Storage and Communication	16,211	16,790
- Real Estate and Business Services	18,618	18,906
- Social and Private Services	3,643	3,855
(2) Financial Enterprises Sector	14,207	16,144
(3) Government Services Sector	24,296	25,990
- Household Services	1,599	1,662
(Less): Imputed Bank Services Charges	4,050	4,422
TOTAL	214,327	217,025
Total Non-Oil Sectors	163,017	169,025

Source : Ministry of Planning *Preliminary Data

Table 3: Sector Shares of Gross Domestic Product

		GDP 1999	GDP 2000	GDP 2001	Non-Mining GDP* 1999	Non-Mining GDP* 2000	Non-Mining GDP* 2001
A.	Goods Production Sectors	51.9	53.4	51.6	36.8	38.7	37.9
	Agriculture, Livestock & Fishery	3.8	4.1	4.3	5.1	5.4	5.6
	Mining	24.1	24.2	22.4	-	-	-
	Manufacturing	13.3	15.5	15.1	17.6	20.5	19.6
	Building & Construction	8.4	7.5	7.6	11.1	10.0	9.9
	Electricity, Gas & Water	2.2	2.1	2.2	2.9	2.8	2.8
B.	Services Sector	48.1	46.6	48.4	63.2	61.3	62.1

* Percentage of GDP after excluding mining sector

ECONOMIC DEVELOPMENT

Table 2: Gross Domestic Product at Base Price by Economic Sectors (at fixed 1995 prices)

2000
- Government Services: 24,296
- Financial Enterprises: 14,207
- Non-Financial Enterprises: 178,275

Non-Financial Enterprises Breakdown (Millions of AEDs):
- Agriculture, Livestock & Fishery: 8,733
- Mining: 51,972
- Manufacturing: 33,120
- Electricity, Gas & Water: 4,487
- Building & Construction: 16,170
- Wholesale/Retail Trade & Maintenance: 20,676
- Restaurants & Hotels: 4,645
- Transportation, Storage & Communications: 16,211
- Real Estate & Business Services: 18,618
- Social & Private Services: 3,643

2001*
- Government Services: 25,990
- Financial Enterprises: 16,144
- Non-Financial Enterprises: 177,662

Non-Financial Enterprises Breakdown (Millions of AEDs):
- Agriculture, Livestock & Fishery: 9,300
- Mining: 48,672
- Manufacturing: 32,785
- Electricity, Gas & Water: 4,748
- Building & Construction: 16,490
- Wholesale/Retail Trade & Maintenance: 21,146
- Restaurants & Hotels: 4,970
- Transportation, Storage & Communications: 16,790
- Real Estate & Business Services: 18,906
- Social & Private Services: 3,855

Legend:
- Non-Financial Enterprises
- Financial Enterprises
- Government Services
- Agriculture, Livestock & Fishery
- Mining
- Manufacturing
- Electricity, Gas & Water
- Building & Construction
- Wholesale/Retail Trade & Maintenance
- Restaurants & Hotels
- Transportation, Storage & Communications
- Real Estate & Business Services
- Social & Private Services

Table 3: Sector Shares of Gross Domestic Product

Percentage of Gross Domestic Product — GDP (1999, 2000, 2001) and Non-Mining GDP* (1999, 2000, 2001)

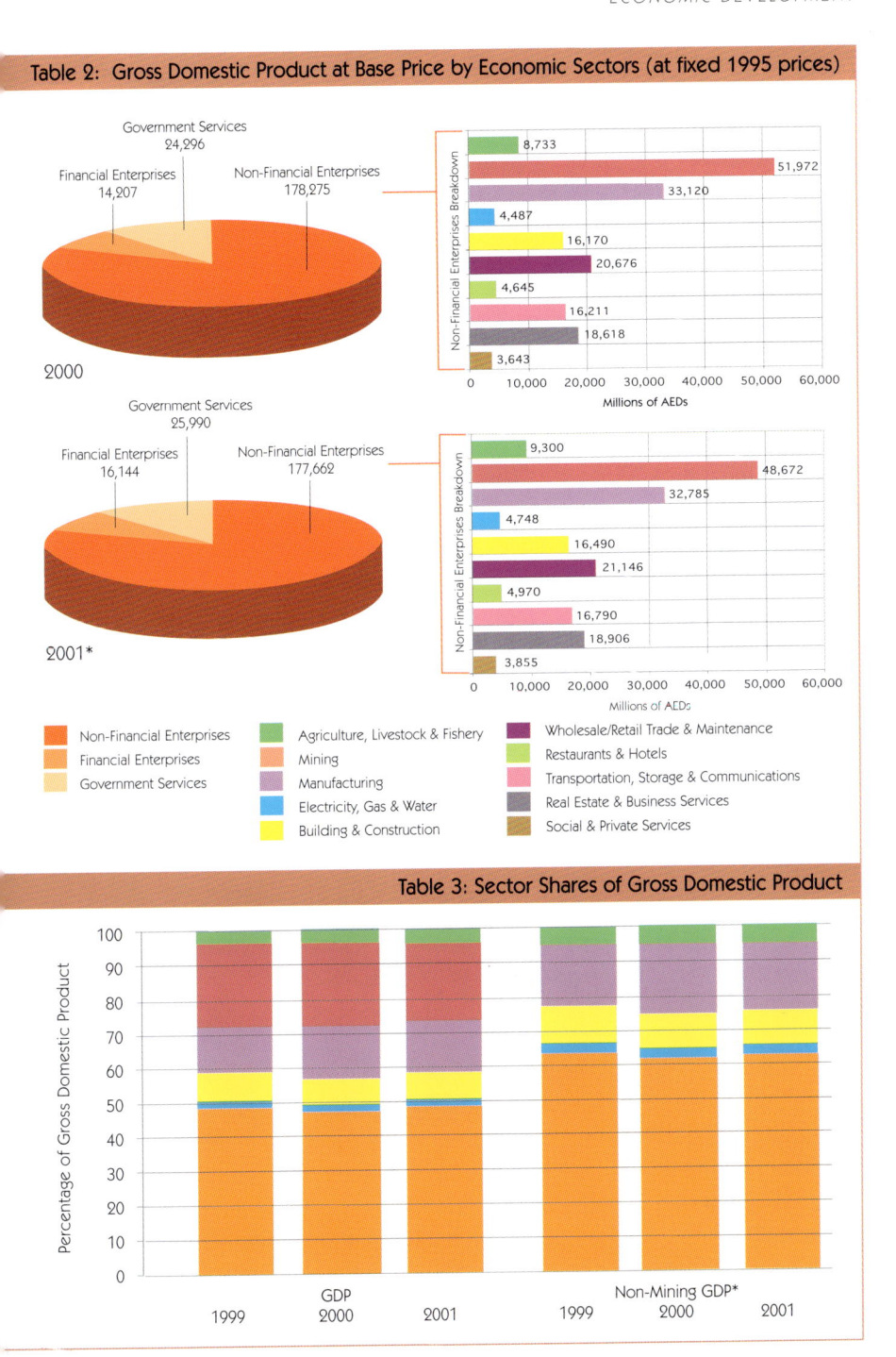

oil prices. The growth achieved in non-oil sectors was mainly attributed to appropriate economic policies, strengthening domestic demand, particularly in the financial enterprises sector and other sectors such as transportation, communication, real estate and construction, in addition to the government's role in supporting public services and providing subsidies to the electricity and agriculture sectors.

Data on growth and contribution of non-oil sectors to output increase in 2001 indicate that the financial enterprises sector achieved the highest rate of increase compared with other sectors, reaching 13.6 per cent. The value added in this sector rose from Dh14.2 billion in 2000 to Dh16.1 billion in 2001. Classified as a major pivot in the process of development in the area of services in the country, the financial sector's contribution to output increased from 6.6 per cent to 7.4 per cent.

Reflecting the state's firm commitment to provide a higher standard of public services to meet the increasing needs of a growing population, the output of the government services sector rose by 7.0 per cent in 2001 compared to the 2000 level. The value of output of this sector reached Dh26.0 billion while its contribution to output increased from 11.3 per cent in 2000 to 12.0 per cent in 2001.

With all the necessary facilities ensuring the effective role of the restaurants and hotels sector, its output rose by 7.0 per cent to Dh5.0 billion in 2001 compared with 2000. This is an increase of more than Dh1.2 billion over four years (the value added of this sector recorded Dh3.8 billion in 1998), reflecting increased focus on tourism.

The agriculture, livestock and fishery sector, which enjoys substantial government subsidy, continued to expand during 2001 with its output increasing by 6.5 per cent to Dh9.3 billion in 2001, although its contribution to output remained at the same level as the previous year. It is noteworthy that the development achieved in this sector over the past years has recently started to have a positive impact domestically, with its output satisfying a greater segment of domestic demand.

In keeping with increasing commercial activity in the country, the wholesale/retail trade and maintenance sector output rose from Dh20.7 billion in 2000 to Dh21.1 billion in 2001. Similarly, the transportation, storage and communication sector grew by 3.6 per cent in 2001 with the value added of this sector reaching Dh16.8 billion. The value added of the building and construction sector increased by more than Dh300 million over the 2000 figure to Dh16.5 billion in 2001. In 2001, all these sectors maintained the contributions to overall output achieved in 2000.

On the other hand, the mining sector (mainly crude oil) output dropped from Dh52.0 billion in 2000 to Dh48.7 billion in 2001 (6.3 per cent). Similarly, manufacturing industries sector output (mainly liquefied gas and petroleum products) declined from Dh33.1 billion in 2000 to Dh32.8 billion in 2001 (1.0 per cent).

With the GDP increasing at a slower rate (1.3 per cent) than population growth rate (7.4 per cent), GDP per capita dropped by 5.7 per cent in 2001 to Dh62,200, against Dh66,000 in 2000.

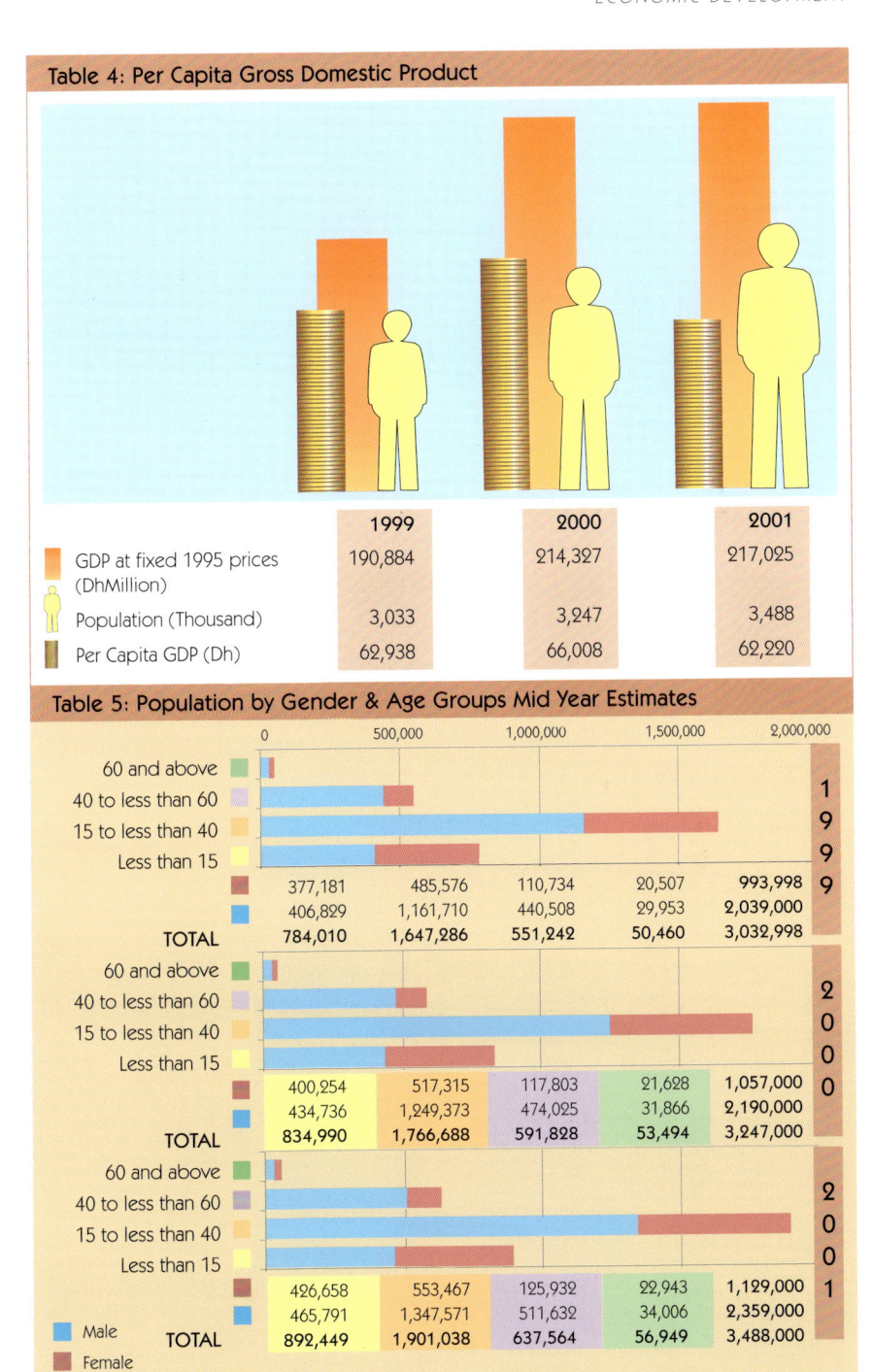

ECONOMIC DEVELOPMENT

Table 4: Per Capita Gross Domestic Product

	1999	2000	2001
GDP at fixed 1995 prices (DhMillion)	190,884	214,327	217,025
Population (Thousand)	3,033	3,247	3,488
Per Capita GDP (Dh)	62,938	66,008	62,220

Table 5: Population by Gender & Age Groups Mid Year Estimates

1999

Age Group	Male	Female	Total
60 and above	20,507	29,953	50,460
40 to less than 60	110,734	440,508	551,242
15 to less than 40	485,576	1,161,710	1,647,286
Less than 15	377,181	406,829	784,010
TOTAL	993,998	2,039,000	3,032,998

2000

Age Group	Male	Female	Total
60 and above	21,628	31,866	53,494
40 to less than 60	117,803	474,025	591,828
15 to less than 40	517,315	1,249,373	1,766,688
Less than 15	400,254	434,736	834,990
TOTAL	1,057,000	2,190,000	3,247,000

2001

Age Group	Male	Female	Total
60 and above	22,943	34,006	56,949
40 to less than 60	125,932	511,632	637,564
15 to less than 40	553,467	1,347,571	1,901,038
Less than 15	426,658	465,791	892,449
TOTAL	1,129,000	2,359,000	3,488,000

Male / Female

PUBLIC FINANCE 2001

Revenues

As a result of the decrease in oil and gas exports' earnings, which ensued from declining prices, total revenues in the consolidated government finance account dropped by 8.6 per cent in 2001 to reach Dh68.0 billion, compared to Dh74.4 billion in 2000.

Tax Revenues

Tax revenues (customs duties and other charges) increased in 2001 by 33.1 per cent to reach Dh9.8 billion, forming 14.4 per cent of total revenues. The increase mainly occurred in other tax revenues, which rose by Dh2.4 billion (42.4 per cent). Likewise, customs revenue grew by Dh67 million (3.8 per cent) in 2001 to reach Dh1.8 billion.

Non-Tax Revenues

Non-tax revenues decreased by 13.2 per cent in 2001, reaching Dh58.2 billion, against Dh67.0 billion in 2000, forming 85.6 per cent of total revenues in 2001 after forming 90.1 per cent of total revenues in 2001. This was mainly attributed to a drop by Dh7.5 billion (13.4 per cent) in receipts from oil and gas exports that recorded Dh48.5 billion in 2001, against Dh56.0 billion in 2000.

Expenditures

Expenditure rose in 2001 by Dh9.7 billion (11.5 per cent), reaching Dh93.7 billion, against Dh84.1 billion in 2000.

Current Expenditure

Current expenditures constituted 80.7 per cent of total expenditures in 2001, reaching Dh75.6 billion, against Dh71.2 billion in 2000. Expenditure on salaries and wages rose in 2001 by Dh252 billion (1.9 per cent) to reach Dh13.7 billion. The increase in expenditures on goods and services reached Dh91 million, bringing it to Dh21.8 billion. Expenditures on subsidies and transfers increased by Dh5.6 billion (39.9 per cent) to reach Dh19.6 billion. Meanwhile, other unclassified current expenditures dropped by Dh1.3 billion (5.9 per cent) to reach Dh20.6 billion.

Development Expenditure

Development expenditures rose by 18.3 per cent to reach Dh13.2 billion in 2001, against Dh11.2 billion in 2000.

Loans and Equity Participations

Loans and equity participations increased by 184.2 per cent compared to its level in 2000, reaching Dh49 billion, of which 12.2 per cent was spent locally.

ECONOMIC DEVELOPMENT

Table 6: The Consolidated Government Finance Account

Items	2000*	2001**
Revenues	74,386	67,971
Tax Revenues	7,373	9,812
Customs Revenues	1,779	1,846
Other	5,594	7,966
Non-Tax Revenues	67,013	58,159
Oil and Gas	56,020	48,526
Joint Stock Corporations	3,936	3,384
Other	7,057	6,249
Expenditures	84,066	93,734
Current Expenditures	71,187	75,645
Salaries and Wages	13,420	13,672
Goods and Services	21,913	21,822
Subsidies and Transfers	14,002	19,587
Other Unclassified	21,852	20,564
Development Expenditures	11,156	13,193
Loans and Equity Participations	1,723	4,896
Local	714	597
Foreign	1,009	4,299
Surplus (+) or Deficit (-)	(-)9,680	(-)25,763
Financing	9,680	25,763
Changes in net Government Deposits with Bank Other(1)	-5,953	2,349

Source : Ministry of Finance and Industry and Local Governments Finance Departments
*Adjusted data
** Preliminary data
(1)Transfers from returns on government's investments.

PUBLIC FINANCE 2001

The Deficit

The deficit widened by 166.1 per cent to reach Dh25.8 billion in 2001, against a deficit of Dh9.7 billion in 2000. The bulk of this deficit (90.9 per cent) was entirely financed by returns on government's investments, while the rest was financed by withdrawals from net government deposits with banks operating in the country. (See also revised figures quoted above issued by Ministry of Planning).

Consumer Price Index Numbers 2001

Data recently published by the Ministry of Planning on consumer price index numbers indicate that the general consumer price index number (1995 base year) rose from 110.7 to 113.1 in 2001 (2.2 per cent).

The increment was due to price rises in all major expenditure groups, albeit mainly in the grouping that includes recreation, education and cultural services, medical care and medical services and transportation and communication, which together formed a total weight of 27.1 per cent. The highest increase occurred in the recreation, education and cultural services group, wherein the consumer price index number rose from 115.2 in 2000 to 125.0 in 2001. The weight of this group equals 10.3 per cent.

It is noteworthy that the price index number for food, beverage and tobacco, housing and related housing services, with a combined total weight of 50.6 per cent in the CPI, rose from 113.4 and 96.1 respectively in 2000, to 113.6 and 98.1 respectively in 2001.

The Balance of Payments 2001

Despite the overall positive image of economic conditions in the UAE during 2001, preliminary estimates of the balance of payments indicated a marked decline in the surpluses of both the trade balance and the current account balance. This was mainly due to the negative developments witnessed in the oil market.

The surplus in the trade balance decreased from Dh54.4 billion in 2000 to Dh38.2 billion in 2001 (29.9 per cent). This was due to a decline (by Dh15.2 billion) in value of exports of the hydrocarbon sector on the one hand, and a substantial increase (by Dh4.5 billion) in commodity imports, on the other.

The decline in proceeds of hydrocarbon sector exports was due to the decrease in crude oil prices during 2001 and hence prices of gas, condensates and petroleum products. The weighted average price of crude oil fell from US$27.2 a barrel in 2000 to US$23.3 a barrel in 2001 (14.3 per cent). Consequently, the value of crude oil exports dropped from Dh79.5 billion in 2000 to Dh66.1 billion in 2001 (16.8 per cent). The value of gas exports also dropped by 9.2 per cent in 2001 compared to 2000, reaching Dh12.7 billion, and so did the value of exports of petroleum products, which decreased by 8 per cent to Dh6.6 billion.

On the other hand, the value of total non oil and gas exports (including non-monetary gold and free zone exports) rose from Dh34.3 billion in 2000 to Dh36.2 billion in 2001 (5.5 per cent). The value of re-exports also rose to Dh49.7 billion in 2001 against Dh48.2 billion in 2000 (3.3 per cent).

The value of total imports (including estimated goods imports of all emirates plus free zone imports and imports of non-monetary gold) totalled Dh133.1 billion in 2001 a rise of 3.5 per cent over 2000. Owing to the improvement in the dirham exchange rate against currencies of the country's major trade partners and the moderate increase in prices of these commodities in countries of origin, the value of imports in 2001 reflected an increase in volume compared to 2000. This is mainly due to a pick-up in activity in domestic non-oil sectors, an increase in number of projects, a rise in domestic demand owing to increases in income levels and population and the increase in value of re-exports, particularly to neighbouring countries.

Despite a 1.5 per cent rise in 2001 in estimated net imports (minus estimated total value of re-exports and exclusive of imports of non-monetary gold and free zone imports) compared to 2000, imports per capita dropped from Dh15,900 in 2000 to Dh15,000 in 2001. This was mainly attributed to a 7.4 per cent growth in population during 2001, which exceeded the increase in net estimated imports.

Within the current account, the balance of investment income achieved by public and private investment institutions fell by half a percentage point in 2001 compared to 2000, reaching Dh18.6 billion. The debit balance of tourism, travel and government services rose by 8.3 per cent compared to 2000, reaching Dh8.8 billion.

As a result of the decline in the current account surplus from Dh50.5 billion in 2000 to Dh32.5 billion in 2001 (35.6 per cent), capital flow of government institutions, private capital flow and net errors and omissions item in the capital account dropped by 26.5 per cent in 2001 compared to 2000, reaching Dh27.1 billion. Private short-term capital also recorded an outflow of Dh3.86 billion.

Meanwhile, the overall surplus in the balance of payments dropped from Dh10.4 billion in 2000, to Dh1.8 billion in 2001. This was mainly due to the decline in flows with the net foreign assets of the Central Bank during 2001.

The goods production sectors' contribution to total output dropped from 53.4 per cent in 2000 to 51.6 per cent in 2001 as a result of the fall in contribution of the oil and natural gas sector. When excluding mining industries output (mainly oil and natural gas), the contribution of the goods production sectors shows a drop from 38.7 per cent in 2000 to 37.9 per cent in 2001, while that of the services sectors continued to represent more than 62.0 per cent of overall output during 2001.

Estimates of GDP at current prices and by major expenditure categories show that it reached Dh248.3 billion in 2001 against Dh258.0 billion in 2000, a drop of 3.7 per cent.

Total final consumption (government and private) rose by 4.0 per cent in 2001 to reach Dh158.7 billion, with its ratio to overall output increasing from 59.1 per cent in 2000 to 63.9 per cent in 2001. As a result of the growth in population and the rise in price levels, private final consumption increased by 3.4 per cent in 2001 to reach Dh116.5 billion and continued to maintain a ratio of more than 73.0 per cent of gross consumption spending. Gross fixed capital formation rose by 2.3 per cent to Dh58.7 billion in 2001 compared to Dh57.4 billion in 2000.

Labour and Population

The UAE population increased by 7.4 per cent during 2001 to reach 3.49 million, 67.6 per cent of which were male. The emirates of Abu Dhabi, Dubai and Sharjah accounted for 39 per cent, 29.5 per cent and 16.1 per cent respectively of the total population in 2001. The number of people in the under 15-years age group reached 892,000 in 2001, a 6.8 per cent increase on 835,000 in 2000. The 15 to 40 age group accounted for 1.9 million in 2001, against 1.77 million in 2000, a rise of 7.6 per cent. Meanwhile, in 2001 there were 638,000 people in the 40 to 60 age group, compared to 592,000 in 2000, an increase of 7.7 per cent. The over-60 age group totalled 57,000 in 2001, up 6.5 per cent from 53,000 in 2000. During 2001 the total number of workers in the UAE rose by nearly 116,000, reaching 1.853 million.

Monetary and Credit Policy 2001

The dirham achieved new gains, benefiting from its fixed peg to the US dollar which improved in its exchange rate against most major currencies in 2001. During 2001, the dirham appreciated against the Euro (3.3 per cent), the Pound Sterling (5.4 per cent), and the Japanese Yen (17.1 per cent), while it depreciated against the Swiss Franc (0.8 per cent), The rate of exchange of the dirham remained unchanged against all GCC currencies in 2001 compared to its level in 2000.

THE ECONOMY IN 2002

A report issued by the Ministry of Planning in late 2002 predicted that UAE GDP would show a 3.5 per cent growth rate for 2002, reaching a total of Dh265.9 billion, compared to Dh248 billion in 2001. The forecast was based on continued economic

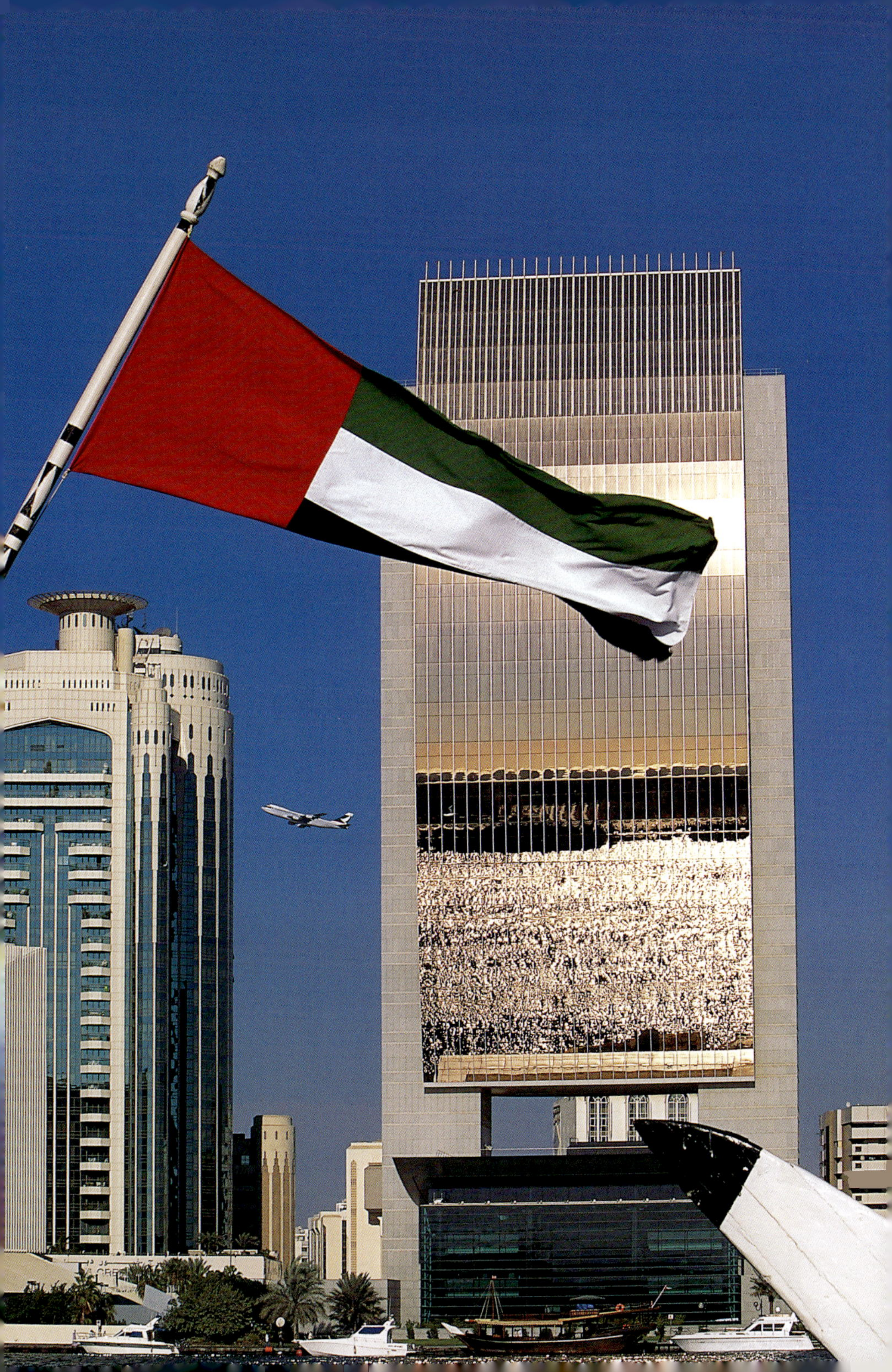

reforms in terms of diversification of national income sources, rationalisation of expenditure and resilience of the domestic economy to global economic realities. Adjusting previous estimates upwards, the report said non-oil GDP would rise slightly to Dh187.1 billion in 2002, from Dh179 billion in 2001.

Total fixed investment was expected to go up in 2002 to Dh60 billion, from Dh58.7 billion in 2001, consumer spending to Dh170.4 billion from Dh158.2 billion, whilst the surplus in balance of payments is expected to decrease to Dh35.2 billion from Dh38.2 billion due to the rise in commodity imports. It further commented that commodity exports and imports could increase to Dh173.7 and Dh138.5 billion, from Dh171.3 and Dh133.1 billion respectively. The report said that the sound economic policies adopted by the country had considerably helped it to resist many pressures faced by other countries, particularly in the developing world.

IMF EXPECTATIONS FOR 2003

The International Monetary Fund issued a report in late 2002 that predicted a 3.1 per cent growth of UAE GDP in 2003 if oil prices maintain their 2002 levels. Whilst the report expected that the relative strength of oil prices in 2002 would reflect positively on the Arab oil exporting countries, it suggested that a military conflict with Iraq would reflect negatively on the whole region. Achieving real economic growth rates in the region is dependent on a number of elements including reducing spending, increasing non-oil revenues and adopting economic reform policies, the report said.

BUSINESS ENVIRONMENT

The UAE is widely perceived as a free market economy that offers secure conditions for investors. It has been highly rated by a number of economic study centres. The World Heritage Foundation (WHF), based in Washington DC, rated it twenty-fourth out of 161 countries and second among Middle Eastern and North African countries. The WHF Index of Economic Freedom defines economic freedom as the absence of government coercion or constraint on the production, distribution, or consumption of goods and services beyond the extent necessary for citizens to protect and maintain liberty.

Meanwhile Euromoney, which specialises in assessing political and economic risks around the world, has classified the UAE as the safest Arab country for investment and the twenty-seventh safest in the world. Euromoney measures political, economic, financial and investment risks for 185 countries twice a year. On a scale of financial safety with 100 being perfectly safe, the UAE scored 79.32 points in the 2002 survey. The index focuses on each country's ability to repay debt and honour its financial and economic commitments, which clearly reflect the investment situation.

A further indication of the strength of the business environment in the UAE is provided by the level of interest in new ventures. The Abu Dhabi Chamber of Commerce and Industry (ADCCI) recorded a rise in the number of registered members in 2001. The total number of new and renewed memberships reached 27,973, 2.7 per cent over the previous year's figure. The business community is assisted by Chambers of Commerce in each of the emirates and by other organised business groups.

FINANCIAL MARKETS

An examination of local financial markets is one way of measuring business performance. UAE's stock market reached a record level in 2002. Market capitalisation of the 56 banks and companies listed on the country's two official bourses in Abu Dhabi and Dubai, gained Dh15 billion (US$4.08 billion) to peak at around Dh119 billion ($32.4 billion) at the end of 2002 compared with Dh104 billion (US$28.3 billion) at the end of 2001. The National Bank of Abu Dhabi (NBAD) index also jumped by 14.1 per cent while turnover in the two exchanges and OTC (over-the-counter) dealing surged to its highest ever level of Dh4.82 billion (US$1.31 billion) in 2002, more than double the 2001 turnover of Dh2.13 billion (US$5.88 million). Several factors help to account for this strong performance in the stock markets including the decline in interest rates as this encouraged investors to opt for high-yield shares and enticed them to borrow more to buy shares. The good performance also reflects growing confidence in the domestic economy and the local stock market following a series of setbacks in global markets. Strong oil prices and good financial results by most listed banks and companies also spurred demand for stocks and boosted overall activity. Another factor was the growing discipline and transparency in the market as most companies began issuing quarterly results.

There was also a return to the local economy of a certain amount of overseas capital and such funds were used mostly in the stock markets. New share flotations by some firms and listing of others, including Gulf companies, also contributed to the upsurge in the market activity and turned the UAE into the second biggest Arab market after Saudi Arabia in terms of capitalisation.

The biggest listing event involved ETISALAT telecommunications corporation, which has a market capitalisation of around Dh35.7 billion (US$9.72 billion), nearly 30 per cent of the total market capitalisation. Another major company listed last year was Qatar Telecom, the first institution from another GCC state to be admitted into the UAE stock market. Dealers cited other positive factors such as a decision by the First Gulf Bank to allow foreigners to own up to 20 per cent of its shares and similar moves by EMAAR, Tabreed and Oasis International Leasing Co. Last year's stock activity involved the trading of a record 247 million shares, more than double the 113 million shares traded in 2001. A breakdown showed service companies, including

ETISALAT, led the market last year with their turnover standing at Dh2.55 billion (US$694 million), nearly 53 per cent of the total value of traded shares. Banks totalled Dh2.07 billion (US$564 million), around 43 per cent.

Both federal and local governments are continually examining ways to encourage investment in the UAE, taking advantage of its strategic location, well-developed infrastructure and safe environment. One recent initiative that will add zest to the business environment is the move by the Dubai Government to clear the way for free zone companies to go public and become listed on the DFM. This will raise new opportunities for many of these companies to finance growth through share offerings. With many Arab and international investors seeking a safe home for their capital, the UAE expects to benefit considerably from such adjustments to the local business environment. DFM is unlikely to fix any lower ceiling of capital to be floated for the public, thus preserving the present freedom of ownership structure. Since free zone companies are normally set up under the sole ownership of foreigners, liquidating their assets can be a real issue. The new arrangements for share listings will create exit routes for investors should they require them.

FREE ZONES

Establishing a business entity in one of the UAE's free trade zones (FTZs) is an attractive option for foreign investors. To date the free zones have been successful in attracting a large number of companies and foreign direct investment, as well as expanding net non-oil exports. By late 2002, there were more than 4000 companies operating in free zones, with an estimated trade of over US$8 billion.

The major advantage in setting up in a free zone is that the business entity is entitled to:
- 100 per cent foreign ownership of the enterprise
- 100 per cent import and export tax exemptions
- 100 per cent repatriation of capital and profits
- No corporate taxes for 15 years, renewable for an additional 15 years
- No personal income taxes; and
- Assistance with labour recruitment, and additional support services, such as sponsorship and housing.

An independent Free Zone Authority (FZA) governs each free zone, and is the agency responsible for issuing FTZ operating licences and assisting companies with establishing their business in the FTZ.

Investors can either register a new company as a Free Zone Establishment (FZE) or simply establish a branch or representative office of their existing or parent company based within the UAE or abroad. A FZE is a limited liability company governed by the rules and regulations of the free zone in which it is established. Under Federal Law No. 15 of 1998, except for acquiring nationality in the UAE, the provisions of

ANNUAL SALES
2000: LOCAL SALES 5,500,000
2000: EXPORT SALES 1,270,000
TARGET
2001 LOCAL SALES 6,500,000
2001 EXPORT SALES 1,600,000
9m
7m.
5m.

the Commercial Companies Law (CCL) do not apply to FZEs, provided that the free zones have special provisions regulating such companies.

Free Trade Zone Licences

Once a legal presence has been established in a free zone, the business is required to lease premises or land and acquire an operating licence from the FZA. Different types of licences apply in the different types of free zone. In general, however, companies with trade and industrial licences can only conduct business within the free zone or abroad. To sell their products in the UAE, a UAE official agent is required. Services and products can be obtained from and within the UAE without an agent. Other types of licence available are service licences (e.g. banking, insurance, air shipment etc) and national industrial licences. For the former the services offered must be the same as those stipulated in the parent company's licence in the UAE or abroad. The share capital of a company applying for a national industrial licence must be at least 51 per cent from the UAE or GCC and 40 per cent of the sale value of the product must be value-added. These licences can be renewed annually as long as a lease agreement is in force with the FTZ.

Jebel Ali Free Zone (JAFZ) (04 8812222; www.jafza.co.ae)

Located in Dubai, JAFZ offers well-structured tax and business incentives in a long established free zone with good manufacturing, warehousing and distribution facilities. JAFZ has more than 2300 companies registered with the free zone. Over 150 of the world's major container shipping lines call at Dubai, including feeder vessels to Iran, Africa and the Indian subcontinent. Dubai International Airport, just 30 minutes by road from JAFZ, is serviced by more than 95 airlines to and from over 137 destinations.

The Jebel Ali Free Zone Authority (JAFZA) runs an exclusive portal for customers in the free zone area. 'MyJAFZA', which is part of Dubai's e-government strategy, was set up to reduce the average time of a transaction by 90 per cent.

Dubai Airport Free Zone (DAFZ) (04 2995555; www.dafza.gov.ae)

DAFZ is an integral part of the Dubai International Airport expansion programme and covers a total land area of 1.2 million square metres, with specially designed facilities for a wide variety of technology driven industries, including retail and light industrial companies as well as commercial distribution services. This free zone, the home of over 200 companies, including some well-known international entities, is a major new step in Dubai's evolution from a distribution hub to a manufacturing centre. In this respect it complements the already well-established Jebel Ali Free Zone. DAFZ has received ISO 9001:2000 certification.

Dubai Internet City (DIC) (04 3911111; www.dubaiinternetcity.com)

DIC is the first complete information technology and telecommunications centre to have been built inside a free trade zone. It is also the biggest IT complex in the

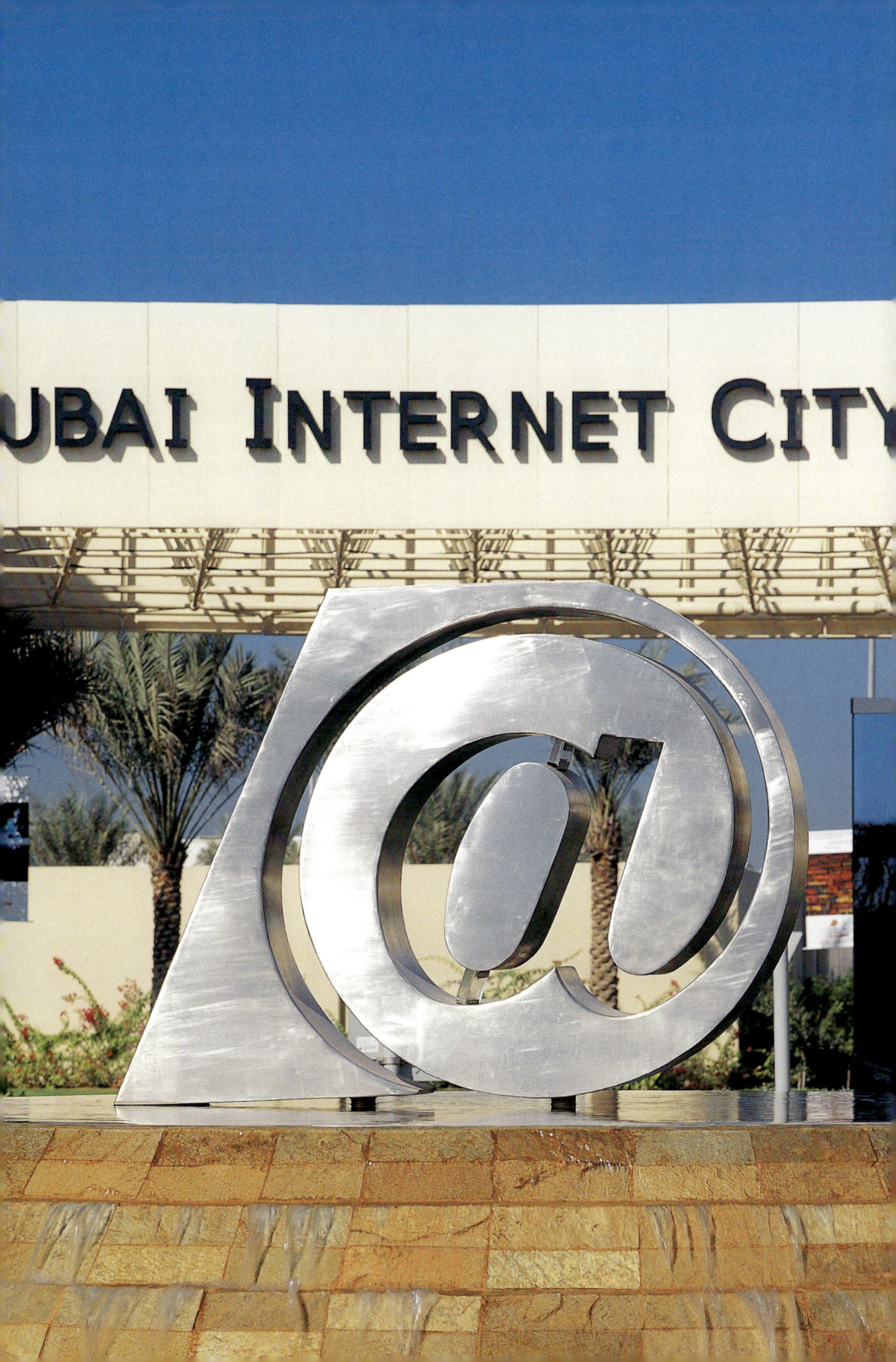
UBAI INTERNET CITY

Middle East, and has one of the largest Internet Protocol telephony systems in the world. Dubai Internet City offers ready-to-operate, fully serviced office space complete with the up-to-date infrastructure that high-tech companies require. Companies can also take land on a renewable lease of up to 50 years and build their own offices.

Dubai Media City (DMC) (04 3994400; www.dubaimediacity.com)
DMC intends to become the region's media hub. Established by the Dubai Technology, E-Commerce and Media Free Zone Authority, DMC offers state-of the-art infrastructure that will enable media-related enterprises to operate globally out of Dubai such as broadcasting, publishing, advertising, public relations, research, music, and postproduction companies.

Dubai Textile Village
This is a new free zone under development on 460,000 square metres of land allocated by the Dubai Government in the Ra's al-Khor area. The facility can accommodate 295 showrooms and stores, available in three sizes, of 230, 460 and 920 square metres. The textile trade in Dubai is expected to continue to record strong growth in coming years, to average between Dh15 and Dh17 billion turnover a year. The Textile Village will feature advanced communication networks and utility systems.

Hamriyah Free Zone (HFZA) (06 5263333; www.hamriyahfz.com)
HFZA in Sharjah comprises approximately 10 million square metres of industrial and commercial land. Included in the free zone area is a 14-metre-deep port which is designed to incorporate dedicated petrochemical bulk handling and general cargo berths. HFZA has extensive facilities, including access to three seaports on the Arabian Gulf and Indian Ocean, combined with a generous incentive framework. The free zone has over 180 companies from 17 countries. It holds ISO 9002 certification, and has recently been awarded ISO 14001 for its quality consciousness in the management of environmental safety.

Ajman Free Zone (AFZ) (06 7425444; www.ajmanfreezone.gov.ae)
AFZ is located adjacent to Ajman Port, between Sharjah and Umm al-Qaiwain. Sharjah's Port Khalid and Dubai's Port Rashid are within 35 minutes drive from the zone. Two international airports are also located nearby.

Umm al-Qaiwain Free Zone (06 651552)
The Ahmed bin Rashid Free Zone was set up within the Ahmed bin Rashid Port in Umm al-Qaiwain, about 50 kilometres north-east of Dubai. It comprises 845 metres of quay wall, 400 metres of which can handle ocean going vessels and 118,000 square metres of land reserved for light industrial development. UAQ Free Zone Authority provides administrative support to the resident companies as well as the usual free zone incentives.

Bur Dubai
Al Maktoum Rd
Deira
Al Sharjah
Za'abeel
Bur Dubai
ARABIAN OUTDOOR
04-7133 33

Fujairah Free Zone (FFZ) (09 2228000; www.fujairahfreezone.com)
FFZ is adjacent to the Port of Fujairah. Companies established there have easy access to all Arabian Gulf ports, the Red Sea, Iran, India and Pakistan on weekly feeder vessels. Mainline services arrive from Northern Europe, the Mediterranean, Far East and North America on a weekly basis, and services leave twice weekly to the Far East and once a week to North America. Fujairah Free Zone is also close to Fujairah International Airport, the only airport serving the UAE East Coast as well as northern Oman. More than 60 new companies were set up in FFZ in 2002, an increase of 25 per cent over 2001.

Ra's al-Khaimah Free Zone (RAKFZ) (07 2280859; www.rakiftz.com)
RAKFZ Authority oversees three new sub zones within the emirate. The 71-hectare Technology Park is designated for capital-intensive, high technology manufacturing and assembly companies. The Park is adjacent to the Ra's al-Khaimah Ceramics Factory and other light manufacturing businesses. The Al Hamra Development, located across the Emirates Highway, is a 325-hectare waterfront recreational and residential development that includes a hotel, waterfront villas, marina and golf course. The proximity of the Technology Park to the Emirates Highway makes it readily accessible to the city centre, international airport, Port Saqr, and destinations southward, such as Sharjah and Dubai. The Industrial Park is located along the Ra's al-Khaimah coastal road approximately 15 kilometres north of Ra's al-Khaimah and immediately adjacent to Hulaylah Island, site of the 100-hectare second phase, and approximately 6 kilometres from Port Saqr. The Free Trade Zone Business Park is centrally located in the heart of Ra's al-Khaimah's business district, between the Industrial Park, 20 kilometres to the north, and the Technology Park, 15 kilometres to the south. Its proximity to the Emirate's Emiri Diwan and other government centres of activity is an additional advantage. The Business Park is also just a short walk from the 1600-square-metres Ra's al-Khaimah exhibition hall, and a new mall, a modern shopping and entertainment complex, and a five-star hotel are only minutes away.

Sharjah Airport International Free Zone (SAIFZ) (06 5570000; www.saif-zone.com)
SAIFZ, located in the vicinity of Sharjah City and adjacent to Sharjah International Airport, is one of the top air cargo operations in the world. This well-appointed ISO 9001 accredited zone is also in close proximity to other major UAE airports and seaports on the Arabian Gulf and Indian Ocean coasts of the UAE.

NEW CUSTOMS ARRANGEMENTS

The GCC Unified Economic Agreement, which came into effect on 1 January 2003 with a three-year transitional period, stipulates that trade within the GCC, and between GCC and non-member countries, will be conducted as a single market under the regulations of a Customs Union and a 5 per cent import tax will apply on foreign imports at the first entry point.

In the UAE, a first step in this process was marked by the issuing of UAE Federal Law No.19 which increased customs duties from 4 per cent to 5 per cent on goods and commodities imported from sources outside the GCC Customs Union with effect from 1 January 2003. The law does not, however, prejudice Federal Decree No.11 issued in 1981 which refers to federal taxes on the import of tobacco and tobacco products. In addition, the new law exempts 53 goods from custom duties in line with the decision made by GCC leaders during their twentieth summit, as well as other exemptions included in the statute of the GCC Unified Customs Union.

Meanwhile, the UAE Federal Customs Authority Law (No.1 of 2003) has been passed. The newly promulgated law supersedes Federal Law No.10 for 1982. The new body will replace the UAE Customs Council and will be responsible for implementing and following-up on matters concerning the GCC Customs Union and supervising customs activities in the UAE.

Under the new arrangements duty will be collected on behalf of the rest of the GCC countries on a quarterly basis, through a clearing system. This is one step in the process towards a Common GCC Market that is expected to come into force on 1 January 2007 with monetary union planned for 1 January 2010. All these phases are interlinked, but the most significant ones in terms of economic integration are the unification of customs tariffs and adoption of a single currency.

E-GOVERNMENT

In an exhaustive global benchmarking exercise aimed at measuring levels of e-governance among the 190 member countries, the United Nations has released a report that puts the UAE in the top league among countries that have successfully introduced e-government. Globally, the index has ranked the UAE as the first in the Arab World and twenty-first worldwide, giving it 2.17 points. This positions it ahead of Japan (2.12), Ireland (2.16), Austria (2.14) and Russia (1.89) and following closely behind Italy (2.21) and Luxembourg (2.20). The top five countries in the list include the US (3.11), Australia (2.60) and New Zealand (2.59). In the Middle East, the UAE is ranked at the top of the list, followed by Kuwait (2.12), Bahrain (2.04) and Lebanon (2.00). Given the fact that the UAE is one of the most 'Internet-connected' countries in the Arab world (claiming the most Internet hosts), with over a million Internet users, and Dubai is home to the world's first Internet City, it is not surprising that both individual governments and the Federal Government have turned to e-government strategies to increase efficiency.

The federal initiative in this field was approved by the Federal E-government Steering Committee in November 2002. The project is to be undertaken in a series of phases, i.e. planning and prioritisation; tendering and contracting, and finally implementation. It will also entail a review of all procedures and services offered by federal ministries, preparation of necessary recommendations on the current status of the IT sector in the Federal Government and specification of best global practices. The new project will include provision of e-services from government to the government; government to citizens; and government to the private sector.

Dubai has already initiated major initiatives in the field of e-government. In October 2002 Dubai e-Government launched a revamped portal www.dubai.ae that gives users online access to a wide range of government services, including a facility for payments to different government departments, together with renewal of visas, ownership deeds and health cards.

Other emirates are also making substantial progress in the field of e-government.

INDUSTRIAL DEVELOPMENT

The UAE's main industrial activities, apart from the oil and gas sector which is covered separately in this chapter, are in construction, aluminium, chemicals and plastics, metals and heavy equipment, clothing and textiles, and food. Dubai has emerged as the primary non-oil industrial centre in the UAE as it steps up its drive to attract capital and expand its manufacturing base to gradually replace its dwindling earnings from oil exports. The emirate is also a major transhipment centre and accounted for almost half the UAE's industrial investment of around Dh28.5 billion in 2001. It also had the largest number of industrial units, totalling 854 at the end of 2001.

Abu Dhabi, whose main focus is naturally on its massive oil and gas industries, ranked second in terms of industrial investment (in the non-oil sector) but fourth in terms of the number of factories (235). Sharjah was the third biggest industrial investor, closely followed by Ra's al-Khaimah. By late 2002 there were over 2330 factories providing more than 188,000 jobs. In terms of investment the hierarchy of industrial sectors is topped by chemicals, followed by food and beverages, metal products, and garments in descending order of importance.

The UAE's manufacturing sector is now focusing on restructuring in order to meet the challenges it will face when new WTO regulations come into effect in 2005. The main thrust is on establishing projects with production privileges that will enable them to penetrate new markets and increase exports.

THE UAE OFFSETS GROUP

The UAE Offsets Group (UOG), created in 1992 to implement the UAE Offsets Programme, is now serving as a commercial and economic think-tank for the UAE, especially for Abu Dhabi. Several multi-million dollar projects including energy-related ventures, shipyards, fish farms, district cooling units and aircraft leasing companies have been created by UOG as joint ventures between local and international investors.

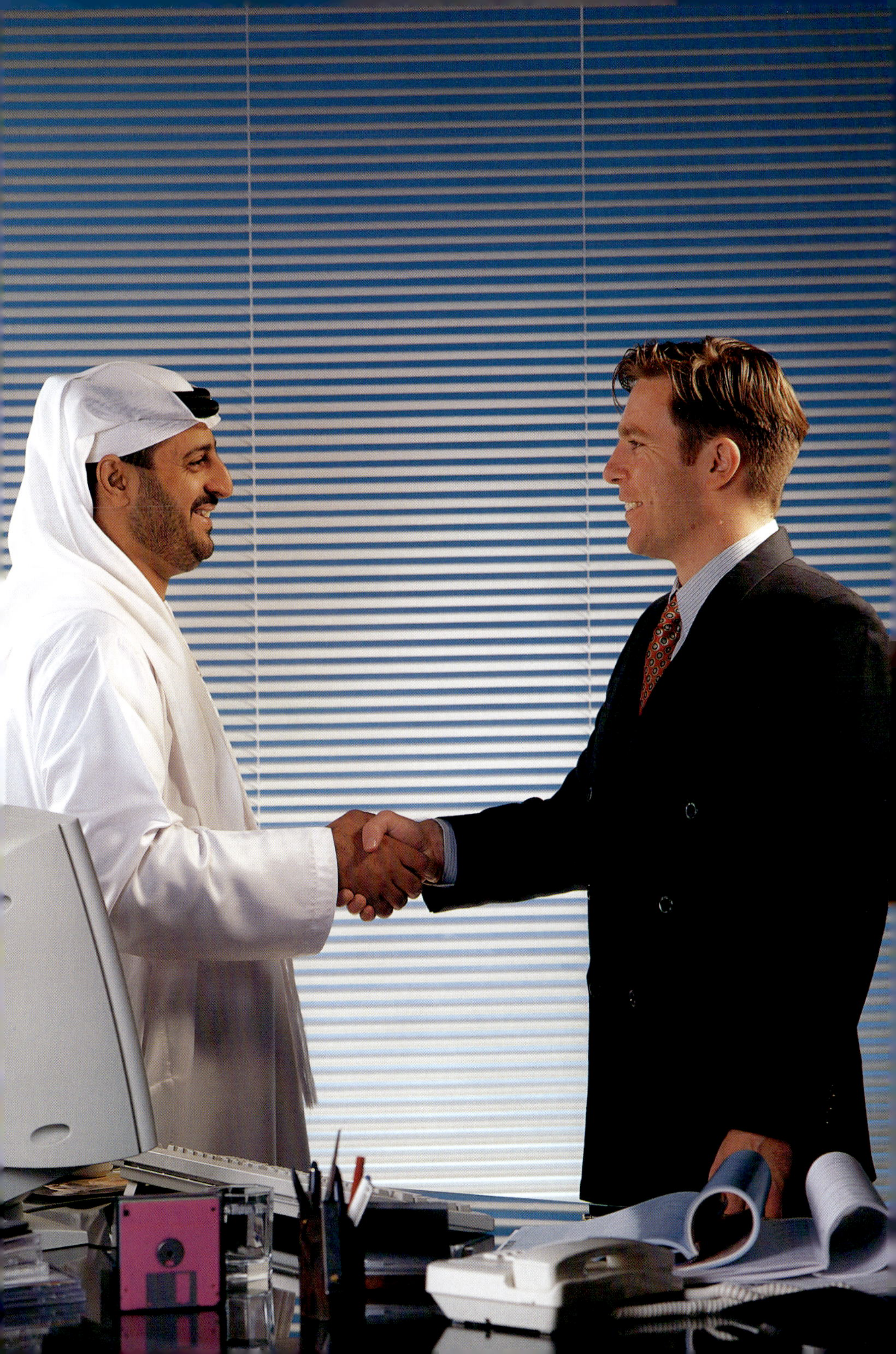

The UAE Offsets Programme requires all defence contractors signing deals worth more than US$10 million with the UAE Armed Forces to fulfil offset obligations and UOG plays the role of a conduit between the joint venture partners. Offsets ventures should yield profits equal to up to 60 per cent of a contract's value over a period of several years (the typical duration of an offset obligation is seven years) and earn offset credits that are evaluated at several milestones during the life of each offset project. The performance of the joint ventures is closely monitored by UOG and if defence contractors fail to fulfil obligations they are required to pay liquidated damages of 8.5 per cent on the unfulfilled portion of the obligation, calculated at each milestone.

To date, the UAE Offsets Programme has resulted in the creation of joint ventures with a combined market value of more than Dh4 billion (US$1.1 billion). The actual contribution of these ventures to the local economy is much higher than the investments and their market values, and is expected to continue to accumulate with the growth and expansion of their operations.

Aside from setting up offsets joint ventures, UOG has also been involved in setting up non-offset related projects. Some defence contractors were of the view that the guidelines and conditions set by UOG were too rigid and hindered the establishment of viable businesses.

UOG overhauled the offsets programme in early 2002 in order to make it more efficient and enable defence contractors to successfully meet their offset obligations. The move followed UOG's organisational restructuring in the second quarter of 2001, which saw the creation of three main operating business units including a dedicated Offsets Ventures Unit to focus on the group's core business, the Offsets Programme.

UOG devised a new strategy to further streamline and facilitate the implementation of the Offsets Programme. Defence contractors can continue to independently identify projects and partners, as they have done in the past, but other options will also be available for them to fulfil offset obligations. After setting up the Chescor Capital Offset Fund (CCOF) in mid-2000, UOG is currently studying new funds that will accept investments from defence contractors, particularly those with small obligations. The new funds will spread investment risk over several projects to get balanced returns. Defence contractors with large obligations may also offset a portion of their obligation by investing in the funds, whose launch will be determined by demand from contractors with outstanding obligations.

UOG also intends to allow defence contractors to set up projects closer to their core areas of expertise, such as training and maintenance, provided they do not rely on a single customer and are commercially driven. On occasion, defence contractors may also be invited to look into investing in other projects initiated by UOG or third parties.

The restructuring is aimed at clearly identifying suitable new offsets and non-offsets projects. Six new business units have been created to ensure that ongoing new projects are implemented on a fast-track basis.

UOG Business Units

Management Services and Capabilities Unit: responsible for planning and research, project development, investment analysis and funding, business commercialisation, legal and technical specialist advisory services, corporate communications and internal audit.

Offsets Ventures Unit: responsible for implementing the UAE Offsets Programme in cooperation with the UAE Armed Forces and international, regional and local defence contractors with offsets obligations.

Government Ventures Division: responsible for setting up new projects under the directives of the government in cooperation with, or on behalf of, government bodies.

New Ventures Unit: responsible for establishing non-offsets projects that add value to the local economy by bringing in new technologies and innovative concepts and ideas to create synergies with the existing resources of the country.

Business Support and Services Unit: responsible for human resources and administration, of the information technology (IT) needs of the group, training and knowledge management to enhance the capabilities of UAE nationals and to assist government-run educational institutions by voluntarily offering work placement opportunities for UAE national men and women.

Finance Unit: responsible for the financial accounting.

Not all the projects managed by the Offsets Group are part of the Offsets Programme. The US$3.5 billion Dolphin gas project is the biggest non-offset scheme being implemented by UOG. It entails the production and transportation of up to 2 billion cubic feet a day (cf/d) of natural gas from Qatar's North Field for the markets of the UAE via a 440-kilometre subsea pipeline. The project is purely a commercial venture, being developed by Dolphin Energy Limited (DEL), 51 per cent of which is owned by UOG through its special purpose Offset Development Company and 24.5 per cent each by TotalFinaElf of France and Occidental Petroleum of the US.

Such projects are being set up as purely commercial ventures where UOG is playing the role of a venture capitalist organisation. The projects aim at stimulating industrial development in the country by providing secure sources of energy.

Under a mandate from the Abu Dhabi Government, UOG also facilitated the development of the 656 MW power generation and 100 million gallons a day (mg/d) water desalination plant at Qidfa, in Fujairah. The US$1.4 billion project, currently under construction, aims at meeting the rising water demand in Abu Dhabi and the growing power needs of the northern emirates. It will also supply 500MW of electricity to the planned Emirates National Grid (ENG).

INDUSTRY NEWS 2002

Ceramics

RAK Ceramics is on track to manufacture 50 million square metres of tiles and two million pieces of sanitary ware per year, which will make it the largest manufacturer of these goods worldwide. Its current Dh140 million expansion programme, including a Dh60 million, 30,000 square metre per day production plant, will raise its capacity to 132,000 square metres of ceramic and porcelain tiles per day. A further Dh60 million will be used to establish a plant in China, while another Dh20 million will be spent on a plant to produce an additional 1000 pieces of vitreous china sanitary ware per day, from an output of 5000 pieces.

Iron and Steel

The US$130 million Emirates Iron and Steel Factory is currently producing 250,000 tonnes per annum of steel reinforcing bars, but plans to double production in 2003. It is planned to export some 15 to 20 per cent of production to neighbouring GCC markets. The design capacity of the plant, the largest such plant in the UAE, is 700,000 tons per year (t/y). The state-of-the-art plant, with German technology, commenced production in November 2001. It produces mainly steel reinforcing bars in sizes of 10 to 32 millimetres. The finished product is used mainly for construction of buildings, bridges and similar projects.

Textiles and Clothing

The UAE has been considering plans to remove an eight-year-old ban on the establishment of new ready-made garment and textile factories in line with rules by the World Trade Organisation (WTO) requiring member states to tear down financial and trade barriers. A study on this topic aimed at finding the best way to re-open the garment industry to new investment. The UAE suspended licences for new clothes factories in 1994 and set export quotas for factories following complaints from the United States and others about dumping of cheap products.

Official statistics show that nearly 150 ready-made garment factories operate in the UAE, with a combined capital of nearly Dh254 million (US$69 million). In the textile industry, there are 57 factories with a total investment of around Dh589 million (US$162 million). The bulk of these investments are concentrated in Dubai and Sharjah, with a combined capital of around Dh637 million (US$173 million), nearly 75 per cent of the total investment.

Garment production in the UAE suffered in 2002 as many local manufacturers switched to overseas factories in order to beat the US quota restrictions on exports. Industry sources believe that local production fell by 15–20 per cent in 2002. Whilst this is not a new phenomenon, the extent of the shift has not previously reached 2002 levels. In the past, there have been moves by the UAE authorities to have the country delisted from the US quota regime but so far these have not been fruitful.

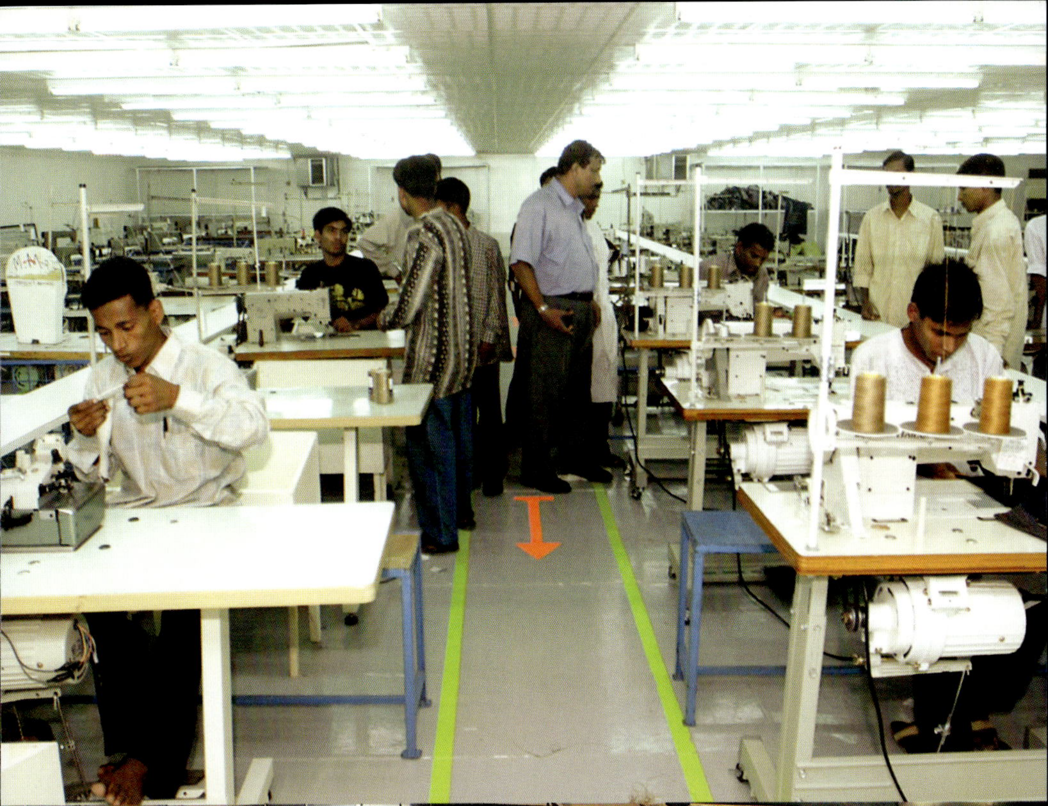

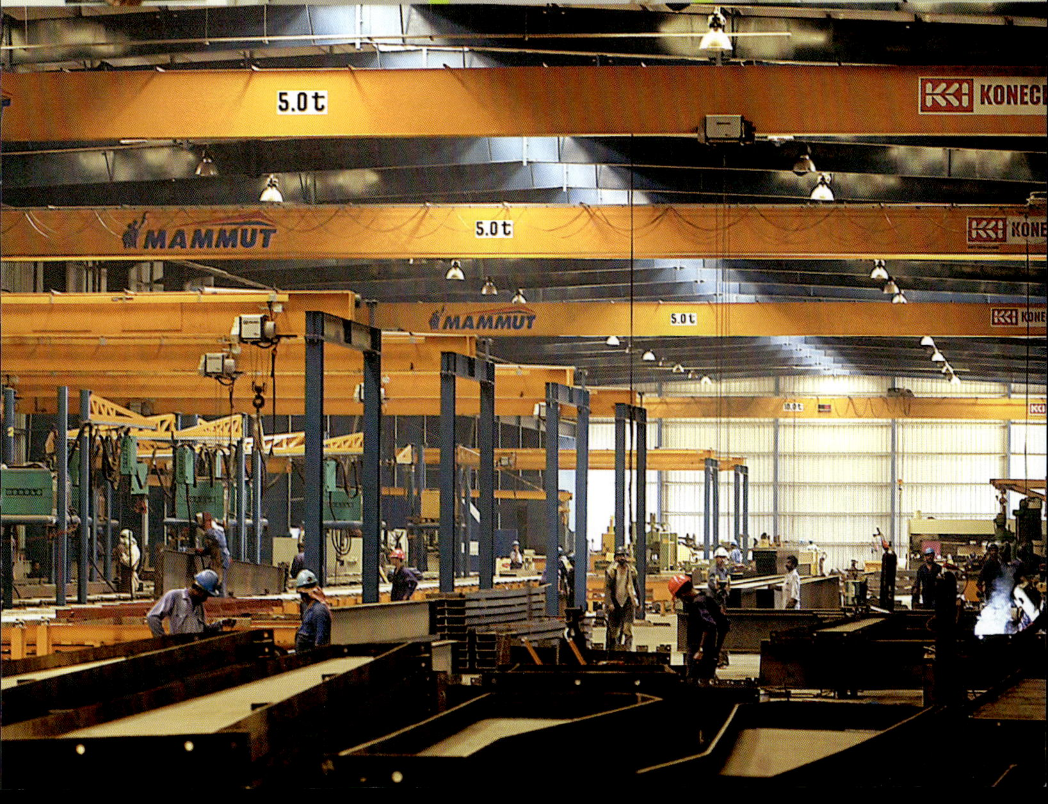
5.0t
MAMMUT
5.0t
MAMMUT
5.0t

Chemicals

A new Dh60 million chlor-alkali plant to produce ultra-pure chemicals is being established in Abu Dhabi's industrial city. The process to be used in the plant is based on environment-friendly technology and will have electrolytic membrane cell modules, caustic soda concentrator and hydrochloric acid absorber. The chemicals produced will be strategically important for oil well management and potable water disinfection. The chemicals to be produced are sodium hypochlorite, sodium hydroxide and hydrochloric acid. The demand for these chemicals is presently met by imports.

Aluminium

Dubai Aluminium Company (DUBAL) plans to expand annual production of the existing smelter at Jebel Ali by 155,000 tons, for an estimated cost of at least US$300 million, proceeded in 2002. An approximately US$41 million contract was awarded to France's Alstom for the first element of the infrastructure development package. The contract covers the extension of kilns 1, 2 and 3. The expansion is being driven by DUBAL's efforts to maximise space available at its Jebel Ali smelter and upgrade existing technology. Called *Kestrel*, the project will be carried out in two main packages, i.e. infrastructure development and power plant and related facilities. The proposed new facilities are due for completion by mid-2003. The new expansion is separate from the company's *Heron* project, which calls for the addition of 350,000 to 400,000 tons/year of new capacity. At present DUBAL produces about 536,000 tons/year of primary aluminium.

Furniture

Figures for 2001 indicate that the UAE furniture and manufacturing industries sector has 236 firms with a total investment of Dh493 million and workforce of 11,418 workers. There were five firms in Abu Dhabi employing 230 workers, 92 firms in Dubai employing 4063 workers, 107 firms in Sharjah employing 5576 workers, 25 firms in Ajman employing 1274 workers, three firms in Ra's al-Khaimah employing 204 workers, three firms in Umm al-Qaiwain employing 54 workers and one firm in Fujairah employing 17 workers.

Cable Manufacture

Dubai Cable Company (DUCAB) recorded a 30 per cent increase in production levels across the entire product range and more than doubled the production of medium voltage (33kV and 11kV) cables in the second quarter of 2002, compared to the corresponding period in 2001. The impressive performance is the result of several initiatives taken by the management to enhance and upgrade working practices within the company, in addition to extensive investment in recent expansion schemes designed to facilitate higher production levels.

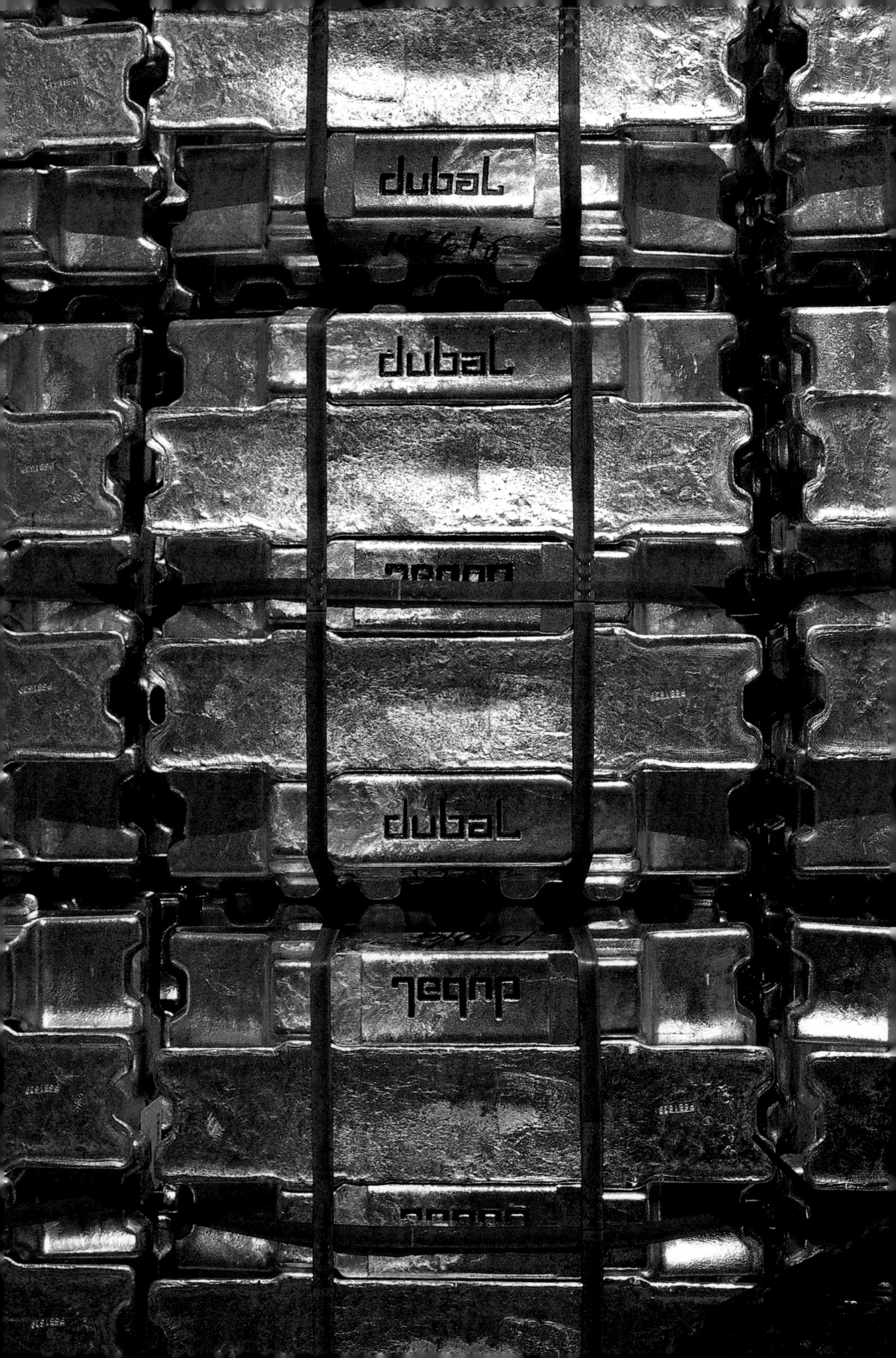
dubal
dubal
dubal

Maritime Industries

Boat-building; ship repair and marine dredging are important maritime industries in the UAE. Information on the Abu Dhabi Ship Building Company (ADSB) and Dubai Dry Dock Company is given under the heading of Seaports and Shipping in the section on Infrastructure. In addition to these two major UAE-based maritime industries, mention should also be made of bunkering which has spawned another important trading industry in the country. In fact, the UAE now ranks among the top five locations in the world for ship supplies and bunkering, with the annual turnover of ship supplies business approximately amounting to US$300 million. There are around 40 ship suppliers in the Emirates.

Dredging

Marine dredging is used to deepen shipping channels and harbours while also mining the soft seabed for sand and gravel to use in land reclamation. The National Marine Dredging Co (NMDC) has been particularly busy in this field, earning a net profit of Dh132.45 million, an impressive 154 per cent increase over the previous year's figures. NMDC is principally engaged in executing dredging contracts and associated reclamation works in the territorial waters of the UAE under contracts from the Government of Abu Dhabi.

OIL AND GAS

UAE's confirmed oil reserves now stand at 97.8 billion barrels, representing 9.1 per cent of the world's reserves. Abu Dhabi Emirate has 92.2 billion barrels of the total bulk followed by Dubai with 4 billion barrels, Sharjah with 1.5 billion and Ra's al-Khaimah with 100 million. The UAE has the fifth largest gas reserves in the world with 212.1 trillion cubic feet. Like oil, Abu Dhabi Emirate has the lion share of 196.1 trillion cubic feet, followed by Sharjah with 10.7 trillion cubic feet, Dubai with 4.1 trillion cubic feet and Ra's al-Khaimah with 1.2 trillion cubic feet.

The federal dimension in the hydrocarbon sector is relatively limited since most of the relevant activities such as oil and gas exploration, production, processing and export activities are controlled by each emirate's own government. One recent exception to this general rule was announced in March 2002 when the federal Ministry of Petroleum and Minerals awarded a Dh37 million contract to the British Geological Survey (BGS) to undertake a comprehensive geological and geophysical survey of the UAE's mountainous zone stretching from Ra's al-Khaimah in the north to the city of Al Ain, in Abu Dhabi, to the south. The project team is also producing both geological and tectonic maps covering the whole of UAE territory. The latter will be used to choose suitable locations for seismic monitoring equipment.

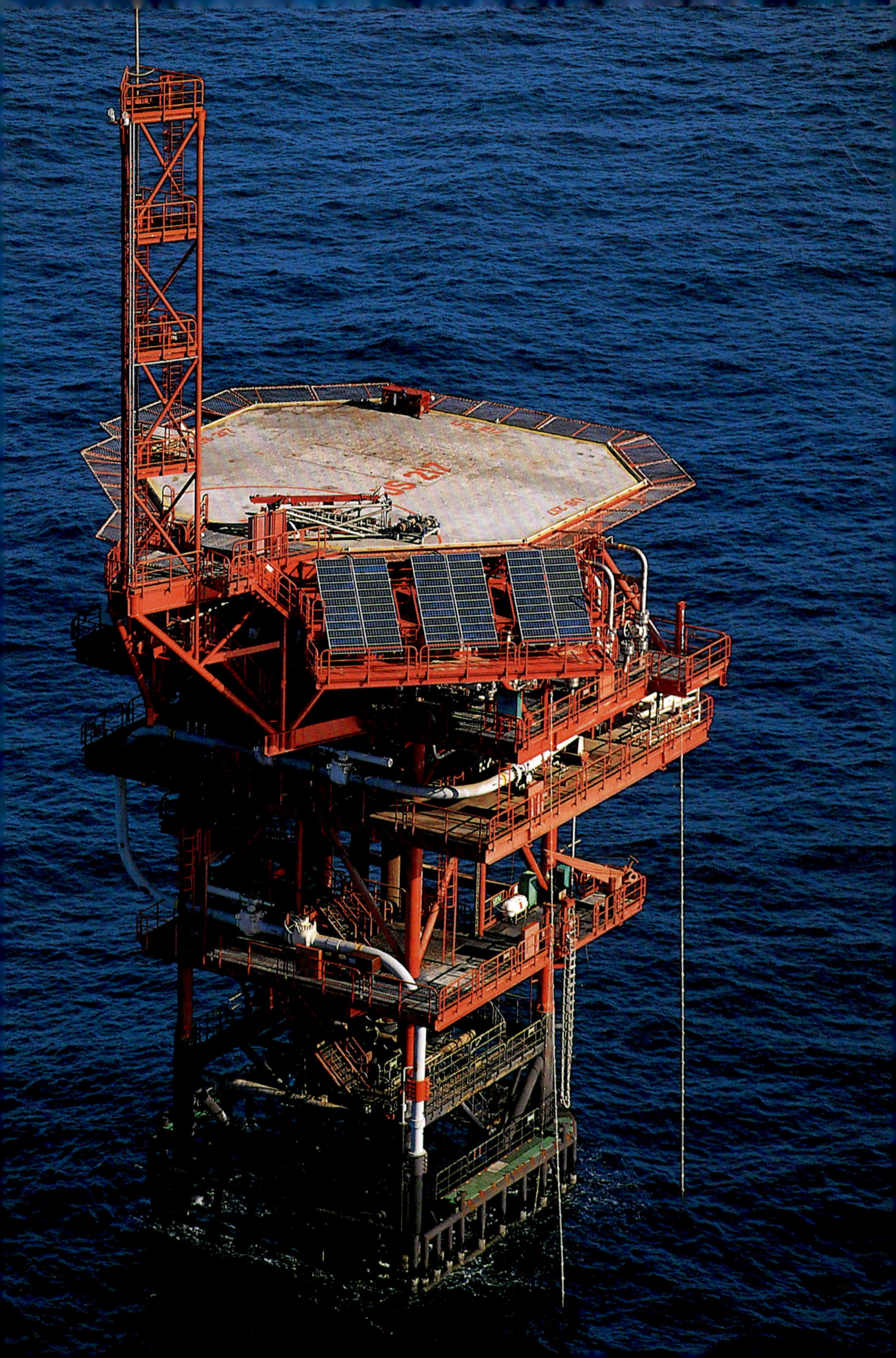

The main focus for oil and gas exploration activities in the UAE in recent years has centered on Sharjah, Ra's al-Khaimah, Ajman and Umm al-Qaiwain where the Norwegian company Atlantis Holdings has exploration licences. These efforts have resulted in several significant finds including a promising gas discovery in Sharjah in 1999, and the reappraisal and drilling of a gas field, originally discovered off Umm al-Qaiwain in 1976 but not previously developed. But the real focus of future growth in oil and gas production over the coming years will certainly be in Abu Dhabi where the vast majority of known reserves are located.

Abu Dhabi is already able to produce considerably more oil than the OPEC quota levels dictate and it is planning to significantly increase its capacity in the near future. Current installed crude oil production facilities permit a production of some 2.45 million barrels per day (b/d), i.e. around 800,000 b/d more than its adjusted production level in 2002 (which was reduced to comply with the OPEC quota). The development programme presently under way calls for an additional 400,000 b/d of capacity by 2005 which will raise its designed capacity to 2.85 million b/d. Approximately half of Abu Dhabi's current oil production capacity comes from offshore fields (1.25 million b/d) and half from onshore fields (1.2 million b/d) and the development programme aims to maintain this balance with an addition of around 200,000 b/d to each system. Sources in the oil and gas industries are acutely aware that Abu Dhabi's hydrocarbon production has been significantly curtailed by its adherence to the OPEC quota system. If it was not for these restrictions, Abu Dhabi could further expand its production capabilities since it possesses vast reserves of both oil and natural gas. It holds 94 per cent of the UAE's total proven oil reserves of 97.8 billion barrels and 92.5 per cent of its natural gas reserves of 212 trillion cubic feet.

At the present time there are oil refineries at Ruwais (420,000 b/d) and Umm al-Nar (88,000 b/d) in Abu Dhabi, in Fujairah (75,000-b/d), in Dubai (a 120,000-b/d condensate refinery) and in Sharjah (75,000 b/d). The UAE thus had total refining capacity of 778,000 b/d at the end of 2001 of which 508,000 b/d was located in Abu Dhabi. Since total refined product consumption in the UAE is around 135,000 b/d, the majority of its refined products are exported.

Most of the major industrial projects in the UAE depend on natural gas for their energy source and consumption of natural gas has increased rapidly over the recent period of development and growth. New power stations, desalination plants and industrial facilities pushed the daily consumption of natural gas from 1.64 billion cubic feet per day (cf/d) in 1993 to over 3 billion cf/d in 2000. The trend is continuing and is placing considerable pressure on the UAE, which has to find solutions to meet the ever-increasing demand for natural gas. It is not that the country lacks the resources — it has the fifth largest reserves of natural gas in the world, but the challenge is to keep production and distribution systems in line with demand. Abu Dhabi exports some 8 million tons/year of liquefied natural gas (LNG) and liquefied petroleum gas

DOLPHIN ENERGY LIMITED (DEL)

The US$3.5 billion Dolphin gas project is now entering an advanced stage of implementation. Dolphin Energy Limited (DEL), a subsidiary of the UAE Offsets Group (UOG) responsible for the first natural gas pipeline network in the Arabian Gulf, is making progress with putting in place the infrastructure for the gas to start flowing to the UAE from Qatar's North Field in 2006.

DEL is expected to award the engineering, procurement and construction (EPC) contracts for the upstream, downstream and midstream work by mid-2003. In June 2002, DEL selected Occidental Petroleum (Oxy) of the US as its second strategic partner and the number of personnel employed by the company has also risen rapidly. Oxy bought a 24.5 per cent stake in DEL from UOG for US$310 million and joined TotalFinaElf of France, which also owns a 24.5 per cent stake in the company, as the second foreign partner. UOG now owns a majority 51 per cent stake in DEL through a special purpose Offset Development Company (Mubadala).

In the meantime, the engineering work for developing the gas fields in Qatar, the processing plant at Ras Laffan and the gas pipeline from Qatar to the UAE has progressed at a rapid pace. Upstream front-end engineering & design (FEED) work has been completed by a partnership of the US's Foster Wheeler Corporation and France's Sofresid, while Halliburton KBR, also of the US, has completed the midstream FEED.

Progress is also being made on the first cross-border gas deal in the GCC under which DEL will buy Omani gas. After signing a memorandum of understanding (MoU) with Oman Oil Company (OOC) in July 2002, negotiations are ongoing to firm up the gas sales agreement for the supply of Omani gas through Dolphin to the power generation and water desalination project of the Union Water & Electricity Company (UWEC) currently under construction at Qidfa, in Fujairah.

The MoU calls for the supply of 120 million cf/d of natural gas from Oman's Fahud field through the Fahud-Sohar gas pipeline by linking it with a gas line being built by DEL from Al Ain to Fujairah. DEL intends to increase the import of Omani gas supplies to up to 300 million cf/d but this will depend on the availability of gas in Oman. Gas supplies are scheduled to begin in late 2003 and will be available for a period of between 42-60 months. The Omani gas will be replaced by DEL's gas from the North Field and the establishment of a link between the DEL and OOC pipelines will facilitate the future supply of DEL gas to Oman.

The Dolphin project involves the development of upstream facilities for the production of natural gas from the Khuff formation in Qatar's North Field, its transportation to a gas gathering and processing plant at Ras Laffan, and the transportation of 2 bcf/d of gas through a 440-kilometre, 48-inch diameter, subsea pipeline to Taweelah in Abu Dhabi and Jebel Ali in Dubai. A separate 179-kilometre, 24-inch pipeline will transport gas from Al Ain to Fujairah for the new 656 MW power generation and 100 million gallons a day (mg/d) water desalination project presently under construction for the Union Water & Electricity Company.

ADNOC GROUP OF COMPANIES AND PARTICIPATIONS (Abu Dhabi/UAE)

ADNOC Company	Share	Activity	Address
Abu Dhabi Company for Onshore Oil Operations (ADCO)	60%	Onshore exploration, development and production on behalf of the partners	PO Box 270 Tel: (971-2) 604000 Fax: (971-2) 669785
Abu Dhabi Marine Operating Company (ADMA-OPCO)	60%	Offshore exploration, development and production on behalf of the partners	PO Box 303 Tel: (971-2) 6060000 Fax: (971-2) 626005
Zakum Development Company (ZADCO)	51%	Development and production from Upper Zakum field; also operates Umm Al-Dalkh and Satah Fields on behalf of the partners	PO Box 46808 Tel: (971-2) 6050000 Fax: (971-2) 669448
National Petroleum Construction Company (NPCC)	70%	Construction and fabrication facilities for the oil industry	PO Box 2058 Tel: (971-2) 6549000 Fax: (971-2) 6549111
Abu Dhabi Drilling Chemicals and Products (ADDCAP)	100%	Production of drilling chemicals and provision of marine base and services	PO Box 46121 Tel: (971-2) 6029000 Fax: (971-2) 6029010
National Drilling Company (NDC)	100%	Provision of onshore and offshore drilling operations	PO Box 4017 Tel: (971-2) 6776100 Fax: (971-2) 6779937
Abu Dhabi Petroleum Ports Operating Company (ADPPOC)	60%	Operating Ruwais, Jebel Dhanna and other oil or industrial ports	PO Box 61 Tel: (971-2) 6777300 Fax: (971-2) 6766903
National Marine Services (NMS)	60%	Owning, operating and chartering or leasing specialised vessels serving the oil industry	PO Box 7202 Tel: (971-2) 6277777 Fax: (971-2) 6268239
Abu Dhabi Gas Industries* Limited (GASCO)	68%	Operation of onshore gas gathering and processing plants	PO Box 665 Tel: (971-2) 6041111 Fax: (971-2) 6047414
Abu Dhabi Gas Liquefaction (ADGAS)	51%	Operation of Das Island gas liquefaction plants	PO Box 3500 Tel: (971-2) 6061111 Fax: (971-2) 6065500
Ruwais Fertiliser Industries (FERTIL)	66.66%	Operation of ammonia and urea plant in Ruwais and marketing its product	PO Box 2288 Tel: (971-2) 6021111 Fax: (971-2) 6728084

ADNOC Company	Share	Activity	Address
Abu Dhabi National Oil Company for Distribution (ADNOC Distribution)	100%	Storage, transportation and domestic distribution of refined products	PO Box 4188 Tel: (971-2) 6771300 Fax: (971-2) 6722322
Abu Dhabi National Tanker Company (ADNATCO)	100%	Transporting crude oil and refined products	PO Box 2977 Tel: (971-2) 331800 Fax: (971-2) 322940
National Gas Shipping Company (NGSCO)	70%	Shipping liquefied gas products from Das Island	PO Box 2600 Tel: (971-2) 6271400 Fax: (971-2) 6274305
Abu Dhabi Oil Refining Company (TAKREER)	100%	Refining	PO Box 3593 Tel: (971-2) 6027000 Fax: (971-2) 6027272
Abu Dhabi Gas Company* (ATHEER)	100%	Gas processing and distribution	Tel: (971-2) 6027533 Fax: (971-2) 6027588
Abu Dhabi Polymers Company Limited (Borouge)	60%	Processing and production of polyethylene	PO Box 6925 Tel: (971-2) 6312333 Fax: (971-2) 6312299

*Gasco and Atheer were merged in April 2001.

(LPG) from its plant on Das Island. Recent developments in the gas sector include work at the Asab field that boosted gas production for reinjection purposes and the new developments at the Bab field that increased marketed production capacity by nearly 1 billion cf/d. This brought Abu Dhabi's gas production up to an estimated 42 billion cubic metres (4.06 billion cf/d) in 2001, accounting for some 76 per cent of the UAE's total gas production of about 55 billion cubic metres.

By June 2001 Abu Dhabi was exporting 500 million cf/d of natural gas by pipeline to Dubai. Additional gas development projects scheduled for completion in 2004 will further enhance the emirate's ability to supply the burgeoning market for gas in the UAE but there are still concerns that these measures alone may not be sufficient to keep pace with demand. As a result of these concerns the UAE Offsets Group (UOG) has established the Dolphin Energy Project that is constructing a supply and distribution pipeline to bring gas from the rich Qatar offshore gas fields to Abu Dhabi, Dubai and elsewhere. The ambitious project is a joint venture between the UAE Offsets Group (UOG) and two foreign partners, TotalFinaElf and Occidental Petroleum. It will deliver the gas through an 800-kilometre gasline to the UAE. The project is due to come on stream in 2006.

OIL PRODUCTION AND CRUDE RESERVES

Abu Dhabi

Abu Dhabi's proven crude oil reserves are estimated at 92.2 billion barrels, which amounts to 94.3 per cent of the UAE's total reserves and gives the emirate a reserve-production capacity of over 130 years at the 2001 rate of output. Its largest oilfield is Upper Zakum, which contains an estimated 48 billion barrels of reserves *in-situ* and estimated recoverable reserves of 16 to 20 billion barrels (using extensive water injection).

Output averaged about 1.82 million b/d in 2001, having been cut from around 2.05 million b/d at the beginning of the year to an estimated 1.76 million b/d at the year-end. Output from ADMA-OPCO's two fields, Umm Shaif and Lower Zakum, totaled 440,000 b/d, while Upper Zakum and the other four fields operated by ZADCO contributed 460,000 b/d and the remaining offshore fields (Mubarraz/Neewat al-Ghalan, Umm al-Anbar, al-Bunduq and Abu al-Bukhoosh) continued to produce about 75,000 b/d between them. In addition, ADCO now produces 130,000 b/d of 57.5° API condensate (0.11 per cent sulphur) from the Thamama formation of the Bab/Habshan field, which started up in 1996.

Dubai

Dubai's proven oil reserves were still officially estimated at 4 billion barrels in January 2002, but the recoverable portion may be less than half this figure, with industry sources estimating them at 1.6 to 2 billion barrels. Meanwhile, estimates

ECONOMIC DEVELOPMENT

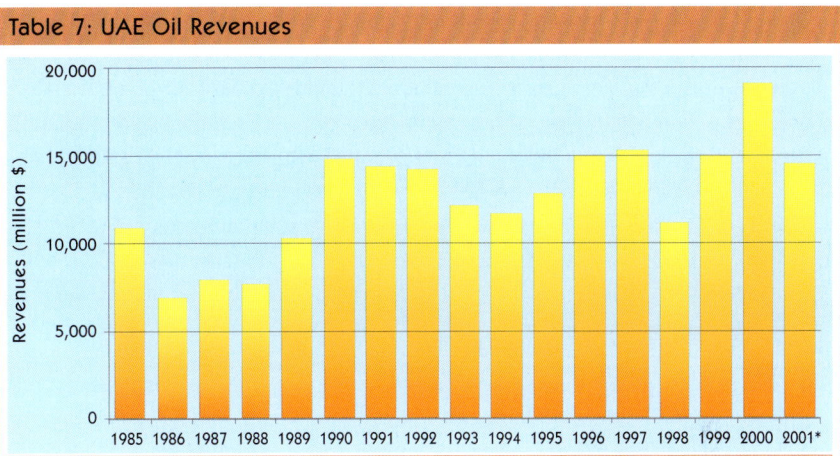

Table 7: UAE Oil Revenues

Year	Revenues (millions$)	% Change	Year	Revenues (millions$)	% Change
1985	10,896	-10.5	1994	11,683	-3.7
1986	6,865	-37.0	1995	12,822	+9.7
1987	7,900	+15.1	1996	14,980	+16.8
1988	7,627	-3.8	1997	15,264	+2.5
1989	10,215	+34.0	1998	11,131	-23.1
1990	14,846	+45.3	1999	15,021	+34.9
1991	14,356	-3.7	2000	19,100	+27.3
1992	14,251	-0.8	2001*	14,500	-24.1
1993	12,118	-17.6			

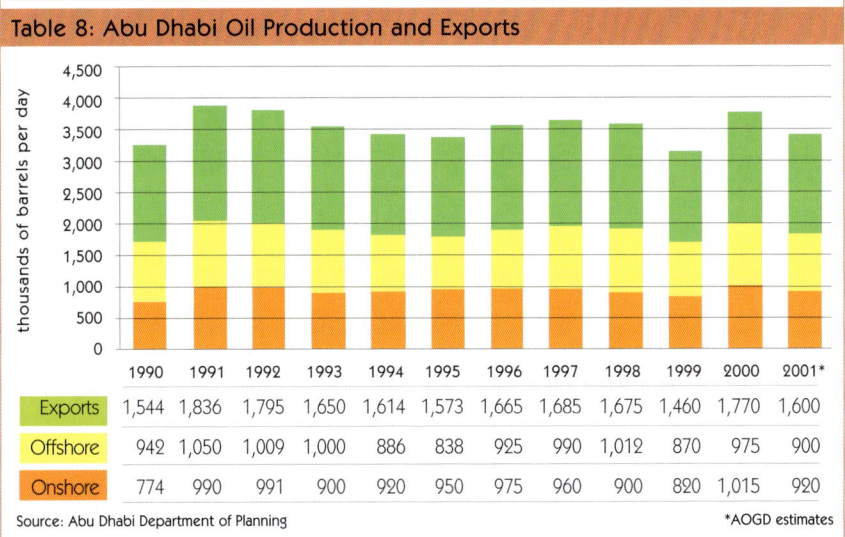

Table 8: Abu Dhabi Oil Production and Exports

	1990	1991	1992	1993	1994	1995	1996	1997	1998	1999	2000	2001*
Exports	1,544	1,836	1,795	1,650	1,614	1,573	1,665	1,685	1,675	1,460	1,770	1,600
Offshore	942	1,050	1,009	1,000	886	838	925	990	1,012	870	975	900
Onshore	774	990	991	900	920	950	975	960	900	820	1,015	920

Source: Abu Dhabi Department of Planning *AOGD estimates

of how long Dubai can keep pumping oil range from 20 to 47 years. Almost all of the emirate's oil reserves are located in the original concession area of the Dubai Petroleum Company (DPC), whose four offshore fields account for its entire output of crude oil and associated gas. Oil output has steadily declined despite a programme of field development, entailing the drilling of infill wells, horizontal production wells and water injectors. The company has installed water and gas injection facilities on a large scale to maximise recovery rates, and all the associated gas produced at its four fields is now reinjected into oil reservoirs.

Sharjah

Sharjah's hydrocarbon reserves are put at 1.5 billion barrels of oil and condensate and 10,700 billion cubic feet of natural gas. The three onshore gas fields account for the bulk of the emirate's hydrocarbon reserves, since the Mubarak field contains less than 50 million barrels of oil and 1500 billion cubic feet of associated gas.

The emirate's hydrocarbon production is now declining. In 2001 it consisted of 45,000 b/d of liquids, down from 50,000 b/d in 2000 and around 70,000 b/d in 1996-97, and about 750 million cf/d of natural gas, compared with 1 billion cf/d in 1997-98. Liquids production was made up of about 5000 b/d of crude and 10,000 b/d of condensate from the offshore Mubarak field and 30,000 b/d of condensate from the onshore Saja'a field, while gas production consisted of 130 million cf/d of associated gas from Mubarak and 620 million cf/d of nonassociated gas from the three onshore fields.

The Mubarak field is exploited under a protocol signed between Sharjah and Iran in 1972, which provides for the National Iranian Oil Company to receive 50 per cent of its net revenues. Sharjah also passes on 20 per cent of the revenues to Umm al-Qaiwain and 10 per cent to Ajman, both of which have claims to the island and the surrounding waters. A continuous fall in production at the Mubarak field led Crescent Petroleum to embark on a secondary development programme which entailed drilling more wells including some horizontal wells, tapping into the Thamama formation and development of a new gas processing platform to handle Thamama gas. After separation, 100 million cf/d of gas is sent through a 16-inch trunk line to Jebel Ali in Dubai. The secondary development programme also impacted positively on Sharjah's oil production and after a temporary surge has levelled out to an estimated 15,000 b/d of liquids (5,000 b/d of crude and 10,000 b/d of condensate) and 125 million cf/d of gas in 2001.

Sharjah onshore Saja'a field, operated by BP, has also experienced some difficulties in maintaining production levels and it produced an estimated 475 million cf/d of gas and 20,000 b/d of condensate in 2001. BP drilled two more horizontal wells at Saja'a in 2000, bringing the total number of wells in operation there to 40, compared with four at Moveyeid and seven at Kahaif.

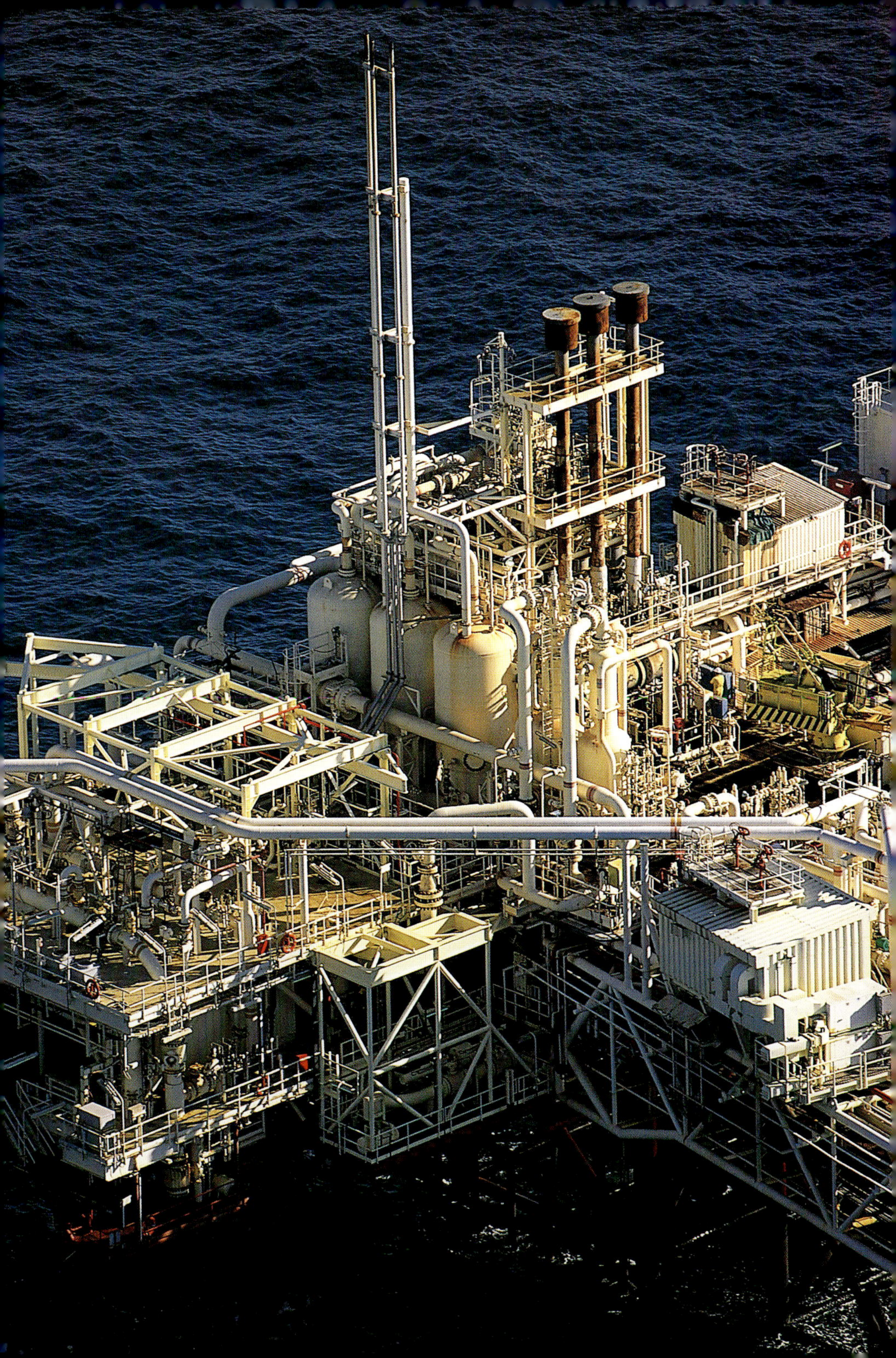

Meanwhile, the Kahaif field has had a gas gathering network and reinjection facilities installed and produces around 150 million cf/d of natural gas and 10,000 b/d of condensate.

Ra's al-Khaimah

Ra's al-Khaimah's hydrocarbon reserves consist of 100 million barrels of crude and condensate and 1.2 trillion cubic feet of natural gas, while it continues to extract 500 b/d of condensate from the Saleh field, the only hydrocarbon structure to have been brought into production in the emirate.

No exploration well has been drilled in Ra's al-Khaimah since 1997, when one was stopped dry. Since then, both operators have preferred to devote their efforts to seismic acquisition and interpretation to improve their chances of success if either should decide to drill another well. One licensee, the Norwegian company Atlantis Holdings, which was taken over by China National Chemicals Import & Export Corporation (Sinochem) in January 2002 and also holds exploration licences in the emirates of Sharjah, Ajman and Umm al-Qaiwain, is reassessing a small offshore tract known as B structure, where a non-commercial find was made in the 1970s.

Ajman

In February 2000 the Government of Ajman created a Department of Petroleum in order to coordinate activities related to exploration and possible future developments in the oil and gas field. Its activities have been primarily confined to carrying out geological and geophysical surveys and producing topographical maps.

An exploration agreement signed in March 1997, by a consortium composed of Atlantis Technology Services Ajman AS, a subsidiary of the Norwegian company Atlantis Holdings (70 per cent) and Scimitar Production International Limited, a subsidiary of Canada's Scimitar Hydrocarbons Corporation (30 per cent), was awarded exclusive rights to explore for crude oil and natural gas throughout the emirate and to exploit any commercial fields it might find. In January 2002 Atlantis Holdings was taken over by China National Chemicals Import and Export Corporation (Sinochem).

Exploration wells drilled in the past were Ajman-1, Ajman-2 and Ajman-3. Ajman-1 was drilled in 1982 and yielded a flow of 639 b/d of 56° API condensate and 2.7 million cf/d of natural gas. The second, Ajman-2, drilled in 1984, encountered traces of oil, but shortly after that a third well was stopped dry. Preliminary appraisal of the Ajman-2 well led to estimates of its recoverable reserves at around 3.5 million barrels of hydrocarbons, but the research team pointed out that, since the well penetrated other formations, the structure could contain total reserves of as much as 20 million barrels of liquids and 50 billion cubic feet of associated gas.

Umm al-Qaiwain

A small offshore gas field discovered in 1976 was redrilled in 2001 by Atlantis Holdings of Norway (which, as noted above, was taken over by China National

Chemicals Import and Export Corporation (Sinochem) in January 2002). UAQ-3 was spudded in April 2001 prior to an announcement of the well's production rate. However, Atlantis commissioned a study from Technip Abu Dhabi for the possible construction of an onshore gas processing plant with a capacity of 150 million cf/d. The study was completed in September 2001.

Atlantis Holdings was assigned its exploration licence, which covers the whole of the emirate's onshore and offshore territory, in April 2000. The company started by carrying out a 3D seismic survey over an 800-square-kilometre onshore area, the first time any exploration activity had taken place in Umm al-Qaiwain since the mid-1980s.

At the present time however, Umm al-Qaiwain's sole interest in hydrocarbon production remains its 20 per cent share of the revenues derived from the offshore Mubarak field in Sharjah, part of which lies under its territorial waters.

EXPLORATION AND FIELD DEVELOPMENT

July 2002 marked the fortieth anniversary of Abu Dhabi's first crude oil shipment to the global market. *British Signal*, a tanker owned by British Petroleum (BP), lifted the first crude oil shipment from Umm Shaif field (now one of the biggest offshore oilfields in the world) and set sail from Das Island on 4 July 1962.

Abu Dhabi

Abu Dhabi National Oil Co. (ADNOC) has drilled 20 exploratory oil wells in the last 20 years. In future, the focus will be on exploration of deep oil and gas prospects. Expansion projects at oil facilities in Abu Dhabi should raise the UAE's sustainable crude output capacity from around 2.5 million b/d to 3.6 million b/d in 2005 and 4 million in 2010. It is expected that more than US$10 billion will be invested in the present expansion programme.

Abu Dhabi already applies the most up-to-date production and drilling technology at its oilfields. Both water and gas injection are in wide use at older fields to sustain reservoir pressure and maintain flow rates. Moreover, operators are drilling a growing number of horizontal wells to improve well productivity and boost recovery rates. Operators in the emirate have acquired considerable expertise in deflected drilling methods and utilise short, medium and long radius drilling techniques in conjunction with both oriented and conventional coring. The longest horizontal hole drilled in Abu Dhabi was a 5500-feet section drilled by ADMA-OPCO.

Gas development projects are continuing at onshore oilfields, and ADNOC is now studying the possibility of utilising acid gas injection to boost flow rates at various oil fields. It currently uses non-corrosive gas, but given its abundant supplies of gas with a high carbon dioxide and hydrogen sulphide content, it wants to develop technologies for extracting these reserves and utilising them for injection purposes, especially at the onshore Bab field. A joint feasibility study carried out by ADNOC and Shell Oil, which explored several options for utilising acid gas, was completed in April 2002.

Abu Dhabi Company for Onshore Oil Operations (ADCO)
An expansion plan due for completion in 2005 calls for the capacity of the Bab field to be increased by a further 50,000 b/d to 350,000 b/d through the development of the Thamama B reservoir. The project calls for an expansion of gas injection capacity at Bab and for an increase in crude handling capacity. In January 2002 ADCO retained the Canadian company Veco Corporation as project management consultant (PMC) for the development of the Bab field.

The other main element in ADCO's capacity expansion programme will be the full field development of the three north-eastern fields (Al Dabb'iya, Rumaitha and Shanayel) to increase their capacity from 10,000 b/d to 110,000 b/d. The work is scheduled for completion in the fourth quarter of 2005 and will provide capacity of 70,000 b/d at the Al Dabb'iya field and 40,000 b/d at Rumaitha/Shanayel.

Work under way at the Bu Hasa field is due to to develop units G and F of the structure, as well as an expansion of unit D. Capacity will remain at 545,000 b/d. A facilities upgrade programme is also planned at Bu Hasa, involving the installation of four new banks of three-phase separation units and a new central control room, as well as the upgrade of instrumentation and control systems. The work is scheduled for completion in the fourth quarter of 2005.

The second phase of the development of the Sahil field will bring a 20,000-b/d increase in capacity by 2004 through the installation of water injection systems. The field currently has a capacity of 55,000 b/d, following the completion of a full field development programme in 1998. The expansion project also calls for the installation of new gas gathering, separation and reinjection facilities and the expansion of the central production station at Asab, to which crude from Sahil is piped for processing.

At Asab itself, a horizontal drilling programme for restoring productivity in Thamama Zone B wells was completed in 1997. Production facilities were also expanded and upgraded to enable them to handle the additional output generated by the installation of gas gathering and injection facilities. As well as expanding production capacity, ADCO continues to invest heavily in enhanced oil recovery (EOR) facilities to maximise recovery rates and maintain pressure in producing reservoirs.

ADCO carries out development of gas production and processing facilities on behalf of ADNOC. It completed three between the end of 1995 and the middle of 2001 and was undertaking others during 2002. Its first gas development project, OGD-1, boosted the production of associated gas at the Bab field from 54 million cf/d to 1865 million cf/d. A second phase, OGD-2, was completed in April 2001 and increased gas production at Bab by 1.13 billion cf/d to almost 3 billion cf/d. Meanwhile, the first gas development project at the Asab field (AGD-1), which entailed the installation of facilities for the production of 826 million cf/d of gas, was completed in April 2000. By the beginning of 2002 onshore gas production capacity totaled nearly 4 billion cf/d.

The two other gas development projects currently under way are both scheduled

ABU DHABI OILFIELDS AND CONCESSIONS

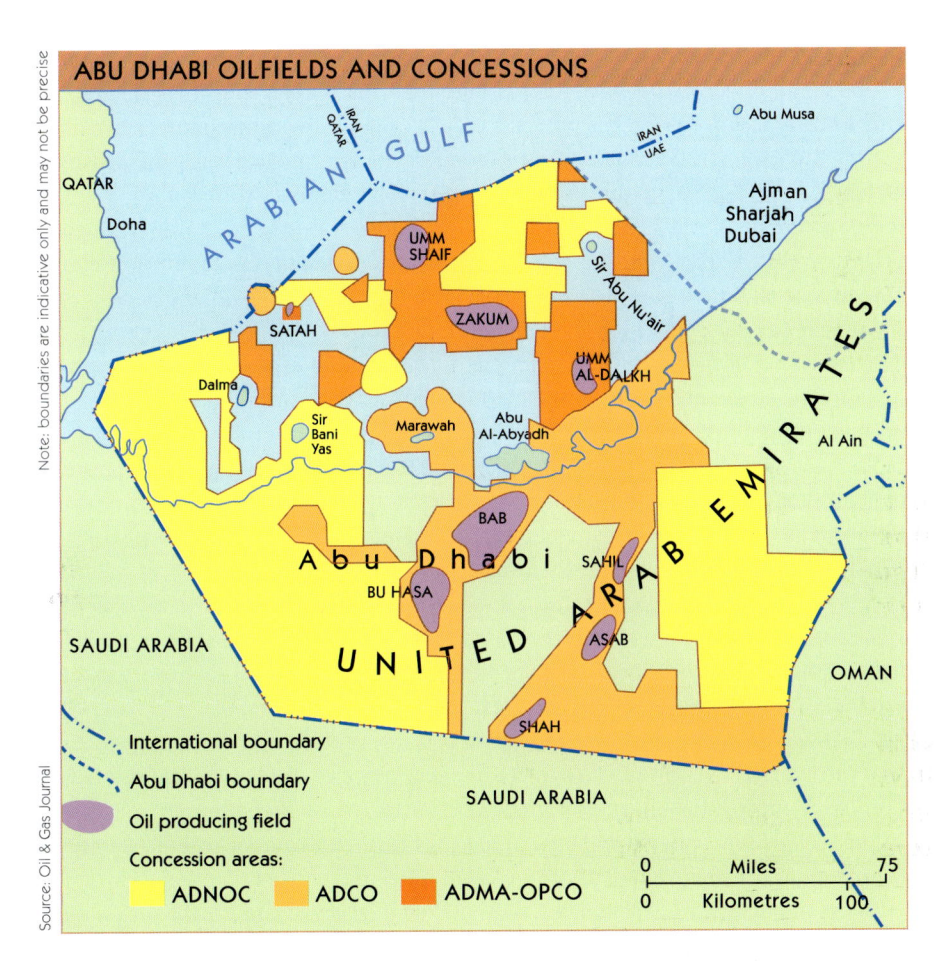

Source: Oil & Gas Journal

Note: boundaries are indicative only and may not be precise

for completion in 2007. OGD-3 calls for the expansion of the Bab Thamama F reservoir to produce an additional 1.2 billion cf/d of gas, as well as for the installation of gas reinjection facilities to recycle the gas into the Thamama F reservoir. The scheme will also result in an increase in condensate production of around 140,000 b/d. The second project, AGD-2, entails an expansion of the Asab gas plant's processing, sweetening and NGL recovery capacity by 800 million cf/d

Abu Dhabi Marine Operating Company (ADMA-OPCO)

The two fields operated by ADMA-OPCO, Lower Zakum and Umm Shaif, are rated at 320,000 b/d and 280,000 b/d respectively. ADMA-OPCO is focused on maintaining capacity at the current level through the drilling of additional production and injection wells and, in particular, the expansion of gas injection systems.

The Umm Shaif crestal gas injection project is the larger of the two, since it entails the installation of facilities for the reinjection of 600 million cf/d of gas from the field's

Khuff reservoir into the Arab C and D oil reservoirs and is scheduled for completion in 2006. The project will double the gas injection capacity of the Umm Shaif field.

The Lower Zakum crestal gas injection project calls for the installation of systems with a capacity of 200 million cf/d. A contract for the project was awarded in October 2001. The gas required by the project will be drawn from the Khuff gas reservoir under the Umm Shaif field, which is to be connected via an 18-inch gasline to the Zakum West Supercomplex, where an additional 200-million cf/d compressor is to be installed on the gas injection platform. ADMA-OPCO expects the project to be completed in the first quarter of 2004.

A milestone occurred in 2001 with the end of flaring at the Zakum oil field. Installation of new and improved pumps enabled all the associated gas produced at Lower Zakum to be processed and pumped at high pressure to Das Island instead of flaring it off above the rig. ADMA-OPCO also built a 10-kilometre, 24-inch pipeline to link Zakum Central to the Zakum West complex, where a new riser platform was installed, as well as an 80-metre long bridge linking it to the gathering/separation platform. In addition, ADMA-OPCO installed a new control and monitoring system at Zakum West, which is powered by a solar generator, whereas the previous system was run by a power plant that burned associated gas. The system is more flexible than a conventional one, since it permits the remote monitoring and control of valves, separation operations and other functions.

A 3-D seismic survey that involved laying of subsea cables for collecting the data was carried out by ADMA-OPCO to study the geology of the Lower Zakum field. Completed in late 2001, it was reported to be the largest ocean bottom 3D (OB 3D) seismic survey ever undertaken over a producing field. The Zakum field 1500–square-kilometre full 350-fold high-density survey has attracted the scientific, technical and business attention of the oil and gas international industry at large. It is anticipated that the high resolution data from this seismic survey will contribute significantly to better structural and fault interpretation of the Zakum field reservoirs, fracture zones density and direction, porosity distribution, horizontal well steering, stratigraphic and facies mapping, development of flanks areas, optimisation of water and gas injection drilling, monitoring of injection and flood fronts and static and dynamic fluids mapping.

Zakum Development Company (ZADCO)

ZADCO operates the supergiant Upper Zakum field, as well as two small offshore fields: Umm al-Dalkh and Satah. ZADCO plans to increase the capacity of Upper Zakum by 200,000 b/d to 725,000 b/d in the coming years. In late September 2002 ZADCO announced that it had completed a pilot phase of the major gas injection project at the field. The project involves the utilisation of a 4000-tonne gas injection platform with a capacity to inject up to 100 million cubic feet per day of high-pressure hydrocarbon gas to each of the Lower and Upper Zakum reservoirs. The Zakum field contains an estimated 50 billion barrels of crude oil in place but, because of

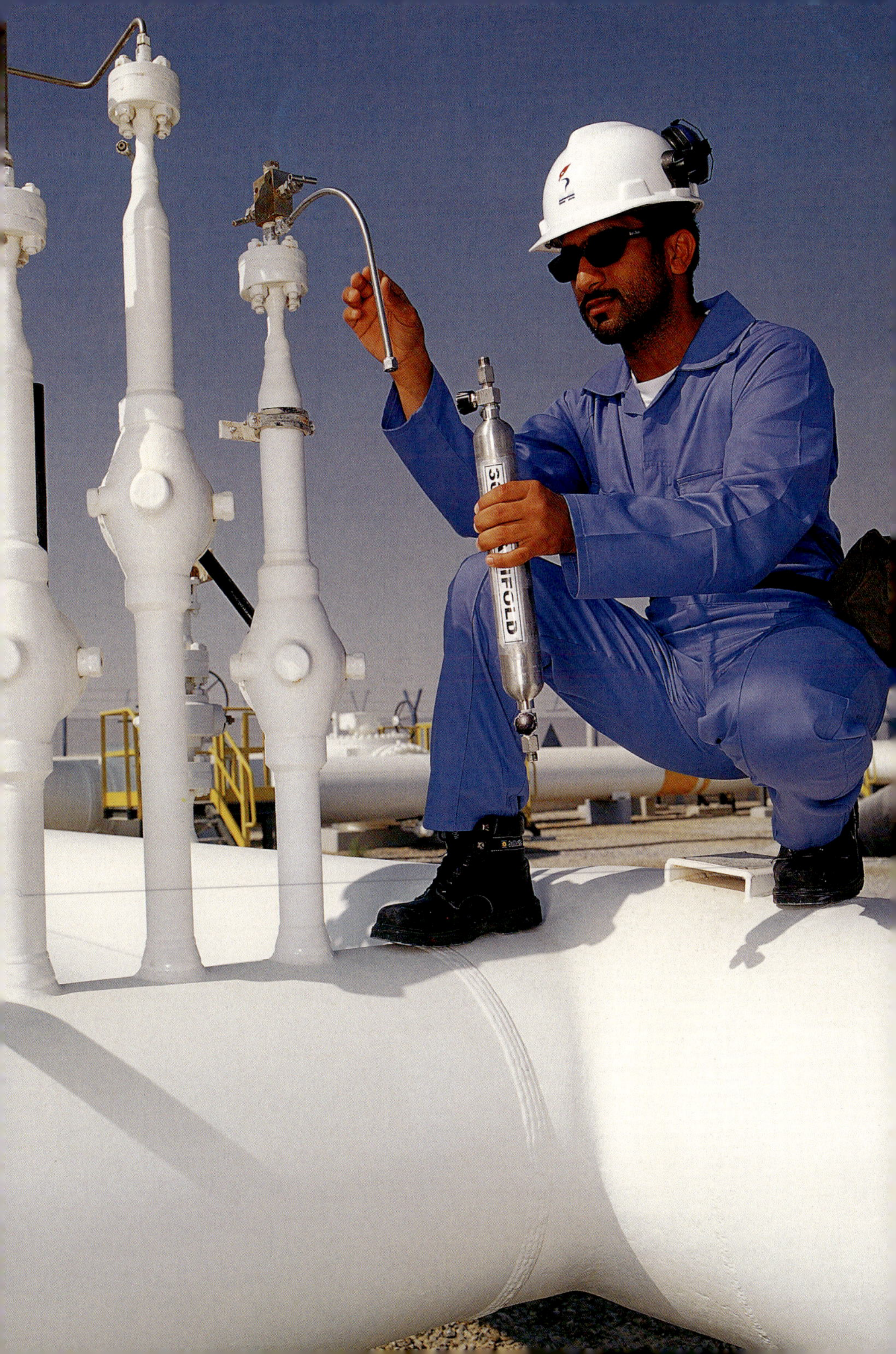

the low pressure and the poor porosity of the rock, the recovery rate is very low despite the large-scale use of water injection as well as gas injection. The field produced an average of 445,000 b/d in 2000 and 435,000 b/d in 2001.

Using gas to inject into oil bearing reservoirs, increasing the pressure and enhancing flow rates is clearly more feasible in the UAE than in countries lacking the UAE's vast reserves of natural gas and oil in close proximity.

Abu Dhabi Oil Company (ADOC)

ADOC operates the Mubarraz field where water and gas injection has been used to increase reservoir pressure. ADOC-GA, a subsidiary of ADOC, brought a nearby field, Neewat al-Ghalan, into production in June 1995. Its output, 4000–5000 b/d of crude, is piped, along with that of Mubarraz, to processing and export facilities on Mubarraz Island, which also handle crude from the Umm al-Anbar field operated by MOCO.

Following ADOC's installation of an acid gas injection system at Mubarraz in 2001, the company reported that oil recovery rates had been substantially increased. Furthermore, the project resulted in the elimination of gas flaring since any recovered associated gas is now reinjected into oil reservoirs. The Mubarraz and Neewat al-Ghalan fields produced an estimated 25,000–30,000 b/d of crude in 2001.

Mubarraz Oil Company (MOCO)

MOCO discovered the offshore Umm al-Anbar field west of Mubarraz Island in 1982. The field came on stream in February 1989 at an initial rate of 7000 b/d. Present crude output is presently approximately 5000 b/d and this is piped to ADOC's processing facilities on Mubarraz Island, where it is blended and exported.

Al Bunduq Oil Company (BOC)

The Al Bunduq field, discovered by ADMA-OPCO in 1965, straddles the border between Abu Dhabi and Qatar. In May 1969 the two countries agreed to share revenues accruing from the field's oil production on an equal basis. In 2001 Al Bunduq produced an estimated 15,000 b/d for Abu Dhabi.

Total Abu al-Bukhoosh Oil Company (TBK)

Total Abu al-Bukhoosh Oil Company was set up to develop the Abu al-Bukhoosh field, an extension of Iran's offshore Salman field discovered by ADMA-OPCO in 1969. The field now yields 25,000–30,000 b/d of crude.

Dubai

Dubai continues to install enhanced recovery systems and other facilities to maximise flow rates at its oilfields in a bid to slow the decline in production, and further development work is now going ahead at the Margham gas field to stem the fall in output there. Dubai Margham Establishment (DME), having assumed operational control of the Margham field at the end of 2000, launched a secondary development programme in the third quarter of 2001 that is aimed at sustaining production and increasing the volume of gas despatched to Jebel Ali. So far, however, these and other efforts have failed to arrest the relentless decline in Dubai's oil production since 1991.

Dubai Petroleum Company (DPC) is by far the largest producing venture in the emirate and operates its four main oilfields, Fateh, Southwest Fateh, Rashid and Falah, which are all located offshore.

OIL REFINING

The UAE has achieved significant growth in the refining sector in recent years with the completion of the Abu Dhabi Oil Refining Company's (TAKREER) Ruwais refinery, which has a full production capacity of 280,000 barrel stream per day (bs/d), in November 2000, and Emirates National Oil Company's (ENOC) 120,000 bs/d condensate processing plant at Jebel Ali Free Zone in December 1999.

Abu Dhabi

Abu Dhabi Oil Refining Company (TAKREER) operates the emirate's two refineries at Ruwais and Umm al-Nar, which have capacities of 420,000 b/d and 88,000 b/d respectively. The Ruwais plant includes two 140,000 b/d condensate processing trains, which came on stream in 2000, tripling its capacity from 126,000 b/d to 420,000 b/d and increasing Abu Dhabi's total refining capacity from 211,000 b/d to 508,000 b/d.

TAKREER is installing unleaded gasoline units at both refineries and expanding and upgrading the Ruwais refinery. The Ruwais upgrade programme is to be undertaken in several stages, starting with the construction of the unleaded gasoline (ULG) unit; installation of a low-sulphur gas oil (LSGO) plant and the expansion of the refinery's hydrocracker. The other units to be added are central environmental protection facilities (CEPF), including for the processing of toxic waste, a 300,000 tons/year base oil refinery (BOR), and additional sulphur loading facilities in the port of Ruwais.

The project for installing unleaded gasoline and low sulphur gas oil units at Ruwais also moved forward in 2001. Scheduled for completion in 2004, it involves installation of a 12,000 b/d reformer, a 19,000 b/d isomerisation unit and a 15,000 b/d gas oil hydrotreater.

Abu Dhabi already produces lubricants at the two oil refineries, as well as at a 30,000 tons/year lube oil-blending plant that started up in the late 1980s and a 4000 tons/year grease plant in Umm al-Nar. The Ruwais BOR provides a further boost to Abu Dhabi's lubricants production.

International Petroleum Investment Company (IPIC), the foreign investment arm of ADNOC, has interests in refining ventures in both Pakistan and South Korea.

Dubai

Dubai has a 120,000 b/d condensate refinery that started up in 1999. It was developed by state-owned Emirates National Oil Company (ENOC) at a cost of Dh 1.3 billion and consists of two 60,000-b/d trains, one for sweet and one for sour condensate.

The plant produces a large proportion of the LPG, jet fuel, gas oil and bunker fuel consumed in Dubai, as well as exporting some 66,000 b/d of naphtha.

Several oil reprocessing and lube oil-blending plants are situated at Jebel Ali, including a lube oil blending and packaging plant that can produce 50,000 tons/year of lubricants, and its output is marketed throughout the Gulf region as well as in the UAE. A lube oil recycling plant (developed by the Western Oil Company of India) produces base stock for processing into lubricating oil or fuel oil. Most of its 60,000 tons/year is exported to India. An oil processing plant for producing gasoline additives and conditioning products has been developed by Ducham, a subsidiary of Abu Dhabi-based Star Energy Corporation, and has a capacity of 20,000 b/d of unleaded gasoline, 360 tons/day of aromatics and 240 ton/day of raffinate. Finally, another Indian company, Gadgil Western Corporation (GWC), runs a fuel oil reprocessing plant with a capacity of 275,000 tons/year.

Sharjah

Fal Oil operates a lubricants plant in Sharjah, which started up in 1979 and produces a variety of products for automotive, marine and industrial use. It was the emirate's second lube oil blending plant, following that developed in 1976 by Sharjah National Lube Oil Company (SHARLU).

A bulk oil products storage facility started up at Hamriyah in April 2001. It was developed by National Oil Storage Company (NOSCO): a 50:50 per cent joint venture between two Sharjah-based companies, Gulf Energy and Union Energy. It comprises six storage tanks, two of 10,000 tons, two of 6000 tons and two of 5000 tons, for holding diesel oil, fuel oil and bitumen.

Fujairah

Despite the fact that Fujairah has never been a producer of either oil or gas, and no exploration is taking place in the emirate, it does possess an 80,000 b/d oil refinery. Fujairah has also succeeded in capitalising on its strategic location on the Gulf of Oman by providing oil storage and bunkering services to shipping. It is the world's second largest ship refuelling centre and has the second largest container terminal in the UAE. The Fujairah refinery had an initial capacity of 35,000 b/d, which subsequently rose to 40,000 b/d before being doubled to 80,000 b/d in October 1997, when a second 40,000 b/d crude and condensate distillation unit started up. In February 1998 however, the operator was forced to close the refinery which was subsequently taken over by Fujairah Refinery Company (FRC), a specially created joint venture between the Government of Fujairah, Swiss-based Glencore International, and a group of financial institutions. The refinery was reactivated in September 2000 with an effective capacity of 52,000 b/d. A second 38,000-b/d unit started up in October 2001, restoring the refinery's capacity to 80,000 b/d. The refinery currently produces only diesel oil and fuel oil, which are sold on the spot market, but there are plans for installing facilities for the production of kerosene, jet fuel and possibly gasoline.

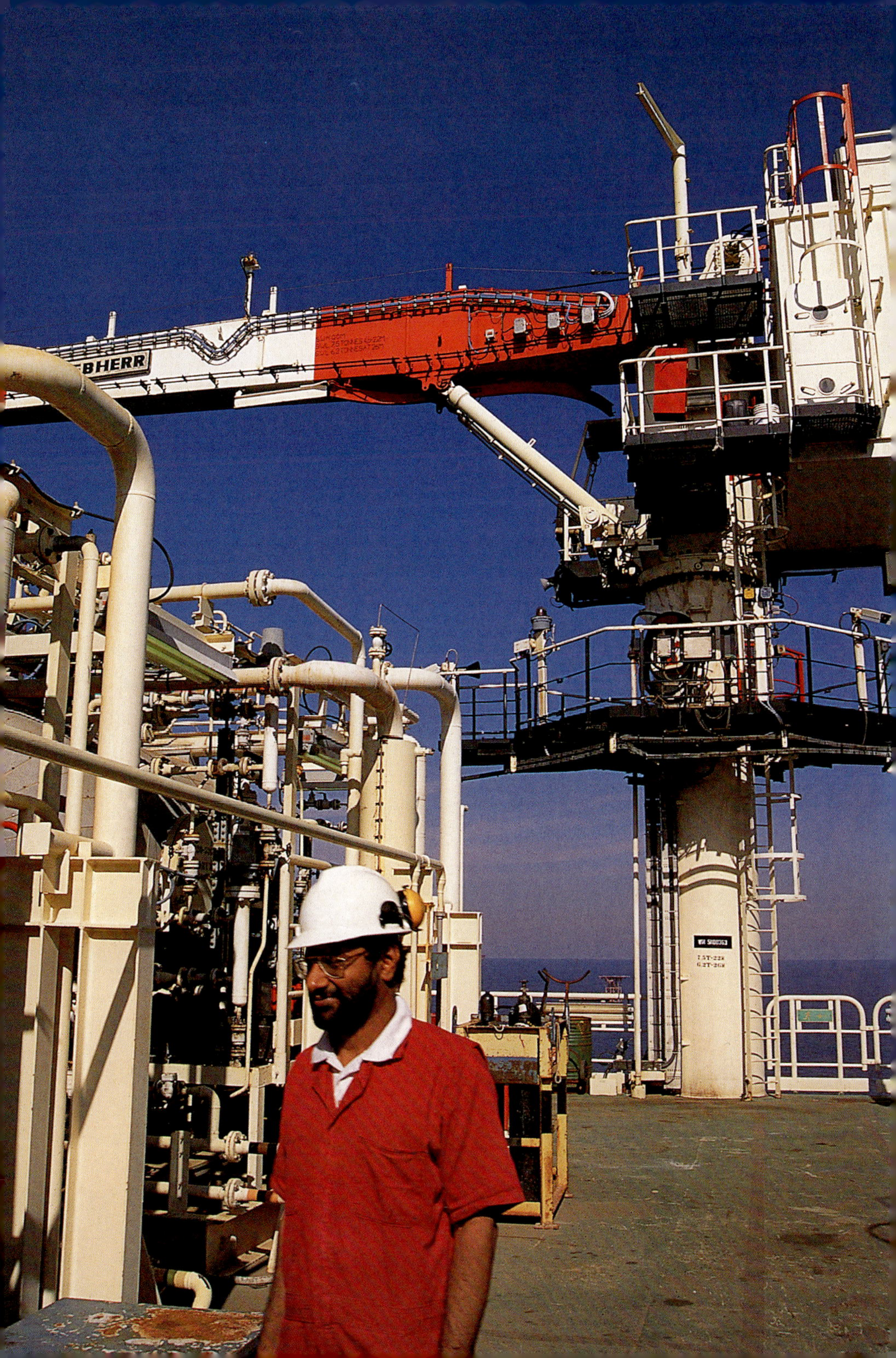

OIL EXPORTS

Abu Dhabi

Japan imports 25 per cent of its total crude oil requirements from the UAE. ADNOC exports four grades of crude: Murban (39° API), Lower Zakum (30° API), Umm Shaif (37° API) and Upper Zakum (34° API). Almost all is sold under term contracts to the Far East. Japanese companies lift around 500,000 to 600,000 b/d; South Korean concerns lift 50,000 to 75,000 b/d, and those with buyers in Taiwan, Thailand, India, Pakistan, Sri Lanka and Bangladesh import 100,000 b/d between them.

As a result of the successive cuts in output due to the reductions in the OPEC quota, ADNOC has been forced to cut term liftings by 5–10 per cent relative to contractual volumes.

Abu Dhabi condensate exports jumped sharply in 2001 due to the startup of the two 140,000-b/d condensate processing units at the Ruwais refinery in the last quarter of 2000. These exports have no effect on the amount of crude that the emirate can export, since condensate is not covered by OPEC's oil production limitation arrangements.

Abu Dhabi's refined products are exported by ADNOC Distribution which sells oil products and lubricants both to the Far East and to Arab and African countries. India is the leading export market for Abu Dhabi's refined products, absorbing over half its gas oil exports as well as substantial volumes of kerosene and LPG. Japan now accounts for about one-third of the emirate's refined product exports, down from 50 per cent in 1993, but remains the largest market for naphtha.

Dubai

Dubai exports all the crude it produces, mostly to the Far East. Dubai crude (31° API) is mainly sold on the spot market, and, despite its very limited volume, serves as a price marker for some other Gulf producers. In 2001 the price averaged US$22.61/b, as against US$26.20/b in 2000, US$19.10/b in 1999 and US$16.10/b in 1998

GAS

Abu Dhabi

The Government of Abu Dhabi is sole owner of all natural gas resources on its territory, both onshore and offshore, whether in associated or non-associated form. The Abu Dhabi National Oil Company (ADNOC) is responsible for developing and marketing these resources on the Government's behalf and is authorised to form partnerships with foreign companies for that purpose, so long as it retains at least a 51 per cent interest in any venture. Abu Dhabi's proven natural gas reserves were estimated at 5.45 trillion cubic metres as at 1 January 2002, representing around 90 per cent of the UAE's total gas reserves of 6.01 trillion cubic metres. During the same period Abu Dhabi's gross gas production stood at 5.76 billion cf/d (59.5 billion cu. m/year)

Table 9: UAE Natural Gas Consumption Forecasts

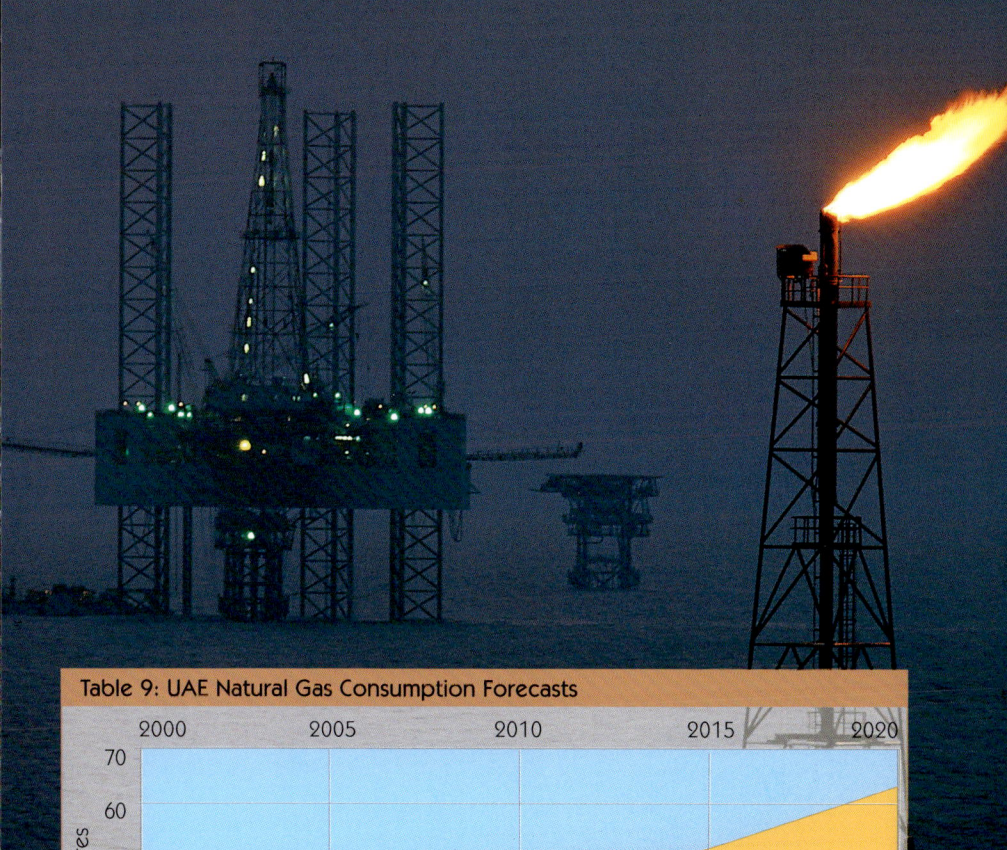

	2000	2005	2010	2015	2020
Electricity/Industry	1.5	8.4	10.5	13.0	16.2
Residential	0.0	0.1	0.1	0.1	0.2
Electricity/Desal.	9.6	13.4	17.7	21.2	25.5
Petrochem. plants	2.1	2.3	2.3	2.3	2.3
Other	8.0	9.9	12.3	15.3	19.0
Total	21.2	34.1	42.9	51.9	63.2

The impressive production figures are the result of a sustained development programme. Three onshore gas projects (OGDs) have been launched in recent years and two more were under way in 2002. These are operated by the Abu Dhabi Gas Company, GASCO, which was established in July 1978 as a joint venture between ADNOC (68 per cent), TotalFinaElf (15 per cent), Shell Gas (15 per cent) and Partex (2 per cent). In May 2001, the company was enlarged by the take-over of a wholly-owned subsidiary of ADNOC, Abu Dhabi Gas Company (Atheer), which was created in June 1999 to take charge of ADNOC's onshore gas development, production and processing operations. The new entity retains the GASCO name.

GASCO operates the massive gas processing plant at Habshan, built in 1983 to process associated gas from the Thamama C reservoir of the Bab oilfield, and which today also processes non-associated gas from the Thamama B, D and F reservoirs and Thamama Units 6 and 7 at Bab. Associated gas from oil production at the onshore fields of the Abu Dhabi Company for Onshore Oil Operations, ADCO, is first separated at GASCO facilities at Bab, Bu Hasa and Asab, and is then sent to nearby processing plants. There, the natural gas liquids (NGLs) are extracted and piped to GASCO's main plant for fractionation into liquefied petroleum gas (LPG). The plant has a processing capacity of some 3 billion cf/d. Some of the gas is reinjected into the oil reservoirs of ADCO fields, while the rest is supplied to the power and water industries, which account for 80 per cent of Abu Dhabi's gas consumption, as well as to the Umm al-Nar and Ruwais refineries, the Al Ain cement works, the Fertil complex and other industrial plants in the Ruwais industrial zone.

As well as producing dry sales gas, the Habshan plant despatches a natural gas liquids stream by pipeline to GASCO's fractionation plant at Ruwais. All output is exported through a dedicated marine terminal at Ruwais, and the company's shareholders are responsible for marketing a pro rata share of the finished products.

The bulk of the sulphur produced by Fertil is exported while, to improve handling of the additional supplies of sulphur being produced as a result of gas and oil development. GASCO is building a pipeline to transport liquid sulphur from Habshan to Ruwais. The 120-kilometre pipeline is expected to cost about US$80 million.

Recent and current developments in the field of onshore gas development include the OGD-2 and AGD-1 projects completed in 2001 and two more onshore development projects at the Bab and Asab fields, OGD-3 and AGD-2. OGD-3 involves extraction of wet gas from the Thamama reservoirs at Bab, from which condensate will be stripped out and the dry gas reinjected into oil reservoirs to maintain pressure. AGD-2 is aimed at increasing the volume of natural gas liquids (NGLs) recovered from the first phase facilities. These projects, being undertaken by GASCO, will yield additional volumes of associated and non-associated gas for supply to the domestic market.

Abu Dhabi began exporting natural gas from its onshore fields to Dubai by pipeline in June 2001, following completion of the OGD-2 project. After an initial rate of 200 million cf/d, the volume sent through the 112-kilometre gasline reached the contractual rate of 500 million cf/d by mid-July 2002. The gas is being lifted by Dubai Supply Authority, whose contract with ADNOC provides for its imports to be increased to 900 million cf/d, the maximum capacity of the gasline, by 2004.

Offshore gas development is also of crucial importance to Abu Dhabi's economy with current work being focused on increasing efficiency with regard to extraction rates. Most of the gas produced offshore is supplied to the Abu Dhabi Gas Liquefaction Company, ADGAS, liquefaction plant on Das Island (see below). Following the doubling of the plant's capacity in 1994, the volume delivered to the LNG plant was stepped up to 800 million cf/d.

One major offshore gas development project currently being undertaken entails further development of the Khuff gas reservoirs under the Abu al-Bukhoosh (ABK) field, 45 kilometres north-east of Das Island. This is now due to be completed in July 2004. It provides for the volume of gas recovered from the ABK Khuff reservoir to be increased by 240 million cf/d to 540 million cf/d. Together with gas production from the Umm Shaif oilfield, this will take total gas production by 240 million cf/d to 1.44 billion cf/d.

Associated gas has been produced at Umm Shaif since 1988, when the existing gas gathering facilities were completed. Two wellhead platforms with a capacity of 150 million cf/d each were installed at the field, as well as two injector/producer platforms. They are all connected to the Umm Shaif Supercomplex, where the Abu Dhabi Marine Operating Company, ADMA-OPCO, recently revamped the gas treatment plant.

ADGAS is responsible for the gas liquefaction plant on Das Island, which began operations in 1977. From the outset, all the plant's LNG and most of its LPG were purchased by Tokyo Electric Power Company (TEPCO) under a 20-year contract that took effect in 1977 and provided for TEPCO to lift 2 million tons/year of LNG and 500,000 tons/year of LPG. In 1990 the company decided to more than double the capacity of its plant to 5.4 million tons/year of LNG, 1.7 million tons/year of LPG and 535,000 tons/year of pentane-plus. The expansion entailed the installation in 1994 of a third liquefaction train with a capacity of 2.3 million tons/year of LNG and 250,000 tons/year of LPG. Like the original units, the third liquefaction train has consistently operated in excess of its design capacity.

In 2000 Japan's imports from Abu Dhabi included US$1.4 billion of LNG, US$712 million of propane and US$50.9 million of butane, mainly from offshore.

The plant's LNG capacity was further increased in August 2001, when ADGAS completed the revamp of the propane compressor serving its third liquefaction train, boosting its production capacity from 320 tons/hour to 380 tons/hour. In early 2002 the company signed a front-end engineering and design (FEED) contract with the Chiyoda Corporation for an additional LPG train with a capacity of around 1 million tons/year. Shortly afterwards, in February 2002, ADGAS signed an agreement with BP

Gas Marketing Company for the supply of up to 750,000 tons/year of LNG. The contract is for an initial period of three years, starting in 2002, and could be extended to five years, depending on BP's requirements. Whilst TEPCO remains ADGAS' major customer, marketing development has considerably broadened the client base in recent years. In addition to the sales to BP mentioned above, the company has sold its gas products to European, American and Asian clients.

Dubai

Dubai's proven natural gas reserves were estimated at 4100 billion cubic feet as at 1 January 2002. The only domestic source of natural gas for end users is the Margham field, since all the associated gas produced at the offshore oilfields is now reinjected. Margham's gas production has been declining for some years and this fall accelerated in 2001. After averaging 330 million cf/d in 2000, down from 350 million cf/d in 1999 and 380 million cf/d in 1998, production was reported to be running at no more than 230 million cf/d of natural gas in early 2002, plus 20,000 b/d of condensate. The slump in output led DME to embark on a further development programme in 2001 to sustain, if not increase, the field's gas production.

Dubai depends heavily upon imported gas to meet its energy needs. Its power stations, desalination plants and factories could not operate without natural gas as an energy source and plans are under way to ensure that future needs are met by ambitious and innovative projects such as the Dolphin Energy gas pipeline network linking Qatar, Abu Dhabi, Dubai, Fujairah and Oman. At present, Dubai is importing gas from Sharjah and Abu Dhabi. Abu Dhabi and Dubai concluded an agreement for the supply of 500 million cf/d of natural gas by pipeline in 2000 and deliveries started in June 2001. The volume will be increased to 900 million cf/d by 2004.

Sharjah

Sharjah LPG Company (SHALCO) operates a gas processing plant in Sharjah. Located in Saja'a, it handles output of the Saja'a and Moveyeid fields and was originally designed to process up to 440 million cf/d of natural gas for the production of 230,000 tons/year of propane, 170,000 tons/year of butane and 220,000 tons/year of condensate. The plant's capacity was increased to 700,-800 million cf/d in 1994 to enable it to handle gas from the Kahaif field as well. The propane and butane produced by Shalco are marketed by Itochu and the condensate by BP. Condensate is carried by a 32-kilometre, 12-inch pipeline to Al Hamriyah on the coast, where BP has its own jetty capable of accommodating tankers of up to 83,000 dwt. The terminal includes two storage tanks with a combined capacity of 110,000 cubic metres. The bulk of the condensate is shipped to Japan, although small quantities are exported to Western Europe and North America. The condensate has a low sulphur content (0.01 per cent) and a naphtha yield of just under 80 per cent.

BP also exports much of the natural gas it produces, although most is supplied to industrial and household consumers within the emirate. Sharjah Electricity and Water

Authority (SEWA) has been developing a natural gas distribution network to supply gas direct to residential, commercial and industrial users. Work on the second phase of this project was scheduled for completion in 2002 and the Hamriyah Free Zone is due to be connected to it in 2003.

Sharjah started exporting natural gas to Dubai in 1986. The initial contract provided for BP to supply 140 million cf/d of gas from the Saja'a field over a three-year period starting in March 1986. A 75-kilometre, 24-inch gasline was built from Hamriyah to Jebel Ali for the purpose. That volume soon proved insufficient for Dubai, and at the end of 1986 a second agreement was signed providing for supplies to be stepped up to 250 million cf/d with effect from the middle of 1987. The capacity of the gasline was increased accordingly through the installation of two additional compression stations. Amoco, the original concessionaire (now part of BP), concluded another gas supply agreement in June 1994, providing for it to deliver natural gas to the Northern Emirates as well once the Kahaif field was in production. Crescent Petroleum also began exporting gas to Dubai in January 1993, following the signing of an agreement with DUGAS for the supply of 100 million cf/d of gas for delivery to its plant in Jebel Ali. The gas is carried by an 87-kilometre, 16-inch subsea gasline from the gas-processing platform that came on stream at the Mubarak field in November 1992.

Ajman

A petroleum production sharing agreement was signed between Sharjah and Ajman in early July 2002 to jointly develop the Zora field, a gas reservoir located around 40 kilometres off the two coasts. Crescent Petroleum and Norway's Atlantis, which hold the concessions from the two respective governments, were also signatories to the agreement. Production, scheduled to start in May 2003, is to be shared equally between the parties concerned.

Umm al-Qaiwain

A survey carried out during late 2001 and early 2002 resulted in discovery of gas reserves off the emirate. The natural gas reserves were confirmed in a letter to the Umm al-Qaiwain Government by Atlantis Holdings. The discovery was made following drilling tests conducted on the UAQ 3 offshore well that revealed recoverable reserves of up to 500 billion cubic feet of gas and 5 million barrels of condensates. The company has prepared plans to develop this new gas well. Subsea pipelines are being laid from Umm al-Qaiwain port to the recent offshore gas discovery.

PETROCHEMICALS AND FERTILISERS

Abu Dhabi

Abu Dhabi has two major petrochemical and fertiliser industrial complexes, the Ruwais Fertiliser Industries company (Fertil) and the Abu Dhabi Polymers Company (Borouge). Fertil was established to utilise lean gas supplied from onshore field of Bab, Asab and Thamama C to produce fertilisers and market them locally and internationally. It brought its existing nitrogenous fertiliser plant in Ruwais on stream in April 1984. It consists of a 1050 ton/day ammonia plant and a 1500 ton/day urea plant, but they have operated at over 130 per cent of capacity in recent years (1310 MT per day and Urea 1850 per day) enabling them to produce 470,000 tons of ammonia and 650,000 tons of urea in 2001.

Borouge is a joint venture between ADNOC (60 per cent) and Copenhagen-based Borealis (40 per cent), established under an agreement signed in April 1998. Its petrochemical complex in Ruwais cost an estimated US$1.2 billion to develop and includes a 600,000 tons/year ethylene cracker. Borouge produces up to 450,000 tonnes of Borstar bimodal high-, medium-, and linear low-density polyethylene per year. Combining good processability with excellent mechanical properties, Borouge Borstar products are stronger, lighter, environmentally friendly and more malleable than conventional polyethylene, resulting in material savings of up to 30 per cent.

Borouge's products are used for the manufacture of plastic film and moulding packaging for industries such as pharmaceuticals, food and beverage, cosmetics, and chemicals. Borouge's products are also suitable for the manufacture of high-pressure pipe used in agriculture, mining, water, gas and sewage distribution, as well as coating of steel pipelines.

In addition to promoting its own polyethylene products, Borouge also oversees the distribution and marketing of Borealis' entire range of polyolefins in the Middle East and Asia Pacific. These products include polyethylene for extrusion coating, moulding, and wire and cable, as well as polypropylene for film, moulding, hot water pipes and engineering applications.

Dubai

Dubai's first fertiliser plant, a joint venture between Kemira Agro Oy of Finland (49 per cent) and the local firm Union Agricultural Group (51 per cent), has the capacity to produce 6000 tons/year of water-soluble compound fertilisers. A second and much larger fertiliser plant developed by the same group, and called the Kemira Emirates Fertiliser Company (Kefco), has a capacity of 60,000-tons/year and was brought on stream in 2001 in the Jebel Ali Free Zone. The first 30,000-tons/year phase of its plant for the production of phosphate and nitrogenous fertilisers entered commercial production in March 2001, followed six months later by the second phase.

Another plant, with a capacity to produce 226,000 tons/year of ammonia and 400,000 tons/year of granular urea is also under construction in Jebel Ali. Meanwhile a 500,000-tons/year MTBE plant, established in 1995, utilises the butane isomerisation process of Lummus, the Catofin dehydrogenation process, and CD MTBE synthesis technology for converting butane into MTBE.

Ajman

Ajman has a 600-tons/day fertiliser plant that came on stream in December 1987.

TOURISM

The tourism industry in the UAE is not only one of the fastest growing sectors in the economy, it is also one of the greatest success stories in the region. Dubai, in particular, has spearheaded tourism development, leading to the phenomenal rise of the country as a major tourist destination. Today, the UAE features in the brochures of most of the top international tour operators. At the core of the country's success has been the ever-present winter sunshine, spectacular sandy beaches and first-class facilities and services. Add to this superlative shopping, manicured golf courses, the allure of the desert, an ancient heritage and a safe environment and you have a recipe that is difficult to beat. Although Dubai started the ball rolling, other emirates have quickly followed suit and are building a tourism industry that will capitalise on their outstanding features. Package operators are also including a choice of UAE locations in their itineraries.

Remarkably, the UAE tourism industry managed to register a positive growth in 2001 despite a serious regional downturn following the September 11 terrorist attack on the United States. The four months after September 2001 had such an impact on the world tourism industry that, for the first time in 50 years, it recorded an annual negative growth. The Middle East as a whole ended 2001 with a 9 per cent drop in international arrivals, whereas in the UAE the impact was confined to a slightly slower annual growth, even though the difficult period coincided with its high tourist season.

DUBAI

Dubai dominates the industry by accounting for nearly 75 per cent of UAE's operating hotels. Nonetheless, this share has witnessed a slight decline since 1996 when it dropped from 76.6 per cent to 72.5 per cent in 2001. Some 92 per cent of the country's hotels are concentrated in Abu Dhabi, Dubai and Sharjah. During 1995–2001, room revenues witnessed the fastest growth in Dubai, averaging 11.8 per cent annually. Although the share of revenues generated from non-room services (catering, conferences and business services) declined slightly in recent years, it remains the source of more than half of the industry's income. In 2001, Dubai generated 69.5 per cent of the country's Dh2 billion total revenues from non-room services. Revenues from room rentals in the luxury hotels dominate the industry's lodging revenues, where they account for more than 60 per cent of such income.

The number of hotel guests in Dubai increased by 6.04 per cent in 2001, whereas guest numbers had been growing at an average of 13 per cent per year in the four preceding years. This continued increase, albeit at a slower rate, was partly due to the fact that tourist inflow from within the GCC countries continued to grow, especially during the summer months,

In 2001, 3,626,625 visitors stayed in Dubai's 403 hotels and hotel apartments for a total of 9.11 million guest nights. The actual number of visitors to Dubai, however, is much higher as a significant proportion of visitors stay with family and friends.

European guests topped the list at 953,064 visitors, generating 3.11 million guest nights. Almost half of the Europeans (46 per cent) stayed in five-star properties. GCC nationals, excluding the UAE, make up the second largest group of visitors to Dubai's hotels and hotel apartments with 845,716 visitors generating 1.65 million guest nights. About 187,555 of this group stayed in five-star hotels. They, however, feature prominently in the hotel apartment list of guests with more than 176,334 staying in apartments. Asian visitors make up the third largest group with 780,604 visitors generating 1.8 million guest nights and 117,739 of these staying in five-star hotels.

Dubai's hotels earned in excess of Dh3.2 billion in 2001, a growth of 7.5 per cent over the previous year. Dubai had reported a 15.63 per cent increase in the hospitality industry's revenues in 2000 on the basis of a 13 per cent rise in the number of guests.

Although the official statistics are not available at the time of writing, it seems clear that well over four million tourists will have visited Dubai in 2002. The number of hotel guests during the first half of 2002 reached 1.91 million, a phenomenal growth of 26.5 per cent over the corresponding period in 2001. Indications are that the number of visitors to Dubai will cross the six million mark by 2010, generating around 23 million guest nights.

Tourism numbers will certainly be helped by an estimated influx of 16,000 visitors from 184 countries in September 2003 for the fifty-eighth annual meetings of the board of governors of the World Bank and International Monetary Fund (IMF). Over 1500 five-star hotel rooms will be added in Dubai in 2002 and 2003 in time to assist in accommodating the delegates. Major new hotel developments include the Grand Hyatt in Garhoud, which will have 674 rooms, Shangri-La on Sheikh Zayed Road with 301 rooms, and the 622-room Novotel and Ibis hotels being developed next to the new Convention Centre where the meetings will be held.

Much of the success that Dubai has experienced is attributable to the Dubai Department of Tourism and Commerce Marketing (DTCM) which was established in 1989. Through its network of overseas offices, DTCM has been promoting Dubai as the best destination for business and tourism worldwide. In 2002, for the third consecutive time, DTCM won the award for 'Best UK-based Tourist Office Promoting the Middle East' at the World Travel Market in London. One of the major focuses for DTCM is the meeting, incentive, conference and exhibition (MICE) segment because it attracts high-yield visitors and the growth of the emirate's MICE sector has been helped by the city's long experience in catering to business visitors.

A comprehensive annual 'Trends and Spends' survey conducted by the UK's *Meetings & Incentive Travel* magazine in June 2002 ranked Dubai as the number one long haul city/state/resort in the world in 2001.

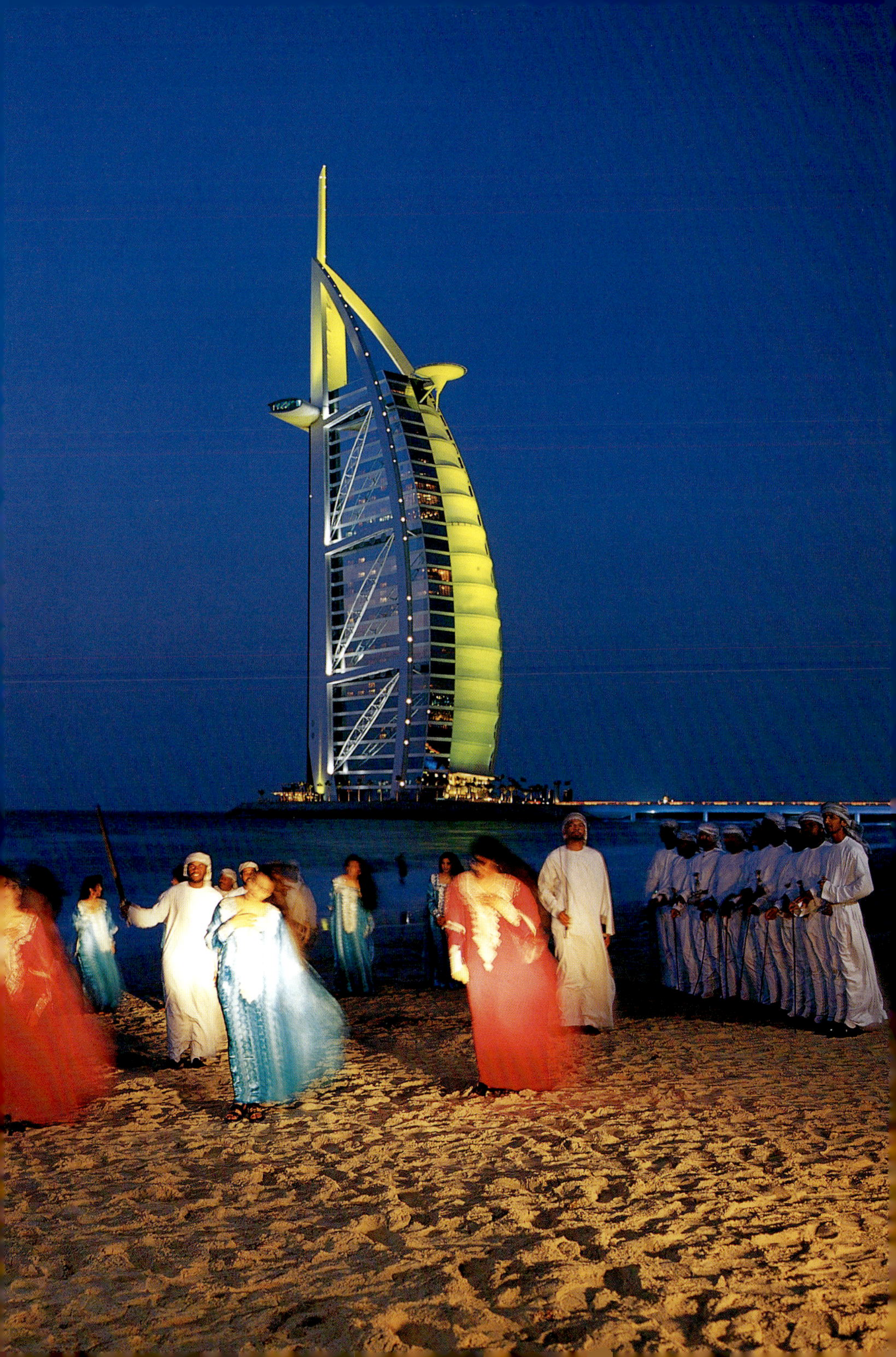

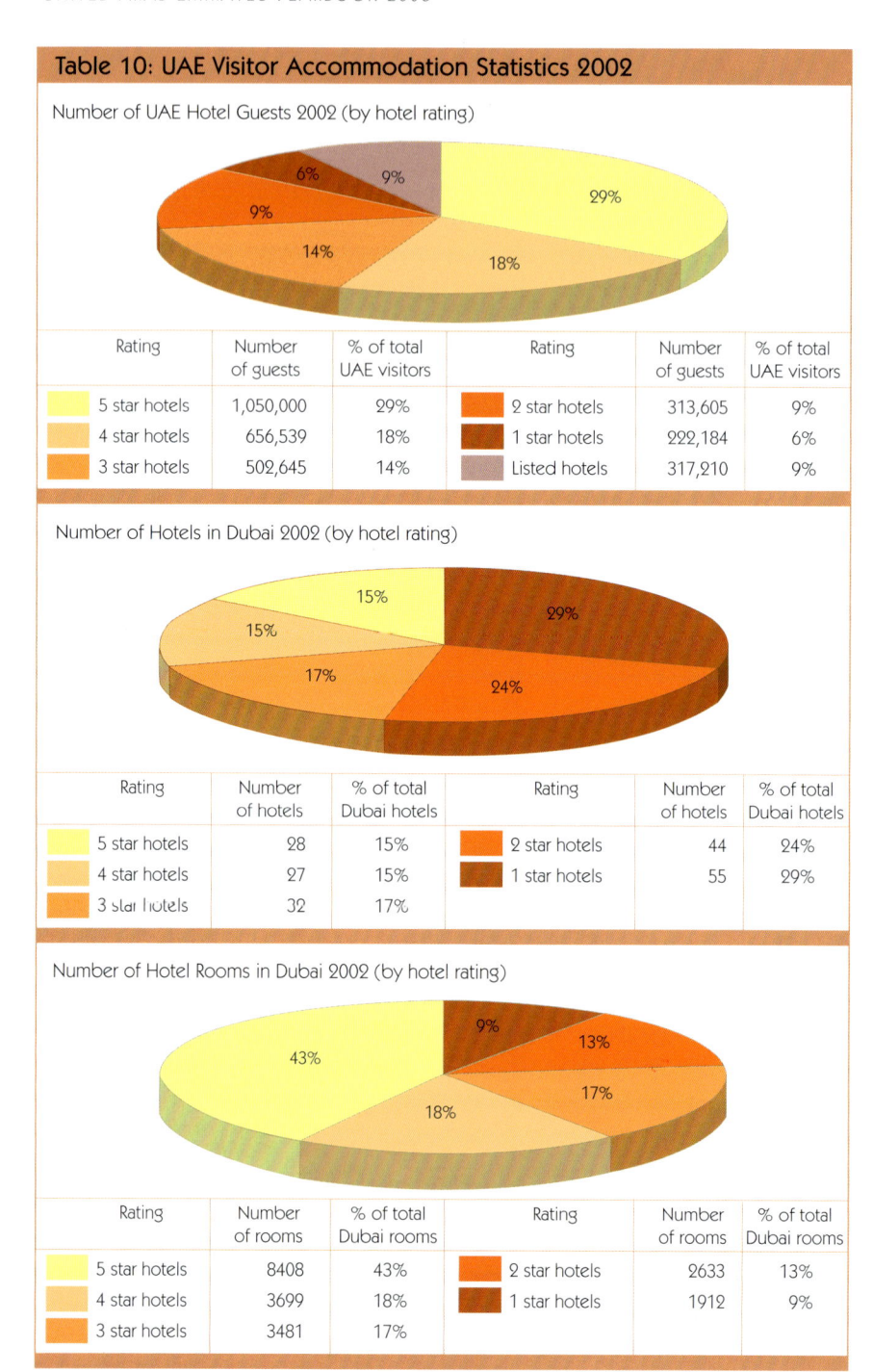

Table 10: UAE Visitor Accommodation Statistics 2002

Number of UAE Hotel Guests 2002 (by hotel rating)

Rating	Number of guests	% of total UAE visitors	Rating	Number of guests	% of total UAE visitors
5 star hotels	1,050,000	29%	2 star hotels	313,605	9%
4 star hotels	656,539	18%	1 star hotels	222,184	6%
3 star hotels	502,645	14%	Listed hotels	317,210	9%

Number of Hotels in Dubai 2002 (by hotel rating)

Rating	Number of hotels	% of total Dubai hotels	Rating	Number of hotels	% of total Dubai hotels
5 star hotels	28	15%	2 star hotels	44	24%
4 star hotels	27	15%	1 star hotels	55	29%
3 star hotels	32	17%			

Number of Hotel Rooms in Dubai 2002 (by hotel rating)

Rating	Number of rooms	% of total Dubai rooms	Rating	Number of rooms	% of total Dubai rooms
5 star hotels	8408	43%	2 star hotels	2633	13%
4 star hotels	3699	18%	1 star hotels	1912	9%
3 star hotels	3481	17%			

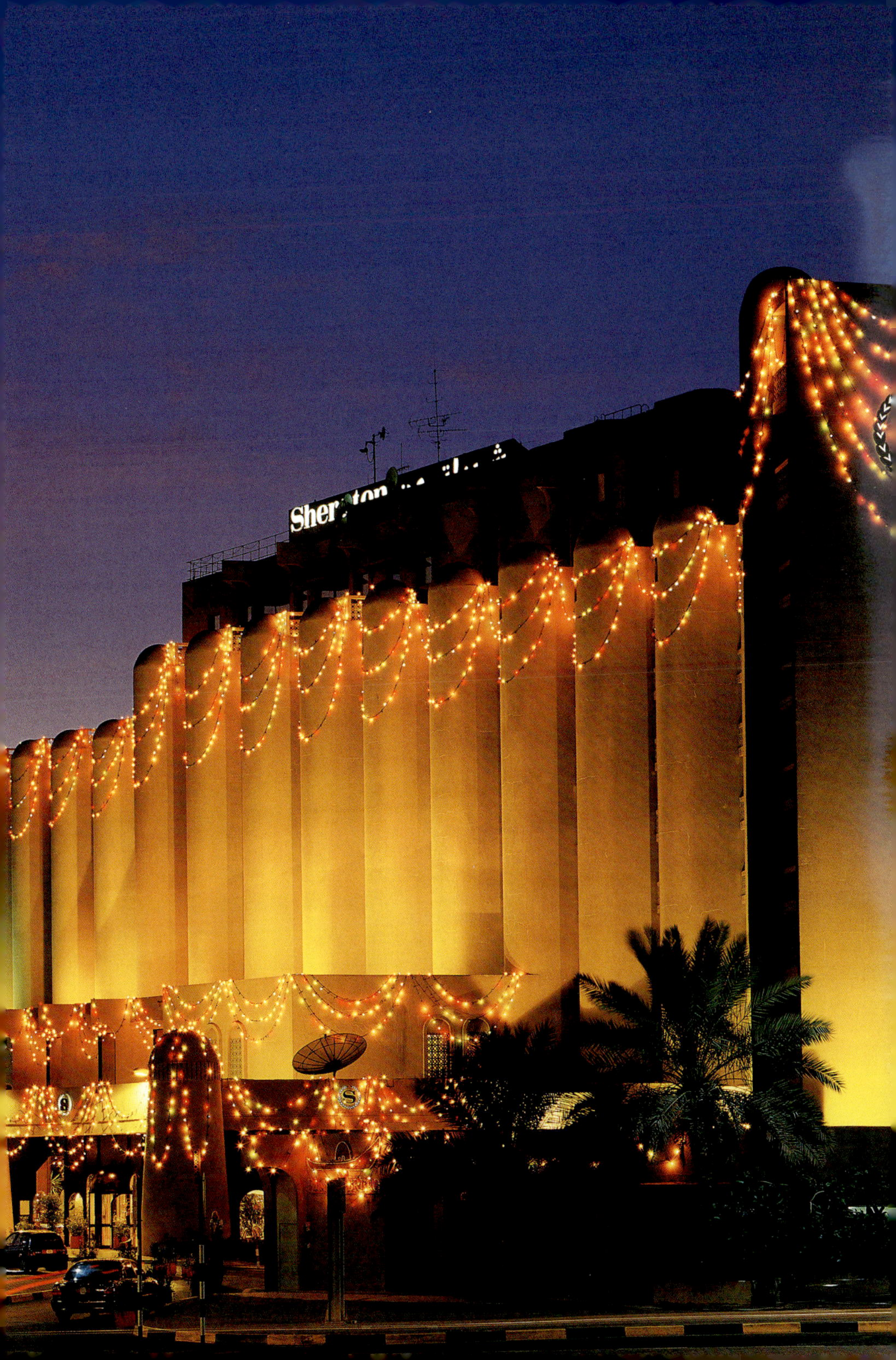
Sheraton

In 2002, all Dubai's 403 hotels and hotel apartments were classified by DTCM, a factor that has contributed enormously towards improving the facilities and standard of service offered to the guests at all the properties in Dubai. Ratings are being monitored on a regular basis. Star ratings for hotels are on a rising scale of one to five and follow an internationally accepted minimum standard. A number of establishments that do not meet the minimum requirements for classification as per the DTCM system but attract a segment of the visitor market were given 'listed' category status.

The DTCM's hotel classification system makes it mandatory for all hotels to indicate their categories by displaying the classification rating plaque near the entrances (denoting their grading) and the certificates in the reception areas.

The UAE's emerging cruise ship industry was one of the areas badly affected by the global slowdown: 7425 passengers used Dubai Cruise Terminal during the first five months in 2001, compared with 2080 during the first five months of 2002. However, the new cruise terminal operated by DTCM was awarded the 'Most Improved Port Facilities' award and 'Best New Terminal Building' award in the Rest of the World category at the March 2002 Seatrade Cruise Shipping Convention in Miami, Florida. Dreamworld Cruise Destinations presented the awards following a comprehensive survey covering 11 categories in the port, terminal and destination sectors of the four major cruising regions in the world. The Dubai Cruise Terminal is the only cruise terminal worldwide to be operated by a government tourism department and offers the very highest standards for passenger comfort and convenience.

The Palm

The Palm, one of the most significant infrastructure projects to come on stream in the UAE in recent years, is destined to take the UAE's tourism industry well into the twenty-first century. Construction of the two man-made islands that make up The Palm is making rapid progress. The project will increase Dubai's shoreline by 120 kilometres and create a large number of residential, leisure and entertainment opportunities. Constructed of around 100 million cubic metres of rock and sand, each island will support 50 luxury hotels, 2500 exclusive residential beachside villas, up to 2400 shoreline apartments, a number of marinas, water theme parks, restaurants, shopping malls, sports facilities, health spas and cinemas. The Palm Jumeirah, primarily a residential area, should be ready by the end of 2005, whereas completion of The Palm Jebel Ali, which is destined to be the ultimate entertainment area in the Middle East, is expected by the end of 2006. Reclamation is on schedule at the Jumeirah site where foundations are expected to be in place by the December 2003 deadline, and reclamation on the second island is also under way.

The huge amount of sand that has been already dredged to build the palm-tree-shaped island off Jumeirah is beginning to be clearly visible in satellite photos taken of the area. Even more visible is the barrier reef of rocks creating the crescent-shaped breakwater around the palm-tree island.

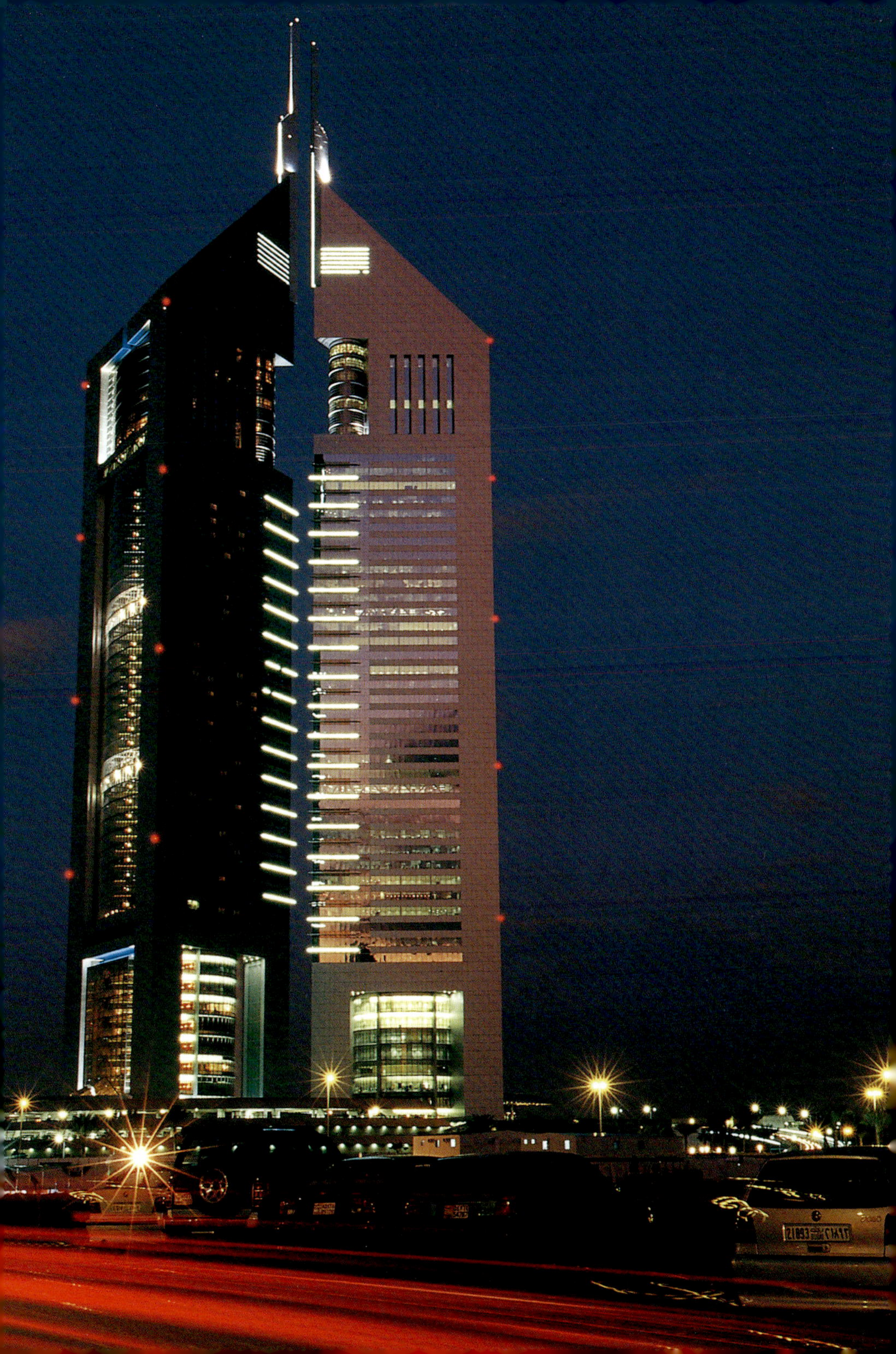

Once reclamation is completed, the project will enter the second phase involving the building of infrastructure and services. This will be followed by the final stage where homes, townhouses and apartments are constructed. A growing list of first-class property developers and hotel groups have signed deals with The Palm.

ABU DHABI

The hotel and restaurant sector in the emirate grew at a rate of 9.9 per cent during 1996–2001, with added value rising to Dh1450 million in 2001, from Dh903 million in 1996. Hotels increased in number from 39 in 1996 to 49 in 2001, while the restaurant sector rose by 9.9 per cent during the same period. Occupancy rates shot up to 78 per cent in 2001, the highest rate ever achieved by hotels in the emirate, from just 60 per cent in 1996. Abu Dhabi's share of UAE hotels increased slightly from 12.8 per cent in 1996 to 13.5 per cent in 2001. During 1995–2001 room charges income in Abu Dhabi grew at an annual average of 6.1 per cent.

Affected by global recession and the after-effects of September 11, Abu Dhabi is making renewed efforts to revitalise its travel and tourism industry. A majority of the 190 travel agencies making up the Travel and Tourism Agencies Committee (TTAC), set up in 2001, are endeavouring to give the trade a promotional boost. In addition, Abu Dhabi allocated over Dh4 billion in 2001 to tourism-related projects. Dh700 million has been earmarked for the Abu Dhabi National Hotels Company (ADNHC) and Dh.1.2 billion for the Rotana Hotel Group. Dh2.4 billion is also being spent on the Abu Dhabi International Airport development project. These amounts do not include the multi-million Corniche expansion programme which will ensure that the area along Abu Dhabi's shores will become a focus for recreation and entertainment in the region (see section on Infrastructure). In recent years, tourism in Abu Dhabi received a major boost with the opening of two mega malls, the Abu Dhabi Mall and the Marina Mall.

The Rotana Hotel Group spent Dh500 million in 2001 on the extension of two properties and the construction of a third with the objective of upgrading their hotels to above five-star level. Their new hotel on busy Hamdan Street, Al Maha Rotana, is catering for both business travellers and tourists.

Abu Dhabi National Hotels (ADNH) has recently upgraded a number of its five-star hotels, while several more are being expanded or new hotels are being built. The company currently owns and administers five five-star hotels in Abu Dhabi and Al Ain, including Le Méridien, Sheraton, Hilton Abu Dhabi and Hilton Al Ain, in addition to six other hotels and resorts of various categories.

The Sheraton Abu Dhabi Resort and Towers is scheduled to complete its Dh130 million building project by March 2003, having already finished a Dh30 million renovation on the resort in 2002. The renovated resort complex has two new restaurants, a snack bar, a three-tiered swimming pool, family pool with beach area, covered children's pool, water sports, fully equipped gymnasium and sauna, steam bath and Turkish Hammam, massage jacuzzis and fitness studios.

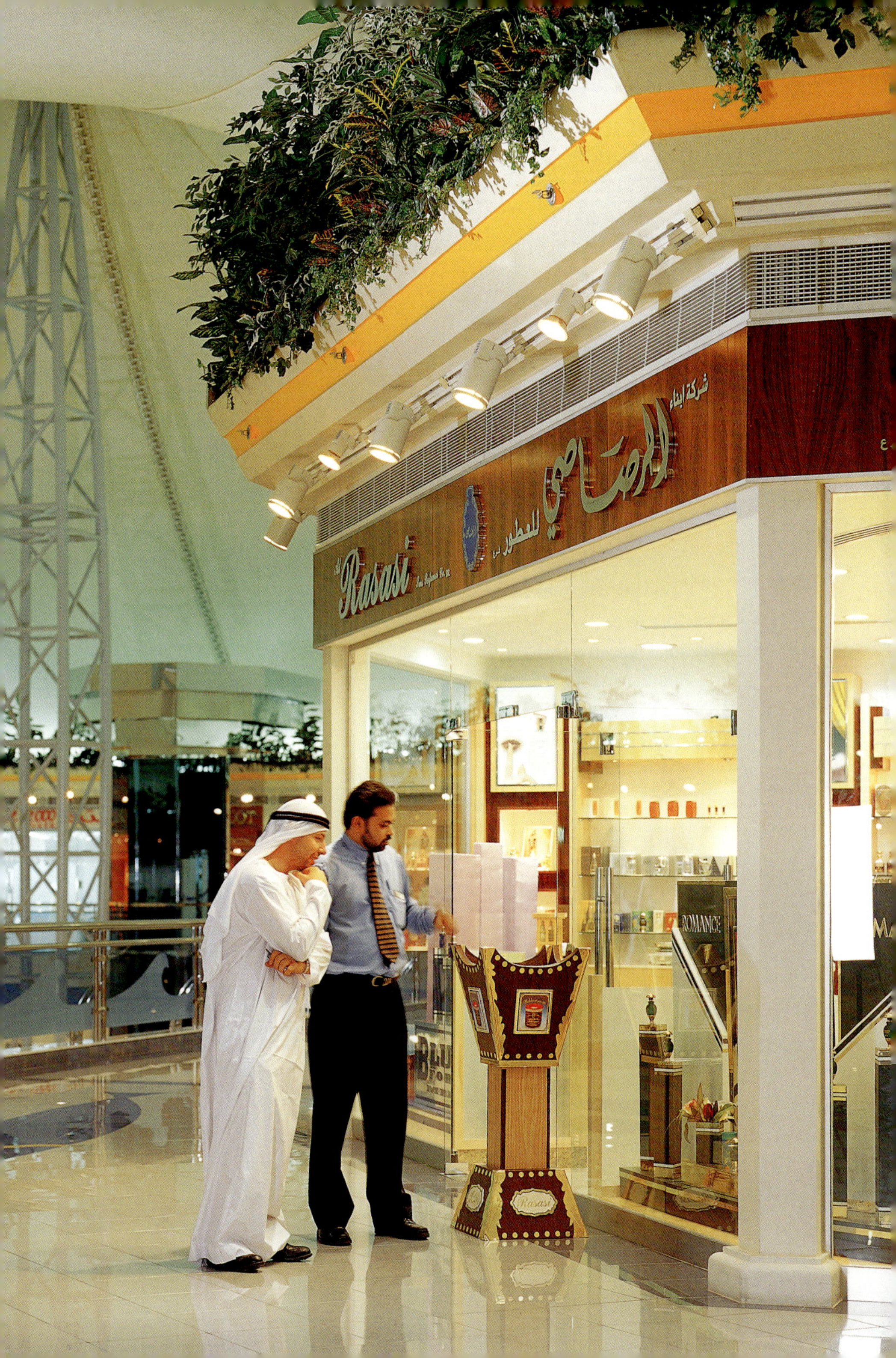

Rasasi
الرصاصي
للعطور
ROMANCE
Rasasi

A new five-star hotel is also being planned for the Abu Dhabi World Trade Centre. Another new project, the Conference Palace Hotel, a 440-room luxury beachfront property, will be run by the Kempinski Hotels and Resorts Group. The new facility has been scheduled for completion by 2004, in time to host the AGCC summit in the UAE capital. It will combine a special auditorium exclusively for AGCC summits and an additional meeting space for up to 1200 delegates. Located diagonally opposite the ADNOC headquarters in Abu Dhabi at the entrance to the Breakwater, the property will include a separate wing built specifically to accommodate heads of state and leaders of AGCC countries. It will be set within 200 acres of landscaped gardens modelled on the intricate design of Versailles and built in the style of an oriental palace.

Dalma Island

Dalma Island, which is located 180 kilometres west of Abu Dhabi, has been selected by Abu Dhabi Municipality and Town Planning, along with other settlements in rural areas, for redevelopment as a tourist centre under the Regional Development Plan.

Dh149.8 million worth of projects are under construction on Dalma, including a new dock for the island's harbour, a state-of-the-art shopping centre to comprise shopping malls, a cinema, entertainment and recreational facilities, improvements at Dalma Hospital, a new mosque and several new infrastructure projects.

AL AIN

Established in 2002, Al Ain Economic Development and Tourism Promotion Authority is making concerted efforts to develop the Al Ain area as a major tourist destination. The creation of a strong city brand that will help with marketing is one of the areas on which the Authority is focusing. The key element, however, is investment in tourism infrastructure. Al Ain Municipality and Town Planning Department, Al Ain Economic Development and Tourism Authority and the Forest Department at the Office of the Ruler's Representative in the Eastern Region are all involved in a multi-million-dirham project to build a tourist resort in the undulating foothills of Jebel Hafit, Abu Dhabi's highest mountain. Le Mercure Grand Hotel Jebel Hafit has recently opened its doors to visitors to the mountain, from which a panoramic view of the entire oasis city is possible. The Jebel Hafit and Wadi Al Mubazzarah area will feature leisure facilities such as lakes and pools, a, clubhouse and lush golf course, visitors' centres, a planetarium, a cableway and a conference centre. The planned golf club will have an 18-hole course and a nine-hole short course along with a media centre.

Al Mubazzarah Park is already taking shape. This green area has a huge beautifully landscaped lake, a restaurant and shop. Next to the park are the natural hot springs that have become a big attraction, drawing people from all over the UAE.

NORTHERN EMIRATES

Although Sharjah, the third largest city in the UAE, also boasts beautiful beaches and excellent shopping, its major strength is its heritage and the many museums and cultural centres that have been built in the emirate. It is no surprise that in recent years Sharjah was named as the 'Cultural Capital of the Arab World'.

Sharjah Commerce and Tourism Development Authority (SCTDA) has done much to develop and market tourism. Tourist inflows to Sharjah rose 70.4 per cent to 743,500 in 2000. Guests spent over 532,700 hotel nights, up 30 per cent over the previous year. Average room occupancy was 51 per cent. At the end of 2000 Sharjah had 23 hotels with 2712 rooms and 4802 beds. The year 2000 also saw the number of visitors to the emirate's 14 excellent museums, scientific, artistic, cultural heritage and Islamic centres increase by 68 per cent to 546,800.

Due to changes in hotel regulations and policies in Sharjah, lodging revenues in the emirate suffered a steep decline in 2001, dropping by more than 10 per cent. Sharjah also witnessed significant decline in its share in total hotels from 7.2 per cent in 1996 to 5.8 per cent in 2001.

In 2002 Sharjah Tourism Advisory Committee was established under the auspices of the SCTDA and a new tourism strategy aimed at presenting the emirate as a tourist destination in its own right was adopted. While the focus will be on regional and international tourism, destination marketing was accorded priority in 2002, with the emirate being promoted as a unique destination through a combination of overseas campaigns, road shows and related activities. Sharjah International Airport is also in the midst of a development phase that seeks to substantially raise its passenger handling capacity.

Ajman and Umm al-Qaiwain, two of the smallest emirates, are more sedate traditional destinations with very little high-rise building and a few excellent hotels. Umm al-Qaiwain, in particular, is well known for its watersports facilities.

Ra's al-Khaimah, whose hotels include two with five-star rating (Ra's al-Khaimah Hilton and Al Hamra Beach Hotel), has further enhanced its attractiveness as a scenic and relaxing tourist destination by awarding a contract early in 2002 to the Dubai-based Hydroturf International to build and operate the first 18-hole golf course in the emirate.

Fujairah on the East Coast is probably one of the most beautiful locations on the Arabian Peninsula, with its long sandy beaches, dramatic mountain backdrops and numerous historical sites. It, too, is making great strides in its efforts to attract more tourists for longer stays. Development of a tourist infrastructure has made considerable progress in recent years, with several new hotels, including a Méridien, built on the northern coast of the emirate, between Aqqah and Dibba. Plans to create a thermal spa and leisure complex at Awhala, in the south, are being developed, while the government-backed Fujairah Tourism Bureau is actively promoting inbound tourism at trade fairs in the Arab world and Europe.

AGRICULTURE

The UAE is an excellent example of how determination and technology can transform a harsh desert environment into a productive zone. The country's unprecedented success in the field of agriculture could not have been possible without the resolve of Sheikh Zayed, who believes that farming and civilisation are two faces of the one coin. Inspired by Sheikh Zayed's visionary leadership, the UAE is currently exporting vegetables and fruits to the USA and UK, flowers to Australia, Qatar, Bahrain, Oman and Lebanon and dates to Japan, Indonesia and Malaysia. Today, the agricultural sector is one of the mainstays of the UAE's programme for economic diversification.

The agricultural sector's contribution to non-oil GDP rose to 6.3 per cent in 2000 from 4.5 per cent in 1995. The value of agricultural production increased by 14 per cent from Dh5.3 billion in 1995 to Dh10.7 billion in 2000, with the share of vegetable output rising from 68 per cent to 77.8 per cent and animal and fish outputs dropping from 20 per cent and 11.4 per cent to 14.5 per cent and 7.7 per cent respectively.

These achievements have won wide international respect, leading in November 2001 to the election of the country to the presidency of the thirty-first summit of the UN Food and Agriculture Organisation (FAO). This was a great honour for the UAE, recognising its role in agricultural development at local, regional and global levels.

Agricultural policies to date have focused on the application of innovative scientific methods to meet local demand for food and upgrade production quality and quantity. So far, this strategy has reaped results with much demand being met locally: the UAE is 83 per cent self-sufficient in vegetables, 100 per cent in dates and fish, 25 per cent in red meat, 21 per cent in poultry, 36 per cent in eggs and 87 per cent in fresh milk. In addition, as already mentioned, in times of excess agriproduce is exported abroad.

INCENTIVES FOR FARMING

Farmers in the UAE are granted land and supplied with every facility to encourage production. A total of 35,584 farms covering an area of 2.7 million donums were distributed in 2000 compared to 11,468 farms (234,349 donums) in 1980. (One donum is equivalent to 1000 square metres.) Of these 35,584 farms, 20,706 are in Abu Dhabi, 1268 in Dubai, 4158 in Sharjah, 596 in Ajman, 314 in Umm al-Qaiwain, 4301 in Ra's al-Khaimah, and 4241 in Fujairah. However, most of the UAE's agricultural production comes from four areas – in and around Al Ain; a narrow but fertile strip along the East Coast; the oasis of Dhaid east of Sharjah; and gravel plains in Ra's al-Khaimah.

Farmers are provided with pesticides, fertilisers, seeds and selected plants, in addition to training in farming methods. Equipment such as spray machines and pumps are provided at 50 per cent discount. Tractors are made available free-of-charge to plough fields. The Ministry of Agriculture and Fisheries' experts devise irrigation systems for farmers to suit their fields and crops and irrigation equipment is also supplied at subsidised rates.

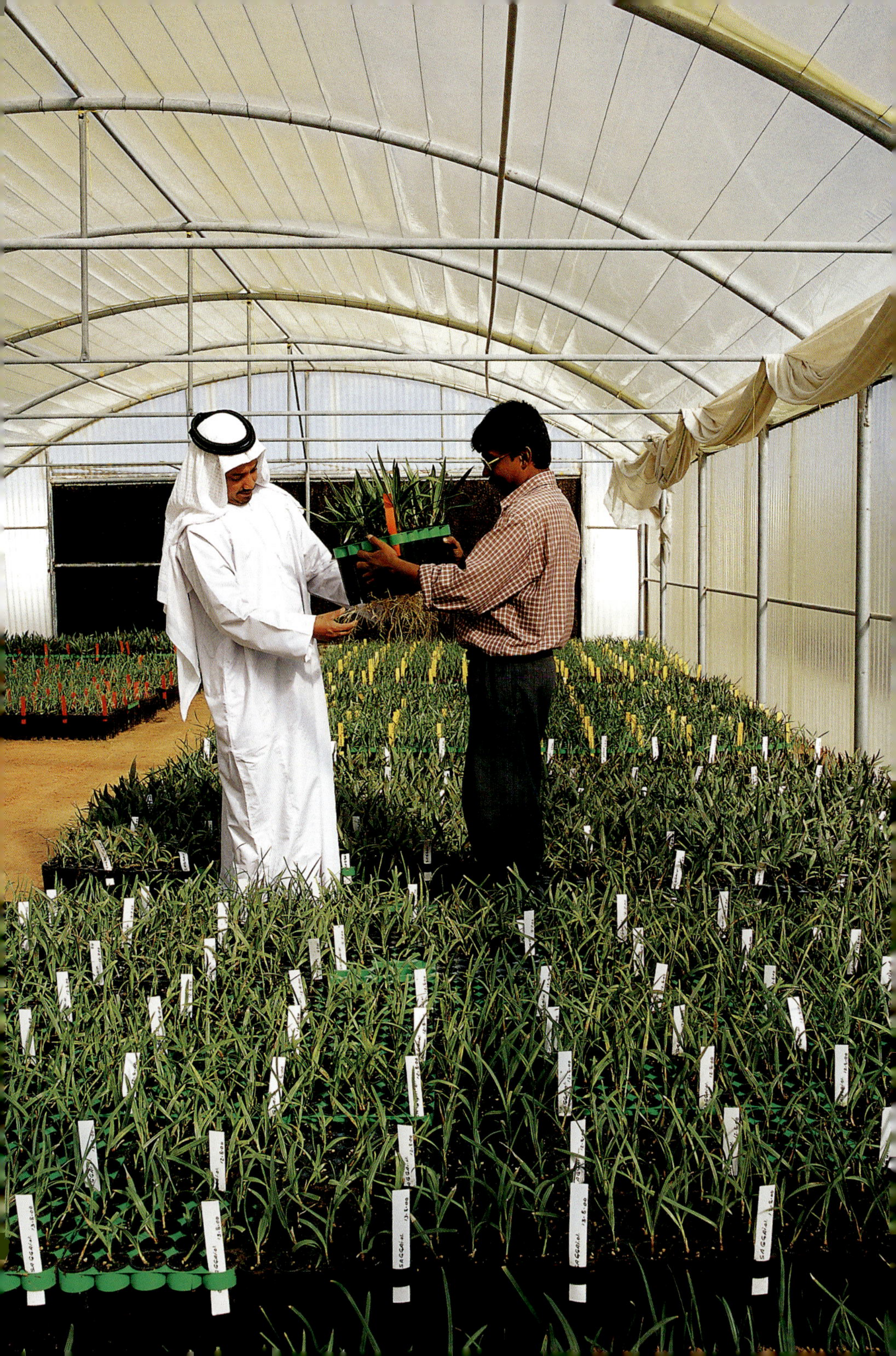

Loans extended to farmers and fishermen over the five years from 1995 to 2000 totalled about Dh1.1 billion, the Abu Dhabi Government providing 93.8 per cent of the funds, while the Federal Government offered the remainder. Assistance to agricultural activities rose by 11 per cent to Dh465 million in 2000 from Dh275 million in 1995. Gross assistance over the five years was Dh2.2 billion, with the Abu Dhabi Government accounting for 95.8 per cent. Cash assistance to cattle breeders in Abu Dhabi stood at Dh507.5 million, while loans to Abu Dhabi farmers accounted for Dh602 million.

VEGETABLES, FRUIT AND LIVESTOCK

One of the greatest agricultural success stories is in the area of date-palm cultivation. Sheikh Zayed's initiatives have led to major developments, including the production of rapidly growing trees and the introduction of effective disease control. The UAE has become a world leader in tissue propagation having established a tissue culture laboratory at the Emirates University for this purpose. The Ministry of Agriculture and Fisheries is also helping to improve productivity through the creation of experimental farms, provision of guidance services and equipment, generation of high quality varieties, and establishment of date processing plants. As a result, farmers were encouraged to plant more trees (currently estimated at 40 million) and the annual date harvest has risen from around 6000 metric tonnes in 1961 to an estimated 318,000 metric tonnes in 2001 (see box on Date Palm Conference). The Emirate of Abu Dhabi, including Al Ain, is estimated to have 33,476,000 date palms, while the Northern Emirates collectively have about 7,224,000 trees.

In second place after the date palm in terms of cultivated acreage and production, vegetables and crops are grown on an area of 398,375 hectares with a yield of 2.6 million tonnes. Overall, whilst 70.3 per cent of all cultivated land is planted with palm trees, 15.7 per cent is dedicated to vegetable production, 6.4 per cent to other crops, and 1 per cent to fruit cultivation. Tomatoes, sweet melon, cabbage, onion, squash and eggplant occupy most of the area allocated for vegetables. Lime, mango, other citrus fruit and guava takes up much of the area allocated to fruit, whilst green fodder, tobacco and wheat are the most popular field crops.

A comparison of 2000 figures with those of the previous year show that while the area set aside for crops (including fodder) increased by 92 per cent, the area allocated to vegetables increased by 15.6 per cent, and the area for palm trees grew by 8.8 per cent, there was a drop of 2.4 per cent in the area set aside for fruit cultivation.

An analysis of the value of agricultural products for the year 2000 shows that at Dh3.5 billion the highest revenue comes from vegetables.. Palm production earned Dh1.9 billion; field crops Dh1.7 billion and fruits brought in Dh2.9 million.

Livestock figures have risen to 2.09 million head, including goats, sheep, cows and camels. Milk production in 2000 was 163,053 tonnes. Red and poultry meat was 24,810 tonnes and 36,310 tonnes respectively. Egg production reached a total of 266 million eggs.

ECONOMIC DEVELOPMENT

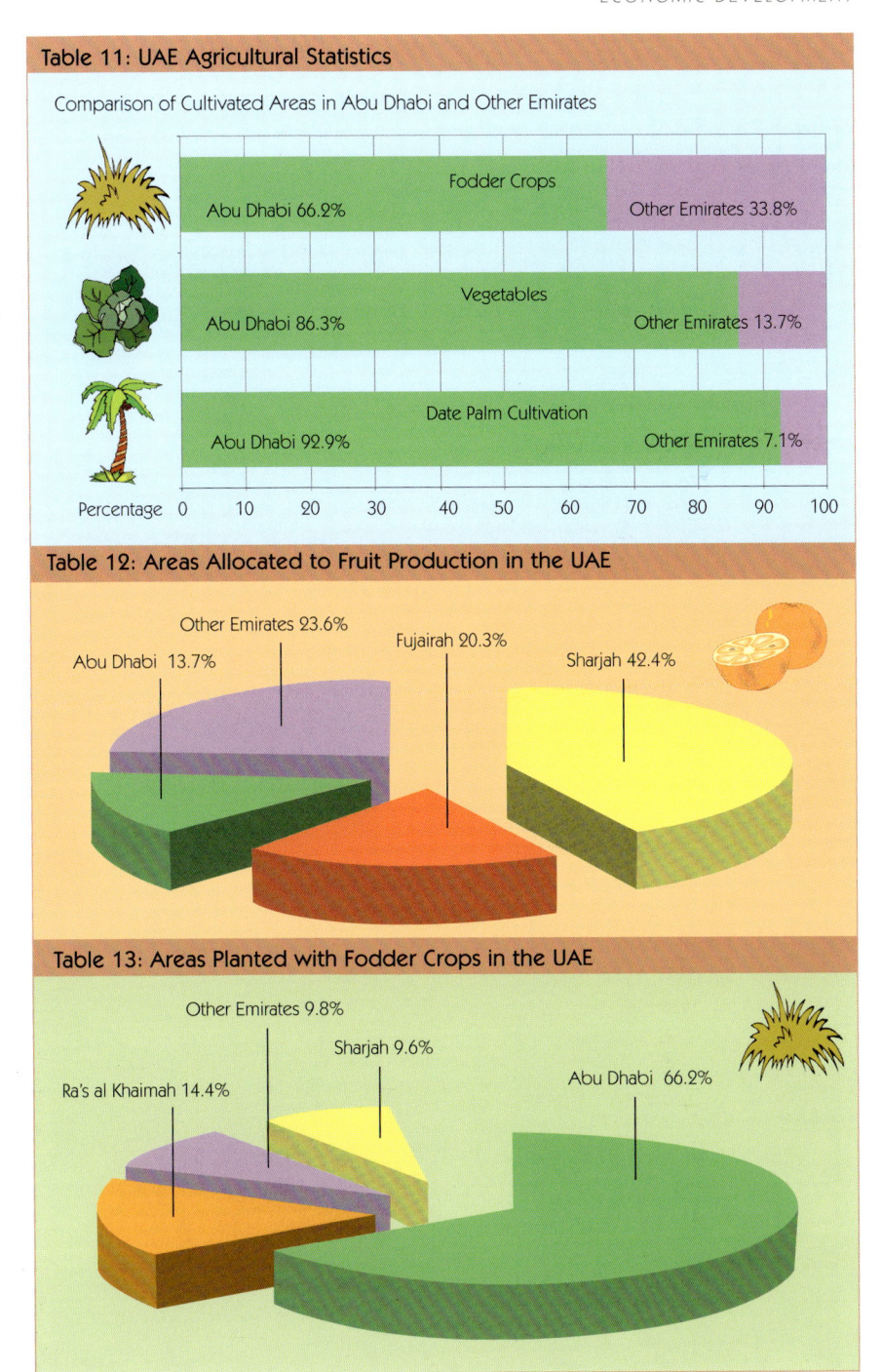

Table 11: UAE Agricultural Statistics

Comparison of Cultivated Areas in Abu Dhabi and Other Emirates

Fodder Crops — Abu Dhabi 66.2% | Other Emirates 33.8%
Vegetables — Abu Dhabi 86.3% | Other Emirates 13.7%
Date Palm Cultivation — Abu Dhabi 92.9% | Other Emirates 7.1%

Percentage 0 10 20 30 40 50 60 70 80 90 100

Table 12: Areas Allocated to Fruit Production in the UAE

- Other Emirates 23.6%
- Abu Dhabi 13.7%
- Fujairah 20.3%
- Sharjah 42.4%

Table 13: Areas Planted with Fodder Crops in the UAE

- Other Emirates 9.8%
- Sharjah 9.6%
- Ra's al Khaimah 14.4%
- Abu Dhabi 66.2%

NATIONAL HORTICULTURE COMPANY

The National Horticulture Company (NHC) was set up under the UAE Offsets Programme in June 1997 as a joint venture between the Abu Dhabi-based Al Hamed Enterprises and Dassault Investissements and TCI, both of France. The Dh50 million (US$14 million) venture is owned 51 per cent by Al Hamed Enterprises, 44 per cent by Dassault and 5 per cent by TCI.

NHC produces about four million roses, plants and other flowers of 18 different varieties at its five-hectare farm in Sweihan, comprising eight glass houses and a shedded area producing a wide range of vegetables and fruits such as eggplant (aubergine), okra (lady's finger), tomatoes and sweet melons.

Rising demand from the local and regional market has triggered a multi-million-dirham expansion program at NHC. The company has added four new glasshouses covering two hectares and increased the area of the open-air plantations. It has also built warehouses and cold stores in Dubai's Al Quoz area to expand its marketing operation which distributes flowers from its 400-square metre warehouse and two cold stores in Sweihan.

The total market for flowers in the UAE is about 100 million (US$27 million) a year. Most of these are being supplied by imports, as local producers are unable to keep up with rising demand. NHC's share of the local market is about 7 per cent and is expected to increase to between 15–20 per cent in 2004.

NHC exports more than 25,000 carnations a week to Australia and is exporting several types of roses and other flowers to Qatar, Bahrain, Oman and Lebanon. Exports to Saudi Arabia are to start shortly. The company has also exported flowers to France and Holland, but due to heavy demand in the local and regional market it was unable to meet demand from those countries.

The technology used by NHC has been imported from the Netherlands, one of the world's biggest and best known flower producers. The computerised glasshouses require fewer workers and make it feasible to have a production facility in the desert. They also have a competitive advantage, especially in the winter season, due to the extremely cold weather and higher production costs in Europe.

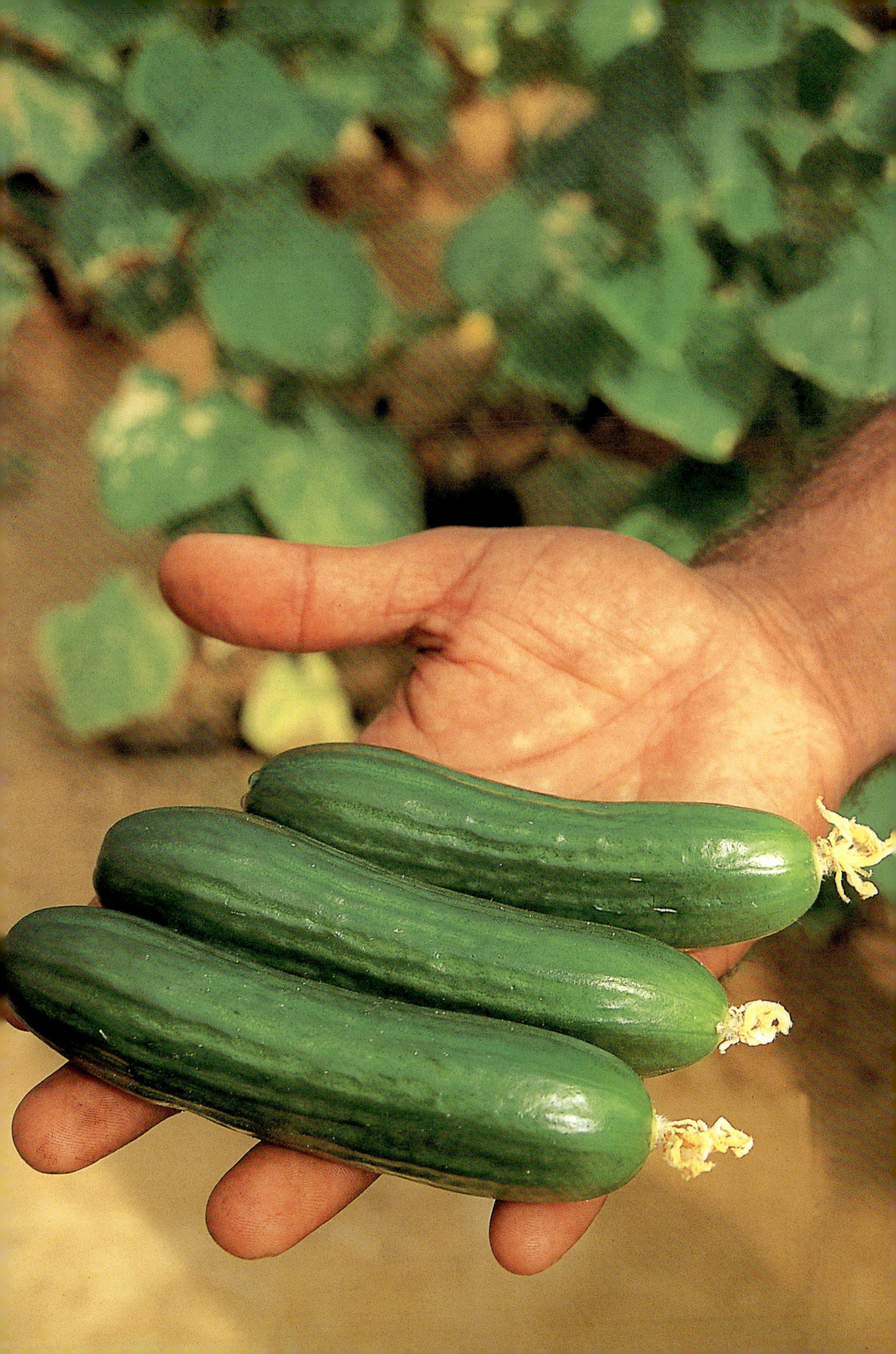

WATER USE

In the UAE, agriculture accounts for a significant proportion of water use. The agricultural water demand stood at 1400 billion cubic metres (bcm) in 2000, and is due to reach 2050 bcm in 2025. Groundwater is still a major source of supply despite the substantial expansion in desalination and the use of treated sewage water for irrigating parks and forests. The number of wells rose from 53,852 in 1982 to 76,256 in 2000 with their output climbing 7.2 per cent a year from 685 million cubic metres to 2.2 billion cubic metres. Consumption of groundwater rose by 6 per cent a year from 95 million cubic metres in 1995 to 241 million cubic metres in 2000. Shortage of groundwater increased 7.9 per cent per year to 2.1 billion in 1999 from 585 million cubic metres in 1982.

In an effort to preserve valuable water resources whilst maintaining development, the UAE has built 45 recharge dams for retaining rainwater with a total retaining capacity of 100 million cubic metres. It is currently constructing 27 dams in 19 valleys in the Northern Emirates, these being funded by Sheikh Zayed. Drip irrigation is also encouraged to conserve water. Today, 80 per cent of the country's cultivated areas (3 million donums) are watered by modern irrigation systems. Farmers are encouraged to grow salt-tolerant crops and use greenhouse cultivation to avoid water depletion.

As well as eliminating water wastage, use of a controlled greenhouse environment assists in reducing the use of fertiliser and pesticides. In addition, the Ministry of Agriculture has banned the use and import of 75 pesticides that have been proved dangerous to the health of humans, animals and the environment. A strict system for registration of pesticides in line with international standards has been established in order to safeguard public health. Special programmes have also been launched to train farmers in the best use of fertilisers and pesticides.

RESEARCH AND DEVELOPMENT

Research on methods of overcoming water shortages and improving crop yields, including the introduction of protected farming systems in greenhouses, drip irrigation systems and experiments on vegetables and fruit trees suitable for the local climate, are being conducted at the Ministry of Agriculture and Fisheries' Dhaid Experiment and Research Centre in the Central Region.

Among wild desert plants currently being studied at the research centre are labath (*Cenchrus ciliaris*), dokhna (*Coelachyrum piercei*), dhai (*Lasium scinelicum*), and thamam (*Dariccum torgidum*). Cultivation is still at the experimental stage but their seeds could be ready for commercial use within the next two years. These plants will not only meet the fodder needs of livestock but also cut water usage by 75 per cent. The indigenous desert plants were chosen after a comprehensive survey. The Ministry is also suggesting that farmers grow more date palms because they are eminently suitable for the UAE's climatic conditions.

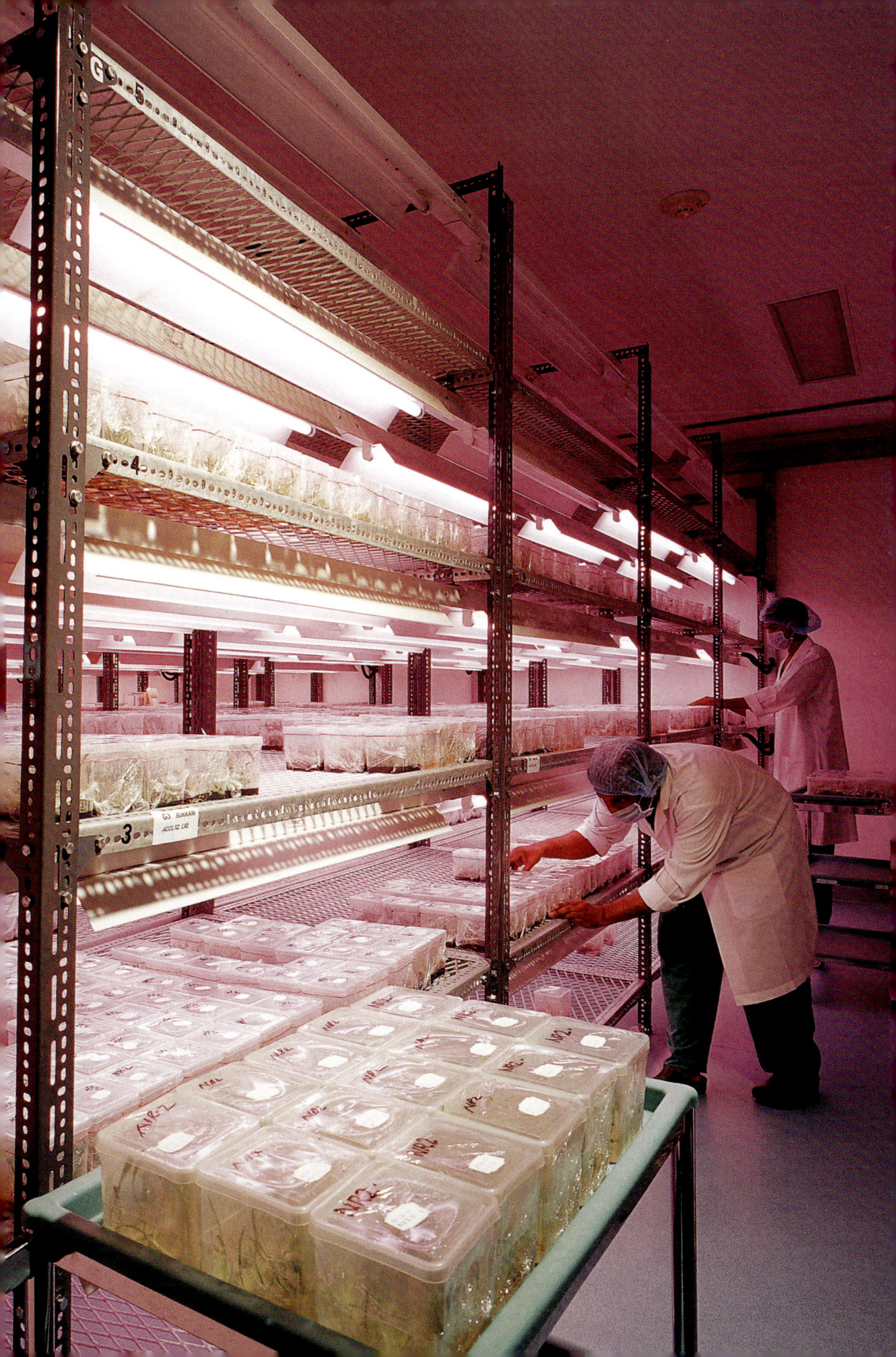
G3 SUKKARI

DATE PALM CONFERENCE

With an estimated 40.7 million date palm trees now planted in the country, the United Arab Emirates is rapidly becoming one of the world's largest producers of dates, responsible for around 6 per cent of total global production. The annual harvest has risen from around 6000 metric tonnes in 1961 to an estimated 318,000 metric tonnes in 2001, with the total amount of land planted with date palms having risen over the same period from less than 600 hectares to 62,000 hectares. Imports of dates into the country have fallen from around 100,000 metric tonnes in 1989 to around 12,000 metric tonnes in 2001, while the UAE, having been partially dependent on date imports to meet local demand, has become a major exporter, with over 50,000 metric tonnes a year now being sold abroad.

Considerable attention has been devoted by Government, and by local farmers, to the date-planting programme, while, at the same time, extensive support has been given to scientific research on date palms, with the UAE now being one of the leaders of techniques of tissue culture, to meet the ever-growing demand for seedlings.

Appropriately, therefore, the UAE capital, Abu Dhabi, was the venue in September for a major international conference on date palms, their history, biology, cultivation and nutritional benefits.

Organised by the Emirates Centre for Strategic Studies and Research (ECSSR) with the support of the Ministry of Information and Culture, the conference was held under the patron of Sheikh Zayed and brought together experts from throughout the Middle East region as well as from further afield. International organisations, too, were represented, such as the secretariat of the UN Convention to Combat Desertification, the Food and Agriculture Organisation (FAO) and the Arab Organisation for Agricultural Development (AOAD)

Native to the Arabian Gulf region and surrounding areas, the date palm, *Phoenix dactylifera*, was originally domesticated several thousand years ago, according to a paper presented to the conference by an archaeo-botanist from France's Sorbonne University. The date of domestication has not yet been determined, but another paper, presented by a researcher from the Abu Dhabi Islands Archaeological Survey (ADIAS) noted that an archaeological site on the UAE's Western island of Dalma had provided some of the earliest evidence anywhere for human consumption of dates.

Radiocarbon dating of charred date stones from old fireplaces on the island showed that they had been consumed around 7500 years ago. By the Bronze Age, around 5000 to 3300 years ago, date consumption was fairly widespread throughout the Gulf and Iraq, according to another paper.

Other papers presented to the conference dealt with issues such as the propagation of dates using tissue culture techniques for mass production, advances in cultivation techniques and date harvesting technology and the use of biological control agents to tackle major pests of date palms, such as the red palm weevil, a voracious insect that reached the UAE from overseas a couple of decades ago.

In an opening address to the conference, Hama Arba Diallo, the executive secretary of the UN Convention to Combat Desertification, noted that the date palm was particularly well-suited as an agricultural plant for desert areas. Not only did it yield a valuable crop, but it also could also be used as a source of timber, while other crops could also be grown in the shade provided by mature date palm plantations. Moreover, since the date palm can tolerate fairly high degrees of salinity, it can be planted in areas that are unsuitable for other cash crops.

At the end of the conference, plans were announced for a major international date-palm festival at the end of December 2003 and early January 2004, to be held in the UAE's inland oasis-city of Al Ain, one of the country's main centres of date production. During the festival, a prize for research into date palms, named after President Sheikh Zayed, will be awarded for the first time.

A film and a book on the life of the date palm and its uses, both entitled *Feast of Dates*, were released during the September conference.

INTERNATIONAL COOPERATION

The Ministry of Agriculture has signed a series of agreements with regional and international organisations on joint cooperation, exchange of data and expertise. The Ministry is working with the Arab Organisation for Agricultural Development on a project to fight red palm weevil. The UAE is also participating in research conducted by the International Fund for Agricultural Development. In addition, the Fund trains UAE date palm researchers.

The United Arab Emirates maintains excellent relations and cooperation with other regional and international agencies, such as UNDP and UNFAO. FAO, in particular, has assisted the UAE in setting up the first Arab Agriculture Information Centre. This will provide information, statistics, reports and research studies on agriculture, fisheries and livestock within the Gulf, the Middle East and around the globe on its website.

The centre will be developed in two phases, the first becoming operational on 10 June 2002, on the occasion of FAO's World Food Day conference in Rome. The second phase will involve additional data collection, as well as presentation of information to make it easily accessible to people.

The centre will be linked to FAO's World Agricultural Information Centre (WAICENT) and other international centres around the globe and will provide information on agriculture not only to researchers and agriculture experts but to the general public as well.

FISHERIES

Considering its productive coastline and its long maritime history, it is not surprising that the UAE has a highly successful indigenous fishing industry. In fact the country has achieved 100 per cent self-sufficiency in fish with the surplus being exported abroad. According to the most recent statistics, 112,561 tonnes, the total fish catch for 2001, was caught by 4589 fishing boats manned by a crew of 12,856 fishermen.

Efforts are being made to increase production within the limitations of the new fishing laws. Federal fisheries law No. 23 for 1999, which came into force in May 2001, is intended to help streamline the fishing industry, encourage traditional fishing methods and curb damaging practices such as harvesting undersize fish, over fishing, and the use of fishing methods that are harmful to fish stocks and the marine environment. The 64-article law is also a very important step towards emiratisation of the fishing profession. Article No. 31 stipulates that no UAE fishing boat shall be allowed to sail without a national captain or owner at the helm. This restriction has already led to an increase in the number of national fishermen registered at the Ministry of Agriculture and Fisheries.

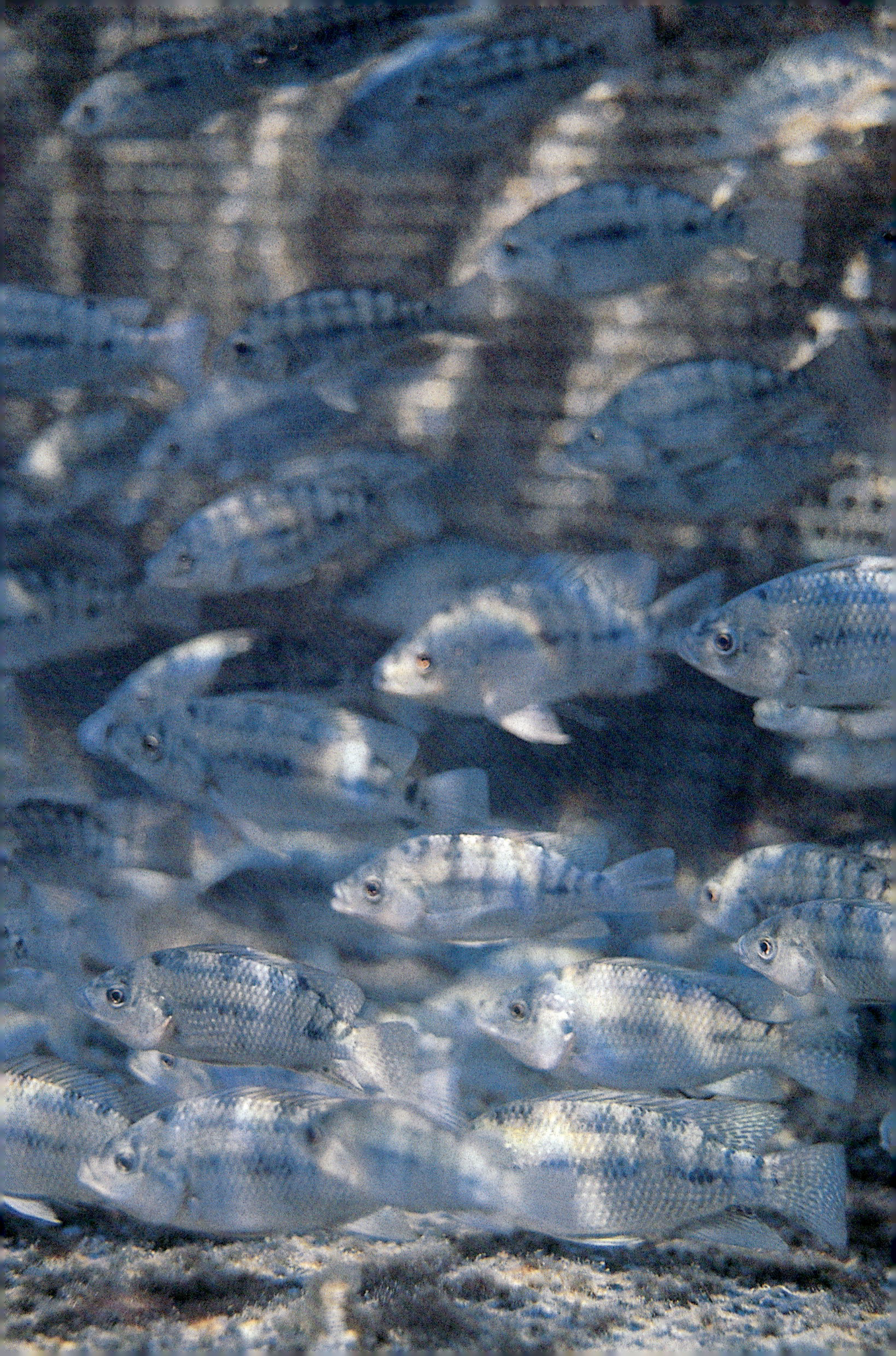

FISHERIES HANDBOOK

In the latter part of 2001 the Ministry of Agriculture and Fisheries issued a handbook detailing a code of practice for fishermen in the UAE based on the new fisheries law. The handbook, published in Arabic, explains the types of equipment to be used, gives information on prohibited fishing areas and seasons, and outlines procedures on how to acquire fishing licences and carry out registration of fishing boats and equipment with the Ministry. Details of special fisheries regulatory committees set up in each emirate to implement the new federal law effectively and coordinate with the Ministry are also explained in the handbook, as well as the regulations on manufacturing and marketing of fish. Special refrigeration facilities on fishing boats going to sea are a pre-requisite. The new law prohibits exports without a special export licence from the Ministry and sets out permitted species and quantities.

The new law also offers incentives and financial assistance to fishermen, particularly the younger generation, to encourage them to carry on this age-old profession.

One of the consequences of the new law is that heavy penalties will be imposed on local fishermen using traditional nets (such as *Al helag*) for fishing pelagic species in UAE waters during the fish-breeding season between 1 May and 30 September.

FISHING LICENCES AND RESEARCH

Following a preliminary assessment of the size of stocks of commercially caught fish species in the waters of the Emirate of Abu Dhabi, the Environment Research and Wildlife Development Agency (ERWDA) recommended in its report for 2001 that the number of commercial fishing licences for the emirate should be limited to 1000. ERWDA is the designated 'competent authority' for implementation of the law in Abu Dhabi Emirate. During 2001, ERWDA issued a total of 639 commercial fishing licences, 409 for boats under 40 feet in length, and 230 for boats of 40 feet and above. It also issued two temporary apprentice fishing licences under a new by-law introduced in August 2001 that permits such licences to be issued to UAE citizens between the ages of 12 and 18 years, to encourage young nationals to enter the industry.

During 2001, ERWDA completed a study on five commercially important species that are found in relatively shallow or inshore waters, including the popular *hamour* (grouper) and *sha'ari* (spangled emperor). Estimates of exploitation rates suggest that the levels of exploitation of the five species in the waters of Abu Dhabi Emirate are 'slightly above the optimum level for their stocks'. Genetic variation among the stocks of the five species is also under scrutiny to provide important information for future management.

ERWDA continued a programme of research into two highly migratory species, kingfish and sailfish. Kingfish were measured and samples taken to permit the genetic make-up of the fish to be determined. During 2001, a total of 1888 sailfish were caught, tagged and released throughout the waters of the UAE, with 945 fish being given tags supplied by ERWDA. Ninety-four fish with tags were re-captured, a rate of 4.88 per cent, which, according to ERWDA, 'is unusually high and probably indicative of over-fishing.' The data collected is being used to develop ERWDA's proposals for management of fish stocks.

In addition, ERWDA has assigned Bruce Shallard and Associates of New Zealand to carry out a major study on fish resources in the UAE waters. The year-long Fish Resource Assessment Survey commenced on 1 February 2002 with the participation of the Ministry of Agriculture and Fisheries, the Federal Environment Agency (FEA) and the Coast Guard. The survey is part of a five-year environment strategy and is intended to assess fish and marine resources in UAE waters and obtain improved estimates of stock size of different fish species.

MARINE RESOURCES RESEARCH CENTRE

Set up in 1984 in Umm al-Qaiwain, the Marine Resources Research Centre of the Ministry of Agriculture and Fisheries (MRRC) is playing an important part in the UAE's efforts to manage its fisheries. The main objectives of the Centre are to conduct biological and hydrographical surveys and research; to produce large quantities of artificial spat of commercially important fish for restocking; to produce commercially important fish and shrimp of marketable size; to provide training and consultancy in aquaculture techniques; and to cooperate with similar regional and international organisations.

The Centre believes that the future of the country's fishing industry lies in farming fish and shrimps. MRRC successfully produced a total of 272,686 fingerlings of various fish species during the 2002 spawning season. Of these, over 98,482 were rabbitfish (*safi*) fingerlings which were subsequently released in lagoons and creeks on the west and east coast of UAE in an attempt to replenish fish stocks, while some have been stocked in the 'grow-out' culture ponds in order to carry out studies at the centre. The project is being implemented with the help of Japanese experts and the Ministry has appointed a number of national graduates of the Faculty of Agricultural Sciences at the Emirates University to work with the Japanese. Centre officials have also been sent for training in Japan, Malaysia, Britain, Tunisia, Philippines, Egypt, and Kuwait.

MRRC has played a major role in the establishment of fish culture projects at Abu al-Abyadh, Shahama and Ajban, in Abu Dhabi. The Centre also has a contract with the international fish farming company ASMAK (see below) for a new hatchery in Umm al-Qaiwain. The aim is to produce 13 million *safi* fingerlings per year – some will be released into Gulf waters, and the remainder will be grown to marketable size by the company.

Another important project at the Centre is research on shrimp. Currently, two species – one local and one from the Red Sea – are being studied and cultured, the plan being to develop shrimp farm projects to meet market demand.

The Centre provides consultancy services on the technical aspects of aquaculture under UAE conditions. It also has a well-equipped laboratory where biological analysis of the samples from larval surveys and the analysis of water samples collected during hydrographic surveys are carried out. In addition, the laboratory has facilities to diagnose and treat common fish diseases. The well-maintained aquarium at the Centre has 29 tanks containing nearly 60 species of fish.

A mangrove afforestation programme is another of the Centre's ambitious projects aimed at protecting the coastline and developing fisheries and fishery resources. Seeds are being sown by the MRRC in many coastal areas of the UAE where there are few mangroves. This project will indirectly help to increase the marine resource potential in the long run. Mangroves are important components of the coastal habitat as they protect the shore from erosion, provide good breeding and nursery grounds for fish and crustaceans, and are also used as fodder.

In addition, the Centre has embarked upon an ambitious programme to study the status of various fish stocks, which necessitates the collection of extensive fisheries data. MRRC is also working on a five-year research plan on the breeding season of important species of fish to determine their catch season.

In 2001, over 9000 visitors from schools, colleges and universities visited the Centre. Training is provided for students and civil servants and the Centre also takes part in marine pollution control programmes and prepares information in English, Arabic, Urdu and Malayalam in order to educate fishermen about fishing rules and regulations.

EU IMPORTS

A European Union (EU) decision in June 2002 allowing the import of fish from GCC states will greatly benefit the UAE since Oman and the UAE are the only GCC states cleared so far for EU imports. The UAE ranks fourth in the Arab world and second in the GCC with regard to annual catch volumes.

The EU had imposed a ban on import of UAE fisheries products in 1998 due to non-conformity with the European Hygiene Regulations implemented in the member states based upon the HACCP system, (Hazardous Analytical Critical Control Point). One of the main stumbling blocks as far as the EU was concerned was that the UAE did not have a sole federal competent authority to certify companies seeking to export their products.

Commission Decision amending Decision 97/296/EC drawing up the list of third countries from which the import of fishery products is authorised for human consumption stated that the United Arab Emirates had now provided information that its fishery products satisfy sanitary conditions equivalent to those of the Community, and it is able to guarantee that the fishery products it will export to the Community meet the health requirements of Directive 91/493/EEC.

ASMAK

ASMAK (plural of fish in Arabic), a joint stock company with a capital base of Dh300 million, was established by an Amiri decree under the UAE Offsets Group (UOG) initiative in 1999. In November 2002, ASMAK released 25,000 fingerlings (*hamour, sha'am* and *sobaity*) raised in the company's hatchery in Kuwait into the sea near Al Jazeirah al-Hamrah. The release is a joint stock enhancement effort between ASMAK, the Ministry of Agriculture and Fisheries and UAE University.

This is the first time that a commercial company has been involved in the Ministry's release programme (see above). ASMAK is keen to develop cooperation with the Ministry on a larger scale and is exploring with UAE University ways to monitor the results of these programmes.

The construction of ASMAK's main hatchery in Umm al-Qaiwain, which will produce 13 million fingerlings a year (see above), will allow the company to work even more closely with UAE authorities to replenish stock for the benefit of fishermen and the economy.

ASMAK has established two modern cage farms with 20 floating cages, each based upon a long-term concession agreement with the Ra's al-Khaimah Government. The farms comprise an offshore sea area of 3 kilometres by 1.5 kilometres near Al Mataf Island and a 2000-square-metre land base at Al Rams. These cage farms produce sea bream, sea bass, sobaity and other types of local species with a production capacity reaching 1200 tons a year.

As well as setting up and commissioning the Umm al-Qaiwain hatchery, ASMAK is developing a pilot plan for shrimp farming and an improvement in existing fish farm production capacity up to 5000 tonnes per year. Plans are under way to raise capacity to four million juveniles a year at the Kuwait hatchery.

ASMAK is in the process of developing its sales in the European market with a gross target of Dh15–Dh20 million. The company, which is implementing the HACCP system at its Ocean Fish Processing plant in Jebel Ali Free Zone, is benefiting greatly from the EU's export approval since a large portion of its production is destined for the EU through its Greek partner Nireus Aquaculture, or directly through its own commercial network.

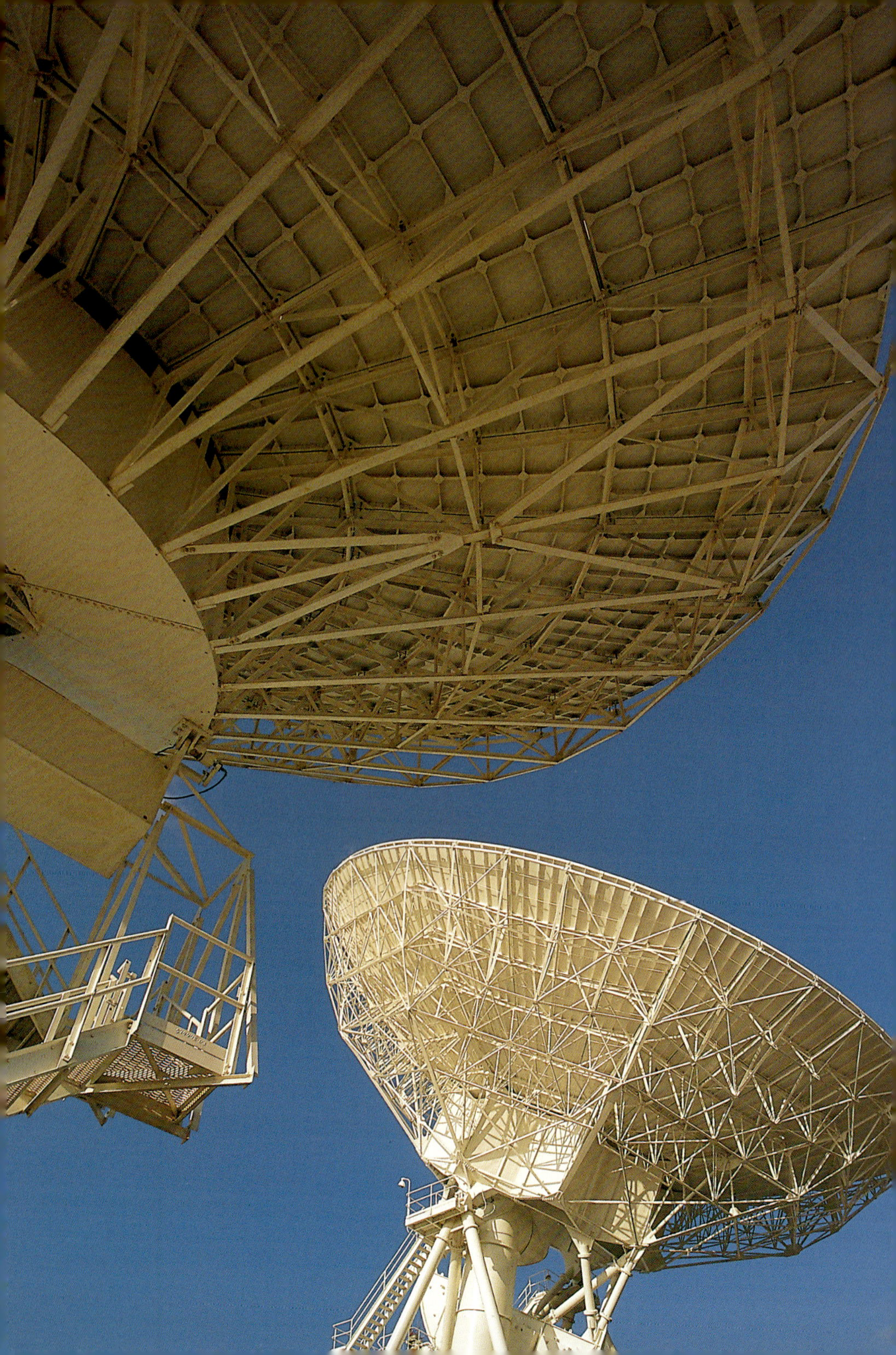

INFRASTRUCTURE

URBAN DEVELOPMENT

THE RAPID DEVELOPMENT OF THE UAE'S TOWNS and villages from small oasis settlements in the 1950s to large modern, fully functional cities has necessitated a heavy investment in infrastructure. Roads, airports, seaports, housing, sewerage, electricity, water, and telecommunications networks have all been developed to meet the demands of a high-tech society. Although this process slowed down to some extent in the late 1990s, a considerable investment is still being made in infrastructure at both federal and emirate level. Dh2.1 billion was allocated for the execution of federal projects in 2002, of which Dh640 million went to the Sheikh Zayed Housing Programme, Dh85 million to maintenance and construction of embassy buildings and UAE diplomats' residences abroad, Dh197 million to construction of roads and bridges, and Dh77 million to maintenance of roads and additional building units. Dh1 billion was earmarked for projects in Ra's al-Khaimah, Dh1.441 billion for Fujairah, Dh1.419 billion for Ajman, Dh1.197 for Sharjah, Dh566 million for Umm al-Qaiwain, Dh554 million for Abu Dhabi and Dh313 million for Dubai.

HOUSING

The unprecedented level of development, increasing urbanisation (the current level of 85 per cent is set to hit 96 per cent by 2030), and a steadily rising population meant that the UAE's housing stock was inadequate to meet the needs of the indigenous population. The Regional Development Plan (RDP), for instance, forecasts that a total of 158,000 new and replacement housing units will be required during the plan's lifetime to accommodate future population growth in the Emirate of Abu Dhabi. To meet these needs the Regional Land Use Plan, the main component of the RDP, provides a coordinated and flexible framework for the location and control of proposed developments.

The scarcity of low-cost housing has been a particular problem. This deficiency is being remedied at one level by a comprehensive grants scheme and the distribution to nationals of land and houses free-of-charge. In October 2002, Abu Dhabi Municipality and Town Planning Department distributed 480 residential plots and 299 low-income houses to eligible nationals in Abu Dhabi Emirate. In the same year the Sheikh Zayed Housing Programme (SZHP), which was established in 2000 to meet the housing needs of UAE nationals, approved construction of over 1600 residential villas in Dubai and the Northern Emirates. Dh800 million was granted to 1812 nationals in 2000 and Dh535 million to 1307 in 2001. SZHP's total budget for 2002 was Dh650 million and applications were up considerably on previous years.

Initially, SZHP applicants could opt for a loan, a grant, or alternatively accept a house that had already been built. But from 2001, on instructions from Sheikh Zayed, SZHP has stopped offering loans, and has converted the loans into grants. The housing programme is being funded by extraordinary funds made available by the UAE Central Bank to which Emirates Telecommunications Corp. (ETISALAT) is also contributing.

Dubai Municipality has allocated Dh5.1 billion for housing projects under its 2015 development plan. Some 32,000 buildings are needed, and each year 1900 will be constructed at a cost of Dh122 million. Of these, 300 will be low-cost houses costing Dh1.5 billion.

In addition, the private sector is playing a major part in the provision of housing, although this is usually at the higher end of the market. One of the more ambitious private sector developments under construction in Dubai is the Dubai Marina complex, an EMAAR project. Dubai Marina promises to be 'a city within a city'. On completion, the 50-million-square-foot project will house luxury residential and leisure facilities covering 2.89 square kilometres. A range of skyscrapers at Dubai Marina will add a new dimension to the Dubai skyline and provide its nearly 50,000 residents with panoramic views of the Arabian Gulf. The first phase of the Dubai Marina project, which commenced in July 2001, comprises six towers housing 1026 residential units.

EMAAR also announced in late December 2002 its Arabian Ranches housing complex, including a golf course and other leisure facilities, to be built at the edge of the desert inland from the city.

The Palm project on two new man-made islands off Jumeirah and Jebel Ali (see section on Tourism) will also have a major residential component.

ROADS, PARKS AND OTHER PROJECTS

A considerable amount of money has been spent by federal and local governments on road building to access newly developed areas and improve traffic flow, on sewerage projects to service increased urbanisation, and on landscaping urban areas, roads and roundabouts to improve the quality of life in the country. The federal government is responsible for inter-emirate roads, whilst local governments take care of transport networks within the individual emirates.

Abu Dhabi

Over the past 34 years Abu Dhabi has spent in excess of Dh150 billion on infrastructure and other development projects. Abu Dhabi Municipality is currently implementing its 20-year plan aimed at improving the transportation system throughout Abu Dhabi, including widening existing roads, building new bypass roads and expanding public transport.

In 2002 the Municipality undertook 200 infrastructure and sewerage projects costing Dh4.2 billion. It also embarked on a major road and park project along the existing Corniche which is already a valuable recreational resource for Abu Dhabi residents. The Corniche roadworks will not only greatly increase available recreational areas but will considerably improve traffic flow. Land reclamation, which commenced along the stretch from Mina Zayed to Hiltonia Beach late in 2001, has been completed.

A realignment of the Corniche Road along the reclaimed land will have three lanes in both directions extending for around 2 kilometres from Al Salam Road to Mina Zayed. Once completed, the Corniche will have parking for 4000 cars, while a flyover will give quick access to the Sheraton Hotel and nearby areas. Pedestrian crossings and bicycle paths will be a feature of the new development. In addition, the Corniche's old landmarks are set to get a facelift. The famous 30-metre clock tower overlooking the sea will be replaced with a new 70-metre tower. Museums, mosques, coffee shops, fountains and parks will add considerably to the attractiveness of the Corniche, whilst extensive planting of trees and shrubs will give the project a natural touch. The total cost of the Corniche expansion programme is expected to exceed Dh700 million. The overall scheme includes the building of a road linking Al Khaleej Al Arabi Street (Arabian Gulf Street) and Eastern Ring Road with Port Zayed via Saadiyat Island to keep heavy goods trucks away from the city.

A number of other structural and landscaping projects will also lend character to the Corniche area. In May 2002 the Geneva Flower Clock, a replica of the original landmark in Geneva, was presented by the City of Geneva to Sheikh Zayed as a token of appreciation of the love and affection the President has shown for Geneva and Switzerland. The clock, which is erected next to the Sheraton Hotel, incorporates a unique display of flowers, rocks and fountains. The work has been carried out by the Agriculture Section of Abu Dhabi Municipality in cooperation with the Parks, Gardens and Environment Department of the City of Geneva and its local consultant, Orient Irrigation Services.

The Public Works Department is also building a wildlife sanctuary on Lulu Island, opposite the Corniche. Planting of date palms and construction of enclosures for introduced gazelle and oryx as well as lakes and ponds for birds are some of the projects under development on the island.

Innovative ways to tackle irrigation are being investigated in order to sustain the extraordinary degree of landscaping that has taken place in recent years. One such project, the Sheikh Zayed Bio-saline Agriculture Project in Abu Dhabi, entered the Guinness Book of Records in September 2002 as the largest sea-irrigated park in the world. Located at Al Jarf Palace overlooking the Arabian Gulf, the 20,000-square-metre park was established in October 1999. The model park uses seawater to irrigate 50 per cent of around 45 species of genetically modified plants, trees and herbs. Its auto-irrigation network has three big water reservoirs filled by water pumps whose pipes extend into the sea for 300 metres. It also has an artificial tidal lake.

Urban centres outside the capital city are also undergoing extensive beautification. In particular work is under way in Al Ain on ten new landscaping, irrigation and park projects at a cost of Dh95 million to complement the new 8.7 hectares family park recently built in Al Sulaimat District. Major development work costing Dh87million has also been planned at Al Ain Zoo to enhance its educational and tourism value. Other major tourism projects include Jebel Hafit Spa and Resort and a new golf course.

Dubai

A five-year (2001–2005) urban development plan and an urban area structure plan (1993–2015) are in place in Dubai. The available urban area measures 604.8 square kilometres, of which 212 square kilometres was already developed by 2001. At the current rate of urban development (3.9 per cent) 504 square kilometres will be urbanised by 2015. The population of Dubai has been growing at a rate of 4.5 per cent per year and currently the density is 42.3 per hectare. Of the total urban area, the major portion, 30 per cent, is being used for residential purposes, industrial areas cover 3256 hectares and roads occupy 19.3 per cent of the land area.

Dubai Municipality is currently implementing its Dh160 million long-term plan to improve the flow of traffic in the emirate. At present, the second phase of the bypass road costing Dh51 million, one of the four main projects in the traffic plan, is under construction. The Roads Planning Section has also undertaken a number of other projects in 2002, including a redesign of interchange numbers 1–6, the Jaddaf roads project, the approach to Al Bustan Road, expansion of Garhoud Bridge and landscaping on Jumeirah Road and at various intersections. Pavement work in Al Wasl, roads in Mizhar 1, Oud Al Mutteena and the northern section of Al Khawaneej Road will be completed in 2003.

Phase One of the major development plan to transform central Dubai's heritage area including waterfront cafes and promenades, which is due for completion early in 2003, will give the city a new living and recreational focus. The second and final phase of the project will be concluded in 2004.

Dubai Municipality also plans to develop the Deira Corniche in 2003, giving the area between Al Hamriyah Port and Rashid Port a new frontage at a cost of Dh3.307 billion. Additional public and private beaches will be provided and the project will offer land for commercial and residential development on the seafront. The road network will also be improved. Space will be reserved for a monorail that will connect the Deira Corniche with Bur Dubai passing near Al Shindagha Tunnel.

Due to the increase in population and the impact of development, it was necessary for the municipal sewage plant on the Al Aweer Road, which was built in 1985, to double its treatment capacity from 45.8 million cubic metres in 1995 to 83.4 million cubic metres in 2001 and it is expected that the plant will receive 112.6 million cubic metres of sewage water in one year in the near future. The treated water is used for irrigation purposes.

Dubai Municipality is also planning to construct a new sewage treatment plant in Jebel Ali. The plant will service various projects in the area, such as Emirates Hills, Dubai Internet City, Dubai Media City, and other residential and commercial complexes.

Dubai Municipality's Parks and Horticulture Department constructed a number of new parks and completed a range of new landscaping projects in 2002. To date Dubai has a total landscaped area of 4,790,852 square metres. In planning new residential districts, the Municipality has reserved 8 per cent of the area for parks or landscaping.

Construction commenced on a new Dh180 million public park in Zabeel that will be phased over a six-year period, with completion scheduled for 2008. This will be the sixth biggest public park in the emirate. The five major public parks attract over 2.5 million visitors a year. New park projects completed in 2002 include seven small parks in residential areas in Al Mezher, Al Garhoud, Hatta, Nad al-Sheba, Umm Suqueim and Al Quoz. Numerous other landscaping projects are also under way in Dubai.

Northern Emirates

Infrastructural development in the Northern Emirates is struggling to keep abreast of population growth in an effort to provide all the amenities that are a feature of modern urban living.

One of the Ministry of Public Works and Housing projects in the Northern Emirates is a Dh300 million highway connecting Sharjah, Ajman and Ra's al-Khaimah. The new road, which will be parallel to the old one, will be completed in two phases, the first phase covering 27 kilometres from the industrial area in Sharjah to Ajman. This will connect with the Sharjah–Ra's al-Khaimah Road, 10 kilometres from the Umm al-Qaiwain interchange. As part of this project, the Ministry is planning to renovate the existing road from Sharjah to Al Shouhada (Martyr's) Roundabout in Ra's al-Khaimah. The second phase of the 90-kilometre road will stretch from Al Sajhah–Al Khawaneej interchange in Dubai to Dhaid in Sharjah and Al Rams in Ra's al-Khaimah. A four-lane flyover is also being built over the busy Al Hamidiyah Roundabout in Ajman, to help ease traffic movement. The flyover will provide uninterrupted progress for vehicles coming from Sharjah to Umm al-Qaiwain and Ra's al-Khaimah, or vice versa.

Beautification continues to be a major focus in all the emirates. Ra's al-Khaimah Municipality, for instance, is implementing an ambitious plan to change the face of the city by 2009. Landscaping, including tree planting and paving of footpaths is already well under way. Other greenery projects, such as the one at Kadrah 70 kilometres south of the city, on the edge of the Hajar Mountains, that will rehabilitate a former quarry, will have a positive impact on the environment.

Sharjah Municipality, which has devoted much time and effort to landscaping its capital city, is constructing three new parks in Khor Fakkan. Al Mudeifi Park covering 46,000 square metres is dedicated to women and children. Facilities will include playgrounds, a train, a mosque and a cafeteria. Luluyyah Park (21,000 square metres) and Al Zabara Park (8000 square metres) will have football and basketball courts among their playground facilities.

ELECTRICITY AND WATER

ABU DHABI

The Abu Dhabi Water and Electricity Authority (ADWEA) continued during the year under review to meet rising demand for water and electricity. Current power generation capacity in Abu Dhabi is 5300 megawatts (MW) compared with 3MW in 1966, while installed water capacity is 400 million gallons (mg/d), with daily usage being around 300 million gallons. According to recent forecasts, the medium term peak demand for electricity is predicted to increase at an annual average rate of 10 per cent. For water the medium average growth forecast is set to be in excess of 8 per cent per annum.

Privatisation initiatives have been a consistent feature in ADWEA's strategy to meet these rapidly growing needs. In the latter part of 2000 there were six generation and desalination companies in the Abu Dhabi water and electricity sector, the most recent addition being a joint venture between ADWEA and Gulf Total Tractebel Power Company (GTTPC) located at Taweelah. GTTPC was the first Independent Water and Power Producer (IWPP) in the emirate to acquire existing assets from ADWEA at the site known as Taweelah A1. Previously, these assets were managed by Bainounah Power Company. In September 2000 the Regulation and Supervision Bureau responsible for overseeing the sector granted a licence to GTTPC to produce 84.76 mg/d of desalinated water with an installed electricity capacity of 1431MW. The existing assets transferred to GTTPC were a desalination plant with a water capacity of 29 mg/d and generation units with an installed capacity of 255MW. Development work at Taweelah A1 and Taweelah A2 will be completed in the summer of 2006.

In November 2001 a seventh production company, Shuweihat CMS International Power (CMS IP), was established and registered in the Emirate of Abu Dhabi and was issued with a generation and desalination licence for the production of 1500MW of electricity generation and 100 mg/day of desalinated water. Shuweihat CMS IP is a joint venture between America's CMS and International Power, the overseas arm of UK-based National Power. ADWEA retains a 60 per cent holding in Shuweihat CMS IP, with the remaining 40 per cent divided evenly between CMS and International Power. The plant is being built on a brownfield site close to Jebel Dhanna in the Western Region of Abu Dhabi Emirate. Commercial production is planned to start in mid-2004.

Plans are also under way to privatise the existing Umm al-Nar facility, east of Abu

Dhabi City. This complex currently has power and desalination capacity of 1100MW and 100 mg/d respectively. A further 62.5 mg/d of desalination capacity is under construction at the complex and is expected to be commissioned before the privatisation agreements are completed. These agreements will cover the purchase of the new 62.5 mg/d desalination capacity and two recently commissioned units of roughly 7 mg/d with associated infrastructure, as well as the development, financing and construction of at least 1000MW of new net electricity generating capacity and potentially additional water generation capacity.

Abu Dhabi has attracted Dh14 billion in investment in the water and power sector since it embarked on privatisation. Currently, 32 per cent of Abu Dhabi's generation and desalination capacity is in private hands and it is expected that privatisation initiatives will continue to dominate the production end of the water and electricity supply chain for the foreseeable future. However, the distribution and supply chain will remain under government ownership.

As far as its own facilities are concerned, ADWEA commissioned a new desalination plant at Al Mirfa Power Company providing an extra 22 mg/day of water in the Western Region. Further developments in the provision of extra generation have seen an agreement between Transco (the transmission company for Abu Dhabi) and TAKREER, part of the ADNOC Group, to receive or transmit power between the two companies at Ruwais. The connection is at a 220kV substation and provides for the import or export of up to 300MW. There are additional advantages for both parties in terms of system security, especially under high load and fault conditions.

ADWEA is currently executing a major transmission project in Al Ain. This includes the construction of 65-kilometre, 400kV and 55-kilometre, 22kV lines. ADWEA is also working on a project that will supply 76 mg/d to the city from the Taweelah 'B' station through a 135-kilometre dual pipeline. In addition, it has completed several water distribution networks in the suburbs of Al Ain.

A new control and despatch centre that enables generation optimising and load forecasting throughout Abu Dhabi Emirate was also commissioned by Transco. Additionally, investment in supervisory, control and data acquisition (SCADA) will ensure a full range of operator focused services.

At the other end of the supply chain are the customers. The responsibility for these rests with two companies, Abu Dhabi Distribution Company and Al Ain Distribution Company. Both entities are joint stock companies, currently wholly owned by ADWEA. Downsizing, investment in networks and improvements in customer service have resulted in these companies shedding their old bureaucratic image. In particular, the purchase of new billing systems and the opening of prestigious customer centres in Al Ain and Abu Dhabi are visible signs of the efforts being made to improve services for the emirate's 300,000 customers. The medium to long-term outlook for the sector is one of rapid changes in order to meet demand and increasing customer expectations.

UNION WATER AND ELECTRICITY COMPANY (UWEC)

The Union Water and Electricity Company (UWEC) was set up by the Abu Dhabi Government under instructions from UAE President HH Sheikh Zayed bin Sultan Al Nahyan to meet the rising demand for water in Abu Dhabi Emirate and the growing power needs of the Northern Emirates. The company came into existence through an Emiri Decree issued on 26 June 2001 by HH Sheikh Hamad bin Mohammed Al Sharqi, Supreme Council member and Ruler of Fujairah.

UWEC is now preparing to build a second power generation and water desalination complex in Fujairah. The new project involves the construction of a power plant of between 800–1000MW and a water desalination plant of 100 mg/d, close to the company's first project a 656MW power generation plant and a 100 mg/d water desalination unit at Qidfa on the Indian Ocean.

UWEC intends to award the engineering, procurement and construction (EPC) contracts in mid-2003 for completion in 30 months. Most of the power produced at the project will go to the Emirates National Grid (ENG) and may also be exported to neighbouring countries through the planned GCC grid.

Construction work on UWEC's first venture, the 656MW power generation and the 100 mg/d water desalination and pipeline project, is scheduled to be completed by July 2003. This project will transport desalinated water to Sweihan through a 179-kilometre dual pipeline, which will also have an 18-kilometre spur to Dhaid in Sharjah. Of the 656MW electricity produced by the project, 120MW will be used to run the desalination unit and 36MW allocated to the transmission system. The remaining 500MW will be supplied to the Northern Emirates – where demand for electricity is rising by between 10–12 per cent a year – through a new 400kV transmission line from Fujairah to Dhaid. The transmission line will eventually be interconnected to the upcoming Emirates National Grid (ENG) to be jointly built by UWEC, the Federal Electricity and Water Authority (FEWA), Abu Dhabi Water and Electricity Authority (ADWEA), Dubai Electricity and Water Authority (DEWA), and Sharjah Electricity and Water Authority (SEWA).

Work on the Dh2.9 billion contract for the construction of the power generation and water desalination unit is being carried out by South Korea's Doosan Heavy Industries and Construction Company. The desalination plant will produce 62.5 mg/d of water by using multi-stage flash (MSF) technology and 37.5 mg/d by using reverse osmosis (RO). This makes the project the only one in the Middle East region and one of the biggest in the world using a combination of the two water desalination technologies.

The Dh1.6 billion water transmission pipeline contract, awarded in August 2001, is being completed by a partnership of Al Jaber Energy Services and France's Technip. The dual pipeline will have capacity to transmit 180 mg/d of water. Trenching work for laying the pipeline is at an advanced stage.

UWEC plans to privatise both projects in line with the ongoing privatisation of the water and power sector in Abu Dhabi. A foreign partner will be offered up to a 49 per cent stake in the project, a structure similar to the one used by the Abu Dhabi Water and Electricity Authority

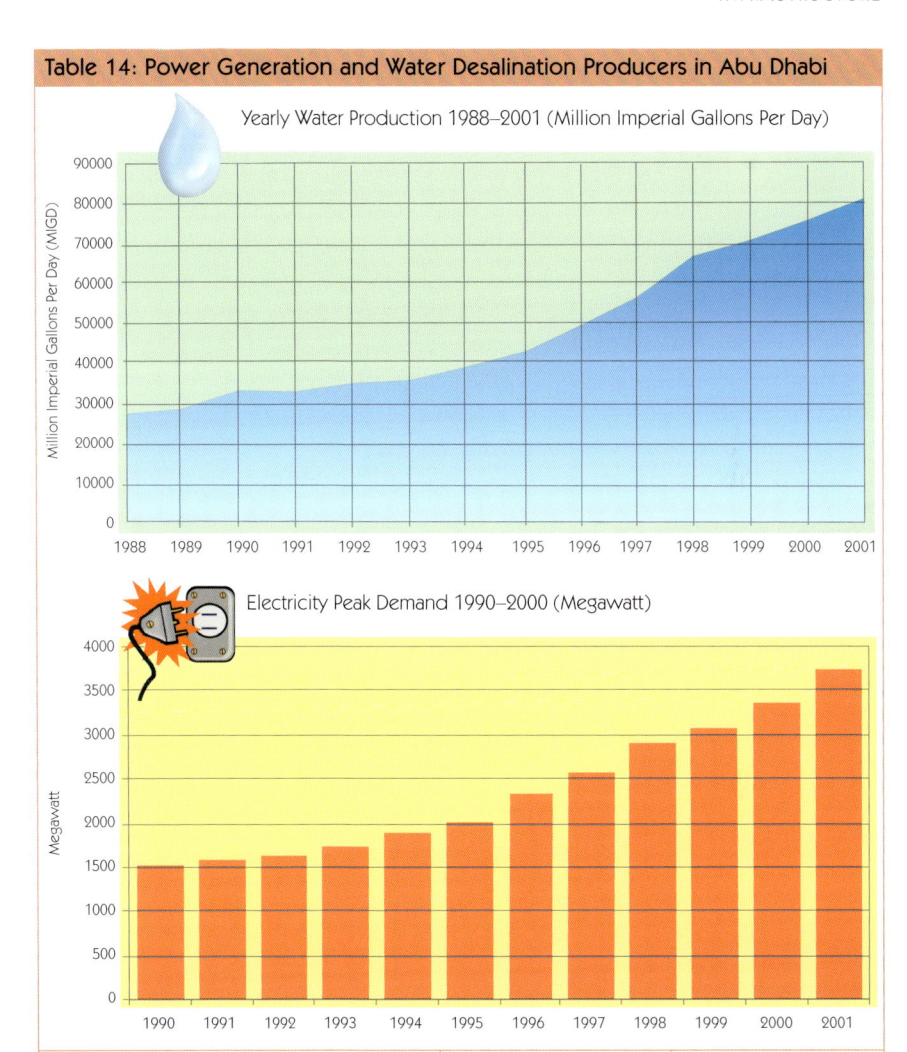

Table 14: Power Generation and Water Desalination Producers in Abu Dhabi

Yearly Water Production 1988–2001 (Million Imperial Gallons Per Day)

Electricity Peak Demand 1990–2000 (Megawatt)

Company's Name	Water in MIGD Licensed Capacity	Water in MIGD Available Capacity	Megawatt Licensed Capacity	Megawatt Available Capacity
Emirates CMS Power Company (ECPC)	50.0	50.0	763	777
Gulf Total Tractebel Power Company (GTTPC)	84.8	30.4	1,431	266
Shuweihat CMS Power Company (SCPC)	100.0	0.0	1,500	0
Al Mirfa Power Company (ATPC)	38.7	16.2	380	300
Al Taweelah Power Company (ATPC)	103.0	95.1	1,220	1,069
Umm al-Nar Power Company (UNPC)	97.0	102.0	1,335	1,148
Bainounah Power Company (BPC)	16.0	15.0	1,001	940
Totals	505.5	308.7	7,630	4,500

Data Sources: Licensed capacity data is from The Regulation and Supervision Bureau.
Availability capacity data is from Abu Dhabi Water and Electricity Company

FEWA

The Federal Electricity and Water Authority (FEWA) has prepared a five-year strategic plan to upgrade and extend electricity and water networks throughout the country. A budget of Dh1583 million was allocated to the project in mid-2002. This includes the allocation of Dh14 million for the supply of power to new houses, as well as Dh8.96 for constructing electricity substations. In addition, the installation of new power lines will cost Dh11 million and a project implemented to increase the generating capacities of existing stations linking the different parts of the central region will cost Dh2 million. In the Western Region, transformers will be installed at a cost of Dh3 million, while Dh89 million will be spent on new water networks. A further Dh40 million has been allocated to construct new premises for the authority in various locations throughout the UAE.

DUBAI

Dubai Electricity and Water Authority (DEWA), the government body that is responsible for the development of the utility sector, continues to invest in new projects in order to meet increased demand in that emirate. As a result, spending on this sector was up 17 per cent in 2002. The emirate is producing 210 million gallon of potable water per day while the daily consumption is 179 million gallons.

Once the new 'L' Station goes into production it will add 880MW of electricity and 70 mg/d of water to the emirate's current power and water supply. In addition, Dh17.3 million is being spent on a new supply network. Due for completion in 2003, the project includes the construction of an extra 185 kilometres of pipeline: 92 kilometres is being laid in Warqa, 13 kilometres in Al Quoz industrial area, as well as 22 kilometres to serve EMAAR and other projects on their completion. DEWA has also laid a 22 kilometre-long water pipeline to the Al Maha nature reserve on the Dubai–Al Ain highway.

DEWA stresses that energy efficiency is given a high priority in supply and demand. On the supply side, fuel utilisation has increased from 30 per cent to 84 per cent through the conversion of existing simple cycle units to combined cycle and cogeneration units. This has significantly contributed to the reduction of specific emissions by 50 per cent. DEWA and Dubai Municipality also cooperate closely to enforce the installation of thermal insulation in buildings, which is expected to reduce the electricity consumption for air-conditioning by about 40 per cent.

SHARJAH

Sharjah Electricity and Water Authority (SEWA) continues to improve and upgrade production and transmission of electricity and water in Sharjah Emirate. Some of the projects currently under development or recently completed include Phase 3 of Wasit Power Station which was concluded during 2002 with the commissioning

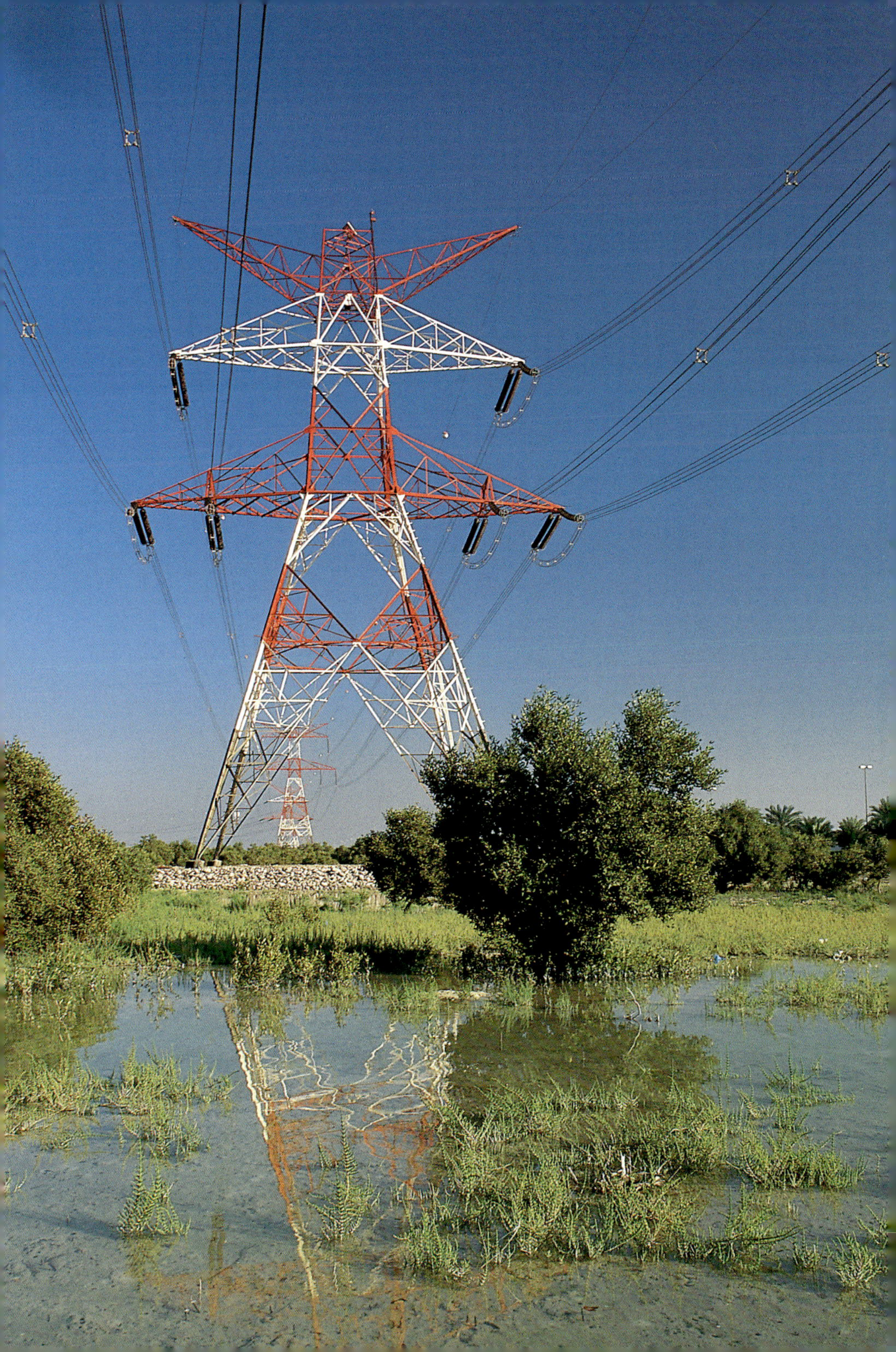

of the seventh (9 Frame) 100MW gas turbine. Phase 4 will cover supply installation and commissioning of 2 100MW (9 Frame) gas turbines costing Dh210 million. The first unit will be commissioned in 2003 and the second in 2004. In 2002 a new (6 Frame) gas turbine of 33MW installed capacity costing Dh40 million was installed at Kalba Power Station on the East Coast.

Money is also being spent on new transmission and distribution substations, as well as transmission and distribution networks in Sharjah, Kalba and Khor Fakkan, the latter two towns being on the East Coast. The new Dh100 million Load Despatch Centre (LDC) at the old site of Nasseriyah Power Station will control and monitor the operation and maintenance of the transmission and distribution substations and acquire information about the network.

In addition, since 2001, 25 new water wells have either been commissioned or are being excavated. Groundwater exploration in Sharjah and the Northern Emirates has been greatly enhanced by a three-year agreement on scientific cooperation between SEWA and Boston University. The agreement involves the use of satellite imagery to identify the potential of groundwater resources. In particular, the programme will emphasise the potential of water resources from two unconventional resources, networks of fracture zones and dried courses of former rivers and streams.

GCC POWER GRID

The first study on a grid to interconnect the six Gulf states was carried out in 1986. This was updated in 1990–92. In 2001, the GCC created an Interconnection Authority to implement the project with a target completion date of 2010. Construction of phase one of the project is scheduled to start in the second quarter of 2004 and involves the interconnection of Kuwait, Saudi Arabia, Bahrain and Qatar. This phase will be operational by the end of 2007. Phase two will integrate the independent power systems of the UAE and Oman. The interconnection will use the UAE grid to link to the GCC North System through Tarif and the UAE to Oman through Al Ain.

The implementation of phase three, which will complete the interconnection of the GCC north and south grids, is conditional on the internal integration of the networks in the UAE.

TELECOMMUNICATIONS AND POST

ETISALAT, the sole telecom provider in the UAE, was established in 1976 to service the local market. In the intervening years ETISALAT has invested more than US$5 billion in building a first-class telecommunications network throughout the country. Sixty per cent of ETISALAT, which was listed on the Abu Dhabi stock market in June 2002, is owned by the government, with the remaining 40 per cent in the hands of UAE investors.

The company earned a net profit of Dh2.5 billion in 2001, its highest net profit ever. Indications are that it has maintained its profitability in 2002 with nine-month figures to the end of September 2002 showing a profit of Dh1.9 billion. ETISALAT earned Dh5.9 billion in total revenues in the nine-month period compared with Dh7.557 billion for the year ended December 2001. The earnings per share stood at Dh6.38. Fixed assets were Dh9.1 billion against circulated assets of Dh6.3 billion. Reserve capital was Dh10.3 billion, while investment over the nine months amounted to Dh512 million.

In accordance with Cabinet decision No. 325/28M of 1998, ETISALAT pays 50 per cent of its net profit every year to the Federal Government. Total royalty payments for 2001 and 2002 were Dh4.976 billion, including Dh1.48 billion paid to the Sheikh Zayed Housing Fund (see above).

As a result of ETISALAT's continuing efforts to improve its services, operating telephone lines nationwide increased from 36,000 in 1976 to 1,065,000 by the end of April 2002. In the same period operating exchanges rose from 28 to 262. Today, the UAE has international direct dialling links with 258 countries, compared to just 36 in 1976. The available circuits for direct international calls rose to 48,000 at the end of April 2002, from only 340 in 1976. ETISALAT has over one million fixed line subscribers. In addition, with current GSM users touching 2.3 million (65 per cent penetration), and Internet users totalling almost a million (over 30 per cent penetration), the UAE has the highest number of mobile phone users per capita in the Arab world, and its mobile network is second in size only to Saudi Arabia. This was borne out by a comprehensive report released in October 2002 by the strategic research service Arab Advisers' Group (AAG), which has analysed the dynamics of the mainline and cellular market in 11 Arab countries. AAG has put the UAE on top of the cellular market share index by a wide margin. (This index is calculated by dividing the share of total subscribers in each country by the share of total population of each country. The higher the score the better the development status of the market, penetration wise.)

The UAE was first with a score of 5.38, Bahrain was second with a score of 3.98, followed by Kuwait (3.87), Qatar (2.72), Lebanon (1.88), Morocco (1.52), Jordan (1.46), Oman (1.2) and Saudi Arabia (1.12). Much lower down the scale were Egypt (0.51) and Syria (0.1). As for the Mainline Market Share Index, the UAE also topped the ranks with a score of 2.96. Qatar at (2.54) was in second place, followed by, Bahrain (2.3), Lebanon (2.04), Kuwait (1.95), Saudi Arabia (1.42), Jordan (1.19), Syria (0.98), Egypt (0.93), Oman (0.85) and Morocco (0.35).

According to the analysts the UAE market still has room for growth. Even at a quite high penetration rate the monthly ARPU (average revenue per user) per GSM user in the UAE is an impressive US$54.

The report, which gives a thorough analysis of ETISALAT and its business divisions, shows that GSM revenues contributed 41 per cent of ETISALAT's total revenues in 2000. The report noted its belief that the GSM revenues in the UAE would continue to grow at a much higher rate than fixed service revenues. Projected growth rates for total PSTN (public switched telephone network) revenues from 2001 to 2006 are only 2 per cent. On the other hand, GSM revenues are projected to exceed US$1.5 billion by year-end 2006, constituting more than 62 per cent of the combined GSM and PSTN revenues in the country.

The PSTN market in the UAE is expected to grow at a rate of 5 per cent, to exceed 1.3 million lines in 2006, a penetration rate of 32.5 per cent. The GSM market is projected to grow at a rate of 14 per cent between 2001 and 2006, to reach close to 3.7 million subscribers by 2006. These projections are grounded on the assumption that a second mobile operator would enter the market to compete with ETISALAT in 2003, an assumption that AAG felt was more than likely, given the global trend towards liberalisation, and the UAE's membership of the World Trade Organisation.

It is estimated that ETISALAT's investment in land lines, 3G and Internet will be between Dh3 to Dh7 billion up to 2006. 3-G networks are claimed to be the networks of the future, providing a complete range of fixed line telecommunications services including telephone, fax, Internet and multimedia capabilities through one line.

The advanced General Packet Radio Service (GPRS) was introduced in January 2002 and ETISALAT is planning to set up a UMTS (Universal Mobile Telephone System) network in 2004. This service and the GPRS system will ensure that the UAE is well placed for the introduction of 3-G, if market testing proves satisfactory.

Other sophisticated services to be introduced to the UAE include MMS (Multi Media Messaging Service). This is a revolutionary technique in messaging as it enables users to send and receive messages with moving pictures and sound. ETISALAT is planning further expansion that will push the GSM lines to more than 2.7 million before the end of 2003.

This constant expansion does not mean that ETISALAT is cutting corners on customer care. The company announced at the end of October 2002 that it has completed the first phase of its ISO 9001:2000 certification programme as part of its drive to increase customer satisfaction. ISO 9001:2000 is a globally recognised standard of excellence. Emirates Internet and Multimedia (EIM), ETISALAT's dedicated Internet unit, became the first business unit within ETISALAT to be awarded this certification. ETISALAT's long-term corporate ISO certification programme encompasses all the corporation's departments and business units.

EIM has been awarded the certification in recognition of the tremendous customer service enhancements made by the ISP in 2002. Extra mail and storage capacity packages announced by EIM in October 2002 follow recent improvements to the entire EIM mail service introduced with the relaunch of EIM's online content sites on 5 September 2002. Useability on the site has been transformed by a new page

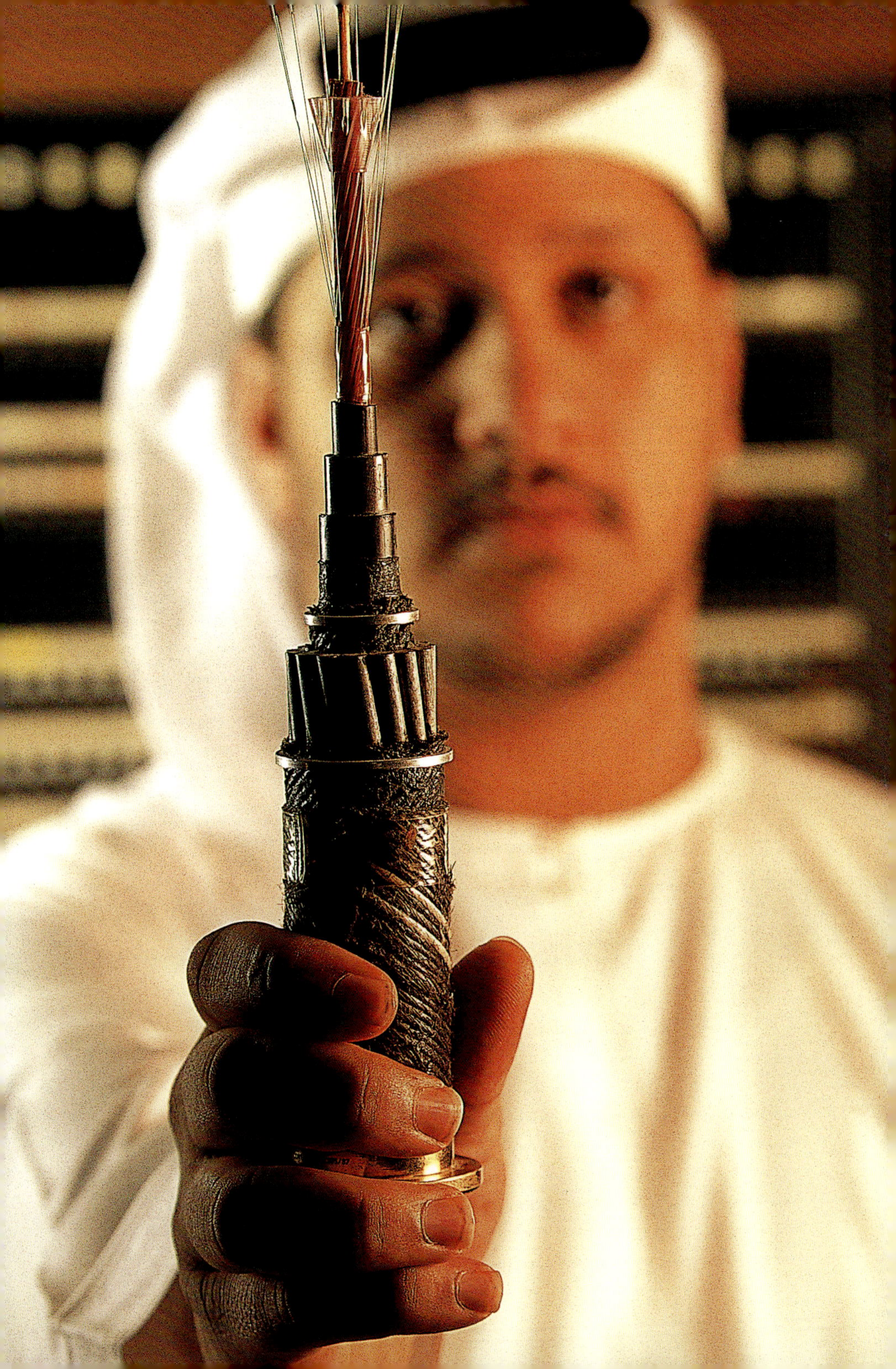

layout that includes fixed navigation icons throughout the site. The company has also introduced an online tutorial to familiarise customers with the new features. This is available on EIM's e-mail service login page (eimmail.ae or webaccess.net.ae).

Figures released by World Paper, a specialised US bulletin, confirm that the Internet infrastructure is well developed in the UAE. The bulletin's global Information Society Index (ISI) for 2001 placed the UAE twenty-eighth among 66 countries surveyed in its index which covers Internet, computer, telephone and other information technology systems. This classification has been confirmed by figures released in October 2002 by the International Telecommunications Corporation that ranked the UAE first among Arab countries in 2001 in terms of Internet penetration rate, with 3,392.39 users per 10,000 inhabitants. Bahrain with 1988.55 users per 10,000 inhabitants was second, followed by Kuwait with 1014.71 users per 10,000 inhabitants. The figures also show that the UAE was at the top of the list of Arab countries in terms of Internet hosts based on 288.53 Internet hosts per 10,000 inhabitants in 2001. (Internet hosts are the number of computers with active Internet Protocol (IP) addresses connected to the Internet.) Bahrain, which ranked second, had a much lower rate of 24.37, with Lebanon in third place with 19.97 hosts. The US has the highest per capita host rate at 3714.01.

ETISALAT, has a highly successful emiratisation policy. Graduates taking up a career in ETISALAT are trained at its own academy before entering the workforce. In ETISALAT Al Ain region, the total number of national employees is 36 per cent, of which 32 per cent are women. All department heads are nationals, while 91 per cent of all senior staff and 31 per cent of junior staff are nationals. Countrywide, the total number of national employees is 38 per cent with the employment of over 1500 nationals in 2000 and 2001, and the company has set a target of 50 per cent emiratisation by the end of 2005.

THURAYA

Key shareholders in the UAE-based Thuraya Satellite Telecommunications Company (Thuraya) which was set up in 1997 include ETISALAT with a 25 per cent shareholding, the Abu Dhabi Investment Co, Arab Corp. for Space Telecommunications, Dubai Investment Co and other Arab investors.

Thuraya entered the satellite telecommunications market in July 2001. At the end of 2002, the service was available in 40 countries and had service provider agreements with more than 60 countries covering an area inhabited by some 3.2 billion people, encompassing the Middle East, North and Central Africa, Europe, Central and South Asia.

Entry to new regional markets, lower cost requirements, higher than forecast revenue per user, the recently launched indoor usage (SATEL) and payphone facilities for remote areas, as well as the world's first international toll-free service to operate over a major satellite network, are all assisting with growth. Thuraya has selected Vertscape's Customer Relationship Management (CRM) solution through the XeRM eBusiness suite to facilitate interactions with service providers and customers. This provides the company with a single web-based interface for quicker communication on a global level.

Thuraya also plans to introduce many more services to enhance the functionality of its handsets, including fixed telephony, fleet management and access to high-speed data. The company is also finalising the software update for its handsets, including the addition of new languages to the menu.

These factors, plus targets of 200,000 subscriber lines in 2003, should help to attain breakeven by 2003. By the end of 2002 the company, which has an equity base of US$500 million, expected sales of handsets to reach 120,000 and working lines to reach about 75,000 to 80,000. Moreover, the launch of the second GEO-Mobile Communications Satellite early in 2003 will widen coverage to include many new markets, especially in Africa. Thuraya launched its first Hughes-built satellite, orbiting 44 degrees east, in October 2000. This second satellite, built by Boeing, will have its orbital location 28.5 degrees east. Thuraya expects revenue from the operations of the two satellites to top US$4 billion over 12 years, yielding a return of between 25 and 28 per cent. The company, which has plans to launch a third Boeing satellite in 2005, eventually aims to provide services to 1.8 million subscribers in the covered countries.

In October 2002, Thuraya paid the first tranche of US$40 million on its debt obligations, which include an Islamic component of US$478 million. The repayment terms required Thuraya to make payouts every six months for a period up to 2005. However, at the time of writing, talks were under way with the creditor financial institutions to restructure the company's remaining debt component.

EMIRATES POST

Emirates Postal Corporation (Emirates Post) celebrated the first anniversary of its launch on 29 May 2002. Previously known as the General Postal Authority, Emirates Post is continuing to improve existing facilities whilst creating innovative high-quality services. Several agreements with similar corporations and postal authorities in countries such as India, Pakistan and the Philippines, and elsewhere in the Middle East are being signed to reduce postal tariffs and offer new and efficient services. Emirates Post has also entered into agreements with international and local companies under which it has been declared the hub for distribution of incoming mail to the Gulf region and the whole of the Middle East.

A new speedy and secure means of transferring money to anywhere in the world through 70 post offices across the UAE was launched in May 2002. Emirates Post's instant money transfer service operates in association with Western Union via a direct link between the post offices in Emirates Post's nationwide systems and Western Union's worldwide network that covers 186 countries and territories across the globe.

May 2002 also saw the launch of 'International Express', a cross-branded product whereby consignors using Emirates Post packaging can utilise DHL's airway bill system and worldwide network linking 120,000 destinations in over 228 countries. Customers using this service are entitled to send a 500-gramme document free anywhere in the world for every five shipments sent through 'International Express' using their Loyalty Card.

The Hybrid Mail Centre, established in conjunction with Abba Electronics LLC, was launched in October 2002. This electronic document centre (EDC) is destined to be a one-stop shop to manage printing, sorting and despatching of documents for private and public sector companies in the region. Services will include the accessing of documents electronically, printing, adding marketing materials where required, enveloping and posting material. The EDC will also encrypt documents to ensure security and distribute via fax, e-mail, SMS or Internet.

New improved versions of previously successful promotions such as Emirates Post's Win-a-Million-Dirhams greeting card launched in 2001 were relaunched in 2002. The 2002 promotion, running from 1 October to 31 December, gave away Dh50,000 in a weekly prize and three grand prizes of Dh200,000, Dh150,000 and Dh10,000.

Other innovative services such as the Al Ramool Automated Sorting Centre and Emirates Post International Transit Hub have attracted the attention of International Postal Corporations like GATS UK and Germany's Deutsche Post.

A surge in profits followed the restructuring of the postal authority. Profits for 2001 were a record Dh97 million, representing a 10 per cent increase over the year 2000. The postal authority is expecting 2002 net profits to exceed Dh100 million with projected revenue of more than Dh245 million, of which Dh222 would come from operations. Dh57 million was allocated for expansion, new projects and completion of ongoing projects.

AIRPORTS AND AVIATION

The UAE has a total of six international airports and, although all are already equipped to a very high standard, most airports are investing heavily in renovation and expansion of their existing facilities. A seventh commercial airport is under construction in Ajman, primarily for business aviation. The aviation industry is also well developed in the UAE with world-class carriers Emirates Airline and Gulf Air, as well as the aircraft leasing company Oasis and aircraft maintenance company GAMCO operating from the UAE.

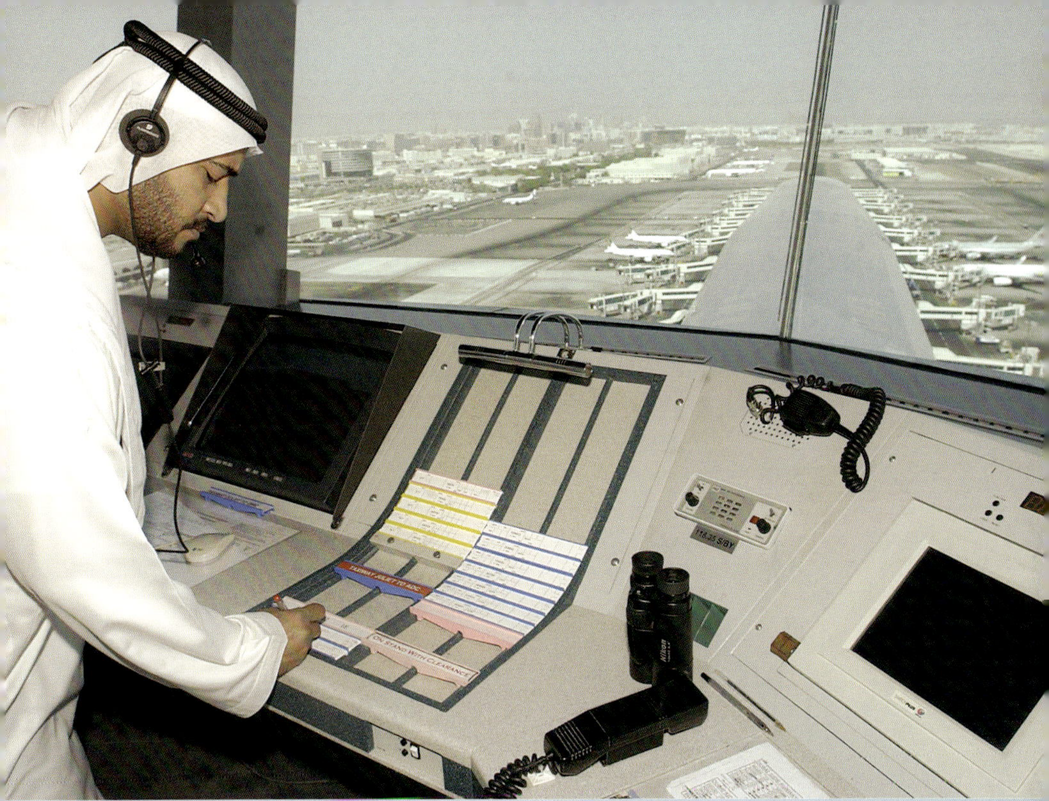
ON STAND WITH CLEARANCE
Nikon

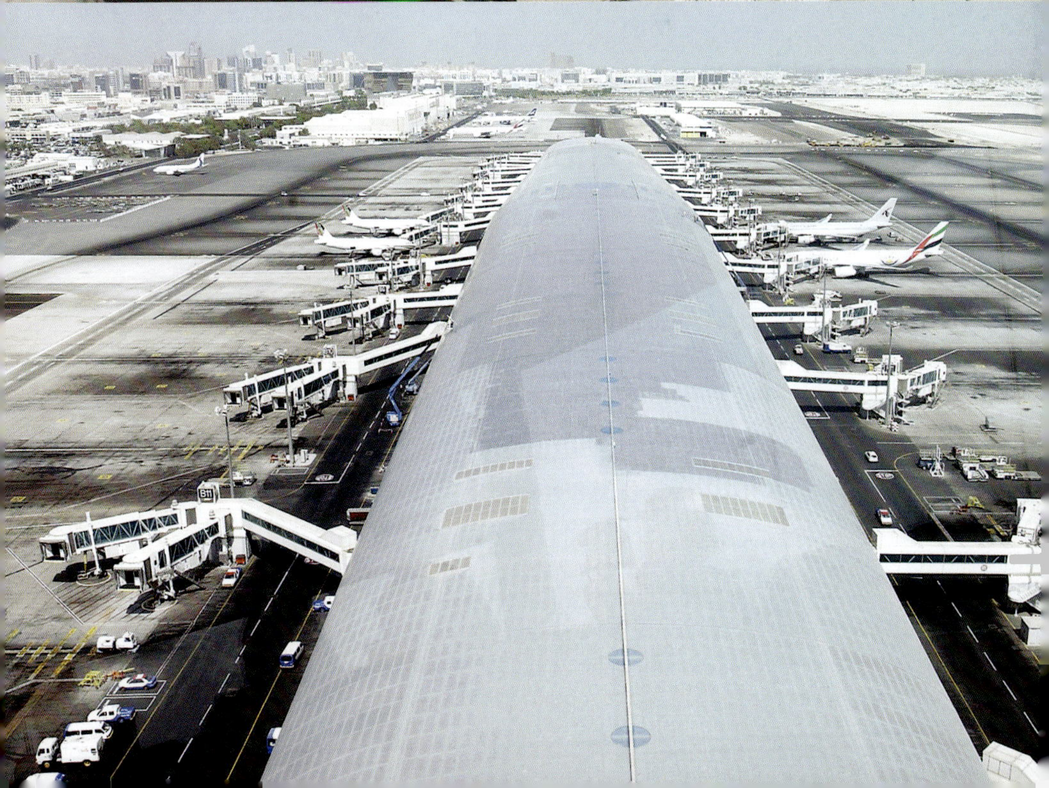

ABU DHABI INTERNATIONAL AIRPORT

Abu Dhabi International Airport (ADIA) is located on the mainland, 35 kilometres east of Abu Dhabi City. Over 40 passenger carriers operate scheduled flights to Abu Dhabi from approximately 90 destinations worldwide. Airport facilities are superb and include an award-winning duty free shop (www.dcaauh.gov.ae/dfs_index.html) a hotel, a golf course 400 metres from the terminal, a gym, VIP lounges, a tourist information centre, car hire, travel agency, hotel reservation, bank, bureau de change, Internet access, and a 24-hour business centre. Aircraft movement at ADIA was up 14 per cent in 2001 to 65,134. The airport handled 3,588,448 passengers and 385,124 tons of cargo.

Work on a new Dh925 million (US$250 million) satellite terminal will start in the first quarter of 2003. Opening is scheduled for the end of 2005 or early 2006. The new terminal will be the airport's second and will increase airport capacity from the current 3.7 million to 7.2 million passengers a year. ADIA is expecting annual growth rates of 12 to 15 per cent in passenger traffic and 15 per cent in cargo throughput.

The terminal will have 7200 square metres dedicated to commercial outlets, 1900 square metres of passenger lounges, and 22,500 square metres of cargo space, enabling a cargo throughput of 350,000 tons per year. It will also have 18 new aircraft stands and will be the first building in the world to have a titanium roof structure. To cope with greater passenger numbers, the airport is planning to install the Middle East's first rapid transit shuttle system to carry passengers between its two terminals.

Other new developments at ADIA include a second 4100-metre runway, five passenger rotundas at the existing terminal, a new 150-room airport hotel with nine-hole grass golf course, and an extension to the existing airport hotel.

Under the new plan Abu Dhabi Duty Free (ADDF), a vital revenue generator for the airport, will host 50 brand name boutiques and 20 specialist shops in an environment designed to recreate a high street shopping experience. For the second consecutive year ADDF won the Frontier Marketing Award for 'Best Marketing Campaign by a Retailer'. The award, widely regarded as the 'Oscar' of the duty free industry, was announced at the eighteenth Tax Free World Exhibition in Cannes in October 2002.

Alongside this massive development plan, Abu Dhabi Department of Civil Aviation (DCA), which is responsible for the running of ADIA as well as Al Ain airport, signed a US$30 million contract with the American company Raytheon in June 2002 for the installation of state-of-the-art air traffic systems at both of its airports. The project is due for completion early in 2004. Air traffic control simulators will also be installed, increasing the local training abilities of the unit.

Safety and efficiency have always been a prime concern of the Department which is working towards application of an integrated management system for all its operations. In 2002 it was awarded the Environment Management Systems Certificate ISO: 14001, a welcome addition to the ISO: 2000-9001 Quality Management Systems Certificate that it was awarded in 2001.

OASIS INTERNATIONAL LEASING COMPANY (AL WAHA)

OASIS INTERNATIONAL LEASING COMPANY (Al Waha) was set up under the UAE Offsets Programme by the UAE Offsets Group (UOG) in May 1997 as a 55:45 joint venture between UAE nationals – who were offered 27.5 million shares priced at Dh10 (US$2.7) each through an initial public offering (IPO) – and founder shareholders. The founders include BAE Systems with a 13.08 per cent stake, Gulf Investment Corporation (GIC) with 2 per cent, ten local institutions with 13 per cent, and 47 private investors with 16.92 per cent.

The company currently owns 15 aircraft leased to nine international airlines and is gearing up to increase its share capital to Dh700 million (US$191 million) from Dh500 million (US$136 million) to fund further expansion in its fleet and operations. Oasis plans to increase its asset and risk profile to Dh5.5 billion (US$1.5 billion) from the current Dh1.7 billion (US$472 million) in the next five years.

The expansion in capital will come in the form of 20 million additional shares through a rights issue, already approved by Abu Dhabi's Executive Council, the company's board of directors and shareholders. The new funds will allow Oasis to make use of opportunities in infrastructure developments and the rising number of power generation and water desalination plants in the UAE.

Recent aircraft leasing deals signed by the company include financing the acquisition of an MD82 aircraft in partnership with Compass Capital Corporation and on lease to Continental Airlines, the purchase and long-term leaseback of two Bombardier CRJ-100ER aircraft to Air Canada, and the acquisition of a new Airbus A321 passenger jet, on lease to Air Canada for ten years.

To diversify its shareholder profile, Oasis changed its articles of association in July 2002 and became only the second company in the UAE – the first is EMAAR Properties of Dubai – to allow non-UAE nationals ownership of shares. Expatriates and overseas institutions can now buy up to 49 per cent of Oasis Leasing shares.

Oasis Leasing also owns a 50 per cent stake in a 172,000 dwt capsize bulk carrier in partnership with the Torvald Klaveness Group of Norway and could pursue further opportunities for investments in shipping, especially in the dry bulk sector. The company is laying the groundwork for diversifying the financial services sector of the Middle East by offering more economical solutions to companies that do not have the capital to buy assets to grow their businesses.

ABU DHABI CARGO VILLAGE

Phase one of a new Cargo Village adjacent to Abu Dhabi International Airport was nearing completion at the end of 2002. With an investment outlay of Dh15 million, the new village will specialise in cargo, storage and re-export operations.

This first phase is capable of handling 200,000 tonnes of freight annually. The new facility is a bonded operation cargo terminal where clients can have their own stores with direct access to both the airside and the landside. The new development has established stores for air cargo over an area of 8700 square metres on the ground floor.

AL AIN INTERNATIONAL AIRPORT

Passenger traffic at Al Ain International Airport (AIA) has been growing at an impressive annual rate of 13 per cent. The airport, which was opened in March 1994, is currently undergoing a US$20.5 million renovation and expansion programme that is scheduled for completion in 2003. The four-phase project includes construction of a large cargo terminal on a site close to the Al Ain–Abu Dhabi Highway, a new dedicated in-flight catering facility, and a new headquarters for ground services equipment. Three new lounges, including a VIP lounge, will be added to the existing terminal to accommodate the growing number of passengers. The existing 450-square metre duty-free shopping complex will also be doubled in size. Completion of the project will increase passenger capacity by 50 per cent.

DUBAI INTERNATIONAL AIRPORT

Almost all the world's leading airlines operate scheduled services to the centrally located Dubai International Airport (DIA). The first-class airport facilities include ATM, bureau de change, bank, post office, medical centre, pharmacy, cafés, restaurants, business and first-class lounges, left-luggage, one of the best duty free shopping areas in the world, tourist information, car hire and Internet access.

The number of passengers using the airport was estimated to be 16 million in 2002, a growth of 18 per cent over the 13.5 million in 2001. This figure is expected to reach 20 million by 2005 and 30 million by 2010. Airport management are continuously seeking new ways to process this high throughput in a fast and efficient manner. For example, in 2002 fast track e-gates, the first in the Middle East, were inaugurated at arrivals and departures. First-time users can acquire the necessary smart cards, which cost Dh150 and are valid for two years, in less than five minutes at the registration offices near the restaurants in the departure area of DIA. An original passport and photographs are required. Fingerprints will be taken at the office. Applications are confined to holders of valid residency visas. The use of the electronic gate is optional and the Naturalisation and Residency Department eventually plans to introduce the system at all entry and exit points in the emirate.

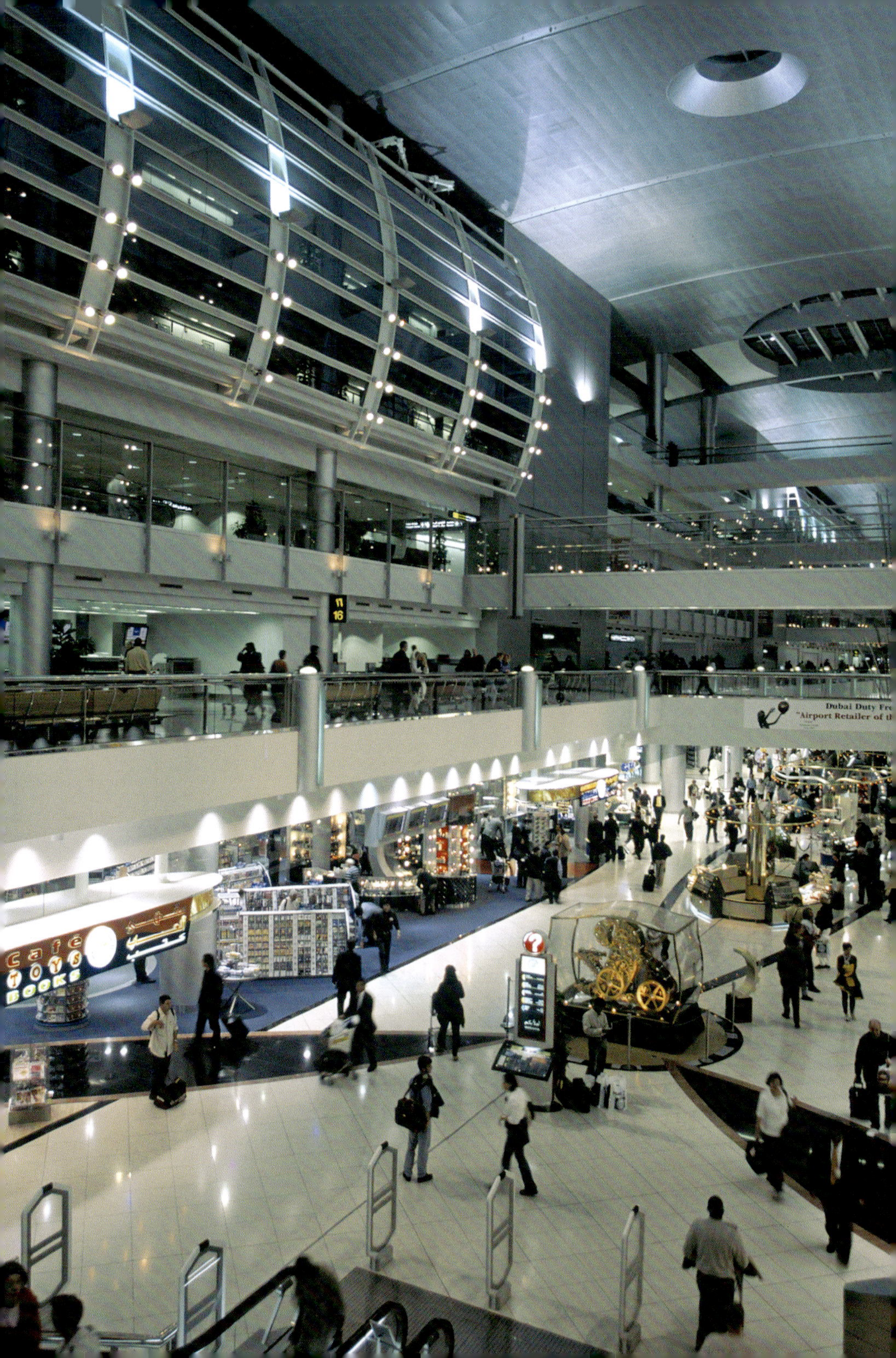
11
16
Cafe
TOYS
BOOKS

Operations based at DIA are benefiting enormously from the increase in passenger numbers: 2002 proved to be an exceptional year for Dubai Duty Free (DDF), with the operation achieving annual sales of Dh1.1 billion, an increase of 23 per cent over the previous year. In addition to its retail success, 2002 was a year of achievements for Dubai Duty Free when it was named by Dubai Quality Awards as the 'Company of the Year – Trade' in the Gold category. It also won the Gulf and Africa Duty Free Award for 'Most Distinctive Retailer of the Year', the Raven Fox Award for 'Middle East Travel Retailer of the Year' and the *Business Traveller* Award for 'Best Duty Free Shopping'.

Executive Flight Services (EFS), a special division of the Dubai Department of Civil Aviation that provides dedicated facilities for private flights, also experienced healthy growth over the ten months to the end of October 2002 and expected 35 per cent growth to the year-end. Total flights handled from January to October 2002 were 1982, compared to 1504 during the same period in 2001. EFS handled 2422 flights in 2002, an increase of 31 per cent over 2001. In the month of October (2002) alone, EFS witnessed an 83 per cent increase in flight movements compared to 2001.

DUBAI CARGO VILLAGE

During the first seven months of 2002, Dubai Cargo Village (DCV) handled over 400,000 tonnes of cargo, including imports, exports and transit, recording a 20 per cent growth over the same period in 2001. July registered the highest ever record in the 11-year history of DCV, showing an increase of 25.50 per cent compared to 2001, with over 65,000 tonnes of cargo handled, including imports, exports and transit. Overall cargo movement at Dubai Airport grew by approximately 24 per cent in 2002 with total freight movement estimated at 784,996.93 tonnes against 632,230.52 tonnes in 2001.

Most cargo airlines and operators at DCV reported a healthy growth in 2002. DNATA Cargo registered a record throughput of 167,076 tonnes in the first half of its financial year from April to September 2002. This represents a 23 per cent increase over the same period in 2001. Exports accounted for 66,945 tonnes, imports for 100,131 tonnes and transit cargo amounted to 12,320 tonnes – a massive 73.4 per cent increase over 2001, caused mainly by a surge in cargo feeder activities from the subcontinent to Dubai for onward connection to Europe and the US. The first phase of Chameleon, a new-generation cargo handling system, was implemented in 2002. DNATA Cargo also completed installation of radio frequency equipment at the airport, and the expansion of the Freezone Logistics Centre (FLC) in the Dubai Airport Free Zone to double its original size. The facility is used by MAS Cargo, UPS and DHL Worldwide Express, amongst others.

NORTHERN EMIRATES

Airport facilities at Sharjah International Airport (SIA), a busy airport located 10 kilometres outside the city centre, include a 24-hour duty free shop, car hire, bar, restaurant, snack bar and bank. SIA reported a 15 per cent rise in passenger traffic in 2001. Scheduled airlines landing at SIA include Gulf Air, Aeroflot, Cathay Pacific, Egypt Air, Pakistan International Airlines, Singapore Airlines and Thai Airways International. Amongst the destinations served are London, Singapore, Frankfurt, Amsterdam, Bombay, Copenhagen, Delhi, Hong Kong, Muscat and Madras.

Sharjah International Airport is building a new terminal to enable it to cope with expansion in passenger traffic over the coming decade. The multi-million dollar project, to be funded internally, is scheduled for completion in 2003. A new arrivals hall will be linked to the existing facility by a bridge.

In recent years Sharjah has emerged as the Middle East's leading cargo airport, and was cited by Europe-based Airports Council International as the top air freight hub in the region for 1999 and 2000. However, cargo throughput fell in 2001 due to difficulties experienced by the freight industry worldwide. Every effort was made to remedy this downturn and the growth rate for the first seven months of 2002 was in the region of 7.2 per cent: 280,306 tons of airfreight were handled against 232, 223 tons for the same period in 2001.

Ra's al-Khaimah International Airport (RIA) is a small but modern and efficient airport whose facilities include a duty free shop, restaurant and snack bar. The main carriers operating through the airport are Gulf Air, Egypt Air, Indian Airlines, Qeshm Air, Centrafrican Airlines and Kuban Air, plus a number of CIS carriers. Destinations served by direct flights are Muscat, Bahrain, Doha, Cairo, Al Ain, Qeshm, Meshad, Uzbekestan, Krasnodar, Calicut, and various destinations in the CIS.

Ra's al-Khaimah Department of Civil Aviation is undertaking renovation and expansion projects costing Dh1.2 million at the airport. These include a new database department, an advanced fire alarm system, new meteorological equipment and improvements to the car park and landscaping.

Fujairah International Airport (FIA), which is served by Gulf Air (flights to Bahrain, Qatar, Muscat), Indian Airlines and Egypt Air, recorded a 54 per cent growth in passenger traffic during the first ten months of 2002 compared to the same period in 2001, with passenger numbers increasing from 34,034 to 52,540. The airport also registered a 6 per cent rise in the quantity of cargo handled from January to September 2002 compared to the same period in 2001: from 25,332 tonnes in 2001 to 26,811 tonnes in 2002. In addition, the airport handled 8593 planes compared with 6869 during the same period in 2001, a 20 per cent rise.

EMIRATES AIRLINE

Profits at Dubai-based Emirates Airline for the first half of its financial year from 1 April to 30 September 2002 were Dh404.2 million, a 140 per cent increase over the same period in 2001. The airline's cash balance for the six months to 30 September also rose to Dh3.9 billion from Dh2.8 billion in 2001. Despite an 18 per cent increase in seat capacity, Emirates raised the load factor to 78 per cent from 74 per cent. Cargo revenues also grew 38 per cent. Emirates posted an operating revenue of Dh4.3

billion, up 27 per cent, from Dh3.4 billion in 2001. In fact, the quarter to end of September 2002 was Emirates most profitable season since it was established in 1985 and Emirates net profits are expected to exceed Dh700 million by the end of the financial year – marking a 15 per cent increase on the previous year's Dh611 million. These impressive results can be viewed against the airline's remarkable achievements in the previous financial year when the aviation industry was plunged into chaos following the terrorist attacks of September 11. Against all odds, Emirates had an 11 per cent increase in its profits from US$115 million to US$127 million for the year ending 31 March 2002. The group revenue increased by 12.9 per cent to US$2.1 billion in the same financial year. Emirates' long-term debt (net of cash) amounted to Dh2.16 billion as of 31 March 2002, an increase of Dh338 million over the corresponding period in the previous year.

Emirates has ambitious aircraft expansion plans that will require financing of around US$5 to US$6 billion. The group announced massive aircraft orders worth US$15 billion at the 2001 Dubai Air Show. Total orders will give Emirates 22 Airbus A380s, 37 Boeing 777s, 6 A340-500s, 8 A340-600s and 29 A330s, with deliveries running to 2010. Given the current fleet and existing orders, Emirates will have 102 of the world's most technologically advanced jetliners by the end of the decade.

Emirates typically financed the acquisition of new aircraft with 15 per cent from internal cash, the remainder being raised externally – around US$3 billion had been raised between 1996 and 2002. As of 31 March 2002, the airline had total borrowings and lease commitments of Dh5.17 billion, up from Dh3.27 billion in the previous financial year. The borrowings for the year included a local currency bond issue of Dh1.5 billion and term loans of Dh40.37 million.

In 2002 Emirates signed a Dh330 million (US$90 million) Islamic financing agreement for an Airbus A330 airliner over a ten-year term. This was the third A330 that Emirates had financed using highly competitive Islamic funding. The aircraft, which was delivered in August 2002, is the twenty-third of the 29 Airbus A330-200s currently on firm order. In 2001, Emirates was awarded the global 'Aircraft Leasing Deal of the Year' Award by *Jane's Transport Finance* for its first-ever Islamic partial aircraft financing facility. Emirates also signed a US$100 million agreement for the financing of the twenty-fourth Airbus A330, using a UK operating lease structure over a ten-year term. The aircraft was delivered in October. This is the third A330 that Emirates has financed using this structure.

Emirates has won over 200 international awards for its service in the 17 years since its launch. Among the important accolades awarded in 2002 was the 'Airline of the Year' award for the second year running from Skytrax Research (UK) following a poll of four million travellers. Emirates' Economy Class was voted number one and the airline was also awarded the 'Best Medium Haul Airline' title for the third year running by readers of the UK's *Business Traveller*. In addition Emirates has been chosen as the 'Airline with the Best Service' in a 2002 survey of readers of two top Middle East travel and business magazines. The airline was also voted 'Favourite Airline for Travel in the Gulf', for 'Travel in the Arab Countries' and for 'Travel to the Far East'.

Emirates launched services to five new destinations in 2002, Casablanca, Khartoum, Perth, Mauritius and Osaka, the latter being the only non-stop flight between the Gulf and Japan. Together, services to these new points will boost the airline's cargo operations with around 250 extra tonnes of capacity in total each week.

With the addition of its new routes, Emirates now flies to 58 destinations in 45 countries in Europe, the Middle East, Africa, the Far East, Asia and Australia. The airline is planning to start operations to New York, Chicago and Los Angeles in 2003, with the delivery of the long-range Airbus A340-500 aircraft.

Emirates expects to double its workforce to more than 35,000 by 2010 as its fleet increases and in the meantime is concentrating on training UAE nationals to take up suitable positions in the company.

GULF AIR

Gulf Air, which is owned by Abu Dhabi, Bahrain and Oman, has a fleet of 32 planes and flies to nearly 50 destinations in the Middle East, Europe, Asia and North Africa. Like many airlines worldwide, the company has been suffering from financial problems that were exacerbated by the post September 11 crisis. However, in July 2002 Gulf Air's new President and Chief Executive, James Hogan, unveiled plans to restructure the company and help it to recover market confidence. Restructuring includes new marketing and sales strategies, the introduction of new divisions, appointment of specialist staff, a reduction in employee numbers and a renewed emphasis on training

Gulf Air has created a Service Division, led by Luke Medley, formerly CEO of Avis in the UK and Australia, and a former Ansett executive. He will be supported by Peter Rowe, who joins as head of Customer Services from his former position in British Midland's Services Division. Gulf Air's new division will focus on improving cost and efficiency in in-flight, catering and other services. The Network Division, headed by Farid Alawi, was set up to optimise schedules, utilisation of aircraft, route profitability and yield management. Alawi will be supported by a team of international airline executives. In addition, the Gulf Air Electronic Frequent Flyer Programme (e-FFP) was launched, allowing the Falcon frequent flyers to monitor their points and rewards online. The company intends to launch an Abu Dhabi-based all-economy airline in June 2003.

Although losses in 2002 amounted to 42 million Bahraini dinars, measures to improve the airline's efficiency and performance have already started to bear fruit, leading to renewed hope that the airline can achieve a successful turnaround in its fortunes and re-establish Gulf Air as a premier world-class carrier in the region.

Gulf Air received an award in 2002 from CFM International (a joint venture company between General Electric and Snecma of France) to mark their ten years of cooperation. CFM56-5A engines power the Gulf Air fleet of ten Airbus A320s that the airline operates on its routes throughout the Middle East. The five Airbus A340s, currently in service on routes to Europe, Africa, the Asia-Pacific region and Australia, are also powered by CFM-56-5C engines. As part of the tenth anniversary celebrations, Gulf Air was also presented with an award for becoming the CFM56-5C fleet leader in terms of engine cycles. To date, CFM engines have achieved 1.2 million flight hours and 600,000 engine cycles on Gulf Air's aircraft fleet.

ABU DHABI AVIATION

Established in March 1976, Abu Dhabi Aviation, the largest commercial helicopter operator in the region, currently has a fleet of 42 aircraft – mostly Bell helicopters. In November 2000 the company moved to a purpose-built facility with 8500 square metres of hangar and workshop floor space at Abu Dhabi International Airport. The bulk of the company's business is in support of Abu Dhabi offshore oil, engineering and construction companies. Abu Dhabi Aviation's specialist skills include such diverse activities as the provision of offshore rescue services and the aerial application of agricultural sprays and fertilisers. The company has expanded its operations in recent years to Oman, Yemen and Saudi Arabia.

Abu Dhabi Aviation announced a net profit of Dh51 million for 2001, down 5.2 per cent from 2000. Shareholders ratified a 30 per cent cash dividend amounting to Dh39 million, proposed by the board at the general meeting of the Abu Dhabi Securities Market (ADSM)-listed company.

The net assets of the company increased to Dh611 million at the end of 2001 from Dh599 million in 2000. Earnings per share (EPS) fell to Dh3.92 in 2001 from Dh4.14 in 2000. Despite a growth in turnover from Dh177 million in 2000 to Dh199 million in 2001, higher operating expenses led to a decrease in operating profits.

In June 2002 Abu Dhabi Aviation was presented with the 'Helicopter Maintenance Centre of Excellence' award by Bell Helicopter, in recognition of its high standards and experience in maintenance and support to ensure safe and consistent operations for over 600,000 hours.

GAMCO

Gulf Aircraft Maintenance Company (GAMCO) was appointed in October 2002 as the Authorised Service Centre for Lockheed Martin Hercules aircraft (military C-130 and civilian L100-30) for more than 16 countries in the Middle East, Africa and Asia. Lockheed Martin's team surveyed the GAMCO facility in November 2001 and subsequently issued a recommendation to appoint GAMCO as the authorised service centre based on its high-quality facilities and trained technical team.

The service centre agreement covers the UAE, Morocco, Algeria, Jordan, Tunisia, Oman, Saudi Arabia, Egypt, Cameroon, Chad, Gabon, Botswana Nigeria, Sri Lanka, Bangladesh and Thailand, among others.

SEAPORTS AND SHIPPING

The UAE has a long history of maritime trade. This is not surprising since the country has over 700 kilometres of coastline, bordering both the Arabian Gulf and the Arabian Sea. Today, it is served by 16 commercial ports (including oil terminals) with a total capacity of over 70 million tons, together with many smaller harbours.

Due to its strategic location, the UAE ranks among the top five locations in the world for ship supplies and bunkering, with the annual turnover in ship supplies amounting to US$300 million.

PORT STATE CONTROL

Vessels from a number of flag of convenience states have been prohibited by decree from trading in UAE waters, unless they hold valid classification certificates issued by the Ministry of Communications. The decree leaves open the possibility for further flag states to be added to the list, with punitive measures for offenders. Port State Control (PSC) is to be set up under UAE Maritime Law in order to allow for the implementation of international conventions to which the UAE is a signatory. This move has led to the possibility of a memorandum of understanding on PSC throughout the GCC region.

The decision was prompted by several cases of marine pollution in recent years caused by the sinking of poorly-maintained ships flying flags of convenience, and will enhance the UAE's ability to crack down on marine pollution in its offshore waters.

MINA ZAYED

The chief shipping ports in Abu Dhabi are Mina (Port) Zayed (which is the main general cargo port located on Abu Dhabi Island) and the oil industry related marine terminals of Jebel Dhanna, Ruwais, Umm al-Nar, Das Island, Zirku, and Mubarraz islands.

With the aid of Emirates Computers, Port Zayed recently completed an upgrade of its entire information infrastructure. The new system will greatly facilitate the efficient working of the port and will also provide shipping agents with the option of instantly following up on their shipments over the Internet, or through the Electronic Data Interchange (EDI) system. The project also involved intensive training of over 200 personnel in various aspects of application, maintenance and database administration.

DUBAI PORTS AUTHORITY

Dubai's main ports are Mina Rashid, close to Dubai City on the south side of the entrance to the Creek, Hamriyah terminal on the north side of the Creek and Jebel Ali, the largest man-made port in the world and home to a highly successful industrial free zone. Dubai's ports are managed by the Dubai Ports Authority (DPA).

Jebel Ali and Mina Rashid handled 4.1 million TEU (twenty feet equivalent units) and 51 million tonnes of general cargo in 2002, with overall tonnage in 2002 recording

ABU DHABI SHIP BUILDING

In 1996 Abu Dhabi Ship Building (ADSB) was set up under the UAE Offsets Programme by the UAE Offsets Group (UOG) as a joint-stock company with a paid-up capital of Dh175.2 million (US$47.7 million). In June 2002 ADSB commissioned new facilities under a US$50 million expansion that has increased the total area of the shipyard to 175,000 square metres from 50,000 square metres at the time of its inception.

The expansion has given ADSB three new ship repair dry berths of 1700 square metres each, a 70-metre quay wall for new ship construction, and outfitting and testing facilities with a total of 320 metres of wet berthing capability. It has also added two 2700-square-metre construction halls serviced by heavy lift overhead cranes – one for building naval vessels and the other for commercial ship construction.

The expansion also saw the commissioning of a new Syncrolift Shiplift comprising two 85-metre shiplift piers, one outfitted for ship repair and the other for berthing and transfer, making ADSB capable of building and repairing vessels of up to 2000 dwt and 85 metres in length.

ADSB is now the only shipyard in the Gulf Cooperation Council (GCC) capable of building naval fighting vessels. It is offering its capability of repairing, refitting, upgrading and building new naval vessels to more regional navies after successfully completing contracts for the UAE, Qatari and Yemeni naval forces. ADSB also undertakes substantial commercial work for ship owners in the oil and gas sector.

The company is now pursuing new building and refit contracts with the Kuwait Navy, which has shown interest in ADSB as a result of the company's services for the UAE Navy. ADSB completed the Dh300 million (US$81.7 million) refit of the UAE Navy's six 45-metre Baniyas Class patrol boats in September 2000, and saved the UAE Government millions of dollars. It is currently upgrading the combat and shipboard systems of the six vessels under a separate contract worth more than Dh184 million (US$50 million).

For the Qatar Navy, ADSB completed repair works on a naval warship and executed a survey for possible refits, which may be carried out in the near future, while for the Yemen Navy it completed the refit of three vessels. Regional navies are increasingly attracted to ADSB due to its ability to complete sophisticated jobs for a lot less than shipyards abroad.

The expertise and lower costs have resulted in the award of more contracts to ADSB from the UAE Navy. They include a Dh110 million (US$30 million) job for the Navy's Ghannatha project, which entails the construction of 12 Amphibious Transport Boats (ATBs) of 23 metres in length to transport combat troops at high speeds, a Dh40 million (US$10.9 million) contract for building three 64-metre landing craft, and a Dh18 million (US$4.9 million) contract for a 42-metre landing craft.

The company is also winning commercial contracts from operators of tugboats, barges and support vessels for the oil and gas industry, with the Abu Dhabi National Oil Company (ADNOC) and its subsidiaries being the biggest customers. Under a US$10 million contract, a 50-metre dredger is being built for a Dubai-based dredging company and more local companies are contemplating using ADSB for their repair, refit and new building programmes to make use of competitive solutions that save costs through shorter delivery schedules when compared with shipyards abroad.

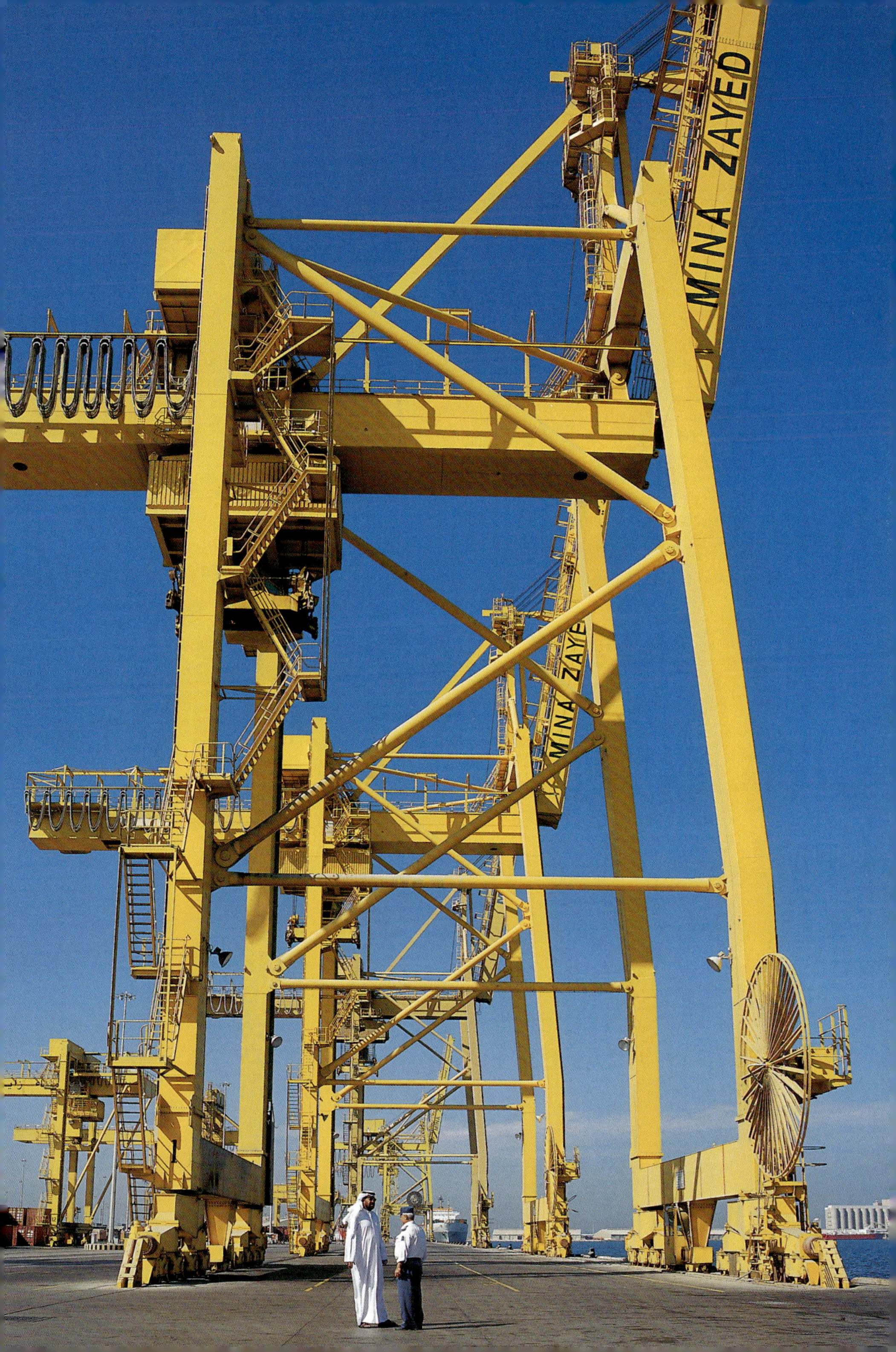
MINA ZAYED
MINA ZAYED

COMBINED CARGO UAE (CCU)

Combined Cargo UAE (CCU) is a joint venture ship investment company set up by the UAE Offsets Group (UOG) in late 1996 with an initial paid-up capital of US$15 million. It owns four bulk carriers and operates a bulker for a Greek shipping firm. The company has aggregate handling capacity of more than 5.2 million tonnes per year (t/y), which is set to increase to 5.5 million t/y in 2003. Its major customers include Aluminium Bahrain (Alba), Saudi Iron and Steel Company (Hadeed), Qatar Vinyl Company (QVC) and Qatar Steel Company (Qasco).

The shareholders in CCU are Abu Dhabi Investment Company (ADIC) (25 per cent), General Investments FZE -(25 per cent), Oman and Emirates Investment Holding Company (OEIHC) (26 per cent), and the Torvald Klaveness group of Norway (24 per cent). Klaveness is also responsible for managing the company's operations and the choice of an experienced partner has minimised the risk of failure and enabled CCU to avoid the pitfalls often experienced by new ventures.

Transportation of aluminium is set to become a major business for CCU. Bahrain-based Alba is to undergo a US$1000 million expansion to increase capacity by 50 per cent to 750,000 tonnes from 500,000 tonnes at present, while Dubai Aluminium (DUBAL) is planning a similar expansion programme, and CCU sees its business growing alongside the expansion of the two aluminium manufacturers' facilities. Aggregates (crushed rocks) are shipped from Fujairah and limestone from Ra's al-Khaimah to customers in Kuwait, while aggregate (pure gabbro) is transported to readymix suppliers in Qatar.

To raise capital for future expansion and growth plans, during 2003 CCU is to launch a US$120 million 'Catalyst Capital Fund.' The maritime opportunity private equity fund will seek US$50 million from regional investors and raise US$70 million of debt from leading maritime banks. It will focus on creating shipping deal flow in Abu Dhabi, mainly through the purchase and sale of second hand and new panamax and capsize vessels. The fund will also invest in long-term lease and new building contracts and place vessels on long-term contracts to major regional and international ship owners.

a 10 per cent increase over the previous year, DPA had registered a 14 per cent growth in 2001 over its performance in 2000. Surprisingly, during the first six months of 2002, the growth rate remained steady despite the events of 11 September 2001. The rapidly developing domestic market and the importance of land cargo have continued to play an important role in DPA's success.

DPA has recently made a number of infrastructure and equipment investments in order to effectively handle the growth of throughput and as part of ongoing customer service. The 'smart rail' system in Jebel Ali container terminal provides RTQs with computerised co-ordinates prior to moving on to their next destination in the container yard which stores approximately 70,000 containers in large stacks. The Spread Spectrum Network has also been installed to improve data communication between the terminal system and equipment. Meanwhile, the Authority has completed the development of pontoons as berthing platforms at Jebel Ali container terminal. These now service the new generation of 6000 TEU vessels that are calling at the port.

Dubai is ranked amongst the leading container ports in the world and was voted the 'Best Seaport in the Middle East' for the eighth consecutive year and 'Best Container Terminal' Operator in the region.

DUBAI DRY DOCKS

Dubai Drydocks provides a ship repair service in compliance with the highest standards of quality and reliability at internationally competitive prices. The company has achieved ISO 9002 Quality Management accreditation for its entire operations. The shipyard dry docks and repairs over 200 vessels per year, including around 50 ULCCs / VLCCs, representing a significant percentage of the total number of these large vessels annually available for dry-docking worldwide. The aggregate deadweight of all ships handled in a single year amounts to over 23 million tonnes. Ship repair business is obtained from throughout the world and Dubai Drydocks is represented by exclusive agents in 28 countries.

The labour force employed at Dubai Drydocks has risen from 300 to over 3500 during its 18 years of operation, giving an indication of the company's growth rate since its inauguration in 1983. Unfortunately, there was an accident at the docks in March 2002 when 29 workers were drowned as the dock gates ruptured and a 12-metre-high wave crashed in, submerging several large vessels under repair.

NORTHERN EMIRATES

Container throughput at Sharjah's twin ports of Khor Fakkan (on the East Coast) and Mina Khalid (on the Arabian Gulf) continued to grow during the first half of 2002 over the comparable period in 2001. Khor Fakkan container terminal experienced a 19 per cent increase over the 513,379 TEU recorded in the first half of 2001, with Mina Khalid also witnessing an 11 per cent rise to over 53,905 TEU in 2001. Most of the extra volume was generated by the ports' existing shipping line clients, underlining the growing importance of the emirate's rapidly developing industrial base.

Sharjah Port Services, a new entity set up under the umbrella of Sharjah Port Authority in 2002, will manage general cargo handling operations at Hamriyah (in Sharjah), Sharjah Creek, and Mina Khalid. Bangkok listed company Thoresen Thai Agencies, holding firm of the Thoresen Group, has a 49 per cent stake in the new entity. From 1 May 2002, the 51:49 joint venture has a 15-year mandate to run stevedoring, cargo handling, storage, cargo delivery, marketing and accounting for general cargo, ro-ro and reefer operations at the three ports.

An estimated 500-strong staff man general cargo operations at the ports which together handle almost one million tonnes annually. Gulftainer Ltd, meanwhile, operates container handling at Mina Khalid and Khor Fakkan on behalf of Sharjah Ports and Customs.

The ambitious inner harbour project at Hamriyah Port adjoining Sharjah's Hamriyah Free Zone was officially launched in February 2002. The project, spread across three phases, will entail a Dh75 million investment in the first phase, which will see the construction of 3.1 kilometres of wharfage across 350 metres, with a draft depth of 7 metres. The complex will include a drydocking facility capable of servicing small- and medium-sized vessels. While the deepwater Hamriyah Port with its 14-metre-draft depth will, in time, double the number of berths to six, the primary thrust in Sharjah will now be towards catering to the needs of small and medium vessels.

Gulftainer starts work on a new Dh30 million inland container park in January 2003, with completion scheduled for June. Strategically located near the University City complex, the 150,000-square-metre site will be capable of holding up to 18,000 TEU, and should be capable of meeting Sharjah's projected demand for the next ten years.

The multi-purpose nature of the facility and the fact that dredging has increased depth from 12.5 to 15 metres have contributed greatly to the success of Fujairah Port which is an important eastern gateway to the UAE. In 2001 the port experienced an almost 100 per cent increase in general cargo to over 400,000 tonnes, a 10 per cent increase in bulk cargo to over 4.25 million tonnes, and a 61 per cent jump in bunkering activity to over 11.5 million tonnes. The Fujairah anchorage, managed by the port, remained in constant demand and continued to sustain a fleet of some 70 supply boats.

A further 600 metres of main berth is being completed to give 1.4 kilometres of continuous straight quay. The port is also completing its major expansion project at the container handling zone aiming to increase its capacity from 700,000 to 1 million containers per year. The port has a special floating quay which is used to supply oil produced by the Fujairah oil refinery to vessels berthing at the port itself or offshore. This quay will be able to supply more than 90,000 bpd to be produced by the refinery.

The port facilities also include two onshore sludge treatment facilities, each with an annual capacity of 10,000 tonnes, offshore and onshore garbage collecting facilities, eight self-propelled slop barges and two slop storage tanker facilities with a total dead weight of 230,000 tonnes.

The Port of Ajman, which had a depth of 5 metres when it was first built, has been dredged to 8 metres. Plans are under way to deepen the port to 10.5 metres, enabling visits by 40,000-50,000 dwt ships of length up to 175 metres. Since 2001 Ajman Port has been managed by Emirates Port Services (EPS) on a ten-year contract. EPS is a joint venture between Emirates Trading Agency (ETA) and the Ra's al-Khaimah-based Union Group.

Umm al-Qaiwain is well-served by Ahmed bin Rashid Port and Ra's al-Khaimah by Port Saqr. The latter is located in the Khor Khuwair industrial area 25 kilometres north of Ra's al-Khaimah City. Cement, marble and gravel from the nearby quarries and factories are shipped from the port.

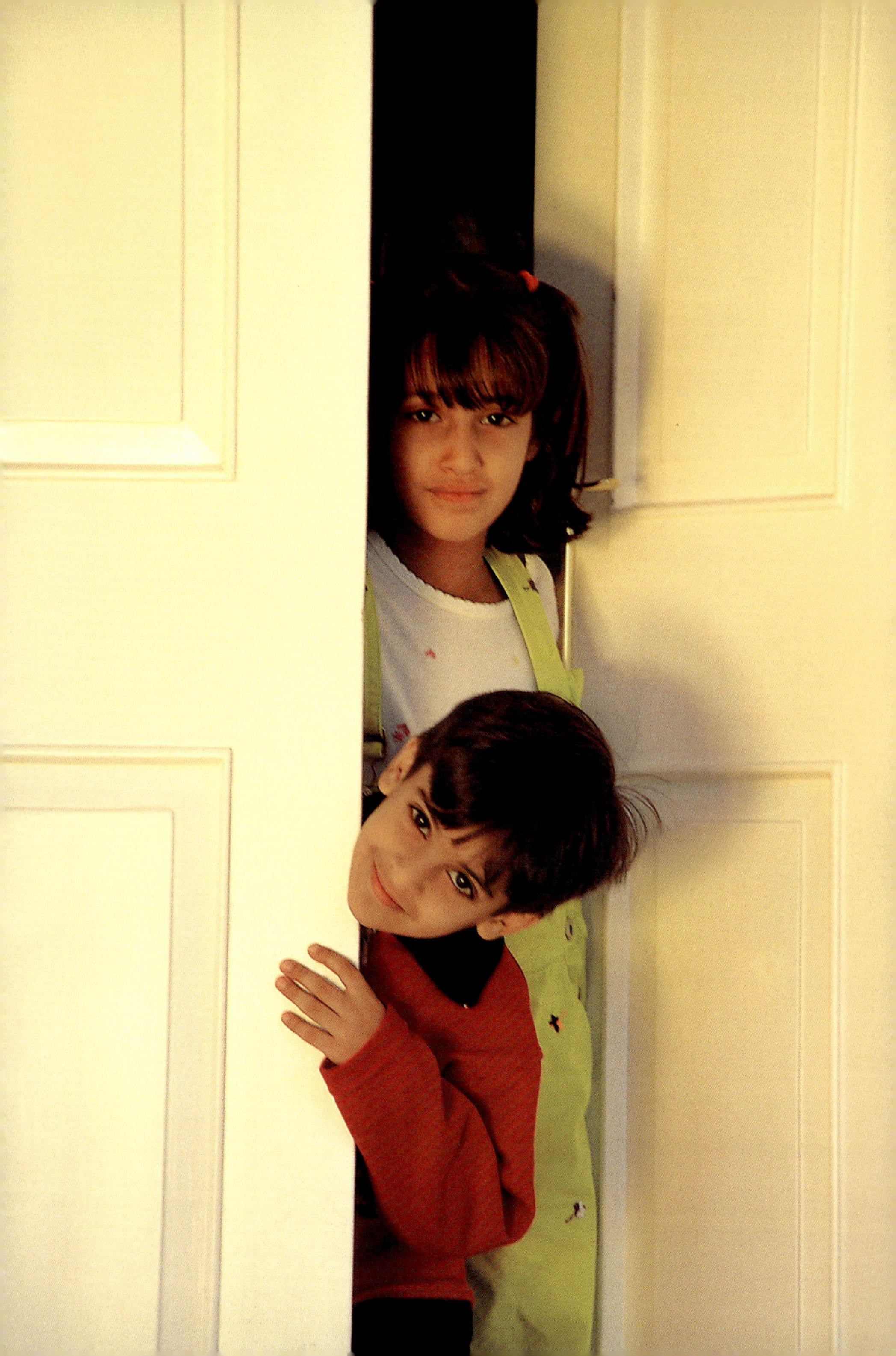

SOCIAL DEVELOPMENT

IN THE MORE THAN 30 YEARS OF ITS EXISTENCE, the UAE has undergone profound social, demographic and environmental change. Revenue from oil, allied to a strong vision for the country's future, has allowed for the swift creation of a country rich in education, medical expertise, housing and infrastructure.

POPULATION

Because of the nature of that oil-driven economy, the UAE has experienced a rapid and unprecedented change in the size and structure of its population. Between 1965 and 1995 it increased fifteenfold and was estimated to be 3.48 million at the end of 2001, with expatriates and their dependents accounting for a substantial percentage of its inhabitants. The Ministry of Planning forecast that this figure would rise to 3.75 million at the end of 2002, an increase of around 7.6 per cent. A noteworthy feature of the population in 2001 was its age structure. The 25–29 year age group was the largest, at around 481,000, followed by the 30–34 year age group at 456,800 and the 35–39 year age group at 426,000. Those in the 10–19 year age group, at 504,578, comprised around 15 per cent of the entire population, a figure which underlines the necessity for job creation through continued economic growth. Those under the age of 50 accounted for 95 per cent of the total population. In the age groups between 20 and 49 years, males accounted for nearly three times the number of females.

With the UAE's low incidence of infant mortality and a life expectancy rate similar to that of other developed countries, further population increase looks inevitable. However, according to *Dubai's Statistical Yearbook 2000*, the rate of that increase may be slowing down. A survey carried out on 4760 national married women, widows and divorcees in the urban and rural areas of Dubai revealed a fertility rate of 4.04 births per national woman, but that rate had fallen by 0.16 compared to the census figures of 1993. It also showed that the fertility rate among illiterate women was more than twice that of women graduates.

Another possible tool in tempering of the speed of population increase is the UAE's policy of emiratisation as the country actively seeks both to reduce its reliance on foreign workers and to preserve its own cultural and religious ethos. The desire to provide a skilled workforce from within its own national population has powered a tremendous expansion in the provision of higher education, with Higher Colleges of Technology accounting for a major part of that growth.

Despite the rapid growth in its population, the UAE retains one of the highest per capita incomes in the world, standing at around Dh19,000 in 2001.

SOCIAL SERVICES

The UAE has, from the outset, been determined that all its citizens should share in the wealth of the country. The sustained effort to ensure essential services to all citizens has placed the UAE at the forefront of Arab countries in terms of its social services. In a trebling of expenditure since 1990, social services expenditure for 2002 is expected to reach US$15 billion. In 2000, the value of social services amounted to one fifth of the UAE's gross domestic product (GDP). Expenditure covers housing, health, education and social aid for nationals besides private investments in schools, medical centres, social programmes and other facilities.

SOCIAL BENEFITS

Despite the broad distribution of wealth that has taken place in the seven emirates, there are those who, for a variety of reasons, remain at risk. The UAE welfare system exists to assist those burdened by intractable problems and to help the vulnerable to realise their full potential as productive members of society. The system is currently administered by the Ministry of Labour and Social Affairs, but the Cabinet has recently given its approval for the establishment of a new authority for development and social welfare.

In July 1999, the Federal National Council approved new legislation regulating social security benefits. Under the law, those entitled to monthly social benefits include national widows and divorced women, the disabled and the handicapped, the aged, orphans, single daughters, married students, relatives of jailed dependants, estranged wives and insolvents. Also eligible for social security benefits are widowed and divorced national women previously married to foreigners.

The amount spent on social assistance has increased steadily since 1994, the total amount allocated during that period being Dh6.27 billion. In 2002, 78, 663 beneficiaries received a total of Dh656 million allocated as follows: Dh174.4 million for beneficiaries in Abu Dhabi, Dh140.6 million for Sharjah, Dh60.177 million for Fujairah, Dh18.5 million for Umm al-Qaiwain, Dh133,600 for Dubai, Dh105 million for Ra's al-Khaimah and Dh33.5 million for recipients in Ajman. An increase in the number of social assistance recipients in 2002 is a result of the broadening of categories under the new law.

The Ministry also attributed a total of Dh2.28 million among nationals whose properties were affected by natural disasters, including Dh174,000 in the form of emergency relief received by 58 beneficiaries in Ra's al-Khaimah and Fujairah because of the losses caused by earthquake in addition to giving Dh273, 000 to 47 beneficiaries

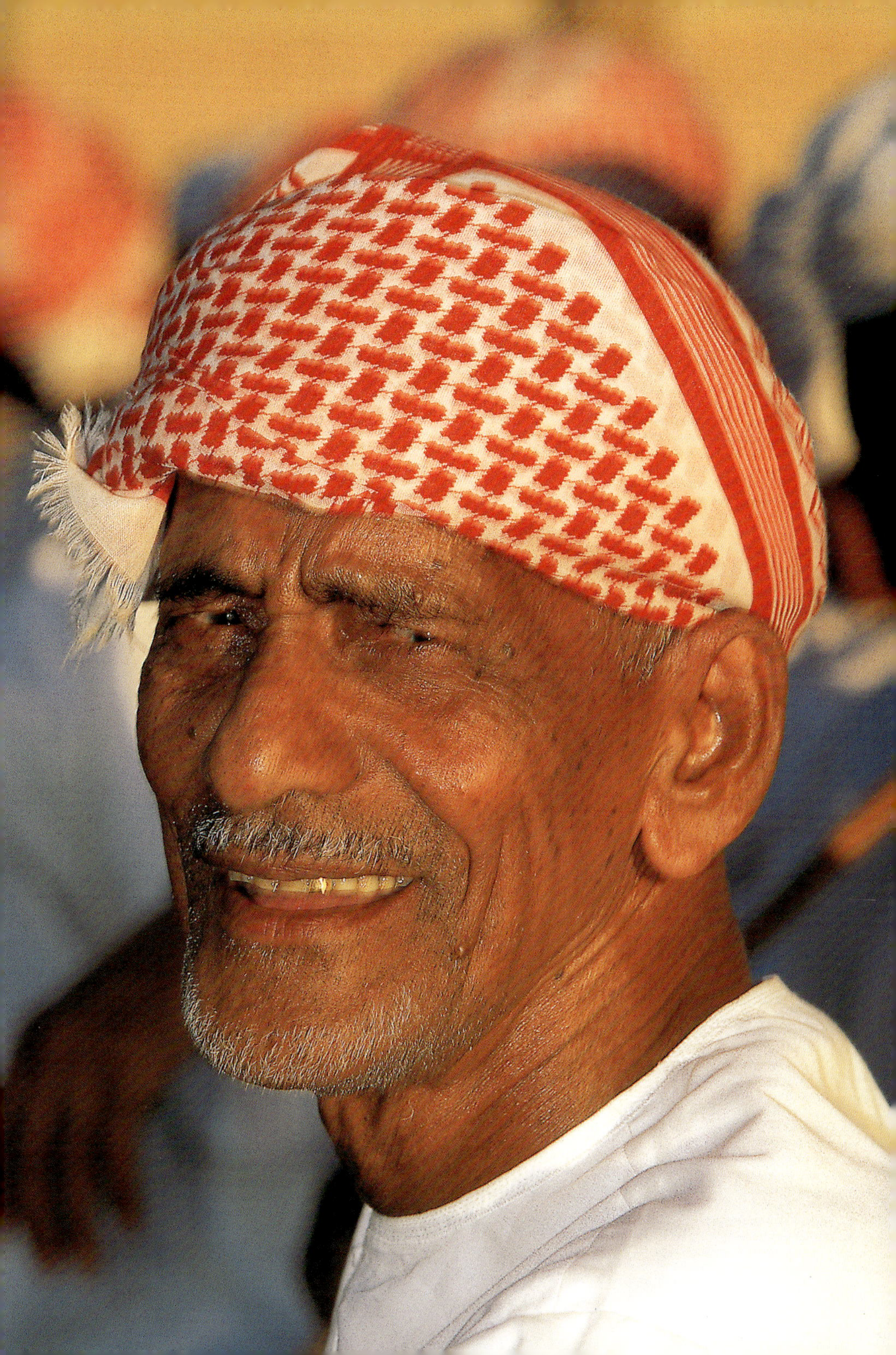

in Fujairah whose properties were destroyed by the collapse of a sand block, besides Dh1.3 million compensation to citizens whose houses and boats were burned.

SOCIAL WELFARE ASSOCIATIONS

Social welfare associations, of which there are more than 100, receive substantial financial aid from the Government. According to the Statistical Abstract of Social Affairs released in late 2002, this amounted, in 2000, to more than Dh6.3 million, of which the greatest amount, Dh2.1 million, was allocated to folk societies. Women's organisations received Dh1.235 million, professional bodies Dh1.010 million, theatre groups Dh810,000, humanitarian associations Dh570,000, cultural bodies Dh540,000 and religious bodies Dh570,000. By the end of the year 2000, the number of social welfare associations had reached 107 with 89 branches and 18,829 working members and 12,849 associate members. The ministry does not grant aid to the 17 licensed expatriate community societies (which include socio-cultural organisations and women's groups representing the many different nationalities present in the UAE).

The Red Crescent Society (RCS)

The RCS, recently set up as an independent authority, is renowned for its international activities (see section on Overseas Aid in the chapter on Government and Foreign Affairs). It is also a major provider of humanitarian relief within the UAE. Its operations (which are diverse) are typical of the tasks carried out by many of the associations and organisations working in the country. In 2002, for instance, it distributed relief in both cash and kind to 400 families in Qurrayah village in Fujairah as part of its annual charity campaign to help low-income sectors of the community. In the same year, it opened a publishing house in Abu Dhabi to produce Braille books for the blind, and established a computer workshop to give blind people access to the latest technical developments. It undertakes other tasks for those in need and cooperates with local authorities in rural areas.

The Al Ihsan Charity Centre

The Al Ihsan Charity Centre, which opened three years ago to assist families in Dubai and the Northern Emirates, has completed a new medical facility that will offer free treatment to disadvantaged patients from all over the country. A team of doctors from the public and private sectors will operate a rotational system, and an ambulance will also be available. Plans are in train to build a hospital and school for the centre.

SOCIAL DEVELOPMENT CENTRES

As the result of an agreement between the Ministry of Labour and Social Affairs and the United Nations Development Programme (UNDP) in 1978, 12 social development centres were set up in various areas of the UAE, including four in Sharjah and the Eastern Region. The centres are under the control of the Department of Social Development Centres (established in 1990). Their main focus has been on improving living conditions for disadvantaged families by encouraging small income-generating projects, upgrading educational and recreational services for youngsters and enhancing women and childcare programmes. As well as running special awareness programmes which help children to absorb sound values and attitudes, the centres also provide families with seminars, lectures and films on health and social issues.

THE ELDERLY

A study published by the Zayed Centre for Coordination and Follow-up (ZCCF) notes that caring for the elderly is one of the new activities the state has found it necessary to undertake. Traditionally, the elderly have been looked after by their own families, but rapid social and economic changes have compelled state intervention in order to meet their needs. Not only are more women, upon whom the task of looking after the elderly would normally fall, entering the workforce, but, because of greatly improved healthcare, people are living longer. It was estimated, in a proposal for the setting up of day care centres for the elderly, that the number of aged citizens will reach 83,000 in 2005, increasing to 150,000 in 2015. To provide for these elderly people and their families, day care centres are to be built throughout the country. Such facilities, along with mobile service units and social and cultural centres, will allow the elderly to remain within the family. A national committee has been charged with integrating appropriate policies for the elderly into the national development strategy.

DISABILITY

The disabled are given specific protection under Article 16 of the UAE Constitution, and, as the Arab Decade for the Disabled (2003–2013) is about to begin, the Ministry of Labour and Social Affairs has revealed the draft of a major new law further safeguarding their rights and increasing their benefits. A new identity card for the disabled will open up many facilities and free services to the holder. Card holders will be entitled to a variety of benefits, including 50 per cent reductions on air and land tickets for themselves and their companions. Five per cent of public transport vehicles are to be modified to accommodate the disabled, and the disabled are to be exempted from all service charges. National authorities must set aside 2 per cent of their budgets to provide new or renovate existing housing for the disabled. Disability cannot be a criterion to deny an applicant a job. Private sector companies with not less than 50 workers must allocate at least 2 per cent of their jobs for the disabled. Failure to do so will (unless no disabled were available for employment) give rise to penalties which offending companies must pay into a central fund for the disabled. Employers employing more than the 2 per cent quota will be rewarded by the Government. The public sector will also be required to allocate 2 per cent of available jobs to the disabled. The law lays out educational rights for the disabled. Finally, 15 per cent of funds raised by private charities will go to the disabled.

The opening of a centre for autistic children in Sharjah during February doubled the numbers of such centres in the UAE. A new Sharjah Autism Centre is planned within the next two years.

ORPHANS

A non-profit, semi-government body offering comprehensive care to orphans, both national and expatriate, is to be set up in Sharjah. The first of its kind, the Social Empowerment Foundation will provide social, psychological, health and financial assistance to orphans living in Sharjah. It is to be run, not as an orphanage but as a support system which will help those in its care to achieve their potential. The facility will be affiliated to the Sharjah City For Humanitarian Services. Although a location for the Foundation has still to be found, it has already begun to operate through the women's committee of the Sharjah Charity International.

EDUCATION

The UAE sees quality education as the main tool for human development. It therefore provides free education to its citizens at all levels of the system. In the academic year 2001–2002, approximately 322,250 students were being educated in 747 government schools, and a further 234,250 in 426 private schools. A further 3784 students attended the 18 centres administered by the General Women's Union (GWU). By comparison, in 1971, the year the UAE Federation was established, there were 74 schools with 32,800 students. The vibrancy of the UAE's education sector is reflected in the record numbers of students who enrolled for higher education courses at the beginning of the 2002–03 academic year. The 11,108 new entrants represented a 5 per cent increase in numbers over the previous year. The expansion in education has been fuelled by enormous investment – around Dh5.4 billion was allocated to education for 2001 alone. It has also been fuelled by the rising expectations of the UAE inhabitants. Women, in particular, are filling university and college places in record numbers, new entrants to the HCTs for the 2002–03 academic year standing at 3768 compared to the figure of 2733 for their male counterparts.

EDUCATION 2020 STRATEGY

Education 2020 Strategy is a series of five-year plans, designed to introduce advanced education techniques and improve innovative skills and the self-learning abilities of students. A Planning, Development and Evaluation Office devises the plans and uses model schools to implement them. The National Centre for the Development of Curriculum and Methodology reviews curricula and developments in educational methodology. All developments take place within the Strategy's framework.

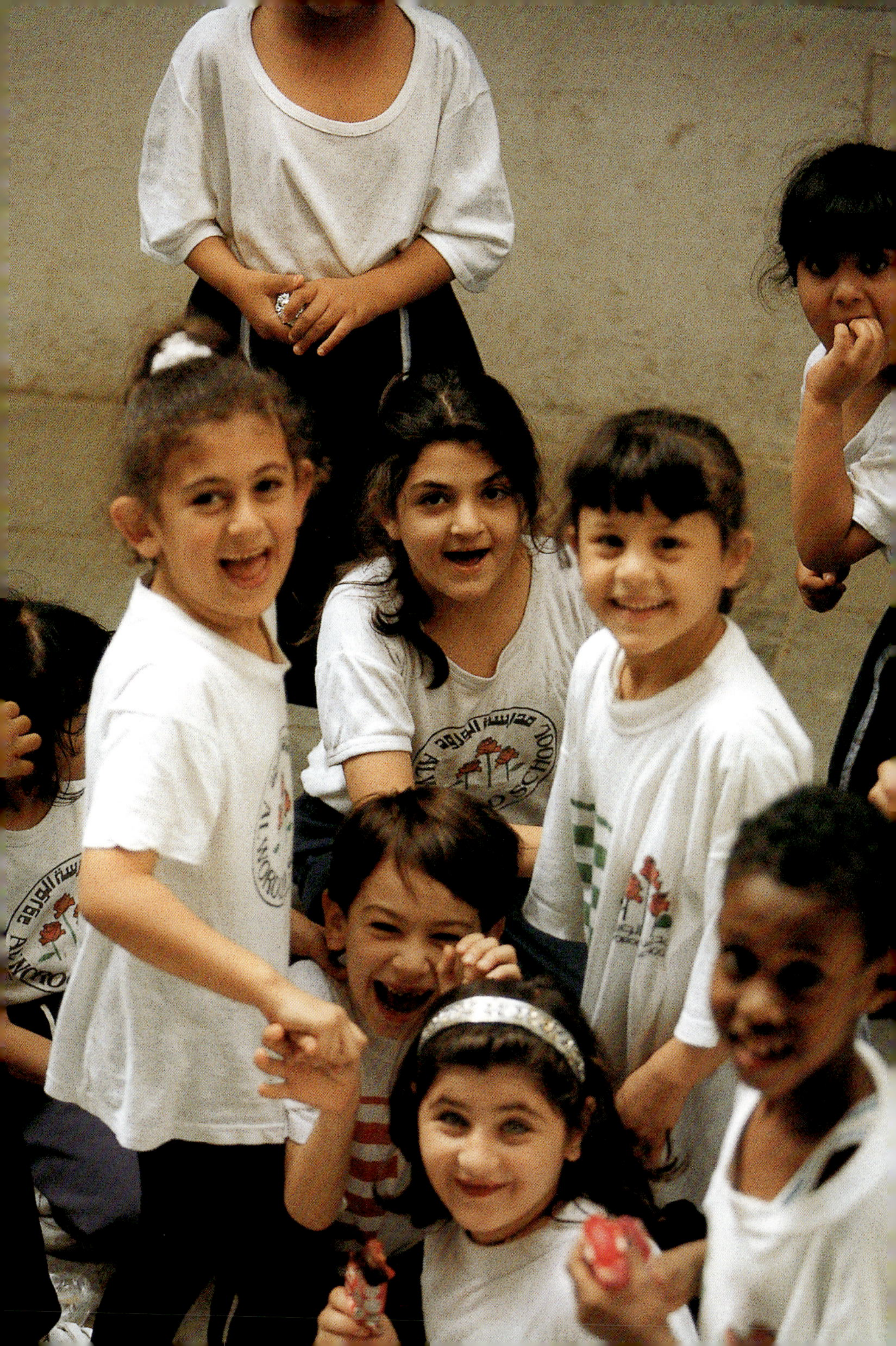
SCHOOL

SCHOOLS

Recognising the crucial importance of keeping abreast with the Information Age, the UAE places great emphasis on Information Technology (IT) literacy at all levels of education, from kindergarten upwards. It is highly innovative in its approach, moving with ease between teaching information technology as a subject and using the technology as a tool of learning and the dissemination of information. The student/computer ratio is 10:1 in kindergarten, 5:1 in primary school, 2:1 in preparatory school and 1:1 in secondary school. Education authorities are switching from textbooks to compact discs – a move which will lighten the physical load for schoolchildren. The move is part of a strategy aimed at upgrading the school curriculum and those who teach it. A teachers' guide to effective presentation of material is also to be put on disc, and this, along with a series of training courses, will provide a complementary upgrading of teacher skills. A questionnaire incorporated into each schoolbook will seek feedback from teachers on the revised curriculum. Another move, which will also lighten the load for children (though not likely to be so popular), is the decision to ban the use of mobile phones by both pupils and teachers in all UAE schools.

Even less popular with schoolchildren will be the reduction in the summer holiday to two months and an increase in study days to a total of ten months currently under consideration by the Ministry of Education and Youth (MoEY).

Primary and secondary education is provided for UAE citizens in a four-stage process and is compulsory at the primary level. The four stages are: kindergarten (ages 4–5); primary (ages 6–12); preparatory (ages 12–15); secondary (ages 15–18). Technical secondary (ages 12–18) provides an alternative to the preparatory and secondary route. Law No. 185/1, 2001, provides special streams whereby gifted students can complete their education in a shorter timeframe. It is planned to change the number of grades at primary and elementary level, reducing those at primary level from six to five and increasing elementary grades from three to four.

Existing student/staff ratios at 17:1 for kindergarten and primary levels and 10:1 for intermediate and secondary levels are well within the government target of 20:1 at kindergarten and primary level and 15:1 at secondary level. In a move to combat teacher shortages in subjects such as English, and Computers and Physics, 1400 new teachers, 691 of whom were UAE nationals, were appointed for the 2002–03 academic year. The move formed part of a five-year plan to create a supply of qualified UAE national teachers sufficient to fill vacant positions.

The MoEY intends to devolve some of its authority to the nine educational zones in line with its decentralisation policy. Under the proposed Act of Authorisation, schools, both public and private, will report directly to their own educational zones. The Act gives wide powers to the individual zones, including the right to prepare their own budgets and those of the schools under their control. They will, additionally, control the issuing of licences to private institutions. The zones will be

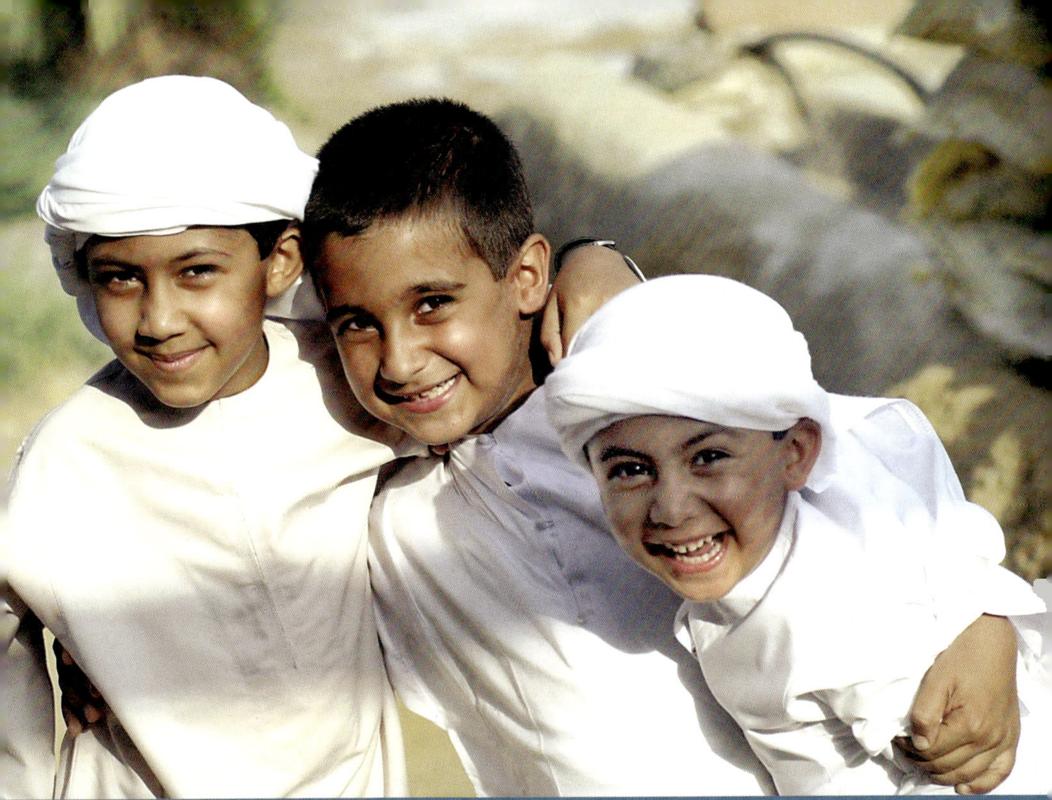
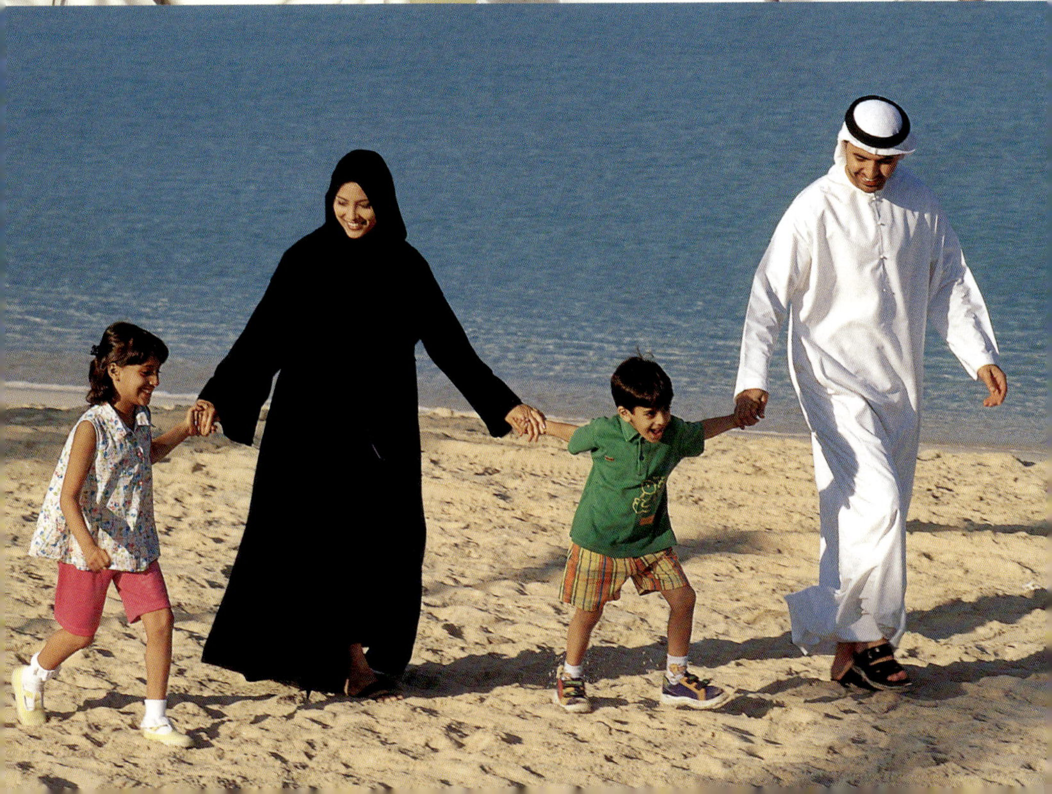

authorised to oversee the running of schools, assessing requirements in terms of expansion or replacement, monitoring feedback from the curriculum, and organising training courses. Sport and health programmes are to be drawn up by the zones, while cultural and technical activities will also come under their remit. The Act will give zones the right to implement new admission criteria for nurseries and to suggest specific numbers of nurseries for each emirate.

In 2001, new by-laws covering private education were introduced to implement Federal Law No. 28 of 1999. The by-laws give priority in appointment of teachers and administrative staff in private schools to UAE nationals, as well as to Arabs and expatriates living in the country. Schools are required to segregate boys and girls from class five onwards, with exemption for non-Arab schools where the majority of students are non-Muslims, provided that they obtain permission from the Cabinet. Student numbers in kindergarten should not exceed 25, while those in higher classes should not exceed 30. All private schools must teach Islamic studies, Arabic language and social studies as compulsory subjects in accordance with the approved syllabus of the MoEY. Non-Arab students are to study Arabic according to the Ministry's special syllabus for non-Arabs. Schools may offer their own social studies course according to the curriculum they follow.

Decree No. 4443 for 2001 is a detailed guide for equating the high school diplomas issued by private schools in the UAE with the Ministry's own secondary school certificate.

In 2002, the MoEY introduced a regulatory manual for private education institutes and training centres. The manual contains details of the rights and duties of employees and employers and specifies the fines for violations. The MoEY has also, as part of its 2020 Strategy, finalised a code of conduct for students in private institutions.

LEARNING FOR FUN

Opening up the avenues of creativity and adventure in education is vital to the encouragement of intellectual exploration. Dubai Municipality's new Dh77 million Children's City offers exciting stimulation for young minds. Lauded as the world's fifth largest infotainment centre, the city boasts a bewildering array of facilities, from a state-of-the-art planetarium, educational facilities and exhibition sites for the applied sciences like telecommunications to exhibitions on the country's cultural, historic and literary treasures. The three-storied futuristic structure will be the venue for year-round educational programmes and workshops.

The Sheikh Mohammed bin Rashid IT Education project was launched in 2000 with the long-term aim of equipping all public secondary schools with computer laboratories, each laboratory to be identical in both design and function. This summer, the project set up an e-Zone at the Modhesh Fun City (one of the most popular attractions of Dubai Summer Surprises) which attracted large numbers of children and parents. The brightly decorated 500-square-metre area was filled with 24 high-end personal computers (loaded with e-games) – and children! A highly-qualified technical team was in attendance to answer queries and to help the children work with Microsoft Office and Web Technology tools.

GSSC RESULTS

A total of 26,792 students took the General Secondary School Certificate (GSSC) examination in 2002. Of these, 10,139 were in the science stream, 16,055 in the arts stream and 598 followed the technical diploma courses. Pass rates were high: 91 per cent in science and 80 per cent in arts. In 2003 the science and arts branches are to be combined to ensure that all students are equipped with a broad-based education.

HIGHER EDUCATION

Higher education is provided by two government universities, 11 Higher Colleges of Technology, as well as numerous internationally accredited institutions and the many specialised colleges, such as that established by the Armed Forces, the Emirates Institute for Banking and Financial Studies (providing highly popular short training courses and two banking diplomas) and the new, online Dubai Police's Electronic Total Quality Management College (eTQMC). Generous grants for overseas courses are available from the federal Ministry of Higher Education and Scientific Research and from other bodies. Over 3000 UAE citizens are currently receiving such scholarships.

In line with the trend in previous years, female students seeking higher education continue to outnumber male students. For the 2002–03 academic year, the UAE University in Al Ain admitted a total of 3972 students, of which 2742 were female, while in the 11 HCT, women comprised 3768 of the 6501 new admissions. The overall intake of students for the HCT showed an increase of 30 per cent over the previous year. Zayed University for women admitted 635 students to its two campuses at Abu Dhabi and Dubai, an increase of 12 per cent on intake for the previous year.

The Universities

UAE University (UAEU), which celebrated its silver jubilee in 2002, comprises nine colleges, the most popular of which, in terms of student admissions for 2002–2003, is the College of Humanities and Social Sciences. The College of Business and Economics, which admitted 510 students (269 were male), became, in 2000, the first business school in the Middle East to be accredited by the American Association of State Counseling Boards (AASCB), and one of only a small number anywhere outside the US to earn accreditation. It also offers a new MBA programme in Global Leadership and Management.

As part of the silver jubilee celebrations, the College of Information Technology organised a two-day International e-Learning Symposium in 2002, with the purpose of exchanging ideas and formulating a strategy for e-Learning in the GCC countries.

The First International Conference on Food Systems is to be hosted by one of UAEU's newest colleges, the College of Food Systems (formerly the Faculty of Agriculture), in April 2003. The Conference will bring together food scientists, producers, food traders, environmentalists, nutritionists, educators and policy makers to discuss concepts and issues of food systems, such as food security, food safety, nutrition, the environmental impacts of food systems and the economic, social and technological trends within food systems.

Zayed University (ZU) was founded in 1998 to meet the needs of human resources development in the UAE. Like its fellow institutions of higher education, ZU continues to forge links with government and private bodies for their mutual benefit. The Institute for Technological Innovation (ITI), for example, is the result of a partnership between Dubai Internet City and ZU, set up in response to an identified need amongst new and developing businesses for innovation in the area of IT. Recognising that scientific, engineering and entrepreneurial skills are all required to harness the full potential of IT applications for the continuing success of the UAE's business market, the initial focus of the ITI's three programmes will be on IT and e-Commerce with emphasis on the building of problem-solving skills. In response to needs expressed by the wider community, ZU has established a Centre for Media Training and Research within the College of Communication and Media Sciences. The Centre will offer training courses and workshops for media and communication professionals in the UAE as well as fostering research into practical issues facing the media in the country and the wider Arab region. The university offers an executive MBA in Managing e-Business, and its International Computer Driving Licence (ICDL) programme is to be certified by the United Nations Education, Science and Cultural Organisation (UNESCO). The programme has been applied worldwide and is currently recognised in 50 countries.

ZU also recognises the importance of fostering international links. The university has been selected as the location for the GCC branch of the International Council on Education for Teaching (ICET) – the first branch to be established in the Middle East. ICET, founded in 1953, is an association of policy and decision makers in education, government and business dedicated to global development through education.

A National Research Foundation to be established at ZU will enhance its role in both the academic and wider communities.

The Private Sector

Higher education is also well-served by the numerous private institutions which have sprung up in answer to the diverse needs of the complex community of people that is the UAE. Institutions include the American Universities of Sharjah and Dubai, Sharjah University and the Ajman University of Science and Technology, while several foreign universities have opened up branches or distance-learning centres within the UAE. The American University of Dubai and Dubai Media City

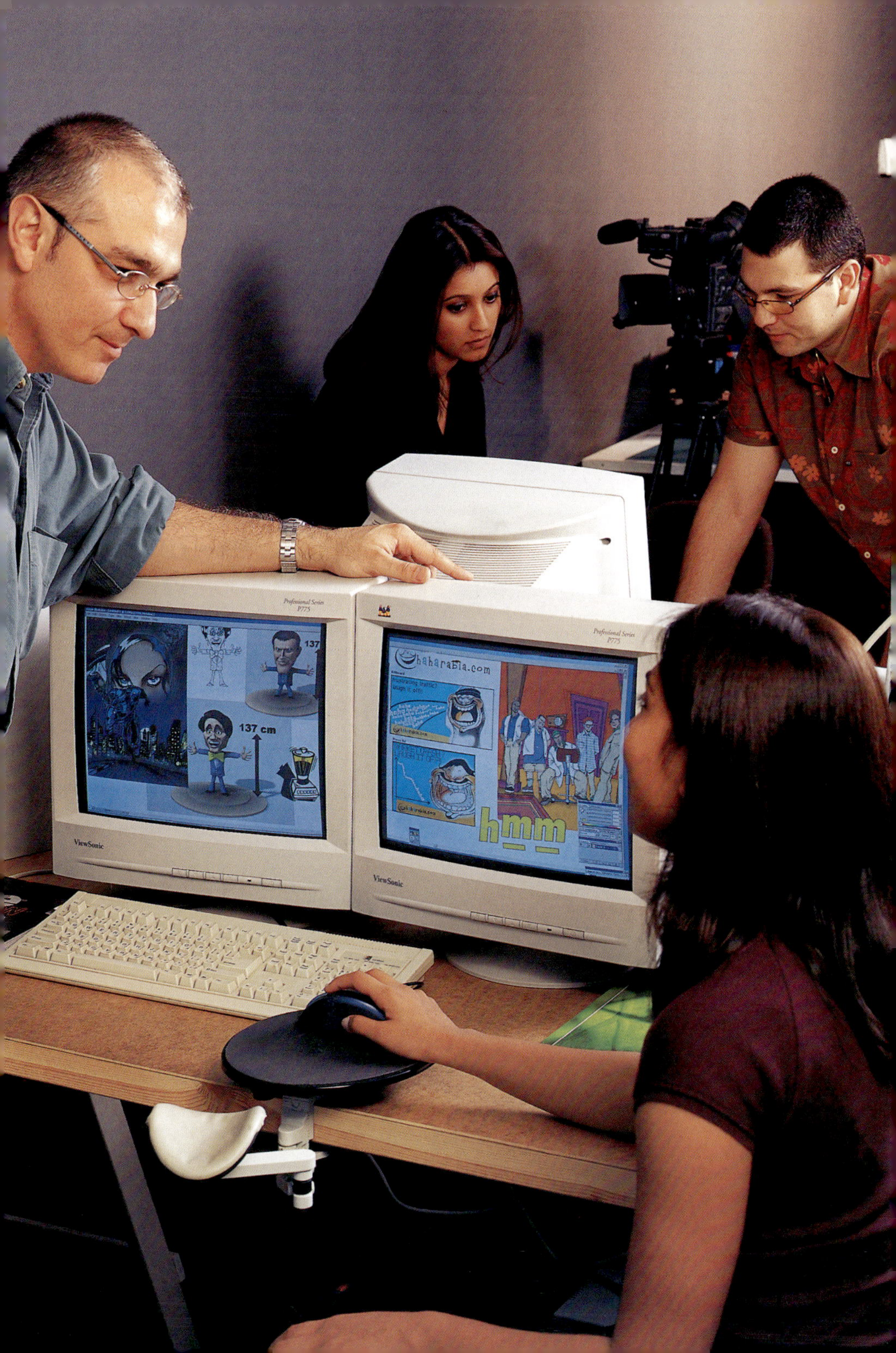
137
137 cm
haharaBia.com
hmm
ViewSonic
ViewSonic

have a cooperation agreement, as part of a strategy to cultivate local talent and provide training for those wishing to take up careers in the media. Many of the private institutions teach in English, as do the government institutions for some courses. Expatriates and citizens alike are benefiting from the increased opportunities for excellent education within the country.

Higher Colleges Of Technology (HCT)

In 1988 a system of government-funded colleges offering a more technically oriented education was devised. The four founding HCTs began the new experiment with an enrolment of 239 students. Demand for the type of education provided has been so high that by the end of the 2001-02 academic year more than 11,550 graduates had received awards from 11 HCTs. With a workforce recruited from over 38 countries, the HCTs offer a diverse study environment and an education noted for its commitment to excellence. Throughout the HCT system, over 950 qualified educators are the backbone of this educational experience, producing graduates who are highly regarded for their IT and communication skills, and their industrial experience, as well as for their strong work ethic. The HCT has formed extremely successful partnerships with industry and more than 85 per cent of its graduates are currently either employed, or studying, or both.

The Centre of Excellence for Applied Research and Training (CERT) – part of the HCT system – has become the location for Intel Corporation's first solution centre, the Energy Competency Centre (ECC). The Centre, a joint venture with IBM, provides access to breakthrough technologies and technical knowledge transfer and is expected to host education forums on how to develop, manage, optimise and exploit distributed computing models that can be used for the oil, gas and energy industry. Exploration and development companies will be first to benefit from the facility. Such initiatives open the way to enhanced communication between industry and educators, allowing each to articulate and assess the needs and the capabilities of themselves and the other and to develop mutually desirable solutions where possible.

In a major initiative for the 2002-03 academic year, 19 online courses have been added to the HCT curriculum. Such courses will allow flexibility for students who would otherwise be unable to participate in further education, perhaps because of their family/work circumstances, or because of their geographic location.

Dubai Women's College (DWC), the largest college within the HCT, offers the only engineering programme (software engineering technology) for women in the HCT. The college aims to equip every student, tutor and administrator with mobile computers and 100 per cent wireless connectivity by 2003. The speed with which the programme is being implemented has put the students on a par or even ahead of many prestigious educational institutions in the world, according to microchip giant Intel. In keeping with its policy of creating strong links with the local community, the college encourages its students to participate in locally-based activities. E-Commerce students and Dubai e-Government, for example, have had extensive exchanges with a view to the promotion of the government's e-services by the students.

Graphic Art students have been in the news this year, with two students from Sharjah Women's College (SWC) winning individual awards, while SWC Design students were finalists in the UAE IT Challenge–Visions website. The quality and originality of the work being produced by SWC design students has attracted the attention of high profile organisations such as Saatchi and Saatchi, Emirates Airlines, The British Council and the British Tourist Authority. Several organisations are undertaking a range of industry focused projects in conjunction with SWC design students.

In an interesting initiative, the Ministry of Higher Education and Scientific Research has signed a two-year Dh1.5 million deal with Reuters News Agency, allowing 30,000 students from ZU, the HCTs and UAEU to read the agency's round-the-clock international and local economic, scientific and political news.

A 'Virtual' College

One of the most innovative new ventures of 2002 has been the inauguration of the Dubai Police's Electronic Total Quality Management College (ETQMC). This 'virtual' college is an online, open study system and will be open to members of the public both within the UAE and abroad wishing to obtain degrees in total quality management. It will provide general training and academic studies, backed up by strong technical support and e-library facilities. It is intended that the college, which is a member of the British Quality Foundation and EFQM, a leading European body for quality, will be a nucleus for future higher educational institutions in the region.

Careers UAE 2003

In order to ensure that the UAE's highly-educated, young population has access to appropriate career information, the Dubai World Trade Centre, in conjunction with the HCTs and the National Human Resource Development and Employment Authority (Tanmia), runs an annual careers fair. Careers UAE 2003 is scheduled for 14–17 April. Tanmia, an organisation dedicated since its establishment in 1999 to ensuring the employment of nationals in all sectors, sees the event as a prime opportunity for those with a stake in the emiratisation process to share information and work in unity to increase the representation of nationals in the UAE's workforce.

FUTURE DIRECTIONS

At the beginning of 2002, Dubai Technology and Media Free Zone announced the establishment of a Dh250 million Dubai Knowledge Village covering 650,000 square feet, an initiative aimed at building a connected learning community which will act as a catalyst for the growth of the new knowledge-driven economy. The Knowledge

Village will facilitate the sharing of the multi-facetted expertise of knowledge-based organisations and the synergy produced from such a sharing through its housing of a Media Academy, an IT Academy, an Innovation Centre, e-Learning institutions, graduate and post-graduate institutions, institutions for research and development, a multimedia library, corporate training institutions, scientific and technology institutes, certification and testing organisations, and incubators. With enterprises such as Reuters (who have recently taken on a group of ZU students as interns), CNN and Sony sharing their expertise on journalism, digital content and production with academics, the success of this venture should see an explosive harnessing of intellect to innovative and competitive ends.

LITERACY

Despite the phenomenal advances in education, some members of society, particularly those of the older generation, remain disadvantaged. Nevertheless, efforts to eradicate illiteracy, defined in the UAE as the inability to read or write in any language (though the multiplicity of languages within the UAE can add to the difficulty of assessing literacy levels accurately), are proving remarkably successful. Between 1995 and 2001, the rate of illiteracy dropped from 16 per cent to 7 per cent for those in the 15–45 age group. In 1972, there were only 54 centres for adult education; by 2001, this number had more than doubled to reach 118, of which 62 per cent were for females. In the same period, the number of teachers and administrative staff in adult education centres more than doubled to 2788 in 2001, of whom 59 per cent were females. The number of learners at the centres increased fourfold from a mere 4912 in 1972 to 19,855 in 2001. Although males outnumbered females in 1972, they comprised only 49 per cent of the total number of learners during 2001.

At present, adult education, which takes place at 122 centres throughout the country, is divided into four levels which correspond closely to the formal schooling system – literacy, primary, preparatory and secondary. In 2000, UAE nationals comprised 72 per cent of total numbers enrolled in adult education classes. Of the 21,461 learners in 2000, 11 per cent were registered in literacy classes, 10 per cent in primary classes, 29 per cent in preparatory classes and 50 per cent at secondary level. While national females outnumbered males at the two lower levels, this was reversed at the two higher levels. This trend is seen as reflecting the demand of the labour market in a country where high qualifications are a prerequisite. Some UAE females do not continue their higher level education because of their perceived social role as mothers and housewives.

To accommodate the changing needs of those seeking its services, plans are under way to upgrade adult education. Among projects is the education programme for illiterate adults working in government bodies whose jobs prevent them from joining evening classes. The 2020 Vision for Education recognises the need to link education to productive work and to create more flexible programmes using modern, informal teaching techniques. It also recognises that, as well as providing literacy classes for educationally disadvantaged adults, it is vitally important to ensure that all children are enrolled for and complete their primary education.

WOMEN

Nothing could delight me more than to see women taking up their distinctive position in society. Nothing should hinder their progress. Like men, women deserve the right to occupy high positions, according to their capabilities and qualifications.

Sheikh Zayed may not have had Mount Kilimanjaro in mind when he referred to a woman's right to occupy high positions, but on 18 August 2002 one woman, Hafsa Al Ulama, became the first UAE woman to reach the summit of Mount Kilimanjaro, as part of a team that included ten Americans and a Palestinian woman. Undeterred by storms and temperatures which dropped to a low of -20°C, she made the journey to the top in seven days. Her magnificent achievement will act as an inspiration to women attempting to achieve their goals in spheres far removed from a 19,340-foot peak in Africa.

Her achievement, it could be said, was born out of Sheikh Zayed's support for the right of women to fulfil their potential which has been central to the progress of women in the UAE over the last 30 years. But women have been instrumental in their own success. From the beginning, they have been prepared to join cooperatively in ensuring their mutual social and educational development, in accordance with their own well-being and that of their families. Women are anxious to play their part in the development of what is still a very young country and, for many years, the General Women's Union (GWU), an organisation funded by the Government, has been the main focal point for the coordination of those efforts. The GWU was established in 1975 as the UAE Women's Federation, under the leadership of Sheikha Fatima bint Mubarak, wife of the President, in order to bring under one umbrella all the women's societies in the country. The Union, which has, amongst its many duties, responsibility for suggesting new laws or amendments to existing laws, researches matters pertinent to women and makes recommendations to the relevant ministries and government departments. The work of the GWU since its inception has brought to the fore many interrelated issues of concern for women, children and the family. It has been instrumental in introducing health education and literacy programmes throughout the UAE as well as undertaking classes in dressmaking and handicraft, household management and childcare, computer and languages. It has offered vocational training, job placement services, family mediation services and religious education.

As the needs of women have developed alongside their educational development, so the range and focus of the GWU's concerns have developed. In a significant move towards coordinating treatment of those concerns at country level, negotiations for the establishment of a Supreme Council for Maternity and Childhood Affairs in 2003 are currently taking place with the Cabinet. The main task of the new council will be to formulate policies and coordinate their subsequent implementation by the different authorities and civil sectors. It will also be tasked with raising public awareness on issues relating to maternity and childhood. It will assist in promoting relevant national strategies and integrated plans devised by the Government and will help to prepare statistics on the actual status of maternity and childhood in the UAE. The Council will also have responsibility for organising conferences, scientific meetings and publications and for strengthening relationships with Arab and international organisations.

The GWU has strong Arab and international links with women's organisations and is affiliated with the Arab Women's Federation, the International Women's Federation and the International Family Organisation. The Gulf Committee for Regional Coordination of Women's Work has chosen Abu Dhabi as its permanent headquarters and 2002 heralded the beginning of the UAE's four-year term of membership of the Women's Committee of the 54-member UN Economic Council. In an interview with *Al Ittihad*, Sheikha Fatima called, on behalf of the GWU, for dialogue with European women and the convening of an Arab-International forum in 2003 for the discussion of common issues.

ARAB WOMEN AND MEDIA FORUM

In 2002, more than 250 Arab women attended the Arab Women and Media Forum (the GWU was one of the joint organisers). The Forum covered a wide range of topics, including the difficulties faced by women seeking a career in the media. The conflict between home and family responsibilities and the flexibility and mobility required for media work was highlighted, as was the tendency towards assigning women to 'women's issues'. One of the most important aspects of the Abu Dhabi Declaration produced by the Forum was the call for equality of opportunity in employment and promotion, and the opening up of issues, be they economic, technological or political, to coverage by both men and women. Sheikha Fatima is in favour of an Arab women's satellite channel – so long as it is not used to create divisions between men and women. The true status of Arab women is not currently reflected by the Arab media, participants in the forum felt, recommending the establishment of a women's channel, not only to present a corrective to the stereotypical image of Muslim women which is evident in the Western media, but to highlight issues of importance to women for home audiences and to publicise women's achievements in public life.

Shortly after that forum, the UAE was the first to sign the convention on the establishment of the Arab Women Organisation, which will come into being on its

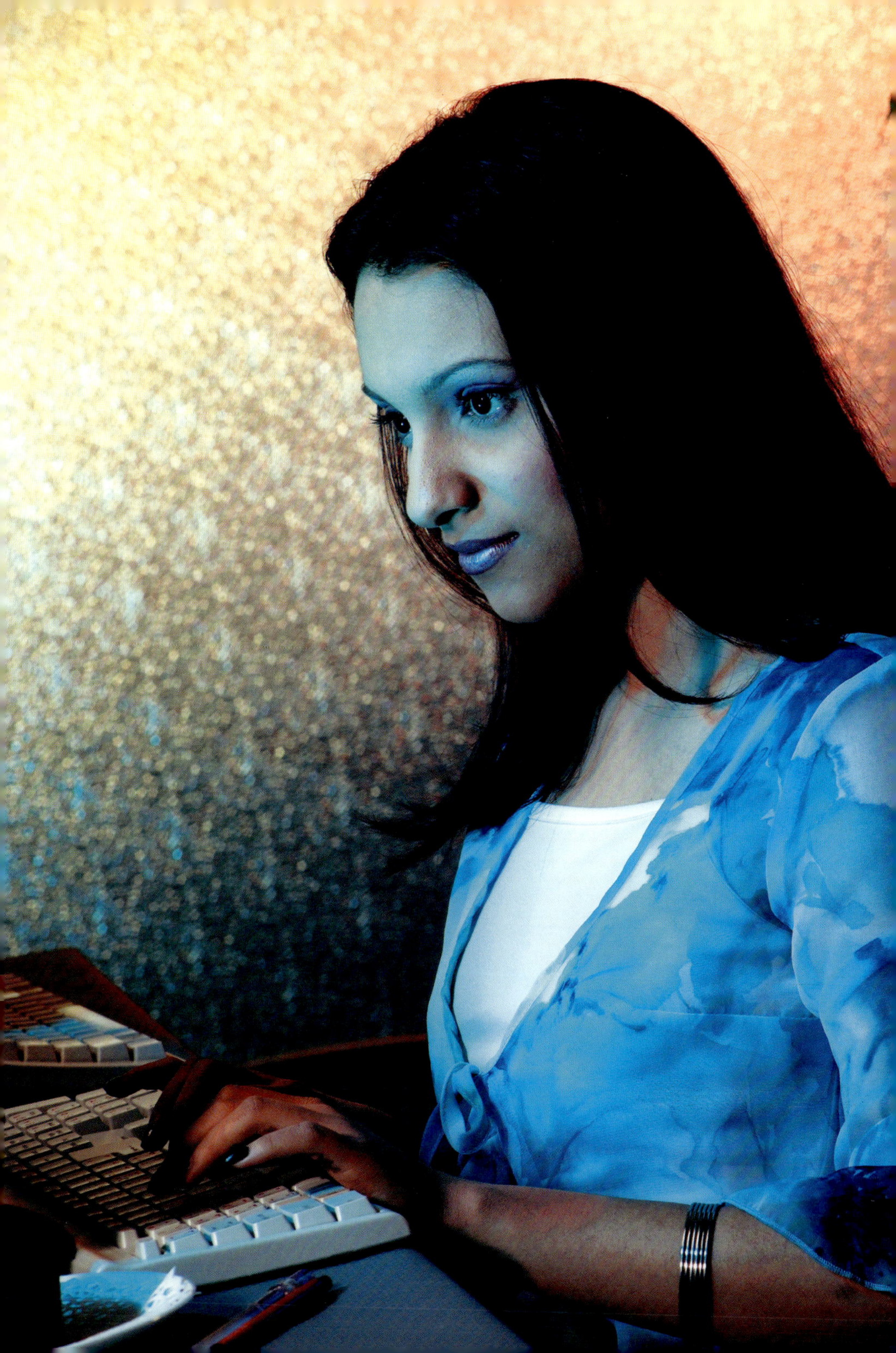

endorsement by seven Arab countries. The agreement emanated from the Cairo Declaration made at the First Arab Women Summit in 2000 – forerunner of the Arab Women in Media Forum, 2002 – and is intended to reinforce Arab women's solidarity and coordination, raise their status and widen the scope of their contribution in various fields.

WOMEN AND EMPLOYMENT

As is apparent from the figures, women have embraced the opportunities for education. But advancement has not been confined to education alone. Women are now a potent part of the workforce of the UAE, comprising 41.5 per cent in the field of education, 34.2 per cent in the health sector and 19.7 per cent in social affairs. In fact, national female employees in 24 federal ministry departments account for nearly 28 per cent of civil servants. UAE national women working in the banking and financial services sector total 1776, or 57 per cent of the nationals working in this field. They also constitute 39.3 per cent of all women employed in the sector. Seventy per cent of UAE women employed in banking are also graduates, or those with higher degrees.

Interestingly, in light of the Arab Women and Media Forum, the executive manager of the Dubai Press Club is female. The Federal Armed Forces accepts women volunteers for its special women's corps – an innovation initiated at the time of the Gulf War – which participates in areas other than front-line combat, and women also form part of the police service. A female taxi service was approved in 2001. While women have been slow to reach senior positions, there is a female undersecretary in the Ministry of Labour and Social Affairs and a female assistant undersecretary for planning and evaluation in the Ministry of Education. In 2001, five women were appointed to Sharjah's 40-member Consultative Council and a female engineer heads the Sharjah Public Works Department.

It is the ambition of the GWU to see women appointed to the Federal National Council (FNC) legislative chapter (names of suitable candidates are being forwarded to the FNC), and Sheika Fatima would like to see women assume the responsibilities of ministerial office, given their constitutionally guaranteed right to participate in political life. The GWU is committed to ensuring that this right is fully utilised for the ultimate benefit of UAE society.

A study by Tanmia on the employment of national women revealed some of the disadvantages experienced by both women and their potential employers. Most of the women looking for jobs are in the 20–30 year age group, with half holding high school certificates, 20–30 per cent university degrees, and less than 20 per cent HCT qualifications. The study identified the need for national women to show a greater commitment towards work (economic prosperity makes work a matter of choice for most, rather than necessity) and to equip themselves with higher, more

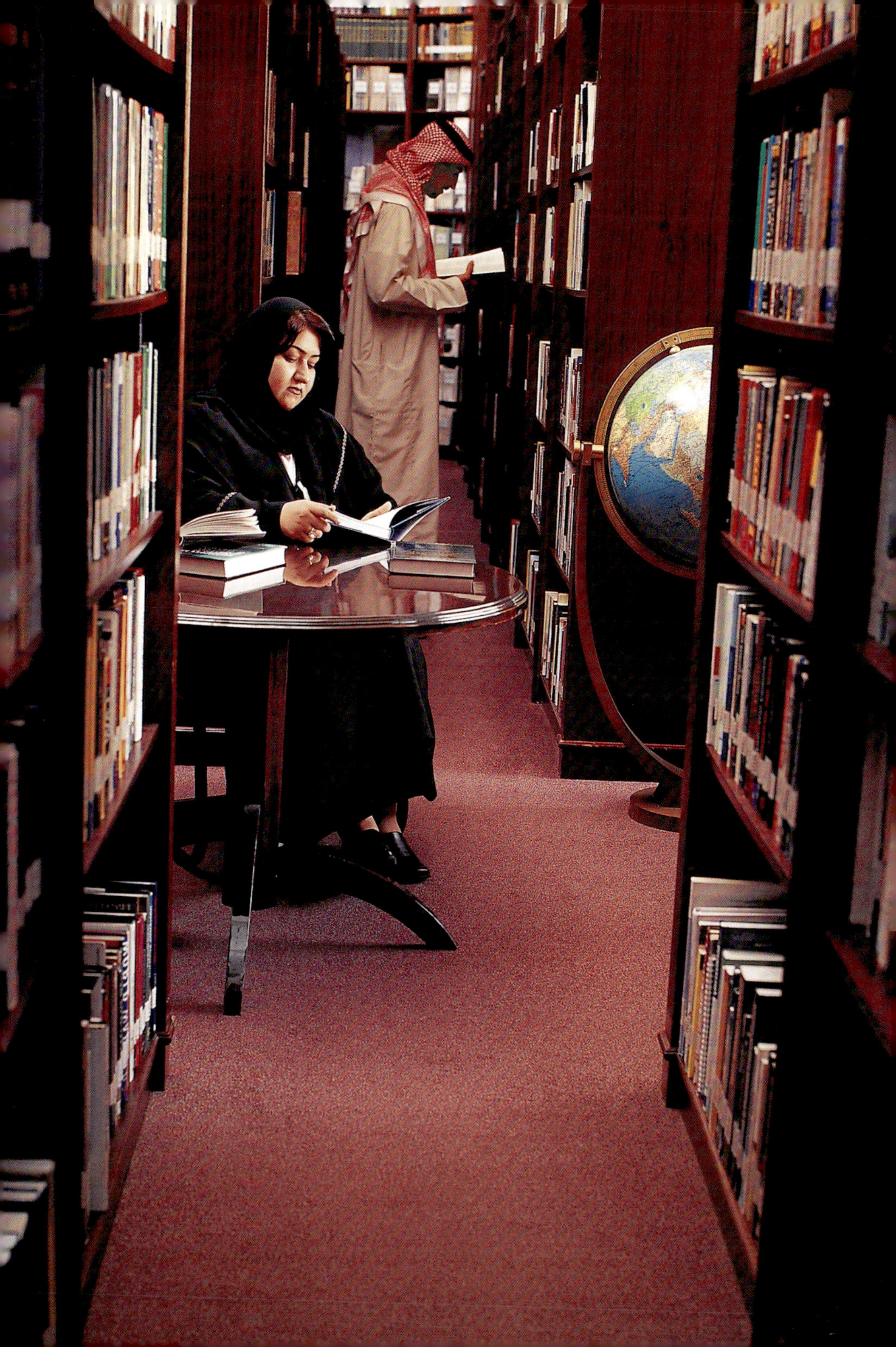

relevant qualifications. Potential employers in the private sector found women lacked proficiency in the English language, computer skills and inter-personal skills. Given the customs and traditions in UAE society, these employers were also apprehensive of possible social problems which might arise in case of perceived misdemeanours in conduct. National women, for their part, saw the two-shift working schedule as one of the main barriers to their participation in the private sector, along with discriminatory practices between men and women, particularly in the area of promotions. Among suggestions for improvement were the provision of free training courses, the elimination of patronage in gaining access to jobs, the upgrading of language skills, reduction in the number of foreign workers and the establishment of a separate department for women in the Government. Nineteen per cent of female job seekers were prepared to set up their own businesses, while 27 per cent of businesswomen interviewed felt that national families needed to provide more support for female entrepreneurs. New technologies also open up possibilities for women to work from home.

The findings show that it will be difficult to woo national women into the labour market without serious consideration being given not only to equipping women with job relevant skills but also to current work practices which do not take account of the circumstances under which women must operate.

The UAE Businesswomen Committee, set up by the Abu Dhabi Chamber of Commerce and Industry (ADCCI) in 2001 to support the position of working women in the Emirate of Abu Dhabi and to widen the opportunities for cooperation between businesswomen in the Arab world, should help to remedy some of the shortcomings. Part of its brief is the provision of training programmes for women on the skills required in the labour market and improving the programme of emiratisation. In 2002 the ADCCI had 1142 businesswomen, representing construction, tailoring, trade, contracting and other companies, on its register.

One of the main reasons for progress being made by women in the UAE is the attention that has been paid to safeguarding their rights, not only in the Constitution itself, but in laws drawn up subsequently to give practical effect to those rights. For instance, discrimination in salary between males and females is forbidden under Labour Law. Sexual harassment is also prohibited. Maternity leave has recently been extended from 45 days to six months – two months on full pay, two months on half pay and two months without pay. On the death of her husband, a woman is entitled to paid leave of four months and ten days, in accordance with Islamic Sharia law.

An issue which has assumed greater importance as more and more women join the workforce is the need for better crèche facilities in the workplace and, at the beginning of 2002, the Department of Family and Child Care undertook the ambitious project of building nurseries in all government departments.

Women in the UAE are trying to forge a future which allows for diversity and choice for themselves and their families. Many women choose to stay at home to

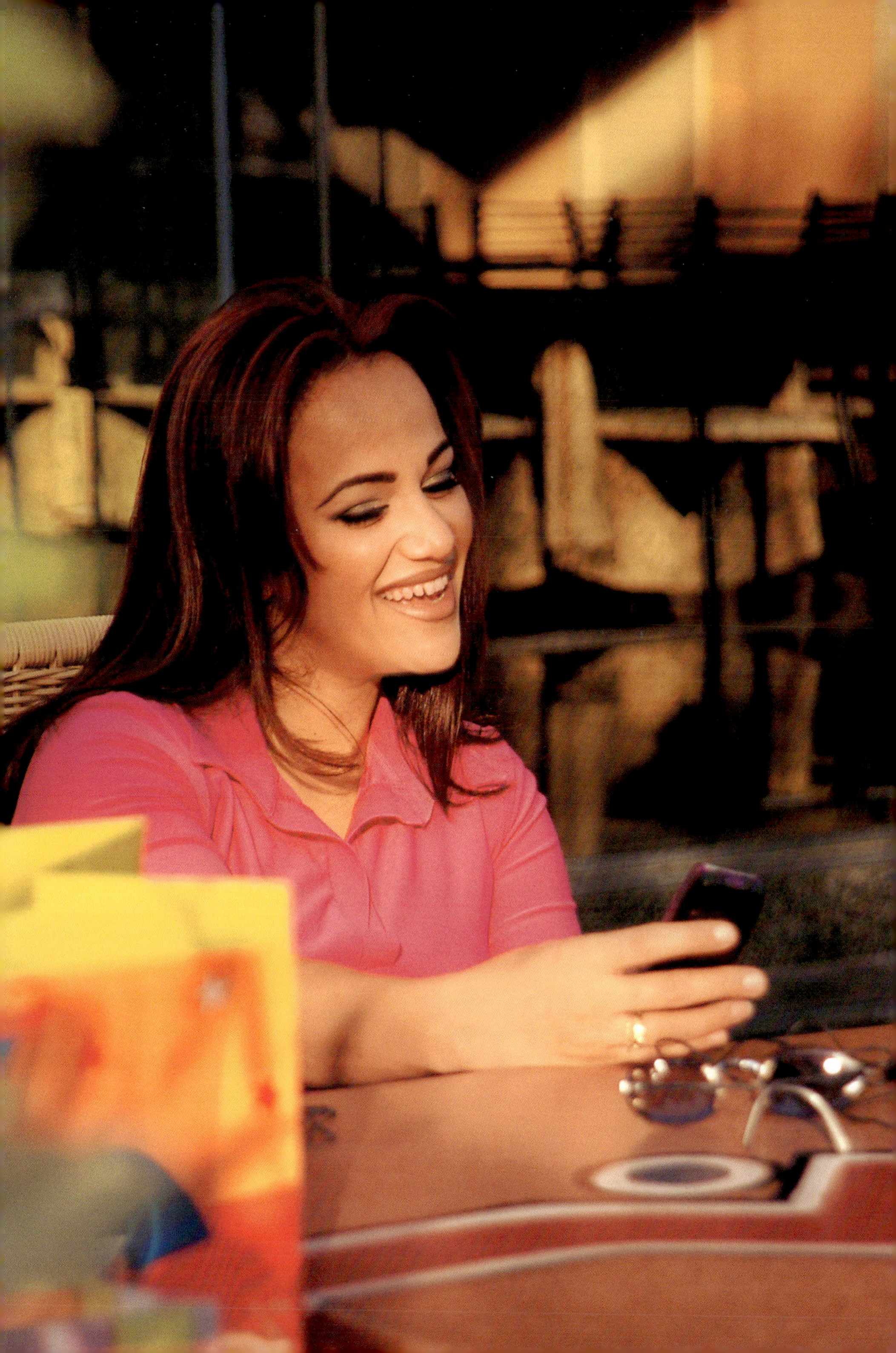

rear their own families, seeing that as their most important social function, but others want to use their education to take part in the forging of the society in which they live. Obstacles still remain in terms of career opportunities and social expectations (both traditional and new) for such women. But UAE women have grown confident in identifying the issues of central significance. While careers are important, of overriding importance is the ability to have not just the right but the means to combine that career with family responsibilities.

MARRIAGE

It was recognised in the early 1990s that growing numbers of UAE women were remaining unmarried. One of the main causes of this problem was the high cost of marriage. A dowry system is traditional to the UAE and, as the country's wealth soared, dowry expectations soared with equal rapidity, making marriage unviable for many young men and their families. The price of wedding celebrations themselves spiralled out of control – costs of US $100,000 were not uncommon – adding an additional financial disincentive to any couple contemplating marriage. UAE men, to avoid the financial difficulties associated with marriage to women of their own nationality, were marrying foreign women, thus exacerbating the imbalance in the demographic structure of society. The Marriage Fund, administered by the Ministry of Labour and Social Affairs, was set up in 1994 to combat this problem. Marriage halls were built to facilitate more economical ceremonies and the Government launched a campaign calling for a reduction in dowry size. Since then, an upper limit of Dh50,000 has been placed on dowry size and the prohibition on extravagant weddings can be enforced by legal sanctions: a prison sentence or a Dh500,000 fine for the couples concerned. In the words of Sheikh Zayed, 'Excessive dowries and extravagance in wedding celebrations and all matters that exhaust the youth at the beginning of their marital life are unjustified things which are against the teachings of Islam and our deep-rooted traditions.'

Young UAE nationals with limited incomes wishing to marry can apply to the Fund for a marriage grant of up to Dh70,000, usually paid in two instalments. Many couples are participating in mass weddings such as that which took place at the Fujairah Exhibition Centre at the end of June 2002. The ceremony for 45 UAE national couples, organised by the Fund, was the fourth such ceremony that year. To date the Fund has organised 38 group weddings.

The number of couples benefiting from Marriage Fund grants increased from 2036 in 1993 to 4027 in 2001. From the beginning of 2002 to the end of August in the same year, 3000 applications had been submitted to the Fund. A total of 60,000 young people will have benefited from the Fund by the end of 2002 at a cost of Dh2.3 billion. Because the applications far outweigh the Fund's resources, the Fund has a deficit. In light of this deficit, an annual budget of Dh300 million

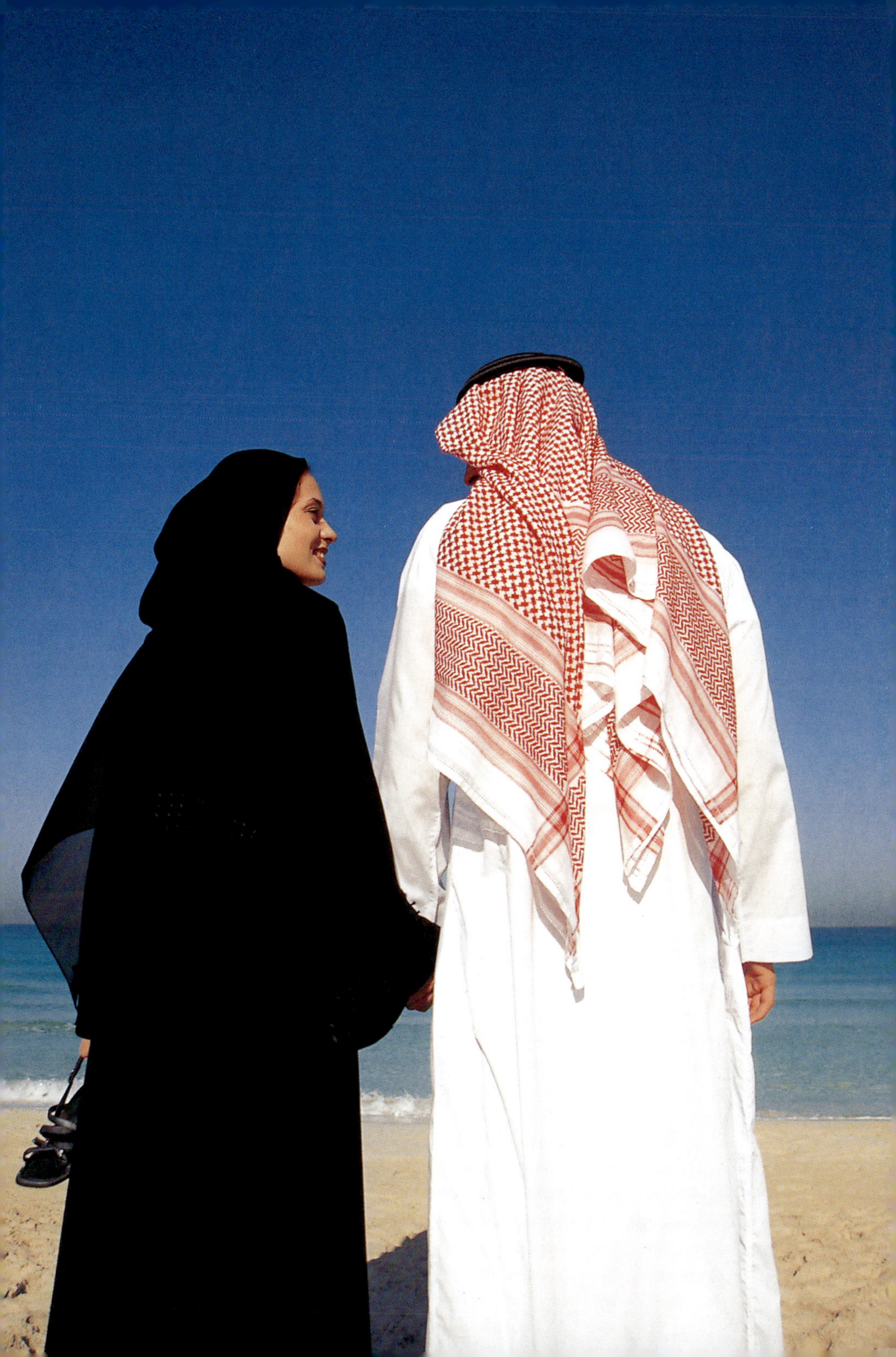

has been proposed (compare this figure to that of 1993, when assistance from public funds was Dh80 million), along with a reduction in the size of the grant to Dh60,000.

Dubai's Statistical Yearbook 2000 showed a high rate of divorce among newly married couples in that emirate, with marriages of 31.85 per cent of local women breaking up within the first nine years. Figures from the Abu Dhabi Marriage Fund showed that in 1999, of 3351 marriages between nationals 21 per cent ended in divorce. This compared favourably with the 31.6 per cent rate of divorce for the 1111 marriages between national men and expatriate women in the same year. The Marriage Fund sees divorce as a very disruptive force in UAE lives and has planned an ambitious programme aimed at producing a divorce-free society. The programme will concentrate initially on the problems of those families who have received the Fund's marriage grant. The Fund is also to conduct courses for those applying for the marriage grant, designed to raise awareness of the negative impact of divorce on society. These courses may become compulsory. A database, monitoring divorce rates, will follow. Amongst the Fund's other plans for the next three years is a media campaign to increase awareness of the importance of family relations. It also proposes opening up a hotline for queries from members of the public.

In a separate initiative, the office of Sheikha Fatima bint Mubarak has introduced a legal service to assist in the resolution of family disputes and other social problems without recourse to the courts. The service will be open to both nationals and expatriates, and will also be open to men.

PERSONAL STATUS LAW

The increasing complexity of family life is placing greater demands on the courts in the UAE. It is hoped that a new personal status law securing social rights for men, women and children, the draft of which is to be reviewed by the FNC, will allow the courts and other institutions to expedite services to citizens. The law is intended to give clear guidelines (within the precepts of Islamic Sharia law) guaranteeing the rights of the different parties in the resolution of family-linked court cases.

HEALTH

The UAE ranks highest among Arab countries in terms of life expectancy (75 years), a figure comparing favourably with that of high-income countries (79 years in 1998), according to the first Arab Human Development Report (AHDR). This is due in no small part to the excellence of its health service. The UAE has been classified by World Health Organisation (WHO) as achieving international health standards in terms of both quality/goodness (the best attainable level) and fairness (availability to all without discrimination).

The Ministry of Health (MoH), which manages a total of 30 hospitals, 115 centres for primary health care and nine centres for preventive medicine throughout the UAE, is planning to construct 17 new hospitals and 25 primary health care centres by 2005. In 2002, the Ministry announced that six new hospitals with a total bed capacity of 1830 are to be opened – a 800-bed general hospital and a 350-bed obstetrics and gynaecology hospital in Al Ain, a 200-bed general hospital in Umm al-Qaiwain, a 180-bed obstetrics and gynaecology hospital in Ra's al-Khaimah, a 120-bed general hospital in Kalba and a 180-bed psychiatric hospital in Dubai. The Corniche Maternity Hospital in Abu Dhabi, run by the Abu Dhabi Health Care Department, is to be provided with a further 300 beds. In addition, three more primary health care centres are to be opened in Ra's al-Khaimah, Ajman and Dibba. This, along with the opening of a new centre for preventive medicine in Dhaid serving Sharjah's central region, shows that the MoH's overall plans for expansion are well under way.

The new hospitals will benefit from the assistance of the revolutionary high-tech tube robot for in-house transport and communication services (the US-made Swisslog Translogic), the first of which has just been installed in a government hospital in Abu Dhabi. The computerised system is connected to large plastic tubes which extend to all sections of the hospital. Items such as blood samples can be transported through the tubes to their destination in seconds.

To satisfy the demand for more nursing staff, five new nursing schools have been created. In 1989, only 30 nationals graduated from nursing school. In 2002, that number increased to 155. The expanded teaching capacity created by the new schools should lead to a considerable increase in those numbers.

Specialised healthcare units were established in 2000 to provide for such complex treatments as open heart surgery, organ transplantation and dialysis units, while comprehensive diagnostic and therapeutic radiological facilities, in addition to surgical treatment, are available at oncology departments in Tawam and Al Mafraq hospitals. Many public health institutions have units for endoscopy.

The Dubai Government is to establish Dubai Healthcare City as a global hub for specialised healthcare and a centre for medical education and research, servicing patients from the entire region. The project, with an estimated cost of US$1.8 billion, includes a university medical complex which will provide specialised medical education and research and be instrumental in attracting medical specialists to the region.

The private health sector is also thriving throughout the country. At the end of 2000, there were 21 private hospitals, with a total of 827 beds, 265 general medical centres, 352 private clinics, and 250 specialist clinics, served by 685 doctors. This year American Healthcare Management Systems Ltd signed an understanding with Emaar Properties to build a 300-bed hospital at a cost of Dh250 million in Dubai.

A multi-million dirham fertility centre offering IVF and related services is to be set up at Zulekha Hospital in Sharjah.

VIRUS DIAGNOSTICS

Increased collaboration between research laboratories round the world is seen by the UAE's diagnostic centres as a key element in combating viral diseases such as HIV, sexually transmitted infections and various strains of hepatitis. A Polymerase Chain Reaction (PCR) research laboratory for AIDS has been established, and the UAE Health Department now has 12 reference and confirmatory laboratories for virus diagnostics, together with three other laboratories established specifically to conduct 'flow cytometry' techniques. The UAE is one of 42 countries participating in WHO's external quality assessment scheme, involving over 900 laboratories. Diagnostic tests for HIV/AIDS and Hepatitis B and C became available in the UAE at the beginning of 2002.

PRIMARY HEALTH CARE

The implementation of a broad programme for the further development of primary health care in the UAE is well under way. Pregnant women are receiving comprehensive care at nine medical and child health centres and more than 80 units at primary health care centres. The initiative's success is reflected not just in the low levels of infant mortality of 6.57 per 1000, a figure in line with that of other developed countries, but also in the very low level of maternal mortality (one in 100,000), a rate below that in many developed countries. Neo-natal services implementing the national immunisation programme, encouraging breast-feeding and providing nutrition advice have also been introduced. A national programme has already proved its effectiveness in the early detection of congenital and hereditary diseases. A screening programme for breast cancer has been launched to cover all women aged over 40 years, and a similar programme for the detection of cervical cancer is to follow shortly.

The school system is used as the basis for continuing primary care. Clinics set up in each school carry out periodical health checks, in addition to administering the continuing vaccination schedule. Pupils undergo regular dental inspections, and the rate of dental caries in schools has dropped by 80 per cent.

Although vaccination efforts have been under way in the UAE since the 1960s, the fight entered a new phase in 1981 with the launch of an new programme to eradicate childhood communicable diseases. This ambitious programme has been remarkably successful, with no cases of polio appearing since 1993, while 2002 should see the UAE achieve measles-free status. Children are routinely vaccinated against hepatitis B, whooping cough, polio, tetanus, diphtheria, measles and TB and in 2002 the authorities achieved 95 per cent vaccination coverage. The country was declared free of malaria in December 2002

To control diseases being imported to the country, the UAE has entered into a tie-up with the Disease Control Centre, USA. Steps are also being taken to restrict the entry into the UAE of animals that might carry diseases that can affect humans.

A NATIONAL HEALTH AUTHORITY

The UAE National Environmental Strategy and Environmental Work Plan has suggested the creation of a national health authority to review laws governing contagious diseases, the quality of human food, animal health, and human capability. Within such an authority would be: a national public health institution to train labourers and health inspectors on all aspects of public health and safety; an environmental health authority; a body to review laws on contagious and transmitted diseases; and a new health department to study diseases common to animals and man. Also recommended were laws to regulate foreign labour, with a view to preventing the introduction to the country of transmittable diseases, and laws to guarantee the quality of human food.

BLOOD AND BLOOD PRODUCTS

The UAE will shortly become the first Arab country to pass a blood transfusion act. The Higher National Committee for Blood Transfusion Services (HNCBT) is currently drafting the final articles of the law, prior to submitting it to the legal department at the MoH. The final three chapters of this five-chapter act have already been completed. Chapter three deals with blood transfusion, its scope, rules and components, as well as with blood transfusion programmes for different pathological cases. Chapters four and five concern the patient to whom blood is transfused, blood transfusion interactions and diseases communicated through such a process. The first two chapters will cover administrative and technical aspects, matters related to blood donors and blood banks, blood donation programmes and policies on blood-transmitted diseases.

In a move to control the quality of its blood transfusion services, the UAE ceased the import of blood in 1983 and has relied on local donors ever since. This and the incorporation of advanced computer systems into blood bank work has caused a major qualitative shift in both safety and accuracy and speed of diagnostic procedures. All aspects of modern technology have been utilised in delivering a high quality product and the results of that effort are evident in the fact that the UAE is now listed by the American Blood Banks Authority on its Internet site as one of ten countries worldwide using safe means of blood transfusion. Along with the US, Canada, France, Austria, Ireland, Germany, New Zealand, Portugal and the UK, the UAE carries out leukocyte filtration of blood, offering 100 per cent filtered blood to all patients. The system of separating white cells from blood units has been applied gradually at Abu Dhabi Central Blood Bank, Sharjah Blood Bank and Tawam Hospital Blood Bank.

Sharjah is acquiring another, specialised centre for blood transfusion and blood diseases, while a brand new blood centre for the extraction of premature blood cells from human umbilical cords for the treatment of leukaemia and thalassemia is planned for Abu Dhabi. The existing blood transfusion centre in Sharjah, along with its counterpart in Abu Dhabi, has been ISO-9002 certified for the past two years.

Artificial Blood Control

Artificial Blood Control, a product created from a mixture of chicken and human blood and used to calibrate blood haematology analysers, is a new success story for the UAE. Imported Artificial Blood Control used to cost the MoH Dh500,000 annually. Now, a locally manufactured product supplies blood banks and government labs as well as 54 haematology labs and the quality is so good that the shelf life of the product has been extended from 30 to 40 days. The move has been praised by WHO.

LIFESTYLE DISEASES

Unfortunately, the affluence which allows for high standards of healthcare poses other, insidious, risks. Lifestyle diseases continue to take their toll on the population, with the three major causes of death in the UAE listed as: cardiovascular disease, traffic accidents and cancer.

Programmes have been organised to prevent and control cardiovascular diseases, hypertension and diabetes, and the MoH has set up a national cancer committee which has been given the task of reducing cancer cases in the UAE by 40 per cent by the year 2020 and improving the cure and survival rates of detected cases by 50 per cent by 2010.

Smoking

That smoking and cancer are intimately linked is shown by the fact that 40 per cent of UAE cancer cases are related to smoking (of which 70 per cent end in death). According to a recent study, the total annual tobacco use and addiction related expenditure in the UAE is estimated at Dh545 million, of which Dh245 million is directly related to the treatment of diseases caused by tobacco use. (Revenue from smokers generated by hospital charges is, on the other hand, less than Dh30 million.) As part of efforts to reduce the use of tobacco, a national taskforce is currently drafting a federal law to ban the sale of cigarettes to those under 18 years of age. The draft also provides for strict control on tobacco advertising, a ban on smoking in public places and a heavy tax on the sale of tobacco.

While most countries try to reduce their smoking populations through deterrence alone, WHO, as part of the International Quit Smoking Competition, came up with the novel idea of tempting smokers to quit by offering a prize to those who could manage to refrain from smoking for a month. The UAE was chosen as one of 100 countries to take part in the competition because of its dedication to intensive quit smoking programmes.

Accidents

The economic and psychological consequences of accidents causing death and those resulting in disability are immense, and the MoH is formulating a comprehensive strategy to cope with the problem, in collaboration with the Traffic Departments of the Ministry of the Interior. The strategy addresses four primary factors: spreading awareness and information, paying attention to vehicles and roads, enhancing medical emergency services and working towards prevention and legislation. Five fully equipped centres to check loads on heavy vehicles (overloading is a major cause of accidents involving such vehicles) are already in operation, and the Ministry of the Interior plans to set up ambulance and rescue units providing quick emergency aid to victims in all UAE cities. One new tool in the fight against speeding is a laser speed gun which cannot be recognised by radar detectors or jammers fitted in cars.

ALTERNATIVE MEDICINE

The use of herbs to combat medical conditions has been traditional in the UAE for thousands of years, but the scientific basis for their effectiveness has not been explored until recently. In 1996, the Zayed Complex for Herbal Research and Traditional Medicine was established by presidential decree and, as well as conducting research on hundreds of herbs and plants, it currently treats 13,000 patients suffering from chronic illnesses. Diabetic Al, used in the treatment of diabetes, is the latest in its range of medicines. In recognition of its success in producing, on a small scale, seven internationally standardised herbal medicines for the treatment of chronic diseases such as diabetes, hypertension, joint inflammation, and ulcers, WHO named the complex as a regional centre for alternative medicine in the Middle East. Tests are under way to produce, for the first time anywhere in the world, antibiotics from herbs and ointment for acne, and the manufacture of medicines on a large scale is planned.

PHARMACEUTICAL PATENTS

Amendments to Federal Law No. 44 of 1992 (Patent Law) protecting inventions, industrial design and models have almost been finalised. The amendments will extend protection to all pharmaceutical products, and will extend a patent's life from 15 to 20 years.

NATIONAL HEALTH INSURANCE

As the cost and range of medical treatment increases, the need for a national health insurance scheme becomes more urgent. The MoH plans to replace the existing health card scheme with an insurance system, and has proposed the establishment of a health insurance authority, responsible for providing free health services to UAE nationals and cost-effective health services to expatriates, who in return must pay a health insurance premium. One insurance scheme under consideration offers three levels of health coverage – economy, standard and high end. Annual premiums would be Dh885, Dh982 and Dh1183 respectively. The economic policy entitles the insured party to free medical treatment at government hospitals for up to Dh2000 annually and covers in-patient hospital treatment for up to Dh25,000 annually. These entitlements rise to Dh5000 and Dh50,000 respectively under the standard policy, while the high-end policy guarantees coverage of Dh10,000 and Dh100,000.

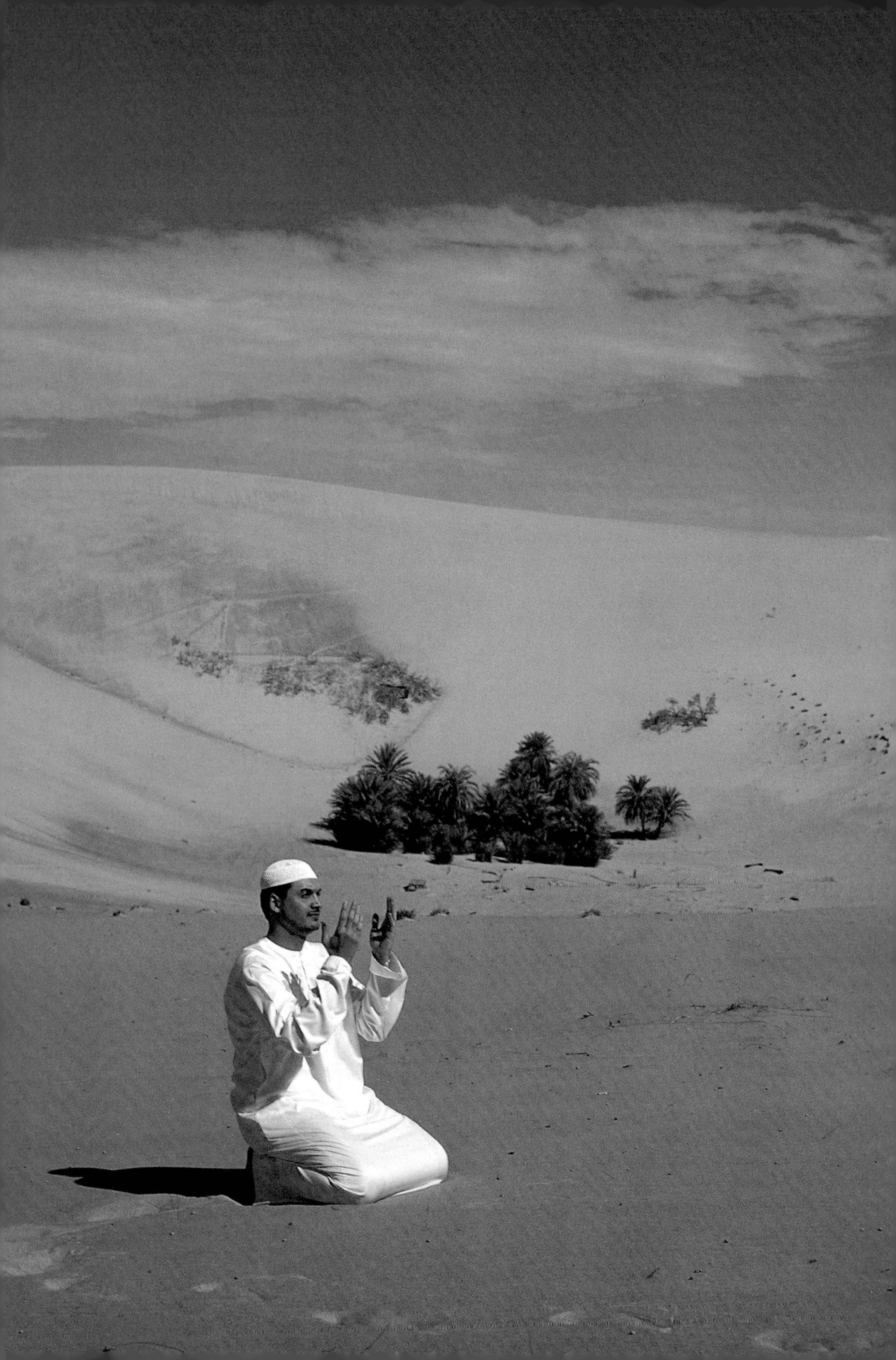

CULTURE AND INFORMATION

CULTURE AND HERITAGE

SINCE BEFORE THE FOUNDATION OF THE UAE, the inhabitants of the seven emirates have been both blessed and challenged by the extraordinary change in circumstances brought about by the discovery of oil. Prior to oil's appearance, the habits of this resilient group of people had, of necessity, been frugal. Conservation and the husbanding of limited resources had been central to survival. The sudden emergence of great wealth brought with it enormous benefits in terms of raising the standard of living, health, education and work opportunities; it also brought with it the potential for great cultural loss. Inevitably, the population explosion led to an unprecedented expansion of cities and towns into their surrounding countryside. Equally inevitably, traditional ways of life disappeared in the maelstrom of progress. Fortunately, the potential for irreparable loss was recognised from the start by Sheikh Zayed and, from the beginning, he took far-seeing and innovative measures to preserve, conserve and reinvigorate. As a result, the UAE has not just managed to preserve many of its unique archaeological and architectural sites, its manuscripts, its literature and its customs, but aspects of life which had disappeared have been faithfully reconstructed, sometimes through the creation of heritage villages, sometimes through the rebuilding of vanished monuments from photographs, local memory and documentary evidence.

Playing a central role in guarding the nation's precious heritage are its many cultural organisations. Prominent among these are the Cultural Foundation in Abu Dhabi, the Cultural and Scientific Forum in Dubai, the Department of Culture and Information in Sharjah, the Fujairah Cultural Organisation, the Studies and Archives Centre in Ra's al-Khaimah and the Juma Al Majid Centre in Dubai. Other institutions of importance to the cultural well-being of the country include Emirates Heritage Club, the National Heritage Revival Organisation and the Marriage Fund.

CULTURAL FOUNDATION

Abu Dhabi's Cultural Foundation (www.cultural.org.ae), a public institution comprising the National Library, the Institute of Art and Culture and the National Archive, is housed in an elegant series of three-storey buildings with arched verandas around a series of courtyards. The Foundation is concerned with the development and promotion of all cultural and artistic activities in Abu Dhabi. Exhibitions, music recitals, cultural and film festivals, book publishing, lectures and conferences, art courses and workshops are all part of the remit of the Foundation.

ZAYED ARAB NETWORK FOR HISTORY AND HERITAGE

The Centre for Documentation and Research (CDR), originally part of the Cultural Foundation, is to set up (with technical assistance from UNESCO) a central electronic network, the Zayed Arab Network for History and Heritage, linking the libraries of all national archives and centres for history and heritage in the Arab world. The CDR, established in 1968, is to be re-housed in a Dh 90 million five-storey, purpose-built building. Custodian of much of the nation's rarest archival material, the CDR is one of the UAE's leading research institutions. The Centre is currently digitising all its archival material. Already a place of prime importance to scholars both national and international, its role in establishing an electronic network of such comprehensive scope can only enhance its standing as custodian of Arabian history.

ZAYED CENTRE FOR HERITAGE AND HISTORY

Established by Sheikh Zayed, the Centre for Heritage and History is a cultural research institution established to encourage research related to tradition and history. Officially inaugurated by Sheikh Sultan bin Zayed Al Nahyan, Deputy Prime Minister and President of Emirates Heritage Club in March 1999, the Centre is affiliated with Emirates Heritage Club, but it has its administrative headquarters in Al Ain.

The Centre pays special attention to the preservation, documentation and publication of the heritage of the UAE, at the same time attempting to create a balance between traditional and contemporary life. Sheikh Zayed is particularly keen to acquaint the younger generation with their authentic cultural heritage since he believes that a 'nation without heritage is a nation without a beginning or an end'. *Zayed: a photographic journey*, a full-colour, large-format, pictorial record of Sheikh Zayed's life, and the *Proceedings of the 2001 Archaeological Conference on the United Arab Emirates*, an invaluable record of archaeological studies in the UAE, are amongst the many useful titles in Arabic and English recently published by the Centre.

ZAYED CENTRE FOR COORDINATION AND FOLLOW-UP (ZCCF)

ZCCF is an independent entity set up in September 1999 as a result of Sheikh Zayed's desire to highlight and foster the concept of Arab solidarity in political, economic and cultural, social and inter-Arab relations. The Centre sees itself as having an instrumental role in reinforcing a common Arab identity and contributing to the formulation of a common Arab strategy in the face of new global challenges. To forward its vision of Arab unity, it is active in the promotion of cooperation with international and regional organisations. Lectures and symposiums organised by ZCCF provide

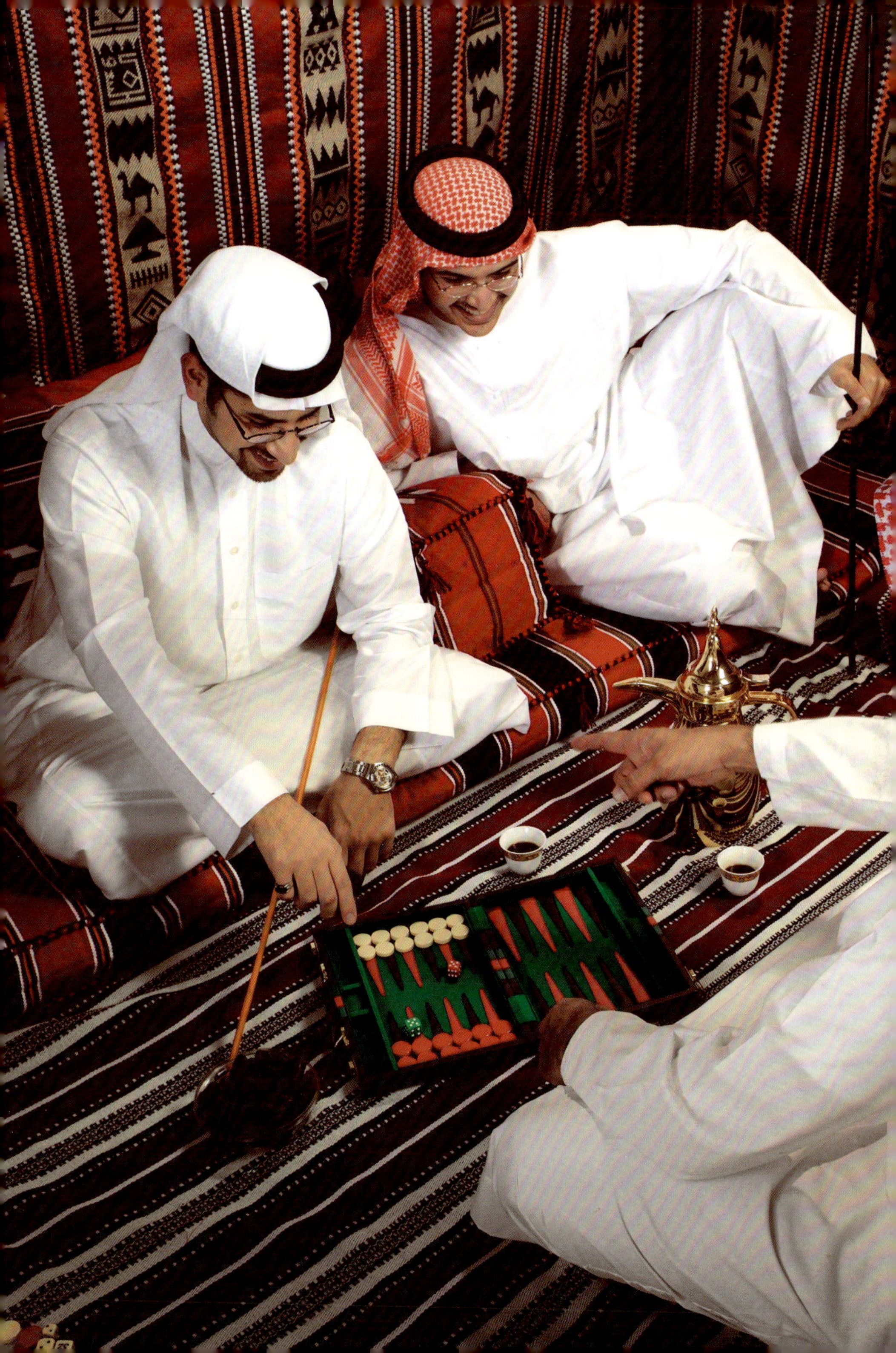

the opportunity for wide-ranging debate with a host of global personalities and its list of publications covers a diversity of issues. Conferences during 2002 explored such varied topics as culture and civilisations, a commemoration of the great Arab philosopher Abdul Rahman Badawi, oil and gas in world politics and an international seminar on the culture of peace and Arab issues. Among international figures hosted by ZCCF since its inception have been former Austrian President and UN Secretary General Kurt Waldheim, former Japanese Prime Minister Ryutaro Hashimoto and Farouq Qaddoumi, Palestinian Foreign Minister. The Centre has won praise for its activities from a number of Arab and foreign leaders, including King Mohammed VI of Morocco, President Jacques Chirac of France (subject of a book issued by the Centre), former US Presidents Jimmy Carter and Bill Clinton, and British Prime Minister Tony Blair.

ZCCF does not neglect the children of the UAE. The Centre's publication *Kharareef: Fairy-Tales from the Emirates*, written by Ibn Madan, is a delightful illustrated collection of stories featuring Sufis, magicians and animals, and introducing children through its pages to the deep well of Arabian culture and tradition. The Centre also produced two studies focusing on the strongly interrelated educational and cultural needs of UAE children: Principles of Education System in the UAE and Child Culture in the United Arab Emirates.

THE EMIRATES CENTRE FOR STRATEGIC STUDIES AND RESEARCH (ECSSR)

The ECSSR, founded in 1994, is an independent research institution dedicated to the promotion of professional research and educational excellence in the UAE and the Gulf area. ECSSR serves as a focal point for scholarship on political, economic, and social issues pertinent to the UAE, the Gulf, and the greater Middle East through the sponsorship of empirical research and scientific studies conducted by scholars from around the globe. The core of its work lies in identifying and analysing issues of vital significance, predicting future trends and devising management strategies to cope with such issues. As well as maintaining and training its own highly dedicated staff of researchers to undertake this work, it hosts conferences, symposia, workshops and lecture series renowned for the international eminence of the participants and the quality of their content and influence. Integral to the strategic success of ECSSR's research programme are the annual Trend Assessment Reports prepared by research analysts in the Centre's different units which, by providing a survey of major international and domestic developments and their possible implications, become a powerful tool in the task of prioritising the goals for the following year.

Current research projects include the 'UAE Economic Diversification Project' (mapping a strategy for diversification in the face of global competition), the 'Influence of the Communication and Information Revolution Upon State and Society in the Gulf' (research involving extensive sampling in several societies of the region is planned) and 'Labour Market and Population Studies' (looking at labour supply and demand together with the social and economic impact of the large expatriate population on the community as a whole).

One of the aims of ECSSR is to forge links with like-minded organisations and it has, since its inception, concluded a number of agreements and scientific cooperation protocols with counterpart institutions at local, regional and international level. By the end of 2000, 17 institutes in Egypt, Germany, Holland, Jordan, Kuwait, Lebanon, Pakistan, Qatar, Russia, Syria, Turkey and the US had signed such protocols.

The ECSSR Eighth Annual Conference, entitled 'Biotechnology and the Future of Society', takes place in January 2003. Participants will include Sir Christopher Evans, founder and CEO of Merlin Biosciences in the UK, Mr Jeremy Rifkin, President of the Foundation on Economic Trends in the US (author of The Biotech Century: Harnessing the Gene and Remaking the World), Dr Michio Kaku, Professor of Theoretical Physics at NYC University (author of the best selling Visions: How Science Will Revolutionize the 21st Century) and Dr Ray A. Goldberg, Professor of Biotech Agribusiness at Harvard University.

The ECSSR's publishing activities have made it one of the major sources of specialised scholarly publications in the region. As well as publishing monographs in its International Studies series, it also publishes the proceedings of conferences, symposia and lectures in Emirates Occasional Papers (an English series) and Strategic Studies (an Arabic series). In addition to these publications ECSSR translates into Arabic works of importance to the Centre and its audience.

A specialised library, state-of-the-art computer and communications facilities help to maintain the standard of excellence achieved by the ECSSR in the less than ten years of its existence. Its future plans include the development of a major database and information bank on Gulf topics.

LIBRARIES

An analysis of numbers visiting Dubai public libraries in 2001 showed a growing interest in reading and a change in readers' habits. A total of 254,341 visitors in 2001 represented a remarkable increase (due in part to a population boom in Dubai) of 100,000 over the previous year. The most prolific readers were Indian, Pakistani and Iranian, with nationals comprising a small but growing number. The numbers of children visiting the libraries almost trebled from 23,799 in 2000 to 62,184 in 2001. Books in the Arabic language proved particularly popular – numbers borrowed in 2001 were 59,491, compared with 20,027 in 2000. The libraries have responded to the increased interest in Arabic publications by increasing their stock of such material. The range of Arabic periodicals, for instance, increased by 100 over the previous year. Internet facilities proved popular, while the new e-Library system by which titles available at all public libraries in the emirate can be accessed through the municipality's website was seen as instrumental in attracting new readers.

THE GROWTH OF MUSEUMS

Tourism, so vital to the economic well-being of the Emirates, does not take place in a vacuum. It must be nurtured. Today's sophisticated visitor is eager for new cultural experiences, and the UAE is alert to the possibilities of its own heritage. But tourism is only one facet of what drives the explosion in cultural renaissance. The UAE's own inhabitants are proud of their heritage and are determined that it should not be lost. Always aware that the key to ensuring the continuity of culture and the nurturing of a population sensitive to its own heritage is education and example, Sheikh Zayed lost no time in starting the process.

In 1971, the first museum was inaugurated in Al Ain at a site chosen by Sheikh Zayed himself. Now, in 2003, plans are under way to make the UAE, described as 'a minaret for cultural radiation', museum capital of the Arab world. Sharjah, with its 15 museums (out of a current total of 21 countrywide), could well stand as a model for such an ambition. In 1998, Sharjah was designated by UNESCO as Cultural Capital of the Arab World for its commitment to art, culture and the preservation of its heritage. Its museums include the impressive, interactive modern Archaeological Museum (among its exhibits is a gold halter, found with a ritually slaughtered horse in a grave near Mleiha), Sharjah Art Museum, an Islamic Museum, Sharjah Heritage Museum, a Science Museum, a Discovery Centre and a Planetarium. Nor is the city content with a mere display of its past cultural achievements – Sharjah Arts Area, with its Art Centre, Art Galleries, the Emirates Fine Arts Society and the Very Special Art Centre for people with disability, provides a shining example of how best to create an environment in which new cultural expression can thrive. Sharjah's visitor figures demonstrate the importance of museums to the tourist industry in the UAE. During a single month in 2002, 21,746 people visited Sharjah museums.

Implementation of the countrywide policy has already begun. A new museum is due to open in Dubai when renovation of a major historic building in the Al Bastakiya district has been completed. The two-storey building, dating from 1918, will house historic coins of the Arab and Islamic era. The renovation itself is part of an overall plan to restore all historic buildings in the Al Bastakiya area (a waterfront quarter where wealthy merchants built their subtly designed windtower houses) to their former glory. The windtowers (*barjeel*) themselves, rising up to 7 metres above the level of the roofs, act to capture the slightest breeze, funnelling this cooling air down into the living areas of the houses and allowing warmer air to escape upwards. The long-term plan includes the opening of more museums, art galleries and restaurants, creating a cultural magnet for tourists.

Abu Dhabi is planning a Dh100 million marine museum – the first of its kind in the Gulf – to complement its famous ship restaurants, the sea sports club and heritage village.

HUMAN RESOURCE DEVELOPMENT
IN
A KNOWLEDGE-BASED ECONOMY
9-11 February 2002
The Emirate
Italian Design
Italian Design
TRIDENT PRESS
NORTHROP GRUMMAN

Other museums can be found throughout the country. Particularly impressive are those of Ra's al-Khaimah, Ajman and Umm al-Qaiwain, all housed in old forts that were once the residences of rulers. The museum in Fujairah, near the old castle, is also well worth visiting.

PRESERVATION THROUGH TRANSFORMATION

If adaptation is the key to survival, then the future of the numerous forts of the UAE is assured for many of them have undergone more than one transformation. The latest guise in which these wonderful forts have appeared is that of museum and exhibition space. From being edifices built primarily to deter, they have become places of enticement for all, enhancing their own intrinsic value through the sheltering of precious artefacts and the display of vanished ways of life. For example, the eighteenth century fort in Ajman switched in 1970 from being the ruler's palace and office to housing the local police force. In 1981 it changed function once again to become a museum housing an interesting collection of archaeological artefacts, manuscripts, old weapons and reconstructions of traditional life. Another fort which reinvented itself as a police headquarters was that of Umm al-Qaiwain. Subsequently restored as a museum, its upper floor includes a high-ceilinged *majlis* (a meeting room and a place to receive guests) elegantly decorated with carved wooden balconies. One of the benefits of having the *majlis* on the second floor was that it took advantage of any available breezes. In Dubai the Al Fahidi Fort has operated as the ruler's residence, an arsenal and a jail. In its current manifestation as a museum it displays in its new underground section some impressively lifelike exhibits of an ancient souq, a Qur'an school, typical Arabic households and an oasis.

Al Jahili Fort (an adobe construction) was built to guard the palm groves and their precious irrigation systems on the gravel plain at the foot of the Hajar Mountains. It had the distinction of being reconstructed as a venue for the UAE pavilion at Expo 2000 in Germany. Even destruction is not necessarily final. Sharjah Fort was torn down in 1969. Undeterred, the present Ruler restored his 1820 family residence with the aid of old photographs and documents, his own notes and the assistance of elderly residents. It is now a museum, with an exhibition area devoted to pearl fishing, education and trade.

The major forts, which were relatively large stone constructions with rounded or square defence towers at each corner, also acted as seats of local government. One of the oldest forts in the UAE is the White Fort (Al Husn) in Abu Dhabi. The original defensive structure of 1793, which served to protect the settlement's well, was the official residence of the Abu Dhabi rulers. Today two sections are clearly distinguishable, a fort dating back to the mid-nineteenth century and a section added in 1936 by Sheikh Shakbut bin Sultan, brother of Sheikh Zayed. The building underwent major renovations in 1983.

HERITAGE VILLAGES

Heritage Villages established throughout the UAE are the custodians of life before oil. Not just for the benefit of tourists, they also provide the inhabitants of the UAE with direct experience of traditional life.

An exciting private venture by UAE national, Ali Al Ghumaish, has resulted in the creation of a new heritage village in Masafi, Ra's al-Khaimah. Already appreciated for the beauty of its man-made waterfall and gardens (plants for which have been imported by another national, Ali Khamis Al Miherizi), the area is further enhanced by the appearance of a cluster of simple *'arish* houses and bedouin tents stocked with traditional handcrafts exemplifying life in the 1940s and 1950s. Plans for the addition of a maritime museum promise to introduce another attractive dimension to this enterprising undertaking.

While heritage villages such as Dubai's Heritage and Diving Villages, Abu Dhabi's Heritage Villages and Hatta Heritage Village answer the need to capture lost or disappearing eras, living traditions are essential to the realisation of a fully functioning culture. Ajman City, for instance, with its natural harbour, is steeped in maritime traditions. A flourishing fishing industry (both traditional and modern) ensures the success of one of the most active dhow-building yards in the country, situated just a few kilometres from the city centre.

SOUQS

Located in all the main towns, souqs (traditional markets) are another absorbing part of the UAE's continuing cultural vibrancy, ranging from the elegant covered souqs reflecting Islamic design in Sharjah to the bustling outdoor market held near Masafi, while Dubai's Electronics Souq is an unashamed combination of traditional and new! A dense array of gold shops, spice shops, craft shops, perfume shops and clothing shops – it is even possible to buy a camel in the market at Al Ain – all grouped together according to speciality make souqs a special delight to the browsing local and tourist alike (particularly those adept at bargaining). Souqs need not be old in order to acquire cultural significance. Sharjah's Blue Souq was built in 1979 and, with its double row of vaulted buildings tiled in blue, linked by bridges and cooled by windtowers, is a fine example of sympathetic architectural design.

SONG, DANCE AND THEATRE

Instrumental music, played on a variety of percussion (two types of drum and a tambourine – *tubool, rahmani* and *daf*), wind instruments (*nai* and the nasal sounding *mizmar*) and strings (*rababa* and *tanboura*), was traditionally accompanied by the human voice. The poetic songs of the bedouin, for example, were sung to the accompaniment of the *rababa*, a one or two-stringed instrument. Music not only formed an essential part of entertainment, it also helped to ease the drudge of daily work. The rhythmic labour required of men working on the pearling vessels was greatly facilitated by the efforts of the *Al Naham*, the vocalist who led the crew through their communal tasks with song, with each task – weighing anchor, raising the sail or diving for pearls – allotted its own particular song. As well as music, there is a strong tradition of dance, be it the mesmerising *na'ashat* in which female dancers sway their long, black hair to the rhythm of a beating drum or the *ayyalah* in which dancing men depict the triumphs and reverses of the battle field. The many folklore groups around the country receive generous support for their dedication to the preservation of these fragile art forms through performance. Such special occasions as weddings and public festivals provide ideal occasions for these revered traditions. Groups sponsored by the Ministry of Information and Culture also perform at functions and festivals around the world.

But of course, in the UAE, love for the traditional does not exclude either the new or the traditions of others. In January 2003, Dubai Media City will host an International Jazz Festival, brainchild of the combined talents of Chillout Productions, The Brass Group, and Prisme International and sponsored chiefly by Philips Electronics. Music will range from Afro, Latin and Oriental Jazz to more contemporary forms of jazz such as blues and funk.

The theatre, too, is strongly supported by the Ministry of Information and Culture which in 2002 announced an annual ceremony to honour those dramatists and playwrights who pioneered the UAE's theatre movement and won awards in GCC and Arab theatre festivals.

HERITAGE AND TECHNOLOGY

The UAE has been quick to realise the potential of new technologies to promote and protect its own cultural wealth. A UAE heritage group, the Emirates Culture Scouts Club, anxious to take advantage of television's potential as an ambassador of the country's cultural assets, has launched a Dh 370,000 project in collaboration with the Ministry of Information and Culture to produce approximately 50 films and documentaries on a variety of social, economic and cultural aspects of the UAE. Four films on the UAE's history, heritage and the strengthening of its Arabic and Islamic identity have already been completed.

The multitude of websites dedicated to publicising and explaining the riches of museums, art galleries, archaeological and historical sites are further evidence of the inventively symbiotic interaction taking place between the new and the old, the technological and the cultural. One proof of the UAE's innovative expertise in this area was the selection of the Sharjah Archaeological Museum's website by the International Council of Museums (ICOM) in 2001 as one of the 11 most important websites in the world posting specialised details on archaeology and pre-historic artefacts.

MEDIA AND INFORMATION

The windows are open for the free flow of information, and those who would wish to close them again are doomed to fail.
(Sheikh Abdullah bin Zayed Al Nahyan, Minister of Information and Culture, Arab Media Forum 2001)

UAE INTERACT

The official website of the UAE Ministry of Information and Culture, UAE Interact (www.uaeinteract.com), was first launched in 1997 and is one of the longest established and most comprehensive Internet sites providing news and information on the UAE. The easily-navigated website is actively managed on a daily basis and contains a substantial database of information that can be searched in a variety of ways. The major sections are as follows: News; Government; Travel Centre; Map Room; Arts Centre; Cultural Centre; The Past; Natural UAE; Educational Centre; Recreational Centre; Books and Shopping. Each of these sections offers comprehensive information sources. The news section, for example, provides a searchable database of over 10,000 news stories together with links to breaking news and information on current and forthcoming events. The travel section focuses separately on leisure and business travellers and provides detailed information on a wide range of topics together with a selectively searchable database of accommodation in the UAE.

From mid-February 2002 until the end of December 2002, UAE Interact's independently monitored statistics indicate that slightly less than a million (981,361) visits were made to the website. These generated over 33 million hits and over 4.5 million page views. The site receives daily visits from over 300 'geographic locations' (North American states are separately listed, along with nation states). The top users were Virginia (USA); UAE; Germany; New York (USA); United Kingdom; California (USA); New Jersey (USA); France; Ontario (Canada); India; Netherlands; Australia; Denmark; Italy; Hong Kong; Singapore; Oman, Texas (USA) and Colorado (USA).

EMIRATES MEDIA INCORPORATED (EMI)

EMI was set up under Federal Law No. 5 for 1999 as the legal successor to the Emirates Broadcasting Corporation and the Al Ittihad Corporation for Press, Publishing and Distribution. As the largest and most diversified media corporation, not only in the UAE but throughout the Arab world, it has interests in all branches of media – television, radio, print, publishing and distribution, and the Internet.

While the Government has relinquished formal control over EMI, ownership is still officially vested in the Government and the corporation remains partially dependent on government funding. Nevertheless, EMI now enjoys editorial and administrative independence and functions very much as a private company. EMI is the parent company of Abu Dhabi Television. In the last year, Abu Dhabi Channel – one of three of the Abu Dhabi Television channels – has been singled out for the excellence of its news coverage (particularly that concerning the Palestinian cause) and the range of issues discussed on its talk shows, while the Abu Dhabi Sports Channel, a pay channel carried on the Showtime platform, has established itself since its launch in 1996 as a leading channel throughout the Arab world, with exclusive rights to the Italian Football League. Emirates Channel, available through terrestrial and satellite transmission, is aimed at a UAE and Gulf audience, concentrating on cultural issues, issues of identity and heritage, as well as political issues. Recently, EMI opened a new office in Cairo, in part of its continuing drive to position itself as a major media player in the Middle East.

Telethon

In April 2002, an EMI-produced telethon campaign, 'For You, Palestine', raised a record-breaking Dh212 million worldwide for the relief of the Palestinian people. The transmission which ran for 13 hours from EMI offices in Beirut, Amman, Cairo, Paris, London, Washington and Jerusalem prompted an overwhelming response from people everywhere anxious to contribute to humanitarian and relief operations.

DUBAI MEDIA CITY (DMC) AND DUBAI INTERNET CITY (DIC)

The creation of DMC, DIC, and Dubai Knowledge Village (see Social Development) situated, as they are, where the Middle East, Africa and South Asia meet, represents an embracing by the UAE of a new world in which information is disseminated so swiftly and so effectively via the Internet, as well as through radio and television satellite services, that the control of information is no longer either feasible or desirable.

While the presence of Microsoft, Oracle, Canon, IBM and HP is an indication of the importance of DIC as a centre of excellence in the world of Information Technology, since its inauguration less than two years ago, DMC has quickly become an international hub for all media-based operations. Among those who have established bases in DMC are such prestigious operations as Reuters, CNN, CNBC (the global satellite channel), Rahbani Productions (one of the largest film production houses in the region), Lintas Middle East North Africa (a major advertising agency network), MBC (the popular Arabic satellite channel), Saudi Research and Publishing Companies (second largest publishers in the world after Time-Warner), Zen TV (a joint venture between DMC and Lebanon's Future Television aimed specifically at the 16- to 35-year age group and focusing on the digital platform), Asianet, Sony TV and Taj TV. The launch of Middle East Television (MET), the first Indian satellite channel to broadcast from DMC, brings to 18 the number of broadcasters operating from DMC. More satellite channels are expected to move into the complex in the near future, attracted by the total solutions on the satellite uplinking front offered through DMC's fully-owned subsidiary, Samcom. It already operates a teleport within DMC and is constructing a new world-class facility at Jebel Ali.

CULTURE AND INFORMATION

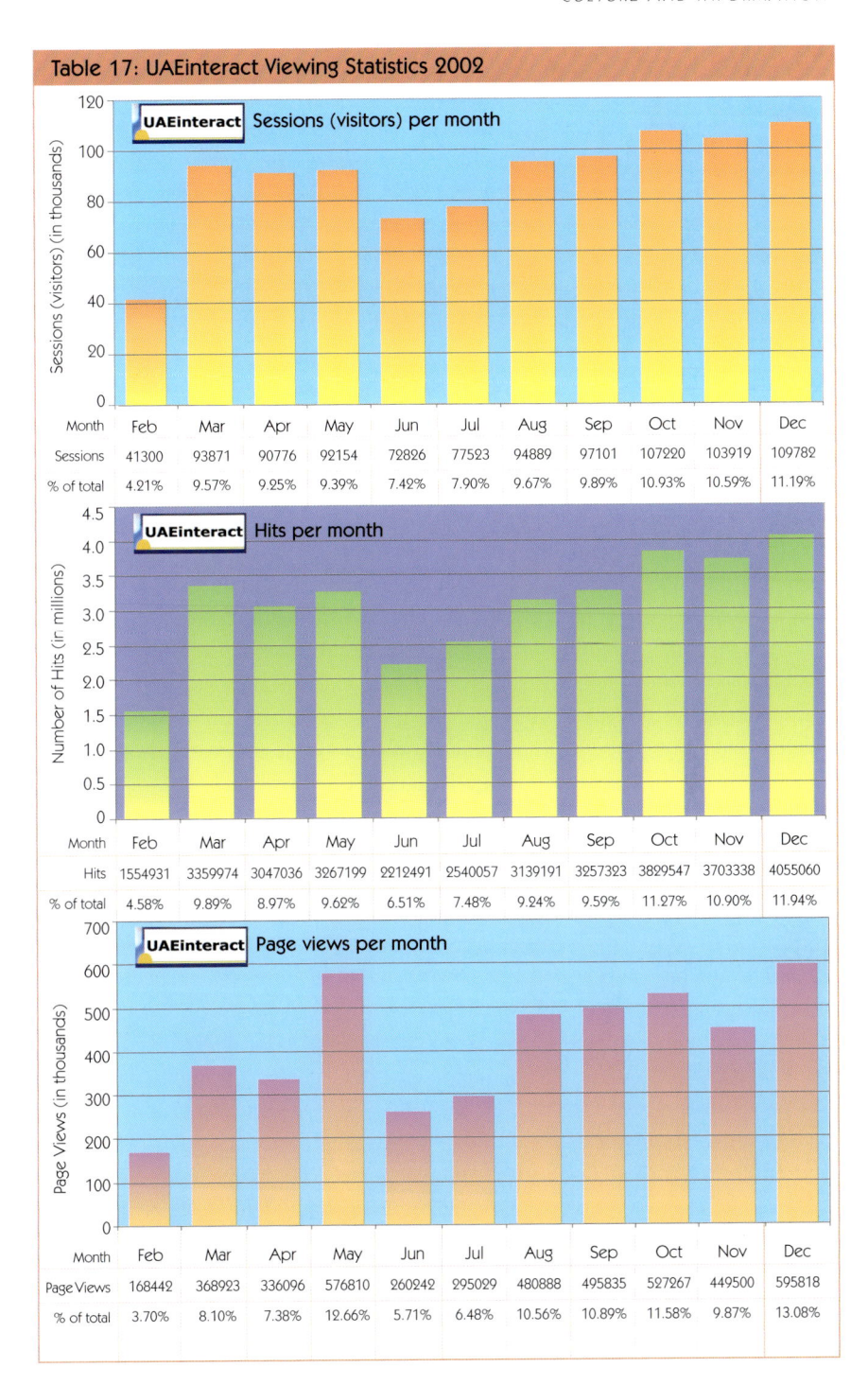

Table 17: UAEinteract Viewing Statistics 2002

UAEinteract Sessions (visitors) per month

Month	Feb	Mar	Apr	May	Jun	Jul	Aug	Sep	Oct	Nov	Dec
Sessions	41300	93871	90776	92154	72826	77523	94889	97101	107220	103919	109782
% of total	4.21%	9.57%	9.25%	9.39%	7.42%	7.90%	9.67%	9.89%	10.93%	10.59%	11.19%

UAEinteract Hits per month

Month	Feb	Mar	Apr	May	Jun	Jul	Aug	Sep	Oct	Nov	Dec
Hits	1554931	3359974	3047036	3267199	2212491	2540057	3139191	3257323	3829547	3703338	4055060
% of total	4.58%	9.89%	8.97%	9.62%	6.51%	7.48%	9.24%	9.59%	11.27%	10.90%	11.94%

UAEinteract Page views per month

Month	Feb	Mar	Apr	May	Jun	Jul	Aug	Sep	Oct	Nov	Dec
Page Views	168442	368923	336096	576810	260242	295029	480888	495835	527267	449500	595818
% of total	3.70%	8.10%	7.38%	12.66%	5.71%	6.48%	10.56%	10.89%	11.58%	9.87%	13.08%

While the cost-effective structure of DMC (a 50-year tax exemption for both organisations – domestic and international – and individuals setting up in the city, free zone regulations allowing operators to fully own the business, the presence in a single geographic location of a comprehensive pool of equipment, facilities and top-to-bottom intellectual expertise) has been vital to its success, the freedom of expression experienced within DMC has been no less important a factor in enticing media organisations such as MBC to relocate from London and Saudi Research and Publishing Companies to relocate from Jeddah and London. This latter factor has been central to DMC's deliberations over the formulation of a code of practice which balances freedom of speech with cultural sensitivities. A tribunal to deal with complaints is also planned. Working within a framework of responsible journalism, DMC has so far established four 'nos': no pornography, no defamatory matter, no preaching of religion other than Islam and no broadcasters owned by political parties.

DMC is not just concerned to attract big companies. Realising that the presence of a strong freelance industry is essential to the cutting of costs and to the generation of a thriving network of talent and ideas, the complex leases units to individuals. A sum of Dh19,000 a year buys a trade licence, resident visa, desk, phone, computer and a shared secretary. So popular was this initiative that the first 150 units sold within two months. In return DMC is benefiting from the presence of a heady mixture of journalists, writers, musicians from the whole of the Arab region and beyond.

The success of both DMC and DIC has given rise to the ambitious expansion programme currently being implemented. In response to unprecedented demand for office space, the Dubai Technology, e-Commerce and Media Free Zone (TECOM) is increasing the total land area of the two complexes by 230 per cent, from its present 1.5 million square feet to 5 million square feet. Of the 650 companies already licensed in the Free Zone (the original target for the close of the first year of operations had been 200), 335 are in DMC, while 315 are in DIC. Web-based companies constitute the largest segment in Internet City (33 per cent) followed by IT support (23 per cent), software development (16.6 per cent), consultancy (6 per cent), application service providers (7 per cent) and back office (7 per cent). In Media City, publishing is the largest sector (25 per cent) followed by advertising and marketing (20 per cent), production and post-production (17 per cent), new media (12 per cent) and broadcasting (9.5 per cent). The rest include music production companies, news agencies, PR firms and companies specialising in recruitment and human resources consultancy. Approximately 80 per cent of the companies setting up in the two complexes are new to the region and, interestingly, TECOM's Director General, Mohammed Al Gergawi, believes that 'Dubai's knowledge economy initiatives are providing the impetus for the growth of the information and communication technology (ICT) and media industries in a vast region stretching from the Middle East to India and South Africa to the CIS countries.'

As a part of this expansion, DMC is poised to become a major production and post-production centre for movies and music. Already, it is home to 20 companies providing such services to the movie and music industry as well as equipment leasing and supply of outdoor units for films and documentaries, multimedia productions, graphic designing for movie production and 3D animations for feature films and cartoons. While up to 25 Indian movies and documentaries were made on location within the UAE during 2001, approximately 90 per cent of equipment and technical skill was outsourced. The creation of a comprehensive pool of equipment and skills within DMC will greatly facilitate the operating and cost efficiency of such projects.

ANNUAL MEDIA STUDENTS AWARDS

These awards, organised by DMC, will encourage young media talent from universities within and beyond the UAE. Students from India, Lebanon, Egypt and South Africa are to be targeted in an effort to increase commitment to mass media and communications and harness talent throughout the entire region. The awards, in photography, radio, TV production, journalism filmmaking, graphic design and advertising, will take the form of either scholarships for postgraduate studies or the payment of fees for intensive training programmes at internationally recognised institutions.

TV, RADIO, NEWSPAPERS AND INTERNET

The UAE has numerous local satellite TV stations. Some focus on Arab culture and identity, others on business and sport. It also has a number of terrestrial stations broadcasting in Arabic and English, including Abu Dhabi TV, Emirates Channel, Abu Dhabi Sports Channel, Dubai 33, Sharjah Channel 22 and Ajman Channel 4.

All of the pay-TV transnational broadcasters such as Orbit, Star, Showtime, and ART have a presence in DMC. Emirates Cable TV and Multimedia (E-Vision), a subsidiary of Emirate Telecommunication Corporation (ETISALAT) and the UAE's only cable television network, offers viewers a total of 90 channels in 14 languages. Now it is introducing a pay-per-view service which will show films in Arabic, Hindi and English, as well as special sports events. E-Vision offers an interactive electronic programming guide (EPG) which allows viewers or subscribers not only to check show schedules on the TV itself, but to programme their TV viewing based on particular categories (e.g. film/actor preference) or genre.

Up to now, only certain parts of the UAE have been able to access E-Vision via hybrid fibre coaxial cable technology. A decision to provide (through the French company, MDS, in conjunction with ETISALAT), wireless cable technology, should see all parts of the UAE brought within the network by the end of 2003.

Radio stations include popular English language stations such as Dubai FM 92, Channel 4 FM, and Emirates 1 and 2 FM.

There are five Arabic and three English daily newspapers in circulation in the country, as well as more than 160 magazines and journals published by local and national organisations, cultural centres, clubs, chambers of commerce and industry, municipalities and educational institutions.

THE EMIRATES NEWS AGENCY (WAM)

Like EMI, WAM too is moving away from its former role of government voice. WAM, which is managed by the Ministry of Information and Culture, transmits news in Arabic and English. It has a staff of 190 journalists, including 23 foreign correspondents covering places as far afield as Cairo, Beirut, Washington DC, Islamabad, Sanaa and Brussels. It has cooperation and news exchange agreements with more than 20 Arab countries and is a member of the Federation of the Gulf Cooperation Council News Agencies, the Federation of the Arab News Agencies (FANA), the Islamic News Agencies Union and the Association of Non-Aligned News Agencies. Seventy per cent of the staff are UAE nationals, while management is 95 per cent emiratised. In six years, the numbers of UAE women journalists in WAM has risen from zero to 20, with most of those joining as graduates on an intern programme. Originally set up to cover topics of national interest, WAM has now broadened its remit to cover topical news events worldwide.

DUBAI PRESS CLUB

The Dubai Press Club (DPC), replete with Internet link-ups, individual earphones for employees and a bank of overhead TV screens tuned in to news stations around the world, was launched in 1999 with the objective of promoting communication and liaison with the international press. In furtherance of this objective, the DPC has formed an International Association of Press Clubs with 20 other press clubs from around the world. Among the prominent press figures to have addressed the DPC this year were Thomas Friedman of the *New York Times*, and Bill Bradley, vice-president of the *Washington Post*. Under the powerful management of the young UAE woman, Mona Al Marri, the DPC has so far established two major media projects – the Arab Journalism Awards (the first such awards in the Arab world) and the Arab Media Summit.

In this, the second year of the Arab Journalism Awards, a special category called the 'Courage Declaration' was created to honour the Palestinian media, currently operating under the most difficult of circumstances, and to help in the rebuilding of their media institutions. A poem by UAE Defence Minister, Dubai Crown Prince Sheikh Mohammed bin Rashid Al Maktoum, shown on a video clip, urged the world to support the Palestinian people in their struggle for justice.

THE INTERNET

Given the investment in Information Technology, it is not surprising to find that the UAE is one of the top 20 countries in the world as far as Internet usage is concerned. Access to the Internet is via Emirates Internet and Multimedia (EIM), the

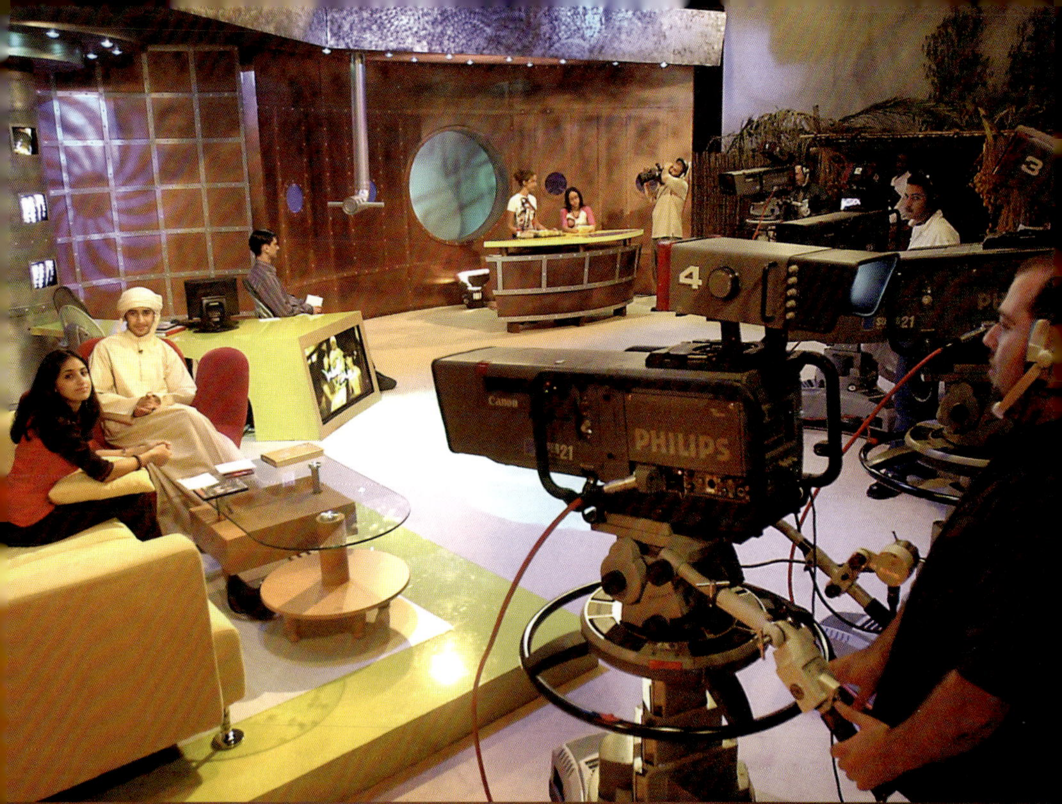
PHILIPS
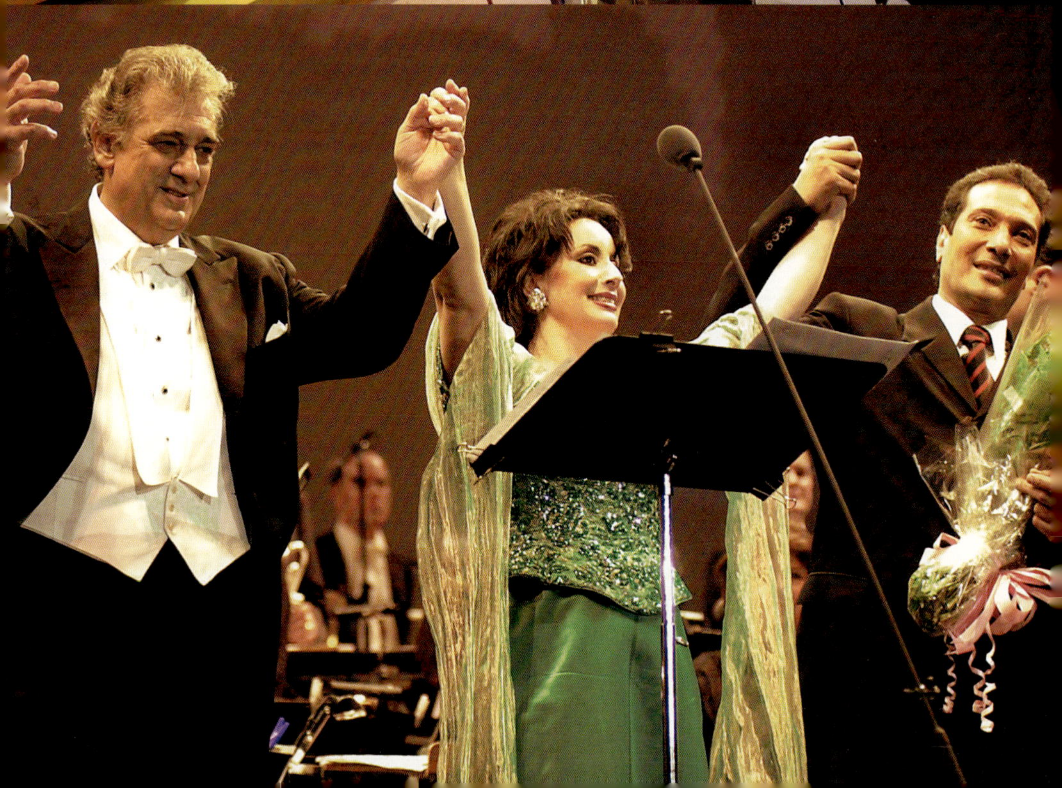

sole Internet Service Provider (ISP) for the country. EIM's multilingual search engine Arabvista, created in 2000, and its bilingual portal Albahhar, launched a year later, are part of EIM's commitment to expanding and improving services to its customers. Both its corporate sites, www.eim.ae/ and www.albahhar.com/, were revamped in September 2002.

Although it has been suggested that the time has come to allow subscribers themselves to choose whether or not to make use of the proxy filtering system currently provided automatically by EIM, a survey conducted by EIM found that 60 per cent of its 14,000 domestic subscribers were in favour of EIM retaining the status of proxy server, indicating that its role in protecting users from offensive material is considered to be an acceptable form of censorship. Fifty-one per cent of customers specifically felt that the proxy server protected family members while surfing online. Business users and others who connect directly to the Internet by a dedicated line are unaffected by the filtering system. The UAE, with Internet penetration rates for 2001 standing above the European average (according to World Markets Research Centre), is not typical of Arab countries. While the UAE has a penetration rate of almost 30 per cent, the average Arab penetration rate was 5.8 per cent, compared with an average European rate of 20 per cent.

One possible reason for the low penetration rates in the Arab world may be the dearth of Arabic websites. This, allied to the fact that 95 per cent of the Internet's websites are English language sites, makes the existence of such sites as EIM's bi-lingual portal, http://www.albahhar.com/, and the EMI website, www.emi.co.ae, vitally important for the expansion of the Internet in the Arab region. While a fine interaction of culture and ideas powered by technological advances and the globalisation of information is demonstrated by such ventures as the online partnership between BBCArabic.com and DMC, offering BBC online news content in both Arabic and English at www.dubaimediacity.com/news, and the new CNNArabic.com site, launched at the beginning of 2002, these are not uniquely Arabic in their provenance. The Albahhar portal, which aims not only to increase the number of Arab Internet users but also to provide a means of introducing Arab and Islamic culture to as wide an audience as possible, is a rich source of Arab-generated news, Arabic literature and poetry, chat services, jokes, career information and a regional classified section. Equally important as an Arabic source in attracting more Arab users is the Emirates Media website, winner of the Golden Web Award (from the International Association of Web Masters), launched in 2000. This website broadcasts news from its own Abu Dhabi Channel and Sports Channel, as well as transmitting live broadcasts of all the EMI radio stations – news, classical music, both Arabic and international, popular Arabic music and international pop (emi.co.ae/sof.ram). Additionally, it displays the newspaper *Al Ittihad* (established in 1969) and the magazines *Majid* (for children) and *Zahrat Al Khaleej* (a popular family magazine).

INTERNET CAFÉS

Internet Cafés have become hugely popular in the UAE. First introduced in 1996, they were an immediate success both as meeting places within the community and as a way of connecting to the Internet. They have proved particularly useful as a means for expatriates to keep in touch with friends and family. By August 2002, there were 191 cafés operating throughout the country, of which 98 had opened in 2002 alone. The number of Internet enabled PCs installed during the same period was 1252, bringing the total number of PCs to 2563. During the single month of July 2002, 28 new cafés opened and 290 PCs were installed.

PROTECTION OF INTELLECTUAL PROPERTY

The UAE operates a strict enforcement policy of its piracy and patent laws, seeing the protection of creativity as a necessity in itself and an essential part of the country's drive towards a prosperous and successful economy. In a recent series of raids, the Ministry of Information and Culture arrested 34 retailers of pirated computer programmes, seizing, during operations, 550 pirated compact discs and 47 computers loaded with a large quantity of unlicensed programmes. A member of the World Intellectual Property Organisation (WIPO), the UAE acceded to the Paris Convention for the Protection of Industrial Property in 1996 following the implementation of three intellectual property laws early in 1993.

Copyright laws – their precise scope and their stringent enforcement – are of particular importance to those involved in any aspect of the media business, and the new Federal Author and Copyrights and Parallel Rights Law No. 7, issued in August 2002, gives copyright protection to authors and artists not only during their lifetime but also for 50 years (an increase from 25) after their death. Variations exist in the case of joint copyright and community copyright. The new law lists the works of art entitled to protection as well as those falling beyond the scope of protection. It defines holders of parallel rights and public performers and stipulates under what circumstances the Court of First Instance may suspend the reproduction, show, display or performance of a work of art, or impound the original work of art together with any copies. The law covers photography (defining the rights of both photographer and person photographed), the misuse of software and their applications, as well as databases. Copyright violations in general attract fines and/or terms of imprisonment varying according to the severity or frequency of the infringement.

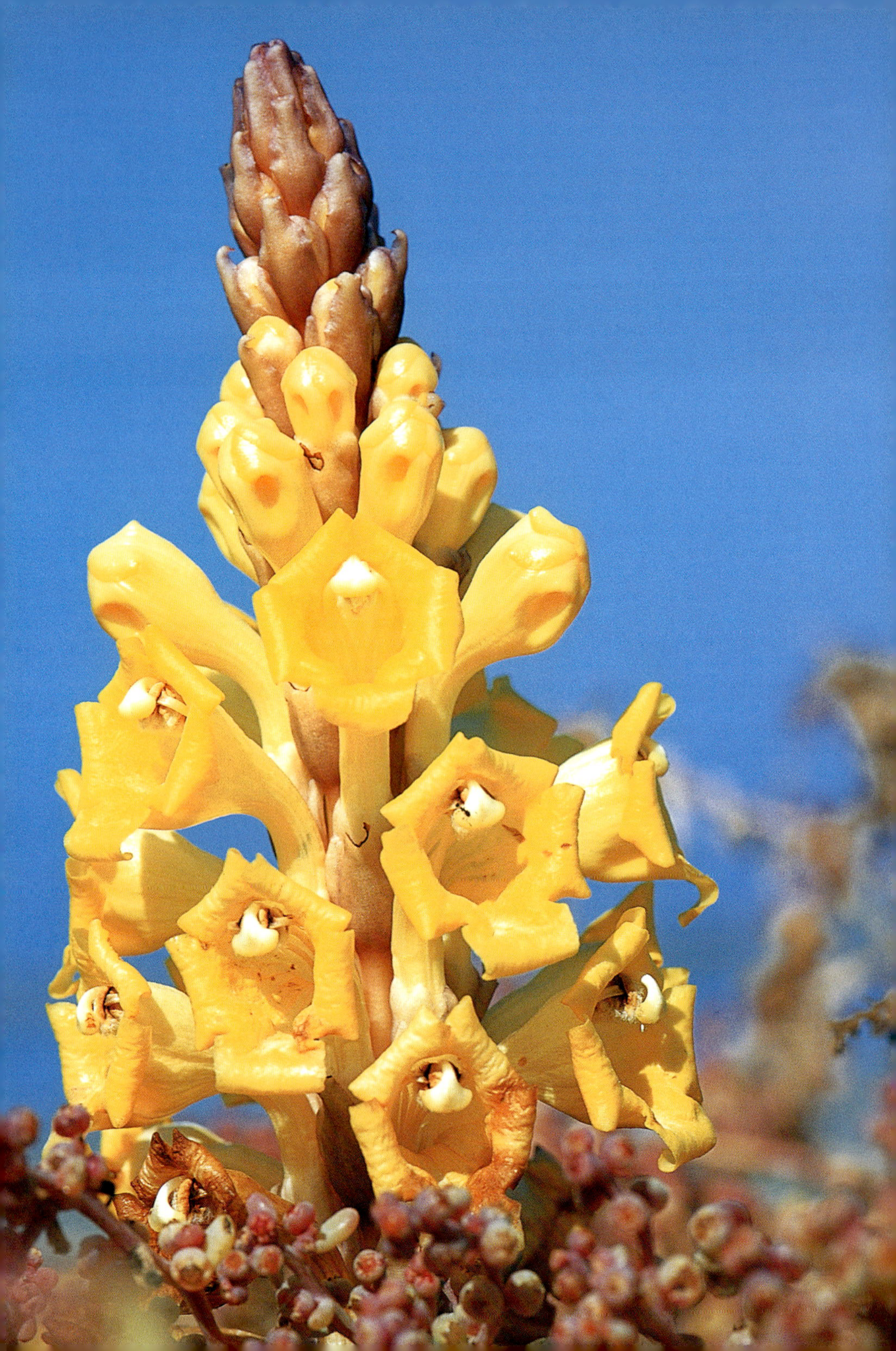

ENVIRONMENT

ENVIRONMENTAL CONFERENCES, SYMPOSIA and other meetings punctuated the past year in the UAE, with messages on eco-friendly and sustainable development coming loud and clear from both the private and public sector. The environment and related issues remain a fashionable growth industry, with research and innovation very much a part of day-to-day operations locally. Whether a hotel performing a green audit, a diving club clearing debris from the seabed or a major oil company installing the technology to eliminate flaring, for example, 2002 has seen a continuing programme of consolidation and the momentum generated over the past few years was maintained. Education and awareness programmes and a healthy amount of coverage by the media continue to spread the word, as well as, equally usefully, the latter highlighting offences and penalties.

Of particular importance in the international arena was, of course, the World Summit. This commenced in Johannesburg, South Africa, in August 2002, and it is only fitting that this should be reported on here first.

WORLD SUMMIT ON SUSTAINABLE DEVELOPMENT

Substantial effort went into preparation of the UAE national report on sustainable development for presentation at the World Summit. This report reviewed the socio-economic trends in the UAE, identified the major factors influencing sustainable development and detailed international and regional cooperation in this field. Also presented for the first time, much of it newly developed, were national environmental priorities, environmental strategies and action plans devised according to the earlier so-called Agenda 21, from 'Rio' ten years previously.

One particular initiative, Abu Dhabi Global Environmental Data Initiative (AGEDI) described later, is a demonstration of the UAE's commitment towards environmental conservation and sustainable development.

GOVERNMENTAL BODIES

The Federal Environment Agency (FEA) established a National Committee for Biodiversity and commenced preparation of a comprehensive national strategy and action plan. This involved consultation with all relevant national authorities and organisations, to some of which particular responsibilities have, or will ultimately be devolved.

New by-laws to strengthen existing federal environmental legislation were drafted by the FEA, concerning, in particular, pollution both on land and at sea, the handling of hazardous materials and medical waste, and pest control substances and fertilisers. Provisions relating to soil and air pollution were also included.

Federal Law No. 11 for 2002, issued in October 2002, was designed to regulate trade in endangered wildlife, as detailed below, with penalties including hefty fines and custodial sentences.

A global initiative on environmental data collection (AGEDI) led by Abu Dhabi's Environmental Research & Wildlife Development Agency (ERWDA) was launched at the World Summit in Johannesburg in autumn 2002. The anticipated benefits to be derived from this bold initiative are considered to be improvement to critical environmental decision-making through the enhanced quality of environmental data held, an improved understanding of the national, regional and global context and the possibility of identifying best environmental practices. Together with improved capacity building and opportunity for analysis and influencing policy making objectively, the initiative makes the likelihood of financial savings and instant information availability very real possibilities.

ERWDA's five-year environmental strategy, 2000–2004, was adopted during the year, its aim being to promote sustainable development throughout Abu Dhabi Emirate. One major part of this exercise has been the commencement of a year-long marine resources survey to assess national fish stocks and recruitment rates amongst commercial species within the Gulf. Short-term fishing bans of various species during the breeding season were also introduced during the year by differing relevant authorities in a move to protect stocks. Also, tighter rules on sports fishing came into effect in Abu Dhabi Emirate this year, with all anglers required by law to obtain a licence. Professional fishermen have required licences since 1999.

Other continuing initiatives from ERWDA included compilation of a national environmental database, an overview of water management and related policy, establishment of a protected area network and oilspill sensitivity mapping and contingency planning. Training in oilspill management was undertaken jointly by Abu Dhabi Petroleum University and ERWDA. Only minor oilspills were reported during the course of the year.

During 2002, ERWDA was selected as the new Middle East and West Asia regional centre for research into mangroves and saltmarsh, working closely with UNDP and other parties.

Sharjah's Environment and Protected Areas Authority (EPAA) was also proactive during the year, hosting seminars on environment protection, awareness campaigns and exhibitions. The Breeding Centre under EPAA, as noted later, continues to have spectacular success with propagation of the critically endangered Arabian Leopard.

The Ra's al Khaimah Environmental Protection and Industrial Development

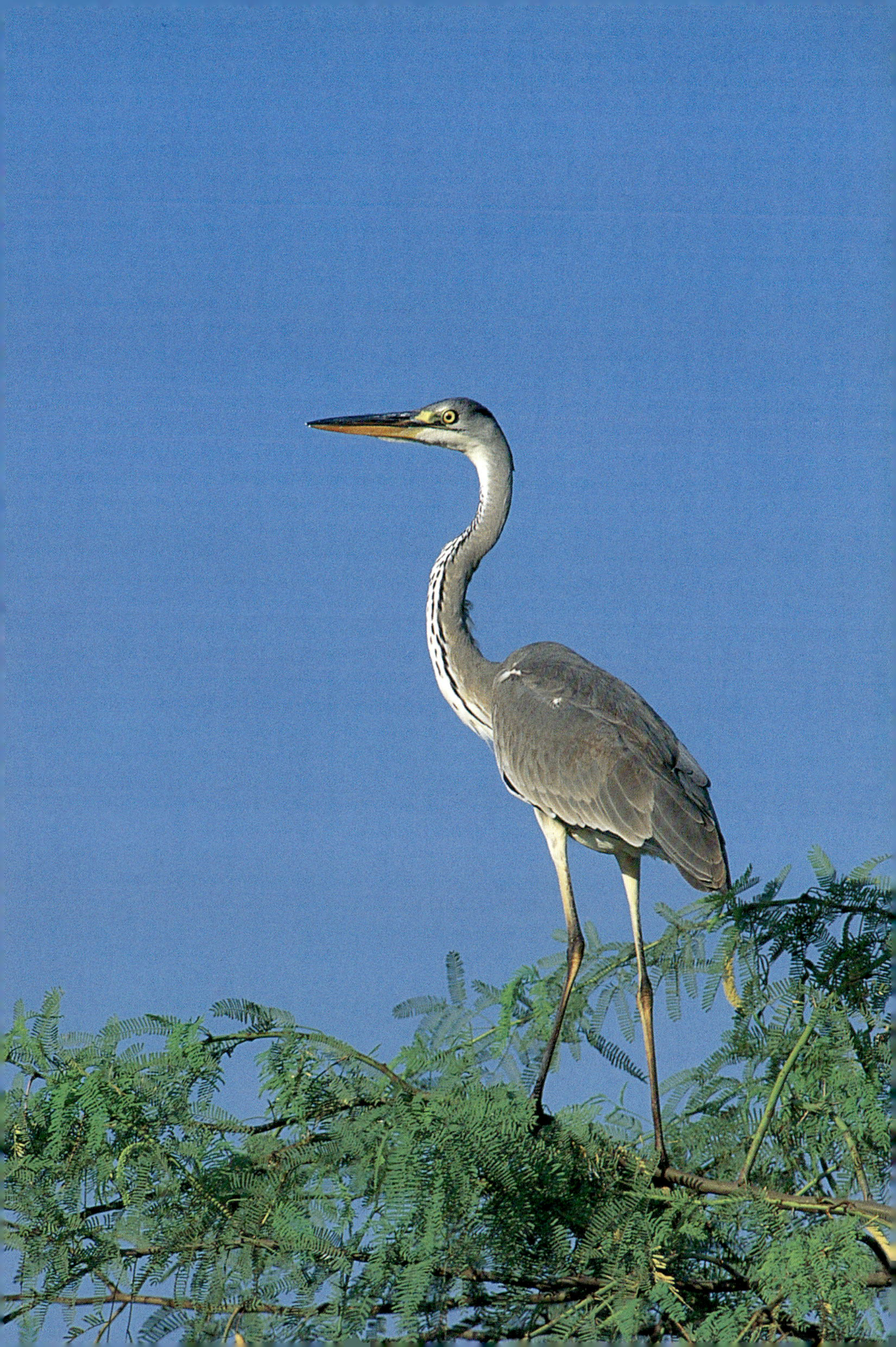

Commission, in only its third year of existence, has the dual function of regulating industrial development and ensuring environmental protection in the emirate.

PROTECTED AREAS

The proposed Bu Tinah-Marawah marine protected area (MPA), which first became a very real possibility last year, has become a reality. Formal designation by the Crown Prince, HH Sheikh Khalifa bin Zayed, of an area of over 4250 square kilometres of coral development and seagrass beds took place by decree early in 2002. Around 75 per cent of the dugong (seacow) population of the UAE is found within the MPA, an area which is also the feeding ground for the largest concentration of green turtles found anywhere in the country. Fishing is now entirely banned in this area. Plans were being prepared at the end of the year for the extension of the MPA to include further areas to the east, around the UAE's largest island, Abu al-Abyadh.

Efforts are also under way by Sharjah's Environment & Protected Areas Authority (EPAA) to establish a marine protected area along the Arabian Sea coast at Khor Fakkan. This would complement the three such areas designated by the Fujairah Government several years ago along the same coast.

During the year under review, Sheikh Mohammed bin Rashid Al Maktoum, Dubai Crown Prince and UAE Minister of Defence, ordered that the area around Al Maha resort, inland from Dubai city, be designated a nature reserve. Dubai Municipality is managing the reserve, and has introduced the necessary regulations to ensure that all potentially damaging activities have been prohibited.

ERWDA was engaged at the end of the year in research designed to designate several further areas of Abu Dhabi Emirate as protected areas.

CONSERVATION

'Save the Dugong' Campaign

The world's second largest population of dugong is found in the Arabian Gulf. It remains, however, an endangered species due to threats to its natural habitat and to its inherent low reproductive potential. It is fully protected in the UAE. Abu Dhabi's Environmental Research and Wildlife Development Agency (ERWDA) continues to undertake research on this species, primarily within the newly created marine protected area surrounding Marawah Island (see above), the core of its range in the UAE. Efforts are also focused on increasing awareness amongst residents of the country on threats to an animal that is seen as a conservation flagship.

Arabian Leopards

The Breeding Centre for Endangered Arabian Wildlife, part of the Environment and Protected Areas Authority (EPAA) in Sharjah, continues to go from strength to strength. Twice during the past year, Arabian leopards (*Panthera pardus nimr*) gave birth to cubs and the centre now houses 12 individuals of this, the most critically endangered

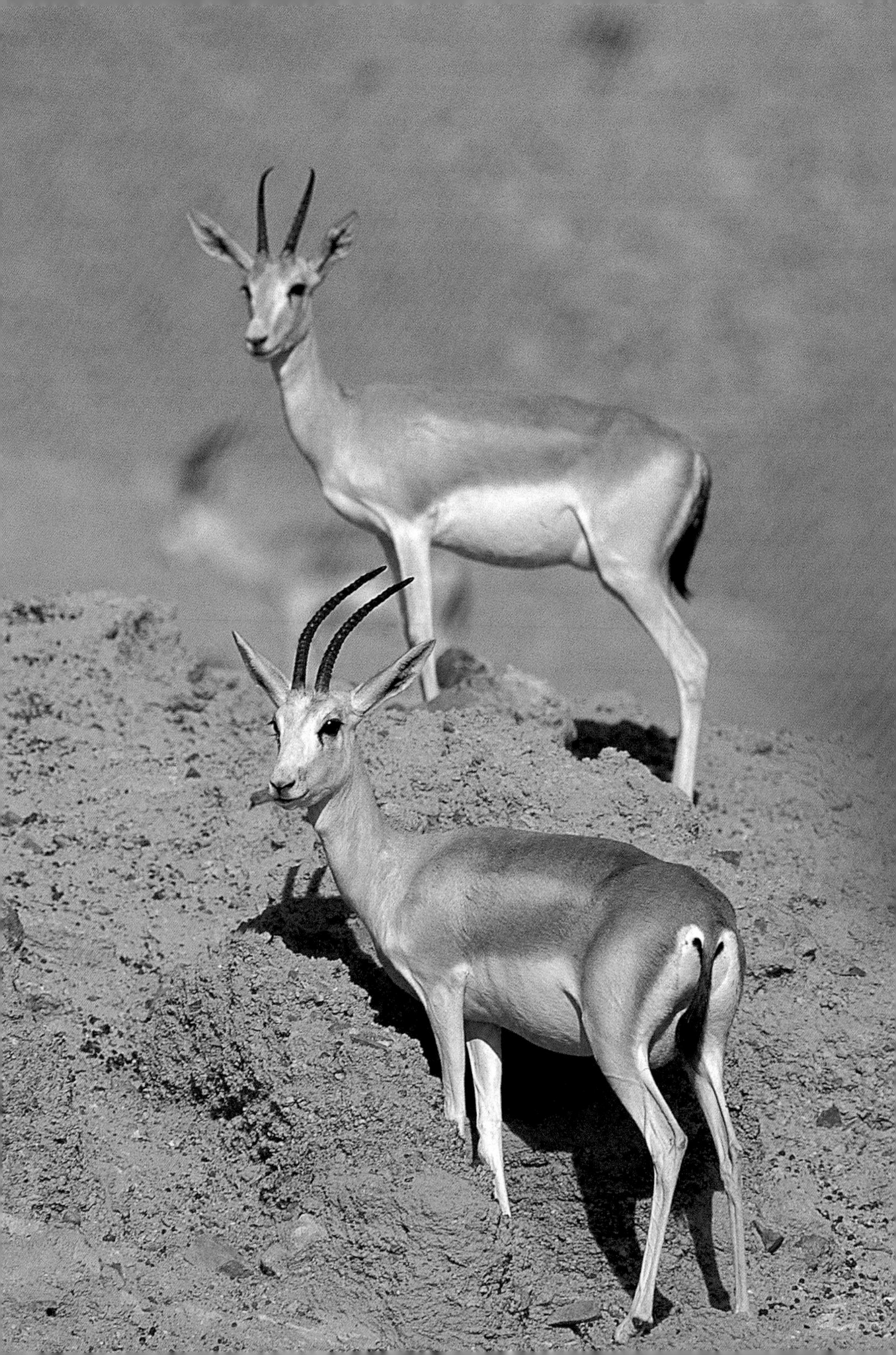

predator in Arabia. International collaboration between the UAE, Oman, Saudi Arabia and Yemen, with breeding loans and exchange of expertise, are part of ongoing conservation effort involving both this and other threatened mountain species such as the similarly rare Arabian tahr (*Hemitragus jayakari*).

Falcon Releases

In April 2002 the Sheikh Zayed Falcon Release Programme again liberated birds in Pakistan, in the North West Frontier Province. A total of 686 sakers and peregrines have been released since the programme commenced in 1995. Satellite and radio-tracking studies continue to provide essential information on the survival, dispersal and recruitment of these birds.

Houbara

Scientific research into the migration and population ecology of the Asian houbara, the favoured prey of falconers, continues along the entire migratory flyway from Asia to Arabia. An alarming population decline continues to be detected throughout central Asian breeding grounds, this being attributable to a combination of hunting pressure, illegal trapping and habitat change or loss.

A new captive breeding facility for houbara opened in Dubai, but the future for the species is still seen in in situ conservation efforts, specifically within its Asian breeding range. The World Conservation Union (IUCN) Species Survival Commission Asian Houbara Specialist Group, the secretariat of which is based in Abu Dhabi, has produced a written strategy for the conservation of the species across the Range States. Management and protection of breeding habitat and areas, the monitoring of annual breeding success and promotion of sustainable hunting practices amongst visiting falconers are all highlighted as paramount for the strategy to succeed.

Arabian Oryx

Increased conservation effort aimed at the Arabian oryx have seen the establishment of a conservation committee consisting of representatives from all the range states, the secretariat being hosted and chaired by the UAE. A bilingual newsletter and website (see: www.whiteoryx.org) have been launched to publicise the committee's activities and foster information sharing.

INTERNATIONAL NGOS

Pre-eminent amongst developments involving non-governmental organisations in 2002 has been the inauguration of an ambitious programme of conservation projects by WWF-UAE through its local partner the Emirates Wildlife Society, now a joined force known as WWF-EWS (email: wwfuae@erwda.gov.ae). EWS operates under the patronage of HH Sheikh Hamdan bin Zayed Al Nahyan, Minister of State for Foreign Affairs and operates from offices provided by the Environmental Research and Wildlife Development Agency (ERWDA) in Abu Dhabi.

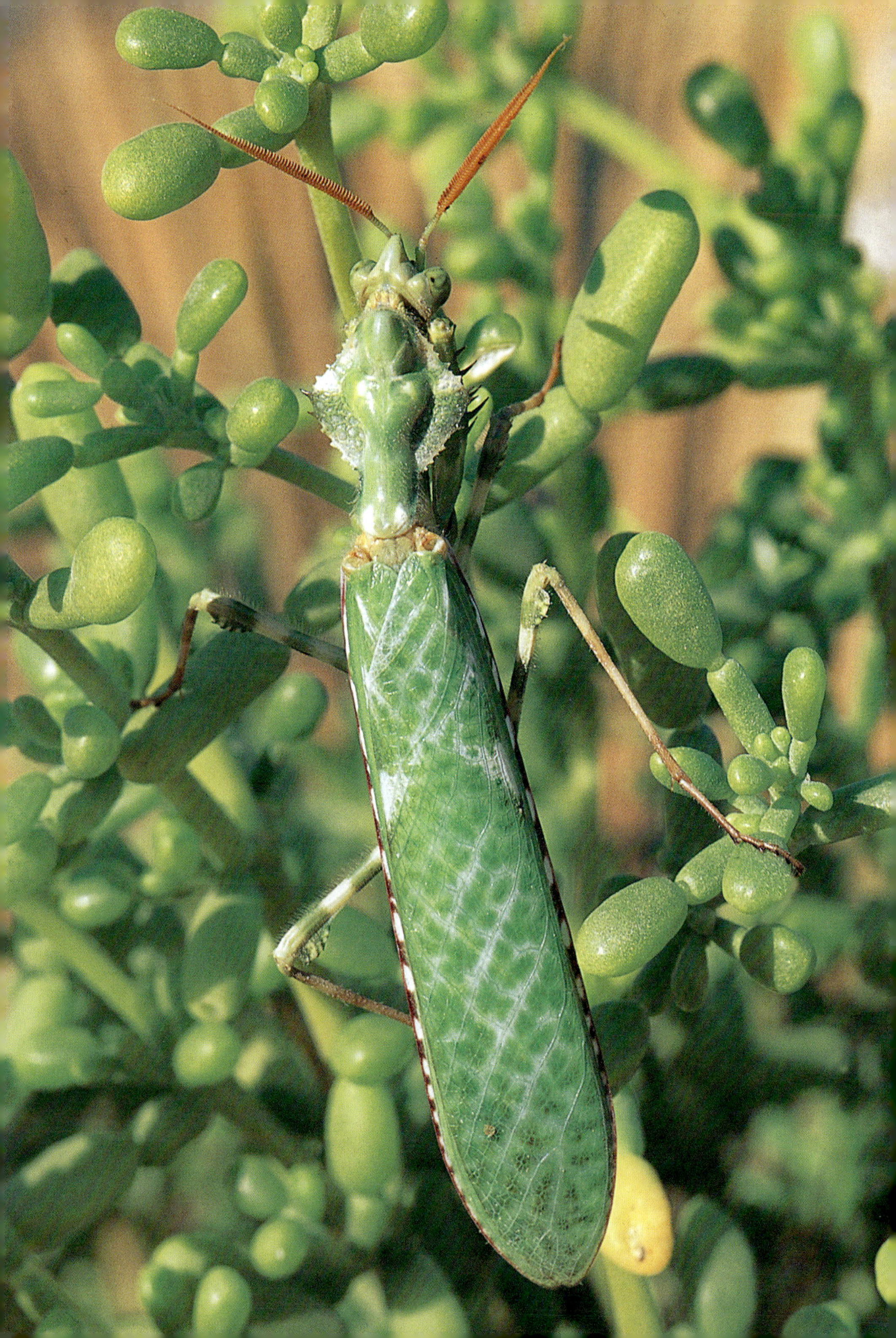

Following the signing of a joint cooperation agreement with UNESCO late in 2001, in May 2002, a UNESCO team visited Khor Kalba, Sharjah, on the UAE's East Coast, to undertake a study of the site's potential for biosphere reserve status. The visit was supported by the Sharjah's Environmental and Protected Areas Authority, with discussions currently ongoing on a timetable for designation of this internationally important site. If successful, this would become the first such reserve in the UAE.

It was announced by Sheikh Abdullah bin Zayed Al Nahyan, Minister of Information and Culture, that the legal framework to permit the UAE to sign the UNESCO administered World Heritage Convention was currently under review.

CITES

With a long and chequered history, the UAE's compliance with the Convention on Trade in Endangered Species of Flora and Fauna (CITES) has posed problems for local environmental officials for a number of years. Problems with controls on the transit trade through the UAE of caviar being illegally exported from the Central Asian states led in November 2001 to a recommendation being issued by CITES to its members of a ban on the import, export or re-export of any CITES listed species to or from the UAE being effectively halted with immediate effect (see www.CITES.org/news). On instructions from senior officials, immediate action was taken to revamp and strengthen the existing mechanism for implementation of CITES rules, and at the CITES meeting in Chile in late 2002, the ban was lifted. Among relevant changes related to the administration of the convention at local level were the selection of the Federal Environmental Agency (FEA) to replace the Ministry of Agriculture and Fisheries as the national CITES management authority, with ERWDA being designated as the scientific authority.

Implementation of Federal Law No. 11 for 2002 was expedited to meet the objectives of CITES through national legislation, and the law will now come into effect in early 2003. Animals found to have been smuggled into the country are being confiscated and taken to designated rehabilitation centres. Education and awareness campaigns targeting the public are under way, with training courses and workshops for relevant officials also concurrent. With the international trade in wildlife becoming increasingly organised and difficult to monitor, the effectiveness of CITES is likely, however, to remain in question, while the UAE's experience over the past year showed clearly that the actions of the CITES Secretariat itself can sometimes contribute to the problems. Thus the temporary ban imposed by CITES on trade with the UAE prevented the import of hitherto legitimately traded captive-bred falcons and raised the market price and demand for smuggled and illegally caught birds.

The International Union for the Conservation of Nature (see www.iucn.org) and the Species Survival Commission (IUCN/SSC) along with the Re-introduction Specialist Group (RSG), which is hosted by the Environmental Research and Wildlife

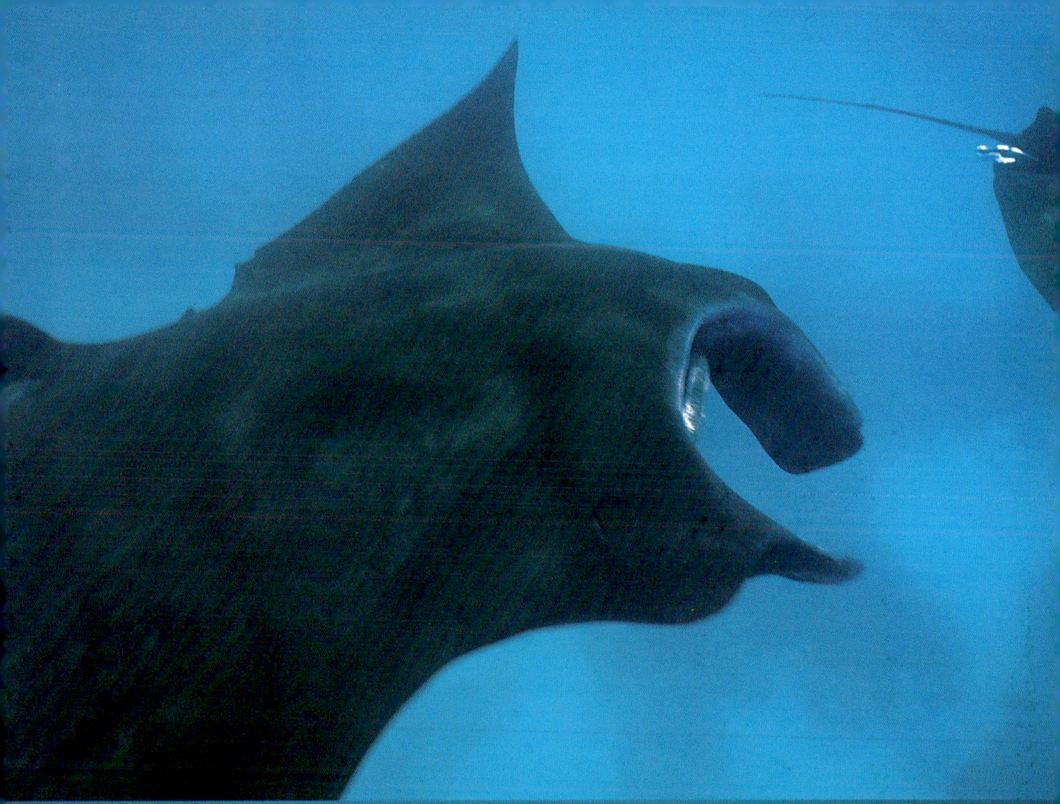

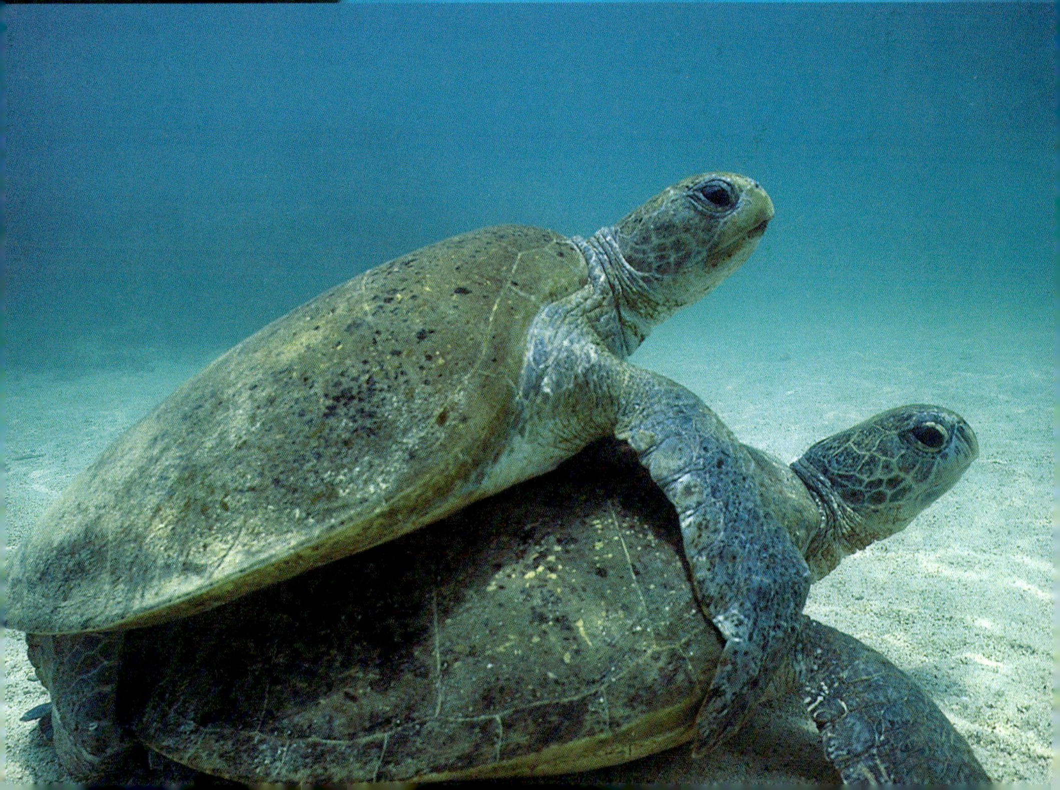

Development Agency (ERWDA) in Abu Dhabi, issued a bi-lingual (Arabic-English) booklet on the Guidelines for the Placement of Confiscated Animals. There are plans to distribute copies to relevant wildlife authorities in Arabic speaking countries in the Middle East and North Africa. It is hoped that this will enable authorities to decide on the best available options to deal with live confiscated animals arising from illegal trade.

A domestic register of falcons held in the UAE for non-commercial purposes was introduced during the year. Each bird is now required to have a so-called 'falcon passport' with which it will be permitted to be taken abroad for hunting trips.

SYMPOSIA AND CONFERENCES

The Second International Symposium and Workshop on Arid Zone Environments was hosted jointly by ERWDA and UNEP in December 2001. The conservation of mangroves and saltmarsh ecosystems was the principal theme of this year's event.

The Water and Energy Technology and Environment Exhibition (WETEX) held in Dubai in February 2002, was timed to coincide with the UAE's fifth National Environment Day which fell on 4 February 2002. The main theme during a week-long programme to mark the latter, now annual, event concerned water sustainability and development. Other important events in 2002 included Arab Environment Day, 14 October and International Day for Biological Diversity, 29 December.

ENVIRONMENTAL AWARENESS

Besides the activities of government agencies already mentioned, a number of other bodies continued during the year to produce valuable educational and awareness material. *Al Bee'ee al Saghier* – the Young Environmentalist magazine produced by the Food and Environment Control Centre of the Abu Dhabi Municipality – has a circulation of up to 10,000 per issue (www.beeeesagheer.com). Two of the UAE's well-known and energetic NGOs, the Emirates Environment Group (EEG) and Environment Friends Society (EFS) remain extremely active in this particular field (www.eeg-uae.org).

Also active in terms of environmental awareness are the three chapters of the Emirates Natural History Group, in Abu Dhabi, Dubai and Al Ain, which continued to organise regular programmes of meetings and fieldtrips throughout the course of the year.

INNOVATION AND RESEARCH

ADNOC, the Abu Dhabi National Oil Company, has introduced solar power generation in its housing complexes, thus making tremendous annual savings on fuel bills. Costs can be fully recovered within six years of installation. The company policy is to promote a clean environment and maintenance of finite resources. In a similar vein, the Abu Dhabi Company for Onshore Oil Operations (ADCO) part of the ADNOC group of companies, remains committed to zero flaring and a reduction in CO_2 emissions.

Biological control methods are being developed to bring the date palm weevil under control in the UAE and in other date-producing nations. In the UAE, the programme is being funded by Government, as is the case elsewhere in the region, while the Islamic Development Bank (IDB) has also contributed to the programme.

The International Centre for Biosaline Agriculture (ICBA) based in Dubai, continues to undertake and support research into what is seen as an increasingly relevant and critical field, the potential for production of salt-tolerant crops on a commercial footing. Technology transfer is seen as an important component to the centre's work. In recognition of the significant future role that biosaline agriculture will need to play both at home and overseas the Dubai Government has waived all water charges incurred by the centre (icba@biosaline.org.ae).

Research into the country's flora and fauna continued throughout the year to be a major focus for ERWDA and the Sharjah EPAA, while voluntary bodies, including the Emirates Bird Records Committee, and individual scientists also continued to study aspects of wildlife, publishing results both locally and overseas. Major new studies on the flora and reptiles of the country are due to be completed early in 2003.

Finally, a novel use for grass cuttings and camel dung has been the focus of an innovative programme of research. The two ingredients are the mainstay of successful bioremediation efforts by BP Sharjah to mitigate residual environmental liabilities from oil spills and oil-based [drilling] mud. An *in situ* bioremediation land farm for receipt of contaminated soil needing cleaning has now been established. The treatment uses the bacteria found naturally in camel dung to bring the soil back to a non-hazardous state, while grass cuttings obtained from the local Municipality provide nutrients and serve to break up the contaminated soil.

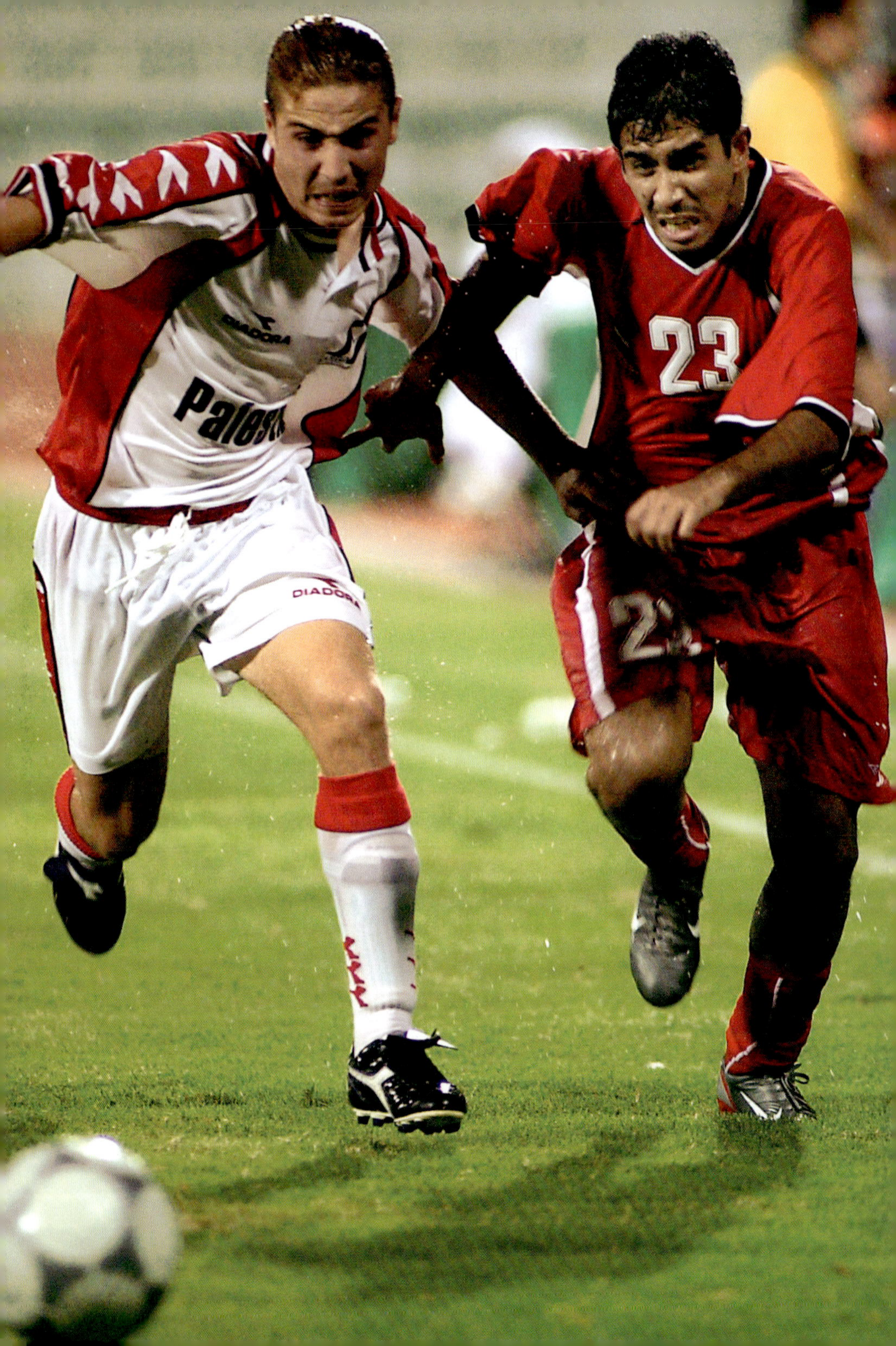

DIADORA
Palest
23
DIADORA

SPORT AND LEISURE

SPORTS PLAY A VITAL ROLE IN THE LIFE of the UAE, fuelled by the innate love of competition and outdoor activities of its peoples. This is reflected in the ongoing and enthusiastic support sport receives from government and private sector sponsors. As a result, the UAE enjoys amongst the finest sport and leisure facilities anywhere in the world, which in turn has made it a popular venue for international events and enabled UAE nationals to compete successfully on the world stage.

Confirmation of the UAE's growing international prestige in sports can be found in the recent decision by the international football organisation FIFA to have the UAE host the 2003 Youth World Cup.

The Public Authority for Youth and Sport (PAYS) has an ambitious programme to upgrade facilities throughout the country. Work is already under way on new sports complexes in Ra's al-Khaimah and Sharjah and similar state-of-the-art sports facilities are being built in Abu Dhabi, Dubai and other emirates. Each complex will have an Olympic-size swimming pool and tennis courts, as well as facilities for indoor games. The goal of this programme is to host the 2006 Arab Games but the upgraded facilities will also be used to encourage school-age children to participate in tennis and swimming.

Sport is also a strong element in the cultural fabric of the UAE and major efforts have been made to ensure that traditional sport and leisure activities such as camel racing and dhow sailing continue to thrive.

In addition, the growth of a sophisticated tourism infrastructure has meant that private sporting facilities in the UAE are among the best in the world.

FOOTBALL

In a year marked by both triumphs and disappointments, football continues to enjoy huge popularity in the UAE with active clubs and associations at all levels from schools and colleges to regional and national.

With 2002 being a World Cup year, football fever was at a high pitch, even though the UAE did not qualify this time around. The UAE did, however, play an important role in the World Cup in the person of Ali Bujsaim, one of only five referees selected for the Asian Group of the contest. This was the third time Ali Bujsaim has refereed in the event, a notable achievement.

Much of the pent up World Cup enthusiasm in the UAE was transferred to the Asian Youth Under 17 Championship, which was played at Al Nahyan stadium in the Al Wahda Club and Maktoum bin Rashid stadium at the Al Shabab Club in Dubai from 6–22 September. Football fans had anticipated great things from the UAE juniors, especially following the team's win in the Iran International friendly junior tournament days before the Asian competition commenced. However, after a strong 4-2 victory over Myanmar (Burma) in the first round, success eluded the youngsters despite their best efforts.

In the UAE First Division, Al Ain continued their spectacular string of victories by being crowned league champions for a record seventh time. Al Ain deserved to win the title after excellent performances in the second round where they posted an unbeaten record in 11 matches. At the end of the season, Al Ain topped the standings with 47 points, nine points ahead of closest rival Al Jazira.

Another disappointment was the Gulf Cup with the UAE finishing last for the second time in their history. This was in spite of a promising opening win against Oman when the team played with great confidence. It was, however, to be their only success in the tournament. Questions around coaching inevitably arose and English football coach Roy Hodgson has since replaced Jo Bonfrere. Hodgson has worked with top clubs in Europe including the Italian Udinese and Inter Milan. In England he coached Blackburn Rovers and Bristol City.

In October, a new programme called the E-sports' Abu Dhabi Junior Football Academy opened under the directorship of Rod Hartshorne, a Football Association qualified coach and a former captain of England's Manchester United's Youth team. The academy has three aims: to give children the opportunity to take part in a professionally structured training programme where they can learn all aspects of the game of football; to set up a Junior Football League with matches throughout the season, allowing children to gauge their progress and enjoy the fun of team competition; and to establish a Centre of Excellence for the more committed players to realise their potential.

The UAE Football Association tournaments committee decided to introduce a new tournament called 'The Reserve League'. This event will commence from the 2002–2003 season.

As the UAE FA prepares to host the 2003 Under-20 World Cup, it received welcome news that ADNOC FOD has signed up as one of the event's major sponsors. The last FIFA Youth World Cup was hosted by Argentina and was watched by 309 million viewers worldwide.

CAMEL RACING

Camel racing is a key focus of Arab social life in the winter, a friendly meeting point enhanced by the sight of highly trained animals racing flat-out down the sand track. The sport is also a considerable tourist attraction; giving visitors a chance to witness a spectacle that is both ancient and unique. The racing season begins in late October

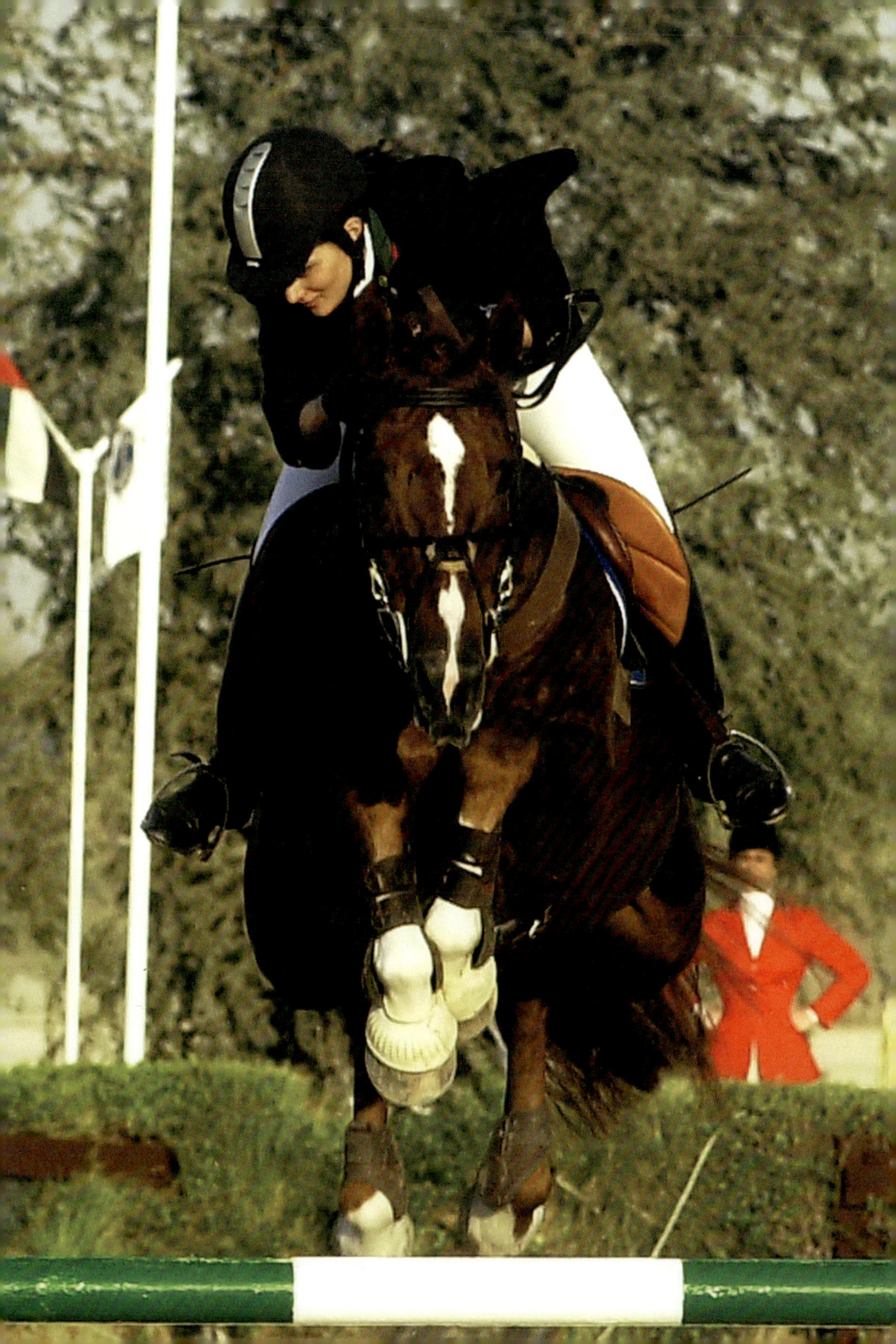

and ends in early April. Race distances vary between 4 and 10 kilometres, and the number of runners in each race can range from 15 to 70.

The 2002 five-day camel race festival at Abu Dhabi's Al Wathba track, concluded with a race meeting of three events, which attracted a large number of camel race fans. In the first major meeting, 'Al Anood', owned by Sheikh Zayed, was placed first. 'Al Shaqra', owned by Dubai Crown Prince Sheikh Mohammed bin Rashid Al Maktoum won the second major event, while 'Al Mashkoor', owned by Abu Dhabi Crown Prince Sheikh Khalifa bin Zayed Al Nahyan, won the third major event in a race meeting which attracted a total cash prize of Dh10 million, to be distributed to the first ten winners of each of the three major events.

In December 2002, the Nad al-Sheba camel racetracks held nine camel races with total prize money of Dh100, 000. The event was organised by the Dubai Department of Tourism and Commerce Marketing (DTCM) to mark the thirtieth National Day and Eid. Based on this year's success, DTCM plan to make the camel race a regular festival fixture.

An important development in the sport was announced by Sheikh Hamdan bin Zayed Al Nahyan, Chairman of the Emirates Camel Racing Federation, in the form of a ban on jockeys under the age of 15. This move will improve further the international standing of the sport, and builds on the earlier rules laid down in 1993 by Sheikh Zayed. This reinforcement of the ban on the use of children as jockeys for camel races has also been praised by the United Nations Children's Fund (UNICEF).

EQUESTRIAN SPORTS

The horse has been an essential part of life in the Arabian Peninsula for over 2000 years. Until recently, the relationship took the form of an enduring partnership based upon survival in one of the world's toughest environments. With the arrival of prosperity, the Emirati's relationship with the horse shifted from survival to recreation. Today, all forms of equestrian sport are enormously popular in the UAE, but the purebred Arabian horse still holds pride of place.

In 1985 the UAE joined the Federation Equestre International (FEI) and in 1992 the UAE Equestrian and Racing Federation under the chairmanship of Dr Sheikh Sultan bin Khalifa Al Nahyan was formed with the mission to promote and sponsor equestrian sport in the UAE. Since the federation's inception, equestrian sport has become focused and highly successful. Racing has already taken its place on the world stage and show jumping and endurance riding are now following its lead. Other equestrian associations, such as the Abu Dhabi Equestrian Club, under the chairmanship of Sheikh Mansour bin Zayed Al Nahyan, also organise equestrian events within the UAE.

Horse Racing

Since its fairly recent beginnings in the UAE during the early 1990s, horse racing has enjoyed phenomenal growth and the country now boasts a number of prestige

DUBAI WORLD CUP
WORLD CUP
mirates
DUBAI WORLD CUP
Emirates
DUBAI WORLD CUP
2002

racing venues where regular meetings are held during the winter months. Both thoroughbreds and purebred Arabian horses are raced.

The UAE has also become an international centre for horse breeding and training with the world renowned Godolphin stables, founded by Sheikh Mohammed bin Rashid Al Maktoum, firmly in the vanguard. Within a few short years the name Godolphin has become legendary in global racing circles, especially for its innovative training methods and its impressive results. For example, at the 2002 Royal Ascot Meeting, Sheikh Hamdan bin Rashid Al Maktoum saw his colours carried to victory in two races including a monumental first place win by 'Malhub' in the £250,000 Golden Jubilee Stakes.

Among the country's equestrian centres, Abu Dhabi Equestrian Club, located a short drive from the city centre, is one of the region's most impressive venues for horse-racing and show-jumping events. The club has two racetracks, one fibre sand and one fibre turf, and extensive training facilities, including an equine swimming pool and an indoor show jumping arena. Up to 16 race meetings are held at Abu Dhabi Equestrian Club from November to April each year, including The President's Cup, National Cup Day and Emirates Championship.

The UAE also boasts the world's richest race meeting, The Dubai World Cup (www.dubaiworldcup.com), which each year awards prizes in excess of US$15 million. It is staged annually in spring at the well-appointed Nad al-Sheba racecourse, close to Dubai city centre. In 2002 champion American jockey Jerry Bailey collected his fourth Dubai World Cup victory and Godolphin their third as 'Street Cry' earned his owners US$2,000,000. Emirates Airline sponsors the Dubai World Cup, which was attended by over 70,000 people.

As well as the Dubai World Cup race itself, the meeting also includes the UAE Derby, the Dubai Kahayla Classic for purebred Arabians, The Dubai Duty Free, Dubai Sheema Classic, Dubai Golden Shaheen and the Godolphin Mile. All the races have Group status whilst the World Cup has been awarded the sport's coveted Group One classification, which places the race on a level with the Derby, Oaks and Arc de Triomphe classics.

The winner of the UAE Derby was another Godolphin-owned horse, 'Essence of Dubai', ridden by Lanfranco Dettori and trained by Saeed bin Suroor. The 2002 Dubai Kahayla Classic for Purebred Arabians, was won by 'Nez D'Or' owned by Sheikh Zayed. The Dubai Sheema Classic winner was Nayef, trained by M. Tregoning, ridden by Richard Hills and owned by Sheikh Hamdan bin Rashid Al Maktoum. In the Godolphin Mile event 'Skoozi', also owned by Sheikh Hamdan, finished second to 'Grey Memo' owned by R. Manzani, R. Sarno and Ridgeley Farm.

Other prestigious events in the UAE racing calendar are the UAE 1000 Guineas, the UAE 2000 Guineas and the UAE Oaks.

A series of international race meetings featuring purebred Arabians, a sport dear to Sheikh Zayed's heart, obtains the widespread support and sponsorship of

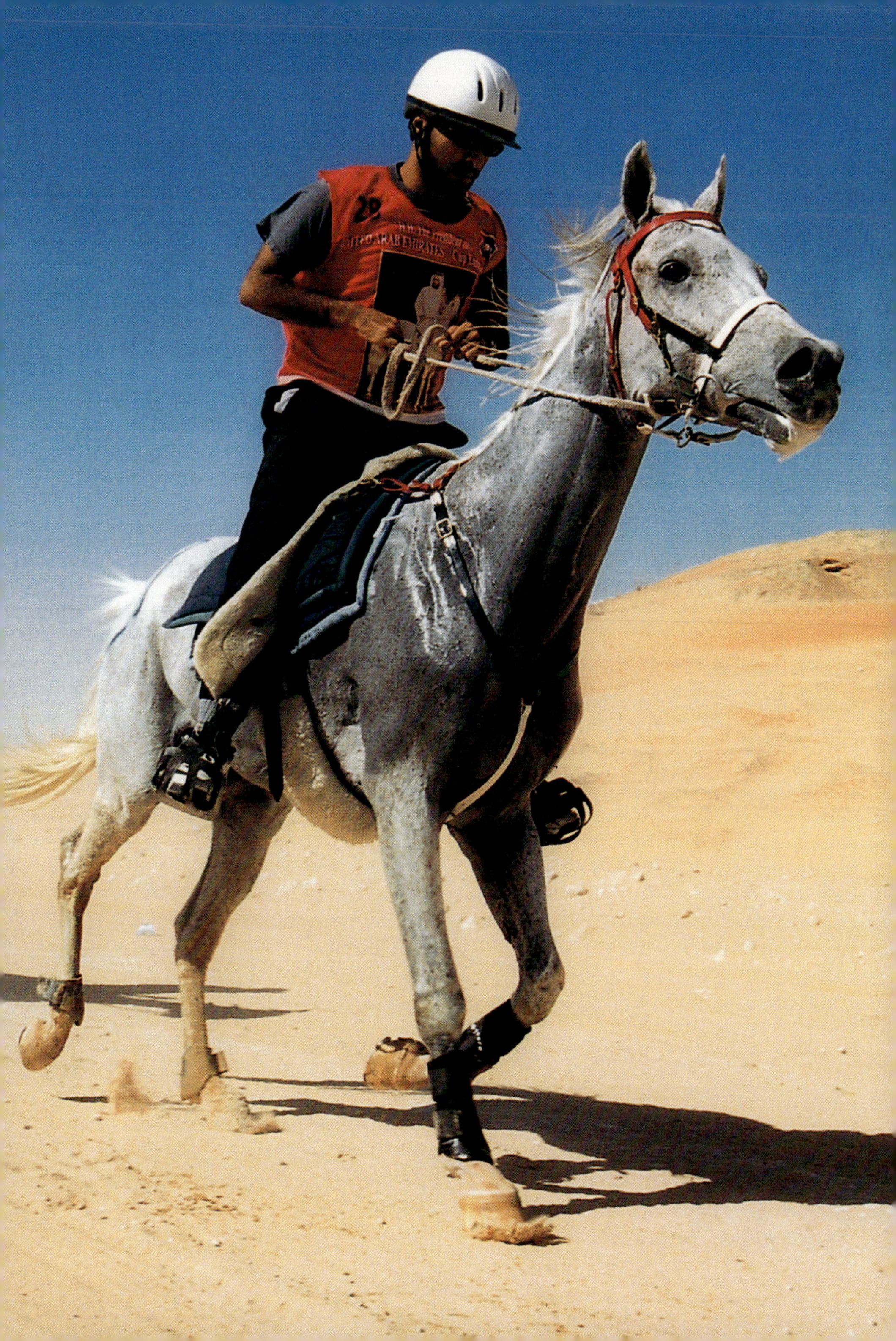

organisations such as the UAE Racing and Equestrian Federation. UAE horses regularly participate and win prizes in these events.

Endurance Racing

Endurance racing has a long and proud history in the Arab world based on the extraordinary strength and stamina of the purebred Arab horses which dominate the sport. Races are typically in excess of 100 kilometres and are run under strictly controlled conditions for both horse and rider.

In addition to enjoying immense popularity within the UAE, the country's national teams have for several years been dominant in international events, this year being no exception. In fact, UAE riders pulled off a clean sweep of all the major world championships culminating in a resounding gold medal finish by Sheikh Ahmed bin Mohammed bin Rashid Al Maktoum at the World Endurance Championship in Spain. Sheikh Ahmed led in the final stage of the notoriously tough competition and crossed the finish line three minutes ahead of his nearest challenger Antonio Rosi of Italy.

This outstanding victory was the first time in 37 years that a rider from an Arab country has received a medal at the World Equestrian Games. The achievement significantly raised the profile of the UAE in international equestrian circles with 999 riders, 800 horses, 52 countries and 1300 journalists attending the event.

The UAE victory at the World Equestrian Games came at the end of a season that saw UAE riders take top honours at all the other major international events, including the 120-kilometre Castiglione del Lago Endurance Ride in Perugia, Italy, which was won in record time by Sheikh Mohammed bin Rashid Al Maktoum. Sheikh Mohammed led a group of UAE riders that included his son Sheikh Hamdan. Among the notable endurance riders beaten by Sheikh Mohammed was the Italian national champion Fosteau who offered fierce competition.

Riders from the UAE also dominated the 120-kilometre international endurance ride at Punchestown, Ireland, where eight of the top ten finishers were horses owned by Sheikh Mohammed. The winner, Sheikh Rashid bin Mohammed Al Maktoum on Lahi da Figeirada, left his rivals far behind when he won the event with more than 38 minutes separating him from the second-placed Sheikh Hamdan bin Mohammed Al Maktoum on Canelle Rio.

In November 2002, UAE riders swept the top four places in the third Al Ahram Al Araby International Endurance Championship held in Egypt. The 120-kilometre ride finished in dramatic fashion with Sheikh Rashid bin Mohammed riding Azzab sprinting to the finish in true racing style. Sheikh Rashid was declared the winner in a time of 5 hours, 16 minutes and 51 seconds. He was followed by Abdullah Khamis Ali Shah (5:16.53) and Sheikh Hamdan bin Mohammed Al Maktoum, aboard Lahi, one second behind in third place. Defending champion Sheikh Mohammed bin Rashid, partnering Yamama, was a close fourth in a time of 5:22.13.

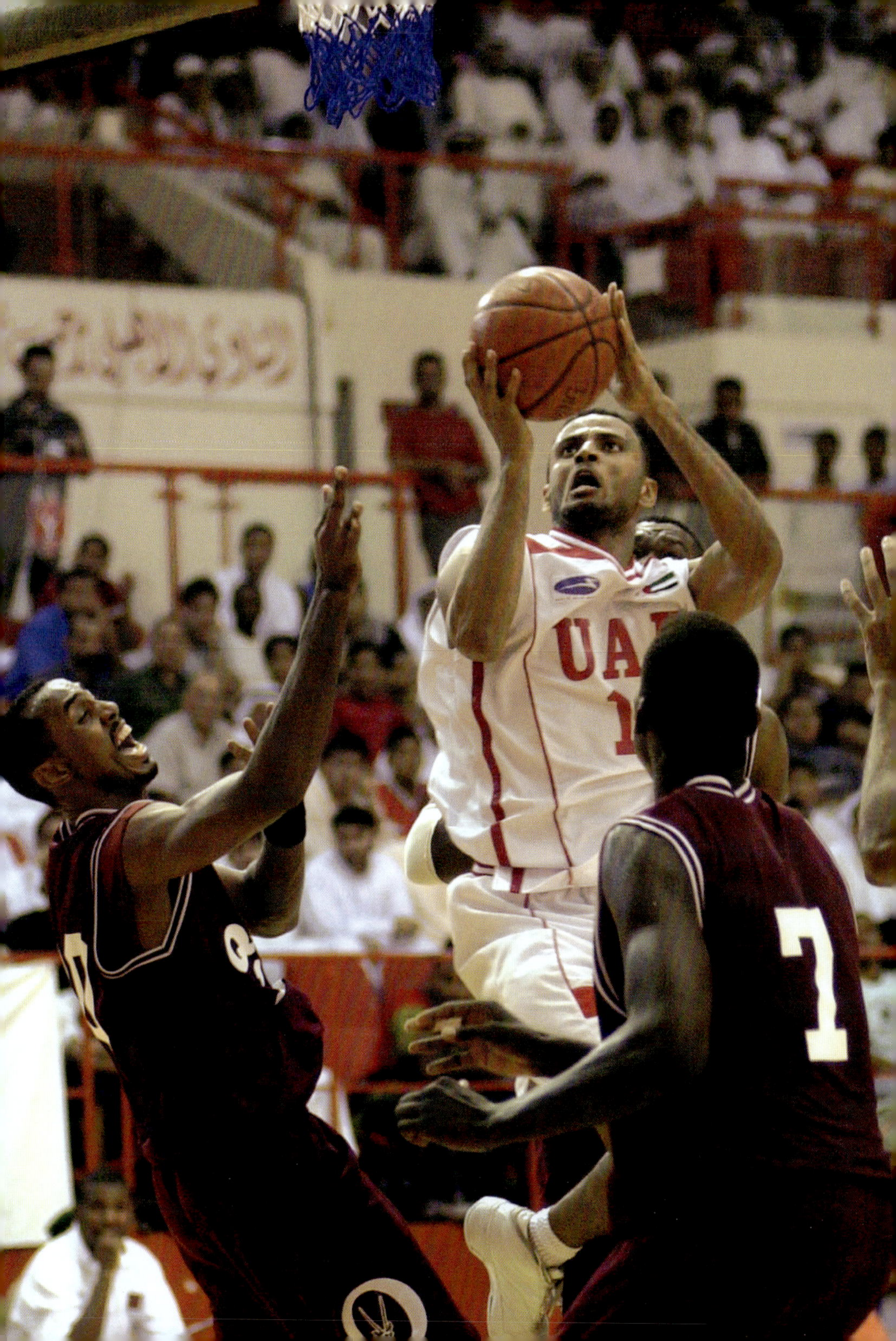

The UAE's endurance racing season begins in late December each year at the Seih Assalem Endurance Village where the biennial world championship was held in 1998. Numerous races are held throughout the year featuring both novices and well-tried champions. The highlight of the UAE season is the FEI-UAE World Cup. This year it was won by Sheikh Hamdan bin Mohammed Al Maktoum riding 'Muneef'. His brother, Sheikh Ahmed bin Mohammed Al Maktoum, finished second place on Southern Exposure. Third place went to Mohammed Ali Al Shafar on ZT Kiavrelle.

Emirates International Endurance Racing (EIER) has also announced a new three-round race series entitled President His Highness Sheikh Zayed bin Sultan Al Nahyan Challenge Series with Dh2million on offer for the three rides

The FEI Emirates Worldwide Ranking was established in 1999 by the FEI in cooperation with the UAE Equestrian and Racing Federation and includes most of the major FEI rides on the international circuit. Sheikh Rashid bin Mohammed Al Maktoum was the lead rider in the inaugural year, 1999. Sheikh Hamdan bin Mohammed replaced his brother Sheikh Rashid bin Mohammed as the world's top-ranked rider in the year 2000/1 and held onto the top position again in 2001/2.

All of the 22 rides sponsored by the UAE Equestrian and Racing Federation in the US, Europe, Australia, New Zealand and South Africa are now held under FEI rules.

The efforts of the UAE equestrian authorities to make endurance racing an Olympic sport received a major boost in 2001 when the FEI formed a subcommittee to examine the feasibility of including it as an Olympic discipline. Faisal Seddiq Al Mutawa, Secretary of the UAE Equestrian and Racing Federation, was named chairman of the subcommittee. The committee's main goal will be to work towards making endurance racing a demonstration event at the Athens Olympics before being finally accepted for the 2008 Olympic Games.

Show Jumping

Show jumping has also increased in popularity in recent years, aided considerably by the impressive developments in facilities such as air-conditioned indoor arenas. This has resulted in a marked improvement in the standard of competition and junior riders are now being given the opportunity to compete abroad.

Show-jumping competitions take place throughout the season at three equestrian centres; Abu Dhabi Equestrian Club, Sharjah Equestrian Club and Dubai Equestrian Centre. In January, the Maktoum International Show Jumping Challenge attracted a stellar field of well known show jumpers from Europe, North America and from other Arab countries and in April, the National Show Jumping Riders Championship 2002 was held at Abu Dhabi Equestrian Club.

The UAE show-jumping team has participated in competitions in other Middle Eastern countries, and in the US and Europe and were particularly successful at the World Equestrian Games held in September 2002 at Jerez, Spain. A team comprising Sheikh Majid bin Abdullah Al Qasimi, Humaid Rashid and Rashid Al Hossani were also declared team champions at the international show jumping championship in Kolkata, India in December 2002. Sheikh Majid and Hossani are among the top 32 show jumpers in the world.

Polo

Polo has been played in the UAE since the Dubai Polo Club was established over 25 years ago. In recent years it has become so popular, especially amongst local players, that the Emirates Polo Association was formed to organise the game on a more professional basis. The UAE is now on the international polo circuit, a remarkable achievement in such a short space of time. The UAE enjoys the major advantage of an eight-month polo season, as compared to an average five-month season elsewhere in the world. Sponsorship is important to the development of the sport, as is the determination to encourage young players.

The plush Ghantoot Polo and Racing Club, about an hour's drive from Abu Dhabi, has four floodlit polo fields, a racing grandstand and polo school, amongst other facilities. Other polo venues include the Dubai Polo Club with two grass fields and one sand field and Dubai Desert Palm Polo, which offers four polo fields and has had professional polo players on staff, such as Adolfo Combiaso and Eduardo Heguy. The polo season featuring regular chukka tournaments and major international events runs from mid-October to April.

GOLF

Golf in the Emirates has come a long way since the not-so-distant days when golfers were restricted to playing on oiled sand, putting on 'browns' rather than greens. Today, enthusiasts of the fastest growing sport in the UAE can take their pick of 18 major golf courses throughout the country, many with distinctive clubhouses, immaculate greens and lush fairways. Some of the courses are of such a high standard that they have been chosen to host major international golfing tournaments.

Three challenging PGA championship golf courses and five additional courses are open to visitors. All the major golf courses have a range of additional facilities, including quality pro-shops and dedicated coaching facilities with PGA qualified professionals.

Al Ghazal Golf Club, one of the newer clubs, is an 18-hole, 6450–yard, par 71 sand golf course situated 400 metres from the Abu Dhabi Airport terminal. It features an English-style hilltop clubhouse, swimming pool and tennis courts and an advanced training facility.

Abu Dhabi Golf Club By Sheraton, another relatively new club, is located in Umm al-Nar, just outside the capital (wwwadgolfsheraton.com). Undulating terrain meandering through pockets of palms and ornamental shrubs and trees, flawless fairways, incredible greenery and seven saltwater lakes are part of two international golf courses, designed by Peter Harradine – the man responsible for some of the best golf courses in the region. The challenging 18-hole, par 72, 7,204-yard National Course and the more forgiving 18-hole, Par 72, 6,498-yard Garden Course feature nine holes floodlit to facilitate night play. Mature date palms and ornamental trees surround a spectacular clubhouse built in the shape of a large falcon swooping down on a golf ball.

Abu Dhabi Golf and Equestrian Club has a nine-hole, 6365-yard, par 70 fully floodlit course located at the club's racetrack that runs through the course, providing a formidable challenge on four holes. Facilities include clubhouse, golf academy, bars and restaurants, floodlit tennis courts, swimming pool and pro-shop.

Dubai Creek Golf and Yacht Club, in the heart of the city, was the PGA European Tour Dubai Desert Classic venue for 1999 and 2000. The Club's 18-hole, par 72 championship course rolls 6839 undulating yards along well-groomed fairways lined with date and coconut palms, attractive water hazards and shrubbery that lend a distinctly tropical air. There is also a nine-hole, par three, floodlit course. A unique clubhouse design echoes the billowing sails of a traditional Arab dhow. Other facilities include a 115-berth marina, tennis courts, picnic and barbecue sites, cycling and jogging tracks.

Emirates Golf Club on Sheikh Zayed Road, just 20 minutes from Dubai city centre, was the first grass course in the Middle East and is a favoured venue of the PGA's Dubai Desert Classic, (including the 2003 event when golfing superstar Tiger Woods will be competing). The club offers two challenging courses. The original 7101-yard, par 72 Majlis course is complemented by the 7100-yard, par 72 Wadi course – the latter featuring a daunting set of bunkers and water hazards. A striking clubhouse is built in the shape of a series of bedouin tents. The club also has a swimming pool, tennis courts, squash courts and snooker room.

Jebel Ali Hotel and Golf Resort, located about 30 minutes from Dubai city centre, is a nine-hole, par 36 course with a large central saltwater lake that comes into play on five holes. Each hole is uniquely landscaped with exotic trees, shrubs, wooden gazebos and panoramic views of the Arabian Gulf. Peacock, guinea fowl, and partridges roam free on the perfectly manicured Bermuda grass greens and fairways. There is also a driving range with bunkers and target greens. A wide range of facilities is available at the resort.

Nad al-Sheba Club, Dubai, features a floodlit 18-hole links-style course playing to par 71. The course has eight lakes and more than 110 pot bunkers. Situated about 15 minutes from Dubai city centre, this is a short course, the emphasis being on accuracy. The first nine holes are located inside the famous Nad al-Sheba racetrack with the second nine outside the track. There is also a large driving range, a practice putting area and chipping greens.

The Montgomerie Dubai, located in the Emirates Hills area just outside the city, combines the course design traditions of truly great Scottish links courses. Covering more than 200 acres, this spectacular golf course provides the player with undulating 'links land' style fairways that challenge and intrigue all levels of player. With 14 lakes and 72 bunkers, The Montgomerie Dubai adds a distinctive variety to the golfing landscape of the region. One of the signature hole designs, the par three thirteenth, boasts the largest single green in the world.

Dubai Country Club (www.dubaicountryclub.com) is the oldest club in the Emirates. It features an 18- and a nine-hole sand course. Golfers are issued with a small piece of artificial turf to play off when on the fairways. Although it is a sand course, there are water hazards and bunkers to be carefully negotiated. The 'browns' are the putting surfaces and are regularly brushed to keep the smooth surface that arguably has a truer roll than grass.

Al Ain, Ruwais and *Sharjah* also have golf courses, with others deep in the desert or on offshore islands used by the oil industry. One of the most dramatic of these is at Shah, just inside the Empty Quarter, where the fairways are overlooked by 200-metre-high dunes. There are no bunkers like that anywhere else in the world!

Dubai Festival City has announced plans to open a new 7250-yards, 72 par, 18-hole recreational golf course designed by Robert Trent Jones II LLC, California's internationally acclaimed golf course architectural firm. The golf course, which will be rich in water features and lush with plants indigenous to the Gulf, will open in September 2003. Dubai Festival City's golfing community will include the clubhouse, golf academy, executive town homes, apartments and a 150-room boutique hotel. This will be Dubai's sixth 18-hole golf facility.

A new 18-hole golf course, the *Tower Links Club*, is under construction in Ra's al-Khaimah. The course will be built and operated by Dubai-based Hydroturf International, and is expected to increase tourism to Ra's al-Khaimah. The area around *Jebel Hafit*, Al Ain will also have a new golf course as part of a major tourist development in the area.

Golfing Events

The Dubai Desert Classic (www.dubaidesertclassic.com), a centrepiece tournament of the European Tour, is staged at either Dubai Creek or Emirates Golf Club in March each year. The hugely popular event offers a total prize of US$5 million. South African Ernie Els won the 2002 Dubai Desert Golf Classic with Swede Niclas Fasth in second place and Carl Pettersson third. Els last won the Desert Classic in 1994. The 2003 Dubai Desert Classic will take place at the Emirates Golf Club's Majlis Course from 6–9 March with the legendary Tiger Woods among the competitors. For the first time since it was staged in 1989, the tournament will be organised by a newly-constituted Executive Committee headed by Mohammed Alabbar, Director General, Dubai Economic Department and Vice-Chairman of DUBAL, the event's official sponsors.

Among the year's highlights for UAE golfers was their outstanding victory at the GCC Golf Championship held at the Dirab Golf Club in Saudi Arabia. The four-man team of Faris Al Mazrui, Ismail Sharif, Rashid Alabbar and Abdullah Al Mosharrekh took five golds and six silver in the six available categories.

Amateur golf in the UAE is organised and promoted by the UAE Golf Association (UGA) (www.ugagolf.com) which was formed in 1996. UGA, with 3500 members, is overseen by a board of directors under the General Authority of Youth and Sports Welfare and is affiliated to the Royal & Ancient Golf Club of St Andrews, WAGC, Ladies Golf Union, the Asia-Pacific Golf Confederation, the GCC Golf Committee and the Arab Golf Federation.

The UAE's reputation as the sporting capital of the Middle East received a major boost when Dubai won a top award at the International Association of Golf Tour Operators (IAGTO) Annual Awards ceremony in South Africa. The emirate picked up the prestigious 'Emerging Golf Destination of the Year' Award beating off strong competition from Malaysia, Turkey, Egypt, Costa Rica, several large US states, and even the home country, South Africa.

MARINE SPORTS

With its 700 kilometres of island-dotted coastline and rich maritime history, the UAE takes a strong interest in both traditional and modern marine activities. New facilities, such as the superbly appointed Abu Dhabi International Marine Sports Club (ADIMSC), a gift from Sheikh Zayed to the youth of the UAE, have made a major contribution to the growing popularity of marine sports. Both ADIMSC and Dubai International Marine Club (DIMC) organise powerboat racing, jetskiing and waterskiing championships, windsurfing, yacht and dingy racing as well as traditional sailing and longboat events.

Powerboat Races

World championship powerboat races are staged every year in the UAE. The penultimate stages of the inshore UIM Formula One are held off Abu Dhabi and Sharjah in October/November, complementing final rounds of the offshore UIM Class One races held off Dubai and Fujairah, also in October/November, and Class II offshore championships off Abu Dhabi. ADIMC and DIMC also organise powerboat races throughout the year.

The UAE's own Victory teams (www.victoryteam.org.ae) have had notable successes on the world circuit over the 12 years that they have been competing. This year however, the local Dubai duo of driver Ali Nasser and throttleman Ali Al Qama, who were the 2001 world champions in Victory 7, faced extremely tough competition from Steve Curtis and Bjorn Gjelsten in Spirit of Norway.

Early in the season, at the Fujairah 101 nautical mile Grand Prix, there was an exciting showdown on the high seas, as Ali Nasser and Ali Al Qama in Victory 7 made it a clean sweep with first place finishes in both the Pole Position and Grand Prix races. In subsequent grand prix races, however, the Norwegians were virtually unbeatable.

The final showdown between the two arch rivals came at the Dubai Grand Prix when Victory 7 won the race to earn the newly introduced Middle East Championship,

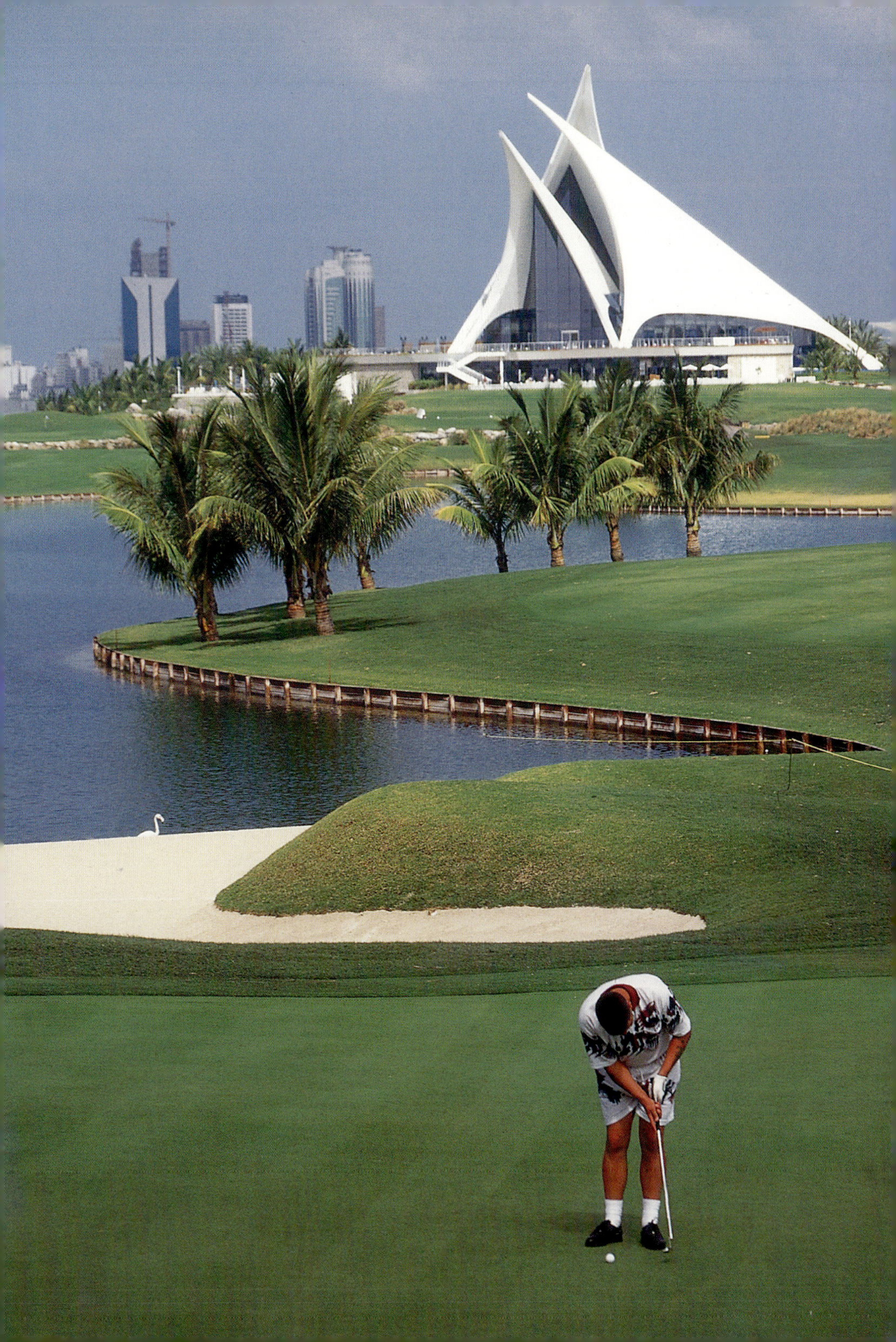

but saw their World Championship hopes die as Spirit of Norway took second place to clinch first place in the points standings. In the final standings, Spirit of Norway earned 131 points to Victory 7's 120. Victory 1 finished in fourth place with 76 points.

In the Pole Position Championship, Spirit of Norway again took top honours but the Victory team clinched second and third places with Victory 7 (118 points) and Victory 1 (102 points) respectively.

In Formula II Powerboat racing *Aqua Man*, Thani Atij Al Qamzi won the President's Cup as well as the Abu Dhabi Grand Prix. Thani was also runner up in the Pole Position standings with 79 points and Al Mansouri was third with 63, all three places on the podium going to the Emirates F-II Team.

Sailing

Competitive sailing is a rich part of Arab maritime culture and an active racing season runs from October to May. The undoubted stars of the UAE sailing world are the majestic wooden dhows, some as big as 60 feet. To see a fleet of them assemble at the start line with their magnificent lateen rigged sails is an awe-inspiring sight. Competition is intense and great attention is paid to the preparation of the boats and their massive rigs. Longboat races also paint an impressive picture as their tightly packed crews labour at their oars, propelling their svelte boats through calm inshore waters under the appreciative gaze of spectators.

Modern sailboat races are also staged throughout the country, both at local and international levels. The UAE National Sailing Championships Series held at the Dubai International Marine Club, is designed to encourage the sport of sailing amongst youth and to select sailors who will represent the UAE in European events. Races were held for two classes – the Optimist and Laser 4.7. In the Optimist class, Omar Shaheen won all six races. In the Laser 4.7 Class, Abdullah Sabah of Emirates Heritage Club took first place, followed by Yousef Khalid of Dubai International Marine Club.

In November, the UAE national sailing team made a clean sweep in the Optimist and Laser 4.7 category races at the Gulf Sailing Trophy held in Doha. Omar Shaheen was the outright winner in the Optimist class by finishing first in all the five races. He was followed by UAE's Jassim Ehab and Abdulhakim bin Dasmal in second and third places overall. In the Laser 4.7, it was UAE's Adel Khalid, who showed tremendous wind judging and boat handling skills to grab first. He was followed by team-mate Ahmed Shaheen, participating in his first international Laser event, and Yousef Khalid in second and third places respectively while Shamsa bin Dasmal, the only female Arab competitor in the event, won laurels for UAE by claiming fourth position.

Diving and Snorkelling

The waters of the UAE offer a range of diving and snorkelling to suit all levels of experience. The reefs and spectacular wrecks along the Abu Dhabi/Dubai coasts, where there is relatively little tidal movement and slack currents, offer relatively

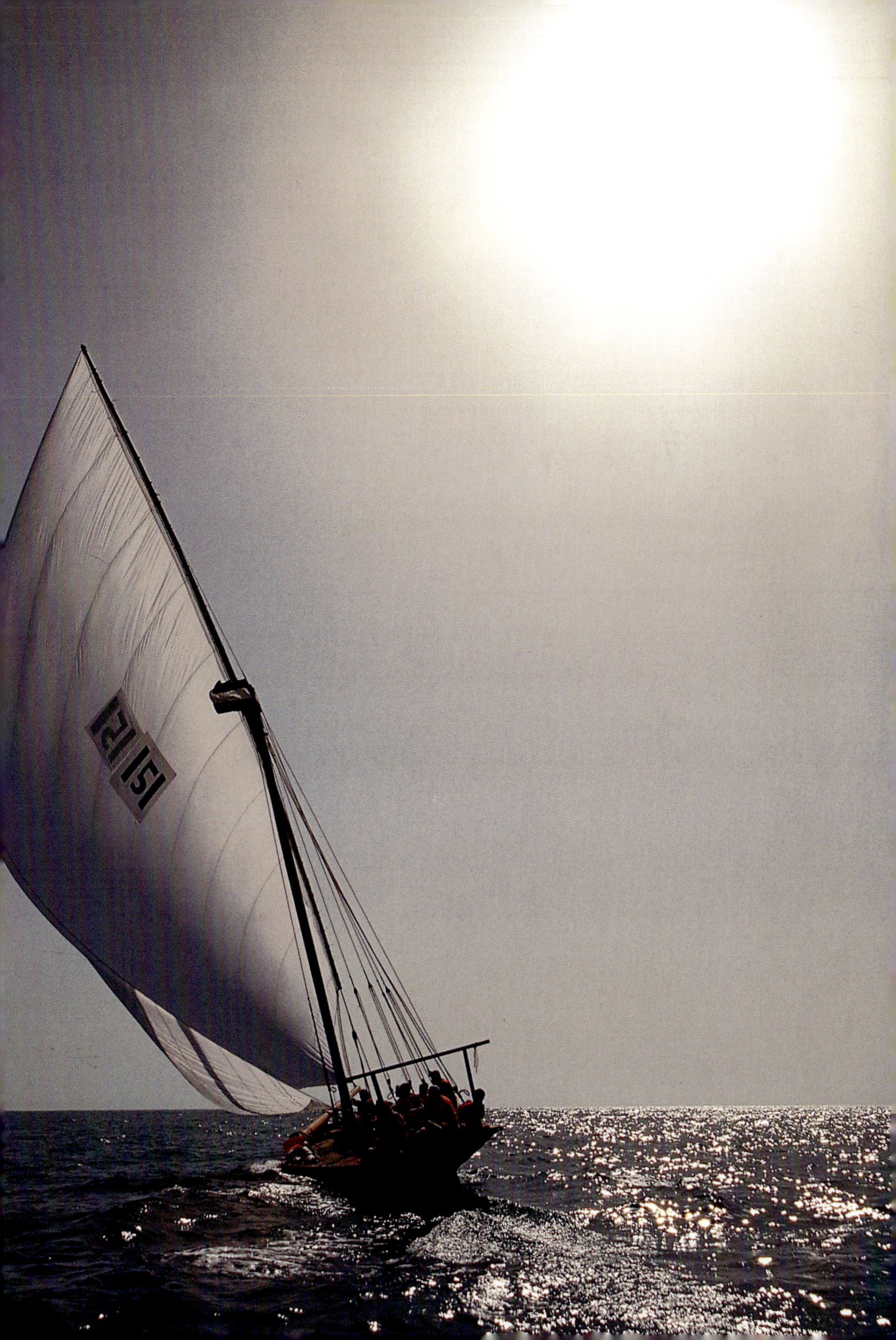
151

sheltered diving. The East Coast is different again with upwellings from the Indian Ocean encouraging a greater diversity of marine life. Off the coast of Khor Fakkan and Fujairah there are more than ten dive sites within just a few minutes' boat ride from the shore. Typically some of the best sites are submerged rocks that have been colonised by soft corals. There is abundant tropical fish life and turtles are commonly sighted. The diving gets steadily more demanding and more varied as the coast runs northwards. From the ancient town of Dibba it is possible to reach a wealth of deeper dive sites off the Musandam peninsula, part of Oman, and within half an hour's boat ride. Mountains that plunge directly into the ocean are covered in soft corals to depths of 40 metres and a cave system offers exciting diving for experienced and suitably qualified divers. The Emirates Diving Association (www.emiratesdivers.com) is responsible for the organisation of diving in the UAE.

MOTOR SPORTS

Motor sports play a big role in the UAE's sporting life. This is particularly evident in rallying in which UAE national Mohammed bin Sulayem has over 60 international rally victories under his belt, including 12 Middle East championships. In 2002, Sulayem continued his winning streak at the FIA Middle East Championship in the Dubai International Rally. It was his fourteenth championship victory and his fifty-fifth career win in the Middle East Championship Rally. Sulayem then went on to win at the Qatar International Rally, where UAE's Abdullah Al Qasimi finished third, followed by a hat-trick of successive victories in the Zayani Motors Mitsubishi Bahrain International Rally.

TENNIS

Thanks to the splendid facilities now available throughout the country and the heavy promotion undertaken by the UAE Tennis Association, tennis is now a much-favoured sport in the UAE, both at amateur and professional levels.

The Dubai Duty Free Tennis Championships is a week of serious competition for the world's top stars as well as a time of entertainment for families in the UAE. Surrounding events help to promote tennis and to show how easy and accessible the game can be for all ages and levels of competence. In this, the tenth anniversary of the event, it would have been difficult to imagine a more appropriate finale than French player Fabrice Santoro, who contested the first Dubai tennis final in 1993, facing the Arab world's number one player, Morocco's Younes El Aynaoui. The unlikely match-up between the two unseeded players, won 6-4 3-6 6-3 by Santoro, brought to an end another two weeks of often spectacular tennis action featuring a star-studded field of players. In women's play, it was also unseeded players who took top honours with Amelie Mauresmo and Sandrine Testud emerging ahead of stars like Venus Williams, Monica Seles and Anna Kournikova to create an all-French final, with Mauresmo taking the title.

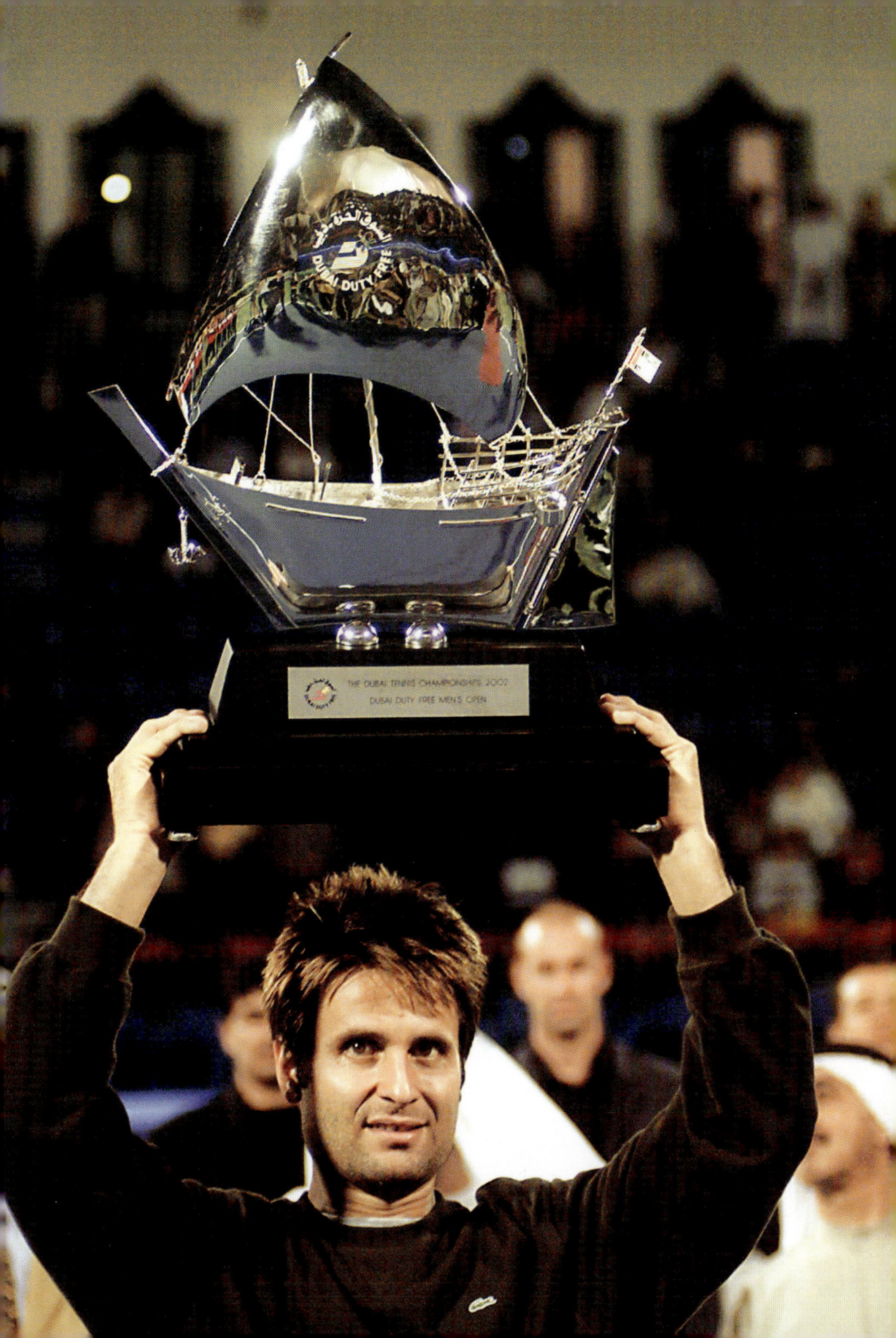
DUBAI DUTY FREE
DUBAI DUTY FREE MEN'S OPEN

CRICKET

Cricket has a growing following in the UAE. Top world teams compete in the Cricketers' Benefit Fund Series at a 27,000 capacity cricket stadium in Sharjah while the Abu Dhabi Cricket Council is nearing completion of the Zayed Cricket Stadium in Umm al-Nar next to Abu Dhabi Golf Club. The ultra-modern floodlit cricket stadium is designed to host both UAE and international matches and will make a major contribution towards establishing the UAE's credentials as a cricketing nation.

Al Ain Cricket Association organises regular matches at its grounds whilst the Darjeeling Cricket Club in Dubai runs matches every Friday, a six-a-side Gulf tournament in March, and regular matches against visiting sides.

Among the year's cricket highlights: UAE retained the Asia Cricket Council (ACC) Trophy with a classic finish in the final against Nepal, captain Khurram Khan cracking a towering six to secure a six-wicket victory. Pakistan won the 2002 Sharjah Cup in a crushing 217 run defeat of Sri Lanka. Pakistan themselves later tasted bitter defeat in a three match to nothing trouncing by Australia.

BOXING

In another major boost for sports in the region the UAE Boxing Federation (UAE BF) has become a full member of the International Boxing Federation (IBF) and the Asian Boxing Federation (ABF) following the ABF general assembly held at the 2002 Asian Games in Busan. The meeting was attended by Sheikh Hamid bin Khadim bin Butti Al Hamid, Vice President of the UAE BF.

CHESS

The UAE has a very enthusiastic Chess Federation that organises domestic tournaments as well as the successful participation of the UAE team in international championships. The President of the UAE Chess Federation, Abdul Rahman Al Shamsi, is also the UAE delegate to the World Chess Federation.

2002 was a landmark year in UAE chess with the inaugural UAE Grand Prix taking place in Dubai Chess Club from 2–10 April. This was the biggest chess event held in the UAE since the 1986 Dubai Chess Olympiad. The Grand Prix winner was Peter Leko of Hungary who defeated Alexander Grischuk of Russia, 3-2, in the sudden death tiebreaker.

In the twelfth Abu Dhabi Chess Festival, under the patronage of Major General Sheikh Saif bin Zayed Al Nahyan, a tie occurred between grandmasters Ulibin, Mikhail, Gleizerov, Evgeny, Safin and Shukhrat all with 6.5 points. Pakistani player Ulibin was awarded the trophy on better technical counts.

A similar tie occurred at the UAE National chess Championship when Nabil Saleh and Taleb Moussa tied for the prestigious title. Nabil took the title on better technical scores.

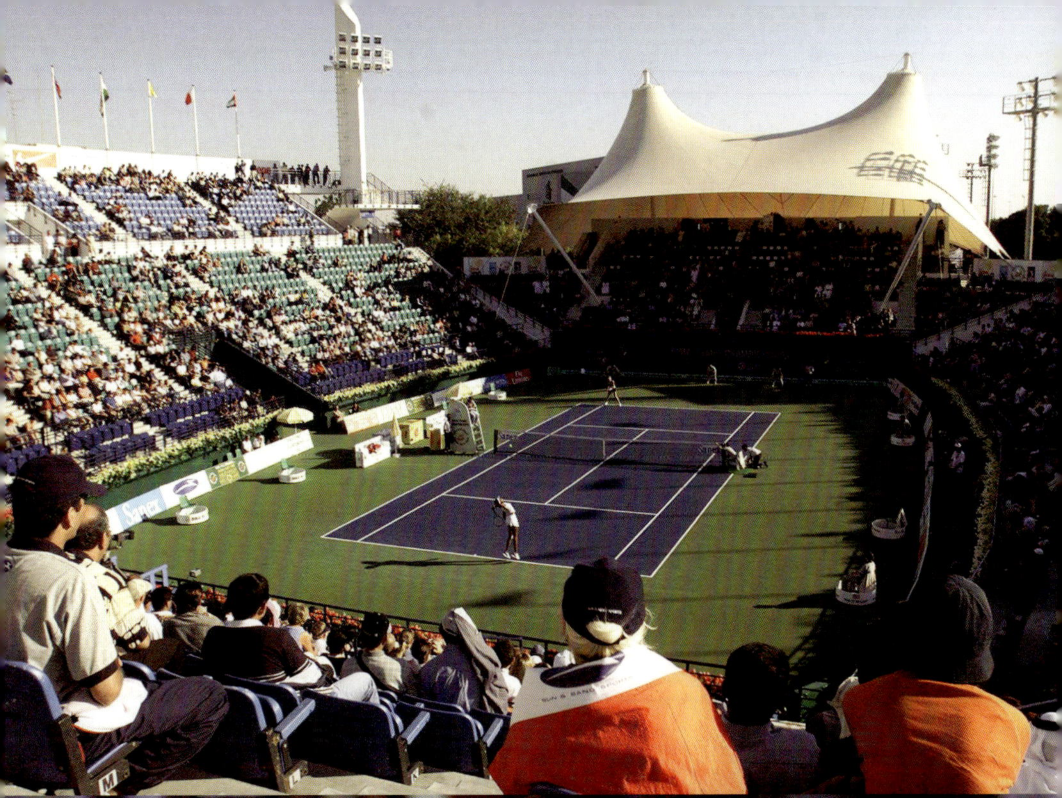

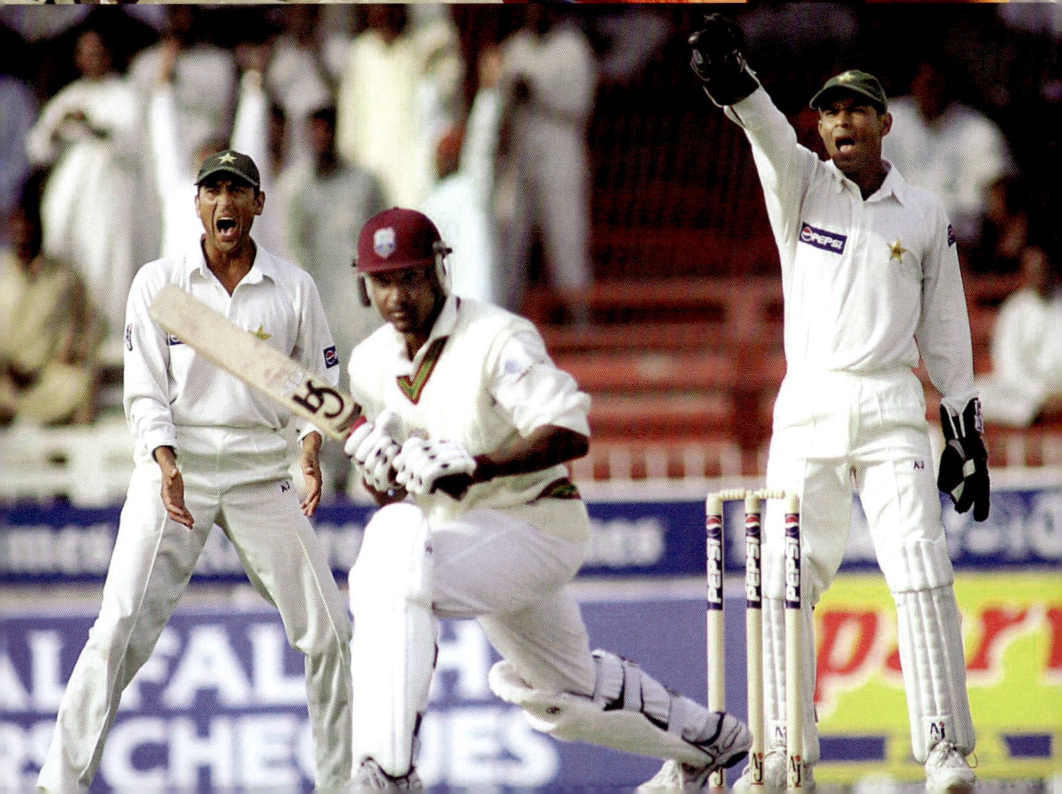
PEPSI

SNOOKER

Mohammed Al Joker made a great comeback to win the 2002 Dubai Snooker Club Open Championship, replacing Mohammed Shahab as UAE number one in the process. Sultan Saqr Al Suweidi, Secretary General of the Public Authority for Youth and Sports, Ministry of Education and Youth, presented the winner with trophy.

ICE HOCKEY AND SKATING

Most surprisingly for a desert state, ice hockey and figure skating are popular sports. Both Abu Dhabi and Dubai have two ice-skating rinks each with another rink located in Al Ain. With the personal participation and support of Sheikh Falah bin Zayed Al Nahyan, Honorary Chairman of the UAE Ice Hockey Association, the UAE national team won the 2001 Asian Championship. UAEIHC was the first Arab ice hockey body to become a provisional member of the International Ice Hockey Federation.

RUGBY

Rugby is another sport with a large following among the expatriate population. Abu Dhabi Rugby Football Club participates in both local and regional tournaments. Games are usually played on a grass pitch provided by the Mina Zayed Port Authority. Rugby is also played in Al Ain at Ambiers Rugby Club and at Al Ain Oasis Barbarians Rugby Club.

World-class rugby sevens teams compete in the Dubai Rugby Sevens in November or December each year for what has become one of the region's top sporting and social events. In 2001, more than 15,000 fans from across the world packed the stands of Pitch One at the Dubai Exiles Rugby Ground to witness New Zealand beat South Africa by 45 to 7 to claim the prestigious Emirates International Trophy. Being sevens, the high-paced action on the pitch is matched by the colourful social scene, with the three-day festival reaching a spectacular climax at the world-famous Rugby Rock, which features top international acts.

BASKETBALL

The UAE team clinched the GCC basketball championship for the second time in style after defeating mighty Qatar 69–58 in the final held at Maktoum bin Mohammed indoor sports hall at the Al Ahli club. The medal hopes of the UAE Cagers ended in disappointment when they were beaten by North Korea 85–64 in the second and final league round match at the 14th Asian Games in Busan.

In the Emir's Cup Tournament it was the surprise outsider An Nahl from Sharjah that took the Cup after 18 years of drought, beating league champions Al Wasl 83–61.

OTHER SPORTS

Many other sports and leisure activities are actively pursued in the UAE. Among them jet skiing and beach volleyball are fast gaining popularity. Other sports such as netball, power lifting, wrestling, handball and softball also have enthusiastic supporters in the UAE.

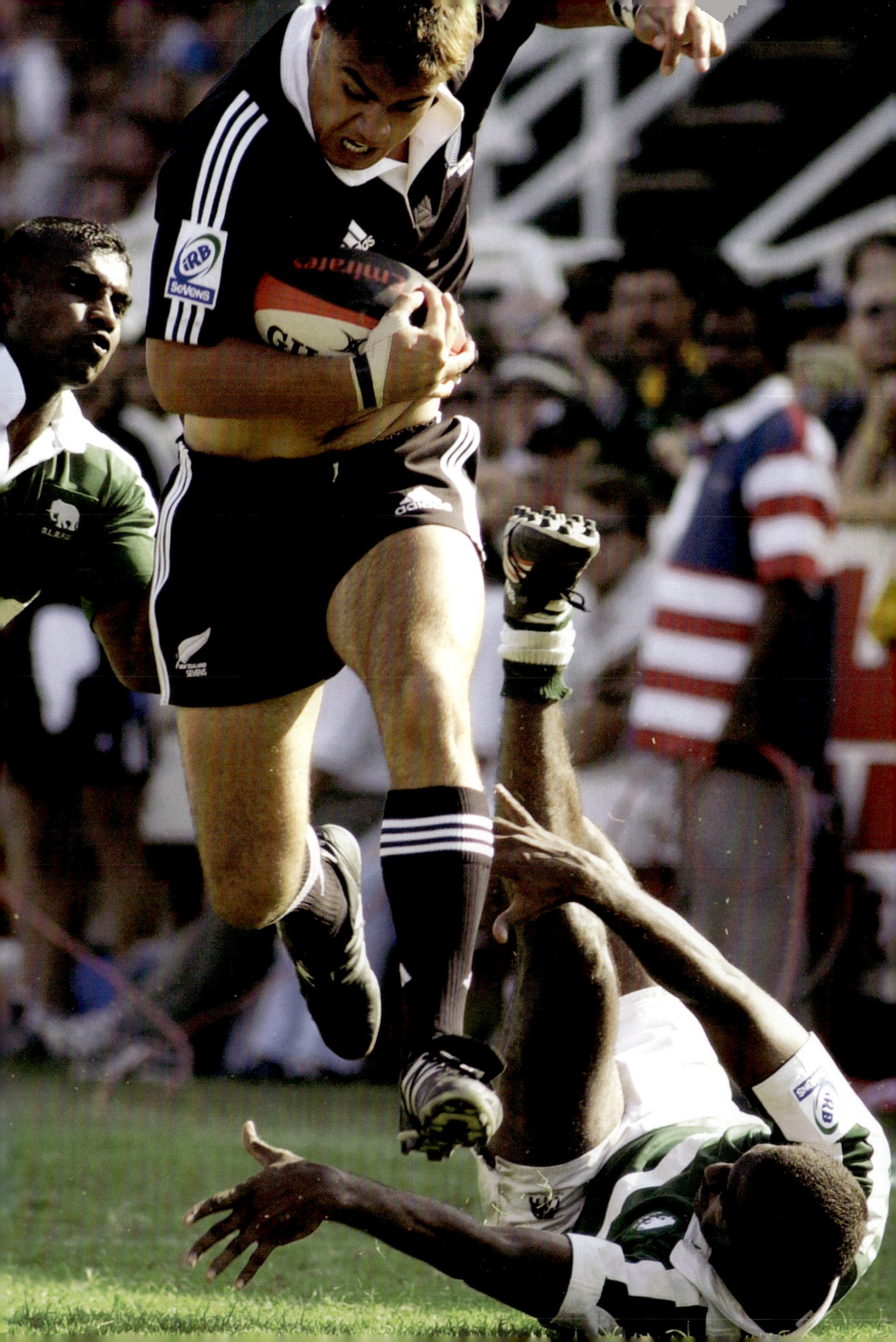
IRB
SeVeNS
adidas

dubai

the city that cares

EXHIBITIONS AND EVENTS

The United Arab Emirates is a major exhibitions and events hub for the Middle East. With its excellent infrastructure, world-class hotels and conference facilities, the UAE is an ideal location for international conferences, conventions and corporate meetings. At the same time, these events attract tens of thousands of visitors annually, providing a valuable economic boost to hotels and other visitor services. Almost 30 per cent of Dubai's total tourist intake originates from this source.

EXHIBITION CENTRES

Abu Dhabi International Exhibitions Centre (ADIEC)
(www.adcci-uae.com/adiecntr)
Abu Dhabi's new multi-purpose exhibition centre has greatly facilitated the staging of major exhibitions in the capital. The state-of-the-art centre provides 16,000 square metres of flexible interior space with all of the attendant services expected in a modern, international exhibition facility.

Some of the Gulf region's most important international exhibitions are held here including: IDEX, a major biennial International Defence Exhibition; ADIPEC, the Abu Dhabi International Petroleum Exhibition and Conference; ADIF, the Abu Dhabi International Fair; MIDCOM, the International Telecommunications Exhibition; Arab Jewellery and Watch Show, featuring precious stones, diamonds, gold and jewellery; and the Building Forum, which covers building and construction, decoration, overseas property and city infrastructure development.

ADIEC is operated by the General Exhibitions Corporation (GEC), which organises a number of exhibitions, including the local and international series entitled 'Made in the UAE'. The latter is designed to open markets to indigenous industries and introduce regional investors to investment opportunities. This exhibition was first organised in 1993 at the Sharjah Expo and has since been staged in several cities in the UAE. The sixth such exhibition, held in Abu Dhabi in 2000, was considered one of the most successful local exhibitions.

Dubai World Trade Centre (DWTC) (www.dwtc.com)
The centrepiece of the Dubai World Trade Centre, its 184-metre-high office tower, is one of the most distinctive buildings on Dubai's skyline. The tower is just part of a complex of large exhibition halls and associated facilities that accommodate approximately 70 exhibitions a year. These include GITEX, the premier information

technology event in the region (see below); GEMEX, global entertainment and media exhibition; the Middle East International Motor Show, the largest international automotive event in the region; INDEX, the biggest furniture and interior design show in the Middle East; along with other international events featuring health, oil and gas, food, construction, fashion, consumer electronics, and education. These events attract thousands of international and regional visitors and exhibitors.

DWTC has developed a wide range of exhibition services and now manages more than 55,000 square metres of exhibition space in two complexes. The new Dubai International Convention Centre (DICC) facility, to be completed in 2003 in time for the 58 board meetings of the World Bank and International Monetary Fund (IMF), will offer more than 7500 square metres of prime meeting space and have the capacity to accommodate up to 6000 delegates. One of its key features is that all the larger meeting rooms are located on the ground level, making access a planner's paradise. The Convention Centre will be linked to the Dubai International Exhibition Centre by a covered concourse that will offer a range of amenities including shops and restaurants and 18 syndicate rooms to accommodate smaller, more intimate requirements.

The Convention Centre's main auditorium, located on the ground level, will be linked to Hall 8 of the Dubai International Exhibition Centre, providing a single venue with up to 11,500 square metres of gross floor space all on one level. The DWTC has also assumed management responsibility for Airport Expo Dubai (www.airportexpodubai.com), the purpose-built exhibition centre adjacent to Dubai Airport where the Dubai Air Show (see below) is staged. The Expo is equipped to host exhibitions to international standards.

Expo Centre Sharjah (www.expo-centre.co.ae/)
In September 2002, Sharjah celebrated the official inauguration by HH Dr. Sheikh Sultan Bin Mohammad Al Qasimi, Member of the Supreme Council and Ruler of Sharjah, of its spectacular new Expo Centre. Designed for functionality and flexibility, the complex covers a total ground area of 128,000 square metres and has been meticulously planned with easy access routes and ample parking space to meet the requirements of its participants. It houses 20,000 square metres of highly functional, column-free, exhibition space and 6000 square.metres of equally useful outdoor space. All of the exhibition areas have been specifically designed for easy move-in and move-out of goods, vehicles and exhibits, ensuring a smooth traffic flow at all times.

The new Centre incorporates the latest advances in communication and information technology. It is first exhibition complex in the GCC region with such cutting-edge features as wireless data, Internet connectivity, turnstile-controlled registration for visitors, and an automated visitor data management system, including an online lead retrieval system for its participants.

The new Centre is also equipped with 1300 square metres of meeting and conference space and is fitted with high-tech audio, visual, theatrical and lighting equipment.

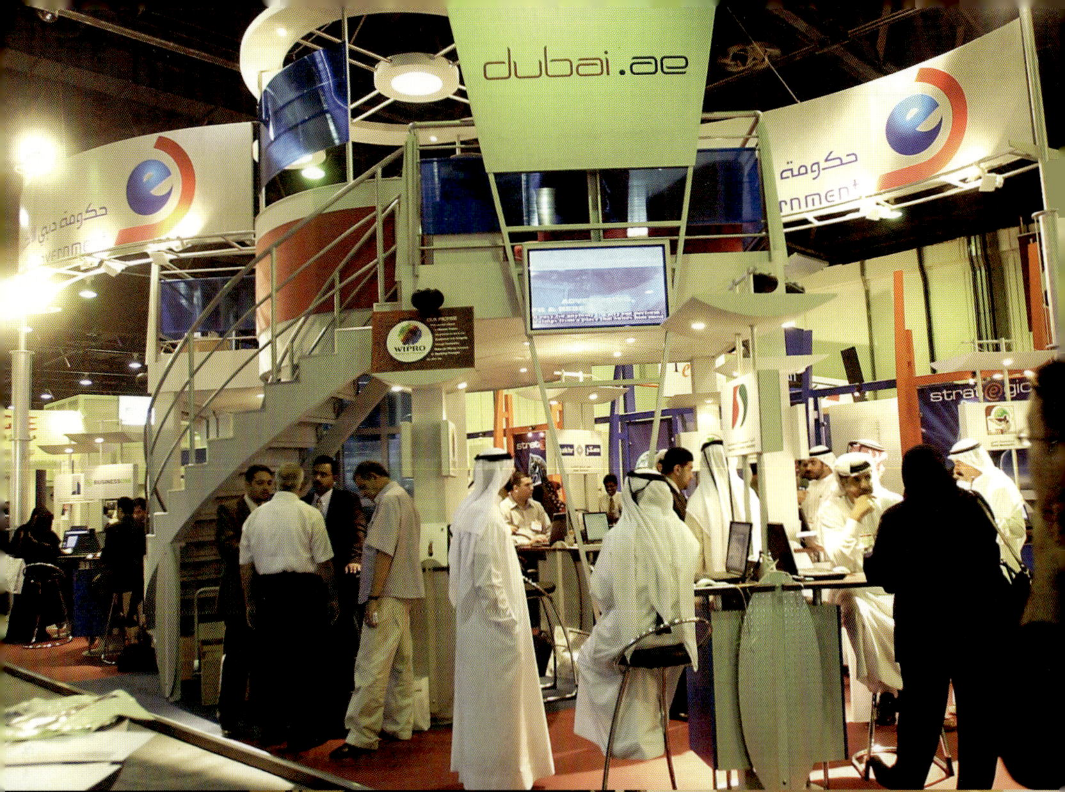
dubai.ae
WIPRO

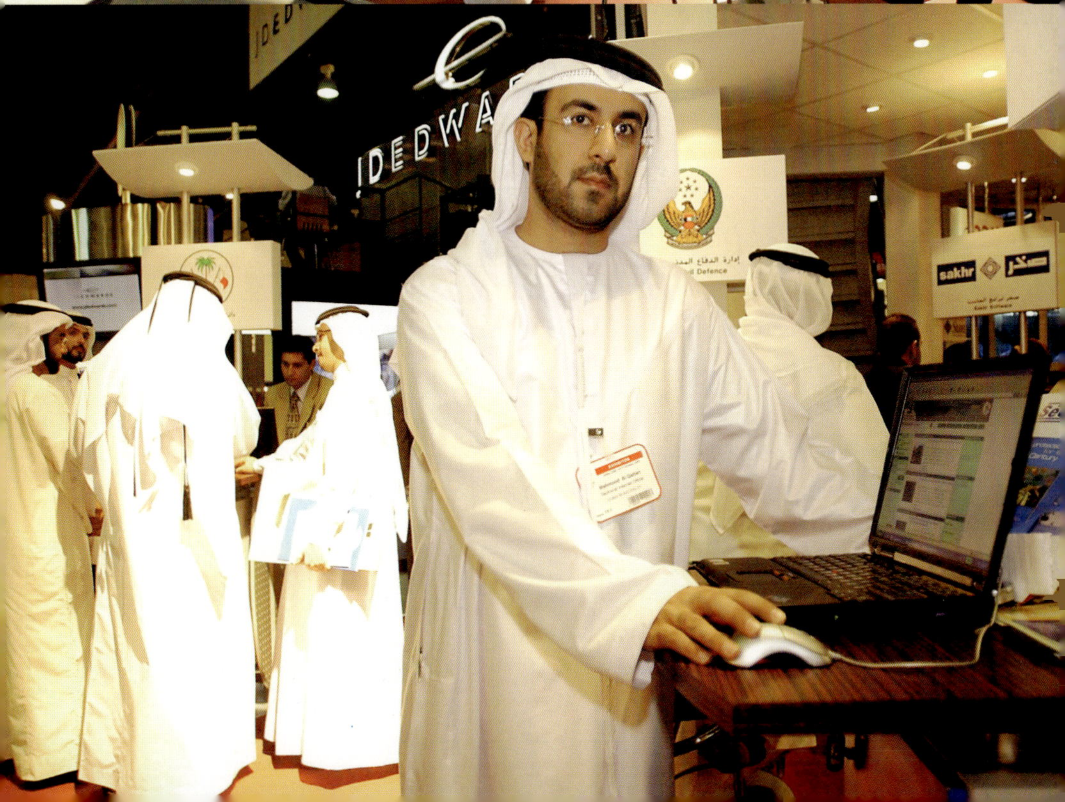
sakhr

Since its inception in 1977, Expo Centre Sharjah has helped to pioneer the exhibition industry in the region. Sharjah Chamber of Commerce and Industry assumed responsibility for the Centre in 1991 and today hosts over 20 exhibitions a year. These include many of the region's premier events, among them: Consumexpo Sharjah, the UAE's unique multi products consumer fair open only to international exhibitors; Gulf Maritime, an international exhibition and conference for the Arab World's commercial, government and military maritime industry; the Mideast Watch and Jewellery Fair, sponsored by the World Gold Council; the International Food Fair which is co-sponsored by the Ministry of Agriculture and Fisheries and the Arab Federation for Food Industries; and the Sharjah Chinese Commodities Fair, China's biggest industrial presentation in the Middle East. In September, the Expo Centre hosts its Thailand Exhibition, a major trade show featuring more than 150 companies, a joint initiative of Thailand's Department of Export Promotion, Ministry of Commerce, Royal Thai Government and the Sharjah Chamber of Commerce and Industry (SCCI). The last show of the season is usually the popular Sharjah International Book Fair. An initiative of the Department of Culture and Information, Government of Sharjah, the event showcases thousands of titles in Arabic, English and other languages.

Ajman Exhibition Centre

Spread over an area of 25,000 square metres, Ajman Exhibition Centre is a newly-constructed, modern, fully-equipped exhibition centre with a range of supporting facilities. The new facility is expected to consolidate the position enjoyed by Ajman as an industrial centre.

Ra's al-Khaimah Exhibition Centre (www.rakexpo.co.ae)

Inaugurated in April 1996, the Centre is located in the Al Nakheel area, very close to Ra's al-Khaimah's business district. The fully-staffed complex, which occupies an area of 37,400 square metres, hosts a number of major exhibitions, including the Egyptian Products Fair; Building and Decoration (BUILDEC); Education and Training Exhibition; and Banking Services and Finance Sources.

Fujairah Exhibition Centre (www.fujairahchamber-uae.com/exhibit.htm)

Fujairah Exhibition Centre, inaugurated in 1996, comprises three major exhibition halls totalling an area of 1080 square metres of indoor display areas, management offices, service utilities for exhibitors and guests as well as an outdoor display arena, altogether covering an area of 55,250 square metres. The Centre is centrally located between the International Airport and the Fujairah Trade Centre on the one hand, and the seaport and Free Zone on the other, and is adjacent to the city's main commercial district. A number of internationally important exhibitions have been held at the Centre since its establishment.

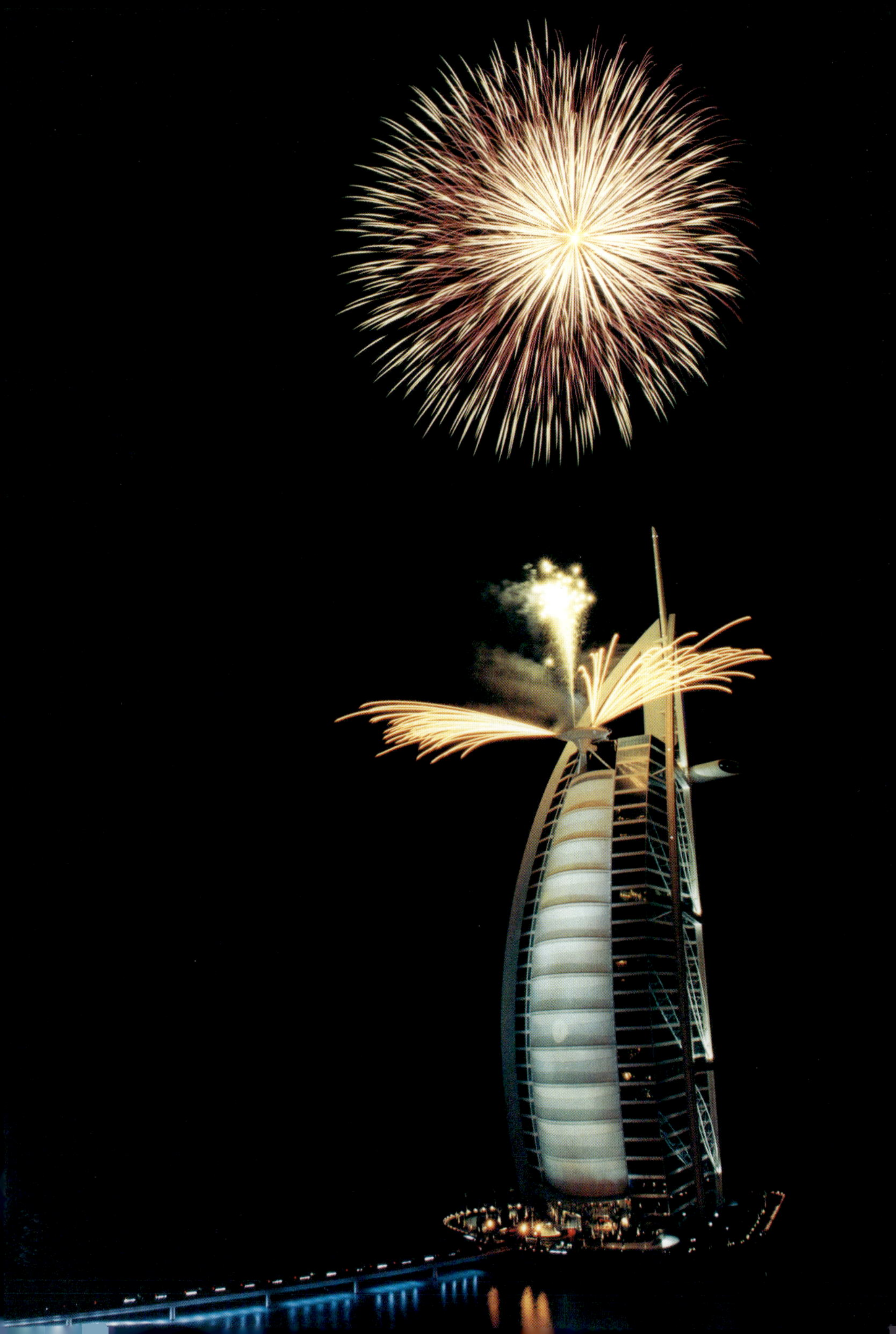

IDEX 2003

In March 2003, Abu Dhabi will once again host IDEX, the prestigious biennial defence industry show held under the patronage of Sheikh Khalifa bin Zayed Al Nahyan, Crown Prince of Abu Dhabi and Deputy Supreme Commander of the UAE Armed Forces. The biennial show is one of the world's leading forums for defence companies to display their latest military, naval and communications hardware. At IDEX 2001, major participants included the United Kingdom (the largest exhibitor with more than 100 companies), the United States, France and Germany, plus newcomers to the event such as Poland, Brazil, Slovenia, South Korea, Turkmenistan, Kazakhstan and Vietnam. Official delegations representing 65 countries and military and defence experts from various parts of the world attended the opening ceremony. The Gulf Defence Conference, at which military experts present papers focusing on military and strategic issues affecting the region, is held in conjunction with the exhibition. Emirates Centre for Strategic Studies and Research, in coordination with the General Exhibitions Corporation, and Jane's Information Group, are the organisers of the conference.

DUBAI AIR SHOW

Due to take place from 7 to 11 December 2003, the Dubai Air Show is a biennial event that is rated among the top three globally, alongside the UK's Farnborough, and France's Le Bourget air shows. The Dubai event is organised at Airport Expo Dubai in collaboration with the Dubai Department of Civil Aviation and the UAE Armed Forces. In 2001, the exhibition featured over 450 companies from 33 countries, and included ten national pavilions. Almost all the aerospace industry majors were represented. Also present was Prince Andrew, Britain's Duke of York, on his first visit to the UAE since he was chosen to lead the British International Trade Organisation. Around 30,000 people visited the air show in 2001.

The event has a 60:40 split between commercial and military participation, with the accent being on civil applications. Some 50 aircraft were on display. Industry experts view the region as an important market, with Middle East and African carriers expected to place orders for approximately 600 aircraft worth an estimated US$50 billion by 2018. Dubai 2001 saw confirmed deals worth US$18.5 billion and another US$6 billion in follow-ups. This includes the US$15 billion historic order announced by Emirates Airline on the opening day. In addition, deals worth Dh462.5 million (US$125 million) were signed by the UAE Armed Forces for development of Puma aircraft with four companies – Romania's IAR, France's Turbomeca, and Rockwell Collins and Cubic Defence System of the United States. At the close of Dubai 2001, 80 per cent of exhibitors had reserved their spaces for the 2003 show.

Among important other activities at the air show was the second Middle East Conference on Aviation Finance which was attended by senior officials of the aviation industry, aircraft leasing institutions, banks, aircraft manufacturers and airlines.

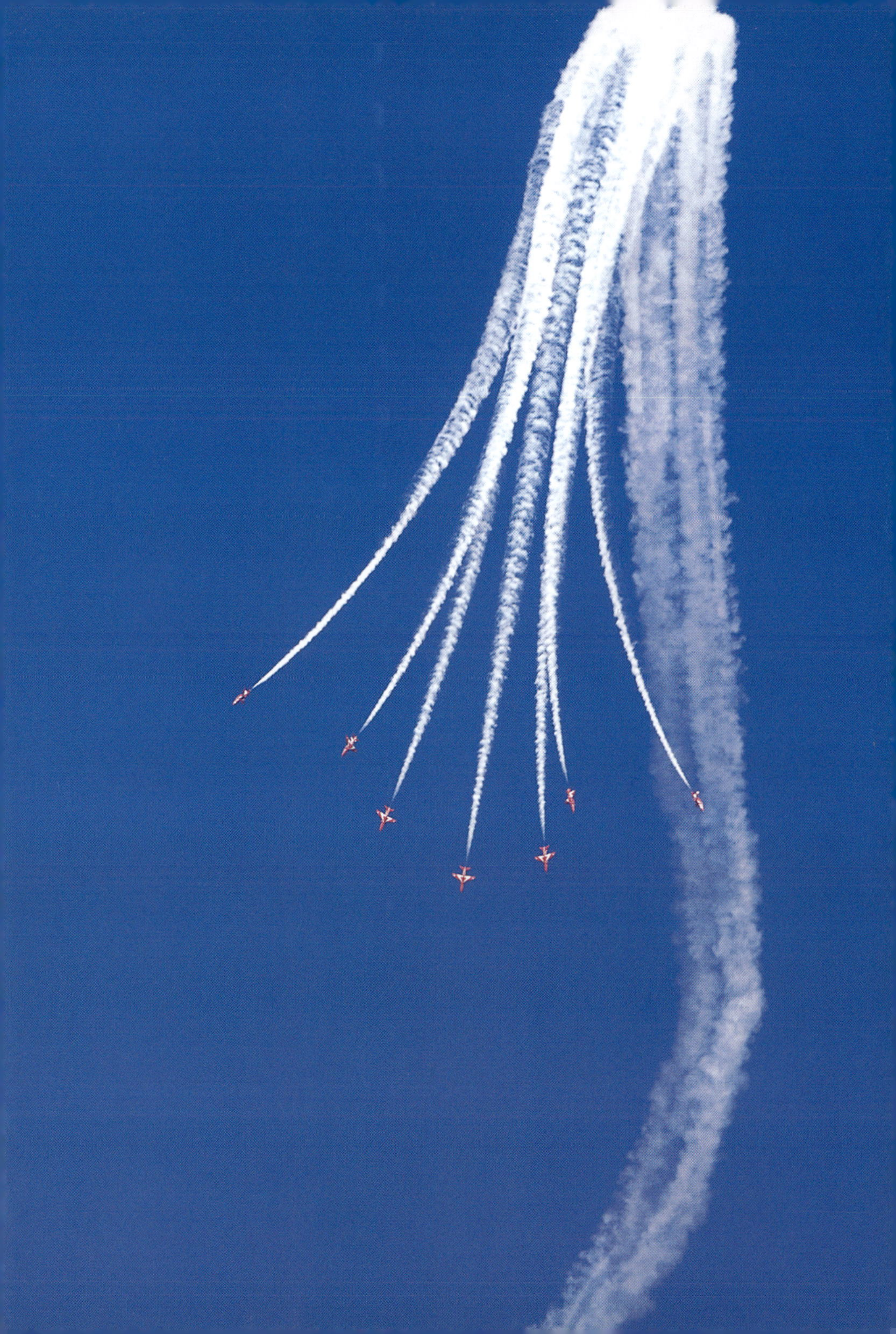

In a move to extend the show's focus into new areas, Dubai 2003 will feature a dedicated ISTAR (Intelligence, Surveillance, Target Acquisition and Reconnaissance) pavilion and conference, as well as an information technology arena and conference.

Dubai 2003 will be held at Dubai Airport Expo from 7-11 December 2003. Though traditionally held in November, the organisers have moved to early December so as not to clash with the Eid holiday celebration at the end of the Holy Month of Ramadan.

GITEX DUBAI

GITEX 2002, the Middle East's largest and most important IT trade exhibition, attracted more than 60,000 visitors as the show continues to grow and develop. At the same time its retail component, Computer Shopper welcomed more than 50,000 visitors. Dubai airport officials reported travel during the same period was up from 484,000 passengers in 2001 to 719,000 in 2002. In addition, numerous hotels reported 100 per cent occupancy during GITEX. The exhibition attracts key industry players who use it to showcase new technologies and demonstrate products that are helping improve business efficiency in a range of sectors, and this year was no exception. Many exhibitors say that the business generated at the event exceeded all previous editions. A notable feature of the GITEX 2002 was the number of African visitors at the show including hundreds of trade professionals from Sudan, Ethiopia and Algeria. Organisers say GITEX Dubai continues to be the DWTC's exhibition front-runner and a model for other events it organises to support various sectors. The 2003 edition of GITEX Dubai will be held from 19 to 23 October 2003.

CABSAT 2002

The eighth cable, satellite, broadcast and communications exhibition (CABSAT), attracting 159 exhibitors and some 4500 trade professionals from the private and public sectors around the world, was both a networking opportunity for those in the cable, satellite, broadcast and telecommunications sectors and a showcase for fibre optics and broadband equipment and services along with wireless cable solutions in a world of expanding satellite and free-to-air technologies. Taiwan, Germany, Korea, Canada, the US and the UK were among the 23 countries represented at the exhibition. Typical of the business generating capacity of this event was the decision by German company, Procast (participating at CABSAT for the first time), to enter negotiations with Orbit to air ten channels in Dubai – the deal is set to be the largest of its kind in the UAE.

Next year, CABSAT is to be integrated into an even more wide-ranging international trade show, GEMEX, the Global Entertainment and Media Exhibition, which will have its debut in March 2003. Dubai Media City (DMC), the Dubai World Trade Centre (DWTC) and the International Conferences and Exhibitions (IC&E) are teaming up to create what is expected to be the region's largest exhibition for the global media and entertainment industry. The exhibition will incorporate the current CABSAT

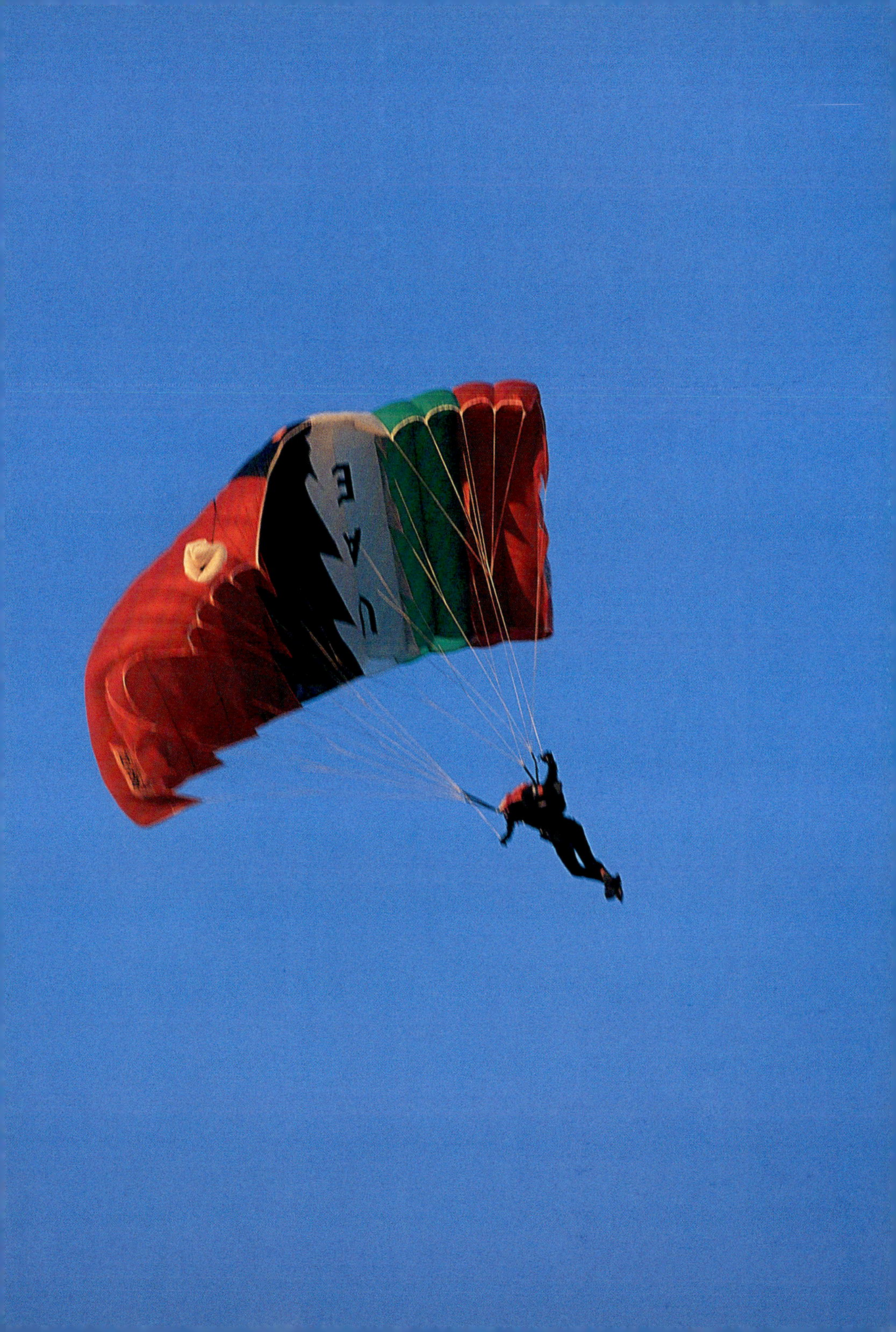

programme into an event covering the entire media spectrum of print and publishing, communication services, new media, music, production and post production, film, entertainment and broadcasting (including cable, satellite and telecommunications). A programme of conferences, seminars and workshops for media professionals and students will focus on the latest developments and opportunities in the media and entertainment industries.

GETEX 2002

The fourteenth Gulf Education and Training Exhibition (GETEX) attracted nearly 320 institutions from approximately 30 countries and saw a significantly increased presence of exhibitors from the UAE. The exhibition, which is the largest student recruitment event anywhere in the Middle East, was attended by nearly 30,000 students, parents, teachers and education professionals. The success of the education sector within the UAE has turned its educational institutions into strong competitors in the academic market. Seventy-three of the institutes attending the exhibition were from the UAE. The fifteenth exhibition will take place in April 2003, where over 50,000 educational and training programmes worldwide will be on display. UAE institutions will undoubtedly have an equally strong presence on that occasion.

DUBAI SHOPPING FESTIVAL (DSF)

By offering 'The world's best brands at the world's best prices,' Dubai has established itself as the shopping capital of the Middle East. The annual Dubai Shopping Festival is a major highlight of the exhibition and events calendar in the UAE, drawing visitors from far afield to take advantage of unbeatable travel offers, spectacular shopping bargains and fabulous raffle prizes in a delightful and entertaining atmosphere.

Dubai Shopping Festival 2002, held from 1 to 31 March 2002, registered a growth figure of 5 per cent, taking the total number of shoppers to 2.68 million and proving that the Festival continues to strengthen its position as a truly global event.

The Global Village remained the most popular and colourful venue of DSF 2002, offering something for every member of the family, from shopping to rides, and stage shows to food courts. It attracted a crowd of over 2.5 million visitors over the 31 days of the event.

The official website of Dubai Shopping Festival, www.mydsf.com, recorded more than 25 million hits during 2002. The site provides a comprehensive and interactive online presence to the world's mega shopping-cum-entertainment extravaganza.

The Dubai Shopping Festival 2002 came to a dramatic close with a massive fireworks display, a flurry of last-minute bargain hunting, grand raffle draws and glittering closing ceremonies at the Creek Park. Thirty-one persons or groups became lucky winners of the three-in-one prize consisting of two Lexus cars and Dh200,000 in cash; 30 people became richer by 1 kilogramme of gold and one lucky person walked away with 10 kilogrammes of gold.

سلسلة
الكتاب الصغير

AL-GHAITH
SNC-LAVALIN
SHELL SOLAR ENERGY BV

Dubai Shopping Festival 2003, which will have the same theme 'One World, One Family, One Festival', will be held from 15 January to 15 February 2003. The period begins with the Spring Break in several GCC countries and concludes with the Eid Holidays. The decision to move the Festival from March to January/February was based upon research done in the retail and hospitality sector that indicated that visiting families like to stay in Dubai for longer periods during the Festival. Feedback from the weekend visitors to DSF 2002 also showed that families based in nearby countries needed more time to enjoy DSF activities and events. So timing the Festival with the holidays was the ideal solution.

DUBAI SUMMER SURPRISES (DSS)

In another record-breaking year, Dubai Summer Surprises (DSS) 2002 posted an 18 per cent rise in visitor numbers, crossing the 1.3 million mark, while total spending rose 19 per cent from Dh1.118 billion in 2001 to Dh1.30 billion in 2002. This outstanding performance confirms the status of Dubai as the premier shopping destination in the region.

Dubai Summer Surprises achieved this success through a combination of special promotions and excellent coordination between DSMG and DSS and also between shopping malls themselves that offered spectacular value-for-money retail promotions worth Dh1.8 million.

Mall traffic registered a sharp increase of 26 per cent to 7.56 million shoppers. Total spending at malls was worth Dh1.15 billion, which is a significant increase of 14.2 per cent. Modhesh Fun City was a huge success throughout the 72-day extravaganza, registering 259,000 visitors including 127,000 children. Modhesh, the festival's mascot, has become a household name and one of the most popular cartoon characters among Gulf children.

The 2002 event was organised into a series of 'Surprises', starting with Food Surprises and followed by Water Surprises; Global Surprises; Ice Surprises; Flower Surprises; Sports Surprises); Heritage Surprises; Art Surprises; Techno Surprises and Back to School Surprises. Plans for Dubai Summer Surprises 2003 are well under way and promise to make the event bigger and better than ever.

DUBAI 2003-WORLD BANK/IMF CONVENTION

In September 2003, Dubai will host the fifty-eighth board meetings of the World Bank and International Monetary Fund (IMF). This high-profile event will inevitably focus global media and government attention on the UAE and presents a unique opportunity to showcase its many attractions. Dubai and the UAE was selected because of its highly developed transportation and logistics infrastructure, its growing importance as a financial hub and its established position as the Crossroads for the New Global Economy. The events will take place in the newly built conference and exhibition facilities at the Dubai World Trade Centre.

INDEX

Abu Dhabi, 2, 7-8, 10, 12, 14, 16, 20-21, 25, 29, 31-34, 36, 46-48, 50-52, 60, 63, 68-69, 72-76, 82, 84-85, 94, 105, 108, 117, 120, 123, 125, 127-132, 136-138, 141-142, 145, 147-150, 152, 159, 161, 163, 165-166, 171, 175-176, 179-181, 184-187, 190, 194, 198-200, 205-208, 210, 216, 218, 225, 232, 236, 240-241, 243, 247-248, 252, 254-255, 257-258, 261, 264, 267-268, 270, 272, 276, 279-280, 282, 284, 288-290, 292, 294, 298, 300, 303, 308
Abu Dhabi Company for Onshore Oil Operations (ADCO) 63, 129, 131, 137, 147, 276
Abu Dhabi Declaration, 232
Abu Dhabi Fund for Development (ADFD), 29, 84-85, 91
Abu Dhabi Gas Company (ADGAS), 129, 147, 148-149
Abu Dhabi Gas Industries Ltd (GASCO), 129-130, 147
Abu Dhabi International Airport, 63, 159, 198, 200, 206
Abu Dhabi International Exhibitions Centre (ADIEC), 303
Abu Dhabi International Marine Sports Club (ADIMSC), 292
Abu Dhabi International Petroleum Exhibition and Conference (ADIPEC), 303
Abu Dhabi Islands Archaeological Survey (ADIAS), 63, 68-69, 171
Abu Dhabi Marine Operating Company (ADMA-OPCO), 129, 131, 136, 138-139, 141, 148
Abu Dhabi National Hotels Company (ADNHC), 159

Abu Dhabi National Oil Company (ADNOC), 69, 129-130, 136-137, 142, 145, 147-148, 151, 161, 185, 208, 276, 280
Abu Dhabi National Tanker Company (ADNATCO), 130
Abu Dhabi Oil Refining Company (TAKREER), 69, 130, 142, 185
Abu Dhabi Securities Market (ADSM), 206
Abu Dhabi Water and Electricity Authority (ADWEA), 184, 186
Abu Dhabi World Trade Centre, 161
Abu Musa, 12, 27, 38, 80
ADGAS, 129, 147, 148-149
ADIAS, 63, 68-69, 171
ADIEC, 303
ADMA-OPCO, 129, 131, 136, 138-139, 141, 148
ADNOC, 69, 129-130, 136-137, 142, 145, 147-148, 151, 161, 185, 208, 276, 280
Adult Education Centres, 230
Agriculture, 7-8, 40-41, 54, 74, 96, 98, 151, 163, 165, 169, 171, 173, 175-176, 178, 181, 226, 274, 277, 306
Ahmed Bin Rashid Free Zone, 113
Airlines, 111, 199-200, 202-205, 229, 308
Airports, 113, 115, 179, 196, 198, 203
Ajman Exhibition Centre, 306
Ajman Free Zone, 113
Ajman, 36, 38, 51, 58, 72-74, 113, 123, 127, 133, 135, 150-151, 162-163, 179, 183, 196, 213, 216, 226, 241, 254-255, 261, 306
Al Ain International Airport, 200
Al Ain, 8, 10, 12, 16, 18, 34, 43, 47, 52, 63, 75, 125, 128, 147, 159, 161, 163, 165, 182, 185,

190, 194, 198, 200, 203, 225, 241, 248, 252, 255, 276, 280, 291, 298, 300
Al Aqsa mosque, 88
Aluminium, 117, 123, 210
Arabian horse, 62, 282
Archaeology, 63, 256
Atlantis Holdings, 127, 135-136, 150
Banks, 50, 58, 94, 103, 108-109, 137, 210, 243-244, 308
Bida Zayed, 34
Business Environment, 107-109
Cabinet, 72-74, 191, 216, 224, 232
Camel racing, 279-280, 282
Cement, 40, 147, 213
Central Bank, 93-94, 180
Centre for Excellence for Applied Research and Training (CERT), 228
Ceramics, 47, 67, 115, 121
CITES, 274
Climate, 7, 32, 43-44, 46, 51, 68, 169
Constitution, 22, 71-76, 219, 236
Council of Ministers, 72-73
Crescent Petroleum, 133, 150
Culture, 2-3, 5, 18, 38, 56, 73, 165, 171, 176, 247, 250-252, 255-257, 259, 261-262, 264-265, 274, 294, 306
Customs Authority Law, 116
Customs Union, 115-116
Date palm, 44-45, 56, 165-166, 171, 173, 277
Date palm conference, 165, 171
DNATA, 202
Dolphin Project, 128
DTCM, 153, 157, 282
Dubai Air Show, 204, 304, 308
Dubai Airport Free Zone (DAFZ), 111
Dubai Cargo Village, 202
Dubai Desert Classic, 290-291

Dubai Drydocks, 211
Dubai Financial Market (DFM), 109
Dubai, 12, 34, 36, 38, 48, 50-52, 66, 72, 74, 84, 88, 90, 93, 105, 108-109, 111, 113, 115-117, 121, 123, 125, 127-128, 131, 133, 141-143, 145, 147-153, 155, 157, 163, 167, 179-180, 182-183, 186, 188, 194, 199-200, 202, 204, 207, 210-211, 215-216, 218, 224-226, 228-229, 234, 240-241, 247, 251-252, 254-256, 258, 260-262, 270, 272, 276-277, 279-280, 282, 284, 288-292, 294, 296, 298, 300, 303-304, 308, 310, 312, 314
Dubai International Airport, 111, 200
Dubai Internet City (DIC), 93, 111, 113, 183, 226, 258, 260
Dubai Media City (DMC), 93, 113, 183, 226, 256, 258, 310
Dubai Petroleum Company (DPC) 133, 142, 262
Dubai Ports Authority (DPA), 207, 211
Dubai Shopping Festival (DSF), 312, 314
Dubai Summer Surprises (DSS), 224, 314
Dubai Textile Village, 113
Dubai World Cup, 284
Dubai World Trade Centre (DWTC), 229, 303, 310, 314
DUBAL, 123, 210, 291
Dugong, 45, 270
E-Business, 226
E-government, 111, 116-117, 229
ECSSR, 171, 250-251
Education, 5, 7, 14, 17, 51, 71, 73-74, 76, 103, 215-216, 220, 222, 224-226, 228-231, 234, 238, 241, 247, 250, 252, 254, 267, 274, 300, 304, 306, 312
Electricity, 68, 74, 96, 98, 120, 128, 146, 149, 179, 184-188
Emirates Airline, 196, 203, 284, 308
Emirates Centre for Strategic Studies and Research (ECSSR),171, 250-251

Emirates Media Incorporated (EMI), 257-258, 262, 264
Emirates National Oil Company (ENOC), 142
Emirates News Agency (WAM), 2, 88, 262
Emirates Post, 195-196
Emirates Telecommunications Corporation (ETISALAT), 108-109, 180, 190-192, 194, 261
Emiratisation, 173, 194, 215, 229, 236
Employment, 10, 17, 50, 194, 219, 229, 232, 234
Empty Quarter, 31, 34, 291
Endurance racing, 286, 288
Environment, 3, 5, 7-8, 20-21, 52, 68, 107-109, 152, 163, 169, 173, 175-176, 181, 183, 198, 228, 252, 267-268, 270, 276-277
Environmental Research and Wildlife Development Agency (ERWDA), 21, 60, 175-176, 268, 270, 272, 274, 276-277
Equestrian Sports, 282
Exhibitions, 3, 224, 248, 268, 303-304, 306, 308, 310
Expo Centre Sharjah, 304, 306
Federal Environment Agency (FEA), 21, 176, 267-268, 274
Federal Judiciary, 75
Federal National Council, 21, 34, 72, 74-75, 216, 234, 240
Federal Supreme Council, 16, 73
Federal Supreme Court, 72, 75
Financial Services, 199, 234
Fisheries handbook, 175
Fishing licences, 175
Fishing, 7, 38, 40-41, 43, 52, 54, 58, 60, 173, 175-177, 254-255, 268, 270
FNC, 21, 34, 72, 74-75, 216, 234, 240
Football, 184, 258, 279-280, 300
Foreign Policy, 12, 24-25, 28-29, 78, 80, 84
Free Zones, 93-94, 109, 111
Fujairah, 40-41, 44, 47, 51, 68, 72-74, 77, 88, 115, 120, 123, 127-128, 143, 149, 162-163,

179, 186, 203, 210, 212, 216, 218, 238, 247, 254, 270, 292, 296, 306
Fujairah Exhibition Centre, 238, 306
Fujairah Free Zone, 115
Fujairah International Airport, 115, 203
Fujairah Tourism Bureau, 162
Gas, 16, 38, 93, 95-96, 98, 100, 102-103, 105, 117, 120, 125, 127-131, 133, 135-139, 141-143, 145-151, 190, 208, 228, 250, 304
GASCO, 129-130, 147
GCC Power Grid, 190
GCC, 25-26, 80, 94, 105, 108, 111, 115-116, 121, 128, 152-153, 177, 186, 190, 207-208, 225-226, 256, 262, 291-292, 300, 304, 314
GCC Unified Economic Agreement, 115
GDP, 94-96, 98-99, 105, 107, 163, 216
General Women's Union, 17, 220, 231
GITEX, 303, 310
Golf, 115, 152, 161-162, 180, 182, 198, 289-292, 298
Greater and Lesser Tunb, 12, 27, 40, 80
gross domestic product, 94-96, 98-99, 105, 107, 163, 216
Gulf Air, 196, 203, 205-206
Gulf Cooperation Council, 25-26, 80, 94, 105, 108, 111, 115-116, 121, 128, 152-153, 177, 186, 190, 207-208, 225-226, 256, 262, 291-292, 300, 304, 314
Hamriyah Free Zone (HFZA), 113, 150, 212
HE General Sheikh Mohammed bin Rashid Al Maktoum, Crown Prince of Dubai and Minister of Defence, 72-73, 270
HE Sheikh Ahmed bin Sultan Al Qasimi, Deputy Ruler of Sharjah, 73
HE Sheikh Ammar bin Humaid Al Nuaimi, Crown Prince of Ajman, 73

INDEX

HE Sheikh Hamad bin Saif Al Sharqi, Deputy Ruler of Fujairah, 73
HE Sheikh Hamdan bin Rashid Al Maktoum, Deputy Ruler of Dubai, Minister of Finance and Industry, 72-73, 284
HE Sheikh Khalid bin Saqr Al Qasimi, Crown Prince and Deputy Ruler, 72
HE Sheikh Saud bin Rashid Al Mu'alla, Crown Prince of Umm al-Qaiwain, 72
HE Sheikh Sultan bin Mohammed Al Qasimi, Crown Prince and Deputy Ruler of Sharjah, 72-73, 81
HE Sheikh Sultan bin Saqr Al Qasimi, Deputy Ruler of Ras al-Khaimah, 73
HH Sheikh Sultan bin Zayed Al Nahyan, 7, 73, 248
HH Dr Sheikh Sultan bin Mohammed Al Qasimi, Ruler of Sharjah, 50, 72
HH President Sheikh Zayed bin Sultan Al Nahyan, Ruler of Abu Dhabi, 72
HH Sheikh Hamad bin Mohammed Al Sharqi, Ruler of Fujairah, 72
HH Sheikh Humaid bin Rashid Al Nuaimi, Ruler of Ajman, 72
HH Sheikh Khalifa bin Zayed Al Nahyan, Crown Prince of Abu Dhabi and Deputy Supreme Commander of the UAE Armed Forces, Chairman of the Executive Council of the Emirate of Abu Dhabi, 72, 74
HH Sheikh Rashid bin Ahmed Al Mu'alla, Ruler of Umm al-Qaiwain, 72
HH Sheikh Saqr bin Mohammed Al Qasimi, Ruler of Ras al-Khaimah, 72
HH Sheikh Zayed, 3, 5, 7-8, 10, 12, 14, 16-18, 20-22, 24-29, 34, 50-51, 72, 77, 80-82, 84-86, 91, 153, 163, 165, 169, 171, 179-181, 186, 191, 231, 238, 247-248, 252, 254, 272, 282, 284, 288, 290, 292
HH Vice-President and Prime Minister Sheikh Maktoum bin Rashid Al Maktoum, Ruler of Dubai, 72-73, 81
Health, 7, 14, 17, 51, 71, 73, 86, 88, 117, 157, 169, 177, 216, 219-220, 224, 231, 234, 240-243, 245, 247, 304
Heritage, 5, 8, 14, 18, 20, 38, 63, 69, 107, 152, 162, 182, 247-248, 252, 255-256, 258, 274, 294, 314
Higher Colleges of Technology (HCTs), 113, 150, 212, 215, 225, 228
Horse racing, 282
Hospitals, 10, 12, 26, 51, 86, 91, 241, 245
Hotels, 34, 96, 98, 152-153, 155, 157, 159, 161-162, 303, 310
Houbara, 60, 272
Housing, 12, 40, 51, 74, 85, 103, 109, 179-180, 183, 191, 215-216, 219, 230, 254, 276
Ibn Majid, 48
IDEX 2001, 308
Illiteracy, 230
Industry, 8, 10, 40, 45, 50, 58, 62, 72-73, 102, 108, 121, 125, 129, 131, 139, 146, 152-153, 157, 159, 173, 175-176, 196, 198, 203-204, 207-208, 228-229, 236, 252, 255, 260-262, 267, 291, 306, 308, 310
International Petroleum Investment Company (IPIC), 142
Internet cafés, 265
Internet, 93, 111, 113, 116, 183, 191-192, 194, 196, 198, 200, 207, 226, 243, 251, 257-258, 260-262, 264-265, 304
Iraq, 25, 43, 46, 78, 82-83, 107
Iron and Steel, 121, 210
Jebel Ali Free Zone (JAFZ), 93, 111, 142, 151, 178
Jenin, 81, 86
Khor Fakkan, 38, 48, 68, 75, 184, 190, 211-212, 270, 296
Leopard, 268
Liwa, 34, 48, 50, 52
Manufacturing Industries, 98, 123
Marawah, 34, 47, 270
Mariculture, 40
Marriage, 238, 240, 247
Media, 88, 93, 113, 161, 183, 192, 226, 228-230, 232, 234, 240, 256-258, 260-262, 264-265, 267, 304, 310, 312, 314
Mina Zayed, 181, 207, 300
Museums, 38, 66, 68, 162, 181, 252, 254, 256
National Horticulture Company, 167
Oil, 8, 10, 12, 14, 16, 34, 38, 40, 51, 63, 69, 75, 93-96, 98, 100, 102-103, 105, 107-108, 117, 123, 125, 127-133, 135-137, 139, 141-143, 145, 147, 206-208, 212, 215, 228, 247, 250, 255, 267, 276-277, 291, 304
Operation Emirates Solidarity, 85
Oryx, 20, 43, 45, 181, 272
Palm project, 180
Pearling, 10, 46-47, 50-52, 54, 58, 256
Political System, 21, 71, 77
Polo, 289
Port of Fujairah, 115
Port Rashid, 113
Port Saqr, 115, 213
Powerboat races, 292
Privatisation, 184-186
Protected Areas, 268, 270, 274
Protection of Intellectual Property, 265
Public Authority for Youth and Sports (PAYS), 191, 248, 279, 300
Public Transport, 181, 219
Qawasim, 50, 66-67
Ra's al-Khaimah Exhibition Centre, 306
Ra's al-Khaimah Free Zone, 115
Ra's al-Khaimah, 12, 31, 38, 40, 47-48, 52, 54, 66, 68, 72-74, 115, 117, 123, 125, 127, 135, 162-163, 178-179, 183, 203, 210, 213, 216, 241, 247, 254-255, 279, 291, 306
Ra's al-Khaimah International Airport, 203
Red Crescent Society (RCS), 29, 86, 88, 90, 218

Roads, 7, 12, 26, 51, 179-182, 245
Ruwais Fertilisers Industries Ltd (FERTIL), 129, 147, 150
Seaports, 113, 115, 125, 179, 207
SEWA, 150, 186, 188, 190
Sharjah Airport International Free Zone (SAIFZ), 115
Sharjah Airport, 115
Sharjah, 12, 38, 40, 45, 50-51, 62, 67-68, 72-75, 88, 105, 113, 115, 117, 121, 123, 125, 127, 133, 135-136, 143, 149-150, 152, 162-163, 179, 183, 186, 188, 190, 202-203, 211-212, 216, 218, 220, 226, 229, 234, 241, 243, 247, 252, 254-256, 261, 268, 270, 274, 277, 279, 288, 291-292, 298, 300, 303-304, 306
Sharjah Arts Area, 252
Sharjah Commerce and Tourism Development Authority (SCDTA), 162
Sharjah Electricity and Water Authority (SEWA), 150, 186, 188, 190
Sharjah Seaports Authority (SPA), 162, 180
Shipping, 41, 51, 111, 125, 130, 143, 157, 199, 207, 210, 212
Show jumping, 282, 284, 288-289
Sir Bani Yas, 20, 32, 34, 47
Social Welfare, 216, 218
Sports, 5, 157, 159, 252, 258, 261, 264, 268, 279, 282, 292, 296, 298, 300, 314
Supreme Council, 16, 72-73, 75, 186, 232, 304
Sustainable development, 267-268
TABREED, 108
Telecommunications, 108, 111, 179-180, 190, 192, 194, 224, 303, 310, 312
Thuraya, 194-195
Tourism, 34, 63, 76, 98, 152-153, 157, 159, 161-162, 180, 182, 252, 279, 282, 291
Trade, 40, 43-47, 50, 60, 68, 93, 95-96, 98, 103, 109, 111, 113, 115, 121, 159, 161-162, 192, 202, 207, 229, 236, 254, 260, 268, 274, 276, 303, 306, 308, 310, 314
Traditions, 3, 43, 45, 47, 51, 63, 66-67, 69, 71, 236, 238, 255-256, 290
UAE Football Association, 280
UAE Golf Association (UGA), 292
UAE Interact, 257
UAE Offsets Group, 68, 117, 119-120, 128, 131, 178, 199, 208, 210
UAE Stock Market, 108
UAE University (UAEU), 178, 225-226, 229
UGA, 292
Umm al-Qaiwain Free Zone, 113
Umm al-Qaiwain, 36, 40, 46-47, 51, 58, 72, 74, 113, 123, 127, 133, 135-136, 150, 162-163, 176, 178-179, 183, 213, 216, 241, 254
UN General Assembly, 81
UOG, 68, 117, 119-120, 128, 131, 178, 199, 208, 210
Urban Development, 179, 182
UWEC, 68-69, 128, 186
Washington, 24, 83, 107, 258, 262
Water, 8, 32, 44-45, 48, 52, 54, 56, 66, 68, 74, 85, 90-91, 96, 120, 123, 128, 131, 133, 136-137, 139, 141, 147, 149, 151, 157, 159, 169, 177, 179, 182-188, 190, 199, 268, 276-277, 290-291, 314
Water use, 169
Wildlife, 8, 20-21, 32, 60, 62, 175, 181, 268, 270, 272, 274, 276-277
Women, 17, 52, 88, 120, 184, 194, 215-216, 218-220, 225, 228-229, 231-232, 234, 236, 238, 240, 242, 262, 296
World Trade Organisation, 121, 192
Worldwide Fund for Nature (WWF), 20
Zakum Development Company (ZADCO), 129, 131, 139
Zayed Foundation, 29
Zayed University (ZU), 225-226, 229-230

CAPTIONS AND CREDITS

4	Mountain gazelle. H&J Eriksen /Trident Press
6	HH Sheikh Zayed. Frank Spooner Pictures
9	HH Sheikh Zayed in Al Ain, 1956. ADCO
11	HH Sheikh Zayed and Sheikh Rashid in 1972. Ministry of Information and Culture
13	HH Sheikh Zayed with young girls. Ministry of Information and Culture
15	HH Sheikh Zayed visiting Egypt in the early 1970s. Ministry of Information and Culture
19	(upper) HH Sheikh Zayed with Mr Kofi Anan, Sec.Gen. U.N. WAM / Ministry of Information and Culture
19	(lower) HH Sheikh Zayed with Rt. Hon. Adrienne Clarkson, Gov. Gen. of Canada WAM / Ministry of Information and Culture
23	(upper) HH Sheikh Zayed visiting citizens on tour. WAM / Ministry of Information and Culture
23	(lower) HH Sheikh Zayed with HM Sultan Qaboos. WAM / Ministry of Information and Culture
30	An old Acacia tree, foothills of Ra's al-Khaimah. H&J Eriksen / Trident Press
33	Among the Liwa sand dunes. Pankaj Shah / Image Solutions
35	New housing project. H&J Eriksen / Trident Press
36-37	Capital cities of the UAE Dubai and Sharjah. Gulf News / Gulf News
36-37	Abu Dhabi, Umm al-Qaiwain, Ajman, Ra's al-Khaimah and Fujairah. Trident Press / Trident Press
39	Dubai Creek with abra and twin shopping centres. H&J Eriksen / Trident Press
42	Exploring an old fort tower in Ra's al-Khaimah. H&J Eriksen / Trident Press
49	A Chinese plate from the Islamic period. Adam Woolfitt / Trident Press
53	Windtowers in old Bur Dubai. Pankaj Shah / Image Solutions
55	Coffee and dates. Pankaj Shah / Image Solutions
57	HH Sheikh Ahmed bin Humaid Al Nuami on endurance horse RM at the old fort in Ajman. Lucy Monro / Lucy Monro
59	Making a shashah boat from datepalm fronds. Trident Press / Trident Press
61	Falconer and falcon. Simon Aspinall / Simon Aspinall
64-65	Removal of fossil elephant tusk from Abu Dhabi desert. ADIAS / ADIAS
70	The flag of the UAE flies over its capital city, Abu Dhabi. H&J Eriksen / Trident Press
79	(upper) HH Sheikh Hamdan bin Zayed Al Nahyan, Minister of State for Foreign Affairs with US President George W. Bush and Secretary of State, Colin Powell. WAM / Ministry of Information and Culture
79	(lower) HH Sheikh Hamdan bin Zayed Al Nahyan, Minister of State for Foreign Affairs, with French President, Jacques Chirac. WAM / Ministry of Information and Culture
87	Demining operations at Operation Emirates Solidarity in Lebanon. Trident Press / Trident Press
89	(upper) HH Sheikh Hamdan bin Zayed Al Nahyan, Minister of State for Foreign Affairs and Chairman of the UAE Red Crescent Society distributing humanitarian aid to children in Niger. WAM / Ministry of Information and Culture
89	(lower) UAE Red Crescent humanitarian aid to Sudan. WAM / Ministry of Information and Culture
92	Headquarters building of ADMA-OPCO in Abu Dhabi. Trident Press / Trident Press
103	Inset: UAE bank notes. Pankaj Shah / Image Solutions
105	Commerce, water transport and aviation at Dubai Creek. Trident Press / Trident Press
109	(x2) Business seminars in Dubai. Pankaj Shah / Image Solutions
111	Dubai Internet City. Trident Press / Trident Press
113	Dubai World Trade Centre. Jumeirah International / Jumeirah International
117	A business handshake in the UAE. Pankaj Shah / Image Solutions
121	(upper) Textile workshop in the UAE. Gulf News / Gulf News
121	(lower) Iron and Steel plant in the UAE. Gulf News / Gulf News
123	Aluminium ingots at DUBAL in Dubai. Trident Press / Trident Press
125	Oil platform off Abu Dhabi. Trident Press / Trident Press
129	Pipework. Trident Press / Trident Press
133	Oil and Gas Platform complex in Abu Dhabi. Trident Press / Trident Press
139	Worker on new gas pipeline in Abu Dhabi. Reinhard Westphal / GASCO
143	Offshore platform and worker. H&J Eriksen / Trident Press

145	Flare on oil field. H&J Eriksen / Trident Press
153	The UAE folklore dancers perform on Jumeirah beach. Reinhard Westphal / Trident Press
155	Sheraton Hotel, Abu Dhabi. Reinhard Westphal / Trident Press
157	Twin Towers Hotel building, Dubai. Pankaj Shah / Image Solutions
159	Inside a shopping mall in Abu Dhabi. Reinhard Westphal / Trident Press
163	Date-palm nursery for plants raised via tissue culture. Reinhard Westphal / Trident Press
166	(insets) Tomatoes and flowers grown in the UAE. H&J Eriksen / Trident Press
167	Cucumbers raised in the UAE. H&J Eriksen / Trident Press
169	Date-palm tissue culture laboratory. Reinhard Westphal / Trident Press
170	Dates. H&J Eriksen / Trident Press
171	A date-palm seedling. Reinhard Westphal / Trident Press
173	Tilapia fish raised in seawater cage, Arabian waters. Peter Vine / Peter Vine
178	Satellite aerials for communications systems, UAE. H&J Eriksen / Trident Press
189	Electricity pylons cross a flooded field in the UAE. H&J Eriksen / Trident Press
193	Optical fibre cable junction. Alex Smailes / Trident Press
197	(x2) Air traffic control at Dubai Airport. Gulf News / Gulf News
201	Dubai International Airport. Walter Bibikow / jonarnoldimages.com
209	Mina Zayed is Abu Dhabi's main commercial port. Reinhard Westphal / Trident Press
210	Cargo is offloaded at a UAE port. Reinhard Westphal / Trident Press
214	Young eyes. Pankaj Shah / Image Solutions
217	Emirati man. Trident Press / Trident Press
221	School girls. Trident Press / Trident Press
223	(upper) Three young Emirati boys. Gulf News / Gulf News
223	(lower) UAE family on the beach. Pankaj Shah / Image Solutions
227	Computer training class. Trident Press / Trident Press
233	Women fill many key roles in the UAE. Pankaj Shah / Image Solutions
235	ECSSR Library in Abu Dhabi. Trident Press / Trident Press
237	Enjoying a coffee break. Pankaj Shah / Image Solutions
239	A young couple on the beach. Pankaj Shah / Image Solutions
246	Prayer time in the desert. Pankaj Shah / Image Solutions
249	Relaxing among friends. Gulf News / Gulf News
253	At the Seventh Annual Conference of ECSSR, 2002. Trident Press / Trident Press
263	EMI Broadcast studio and concert presentation. Gulf News / Gulf News
266	Desert hyacinth. H&J Eriksen / Trident Press
269	Heron on mangrove bushes. H&J Eriksen / Trident Press
271	Two sand gazelle on Sir Bani Yas. H&J Eriksen / Trident Press
273	Camouflaged grasshopper. H&J Eriksen / Trident Press
275	(upper) Manta ray in Arabian waters. Peter Vine / Peter Vine
275	(lower) Mating green turtles in Arabian Gulf waters. Peter Vine / Peter Vine
278	Footballers. Gulf News / Gulf News
281	Showjumper. Gulf News / Gulf News
283	(x2) Dubai World Cup. Gulf News / Gulf News
285	Endurance – Action on the trail at Al Wathba in Abu Dhabi. Lucy Munro / Lucy Munro
287	Basketball game. Gulf News / Gulf News
293	Golf is one of the favourite sports in the UAE. Trident Press / Trident Press
295	A sailing dhow. Pankaj Shah / Image Solutions
297	The winner of Dubai Tennis Championship Fabrice Santoro of France with his trophy. Gulf News / Gulf News
299	(upper) Dubai Tennis Championship semifinals between Venus Williams of USA and Sandrine Testud of France. Gulf News / Gulf News
299	(lower) Second Test match between Pakistan and West Indies, Sharjah Cricket Stadium. Gulf News / Gulf News
301	New Zealand against Sri Lanka during the Emirates Airline Dubai Rugby Sevens 2002, Dubai Exile Rugby Club. Gulf News / Gulf News
302	Dubai Exhibition Centre. Trident Press / Trident Press
305	(x2) Exhibition scenes in the UAE. Gulf News / Gulf News
307	Fireworks over Burj Al Arab. Pankaj Shah / mage Solutions
309	Aerial display. Pankaj Shah / Image Solutions
311	Parachutist during Dubai Shopping Festival. Gulf News / Gulf News
313	Exhibition scenes. Gulf News / Gulf News